STRANGERS IN HIGH PLACES

BOOKS BY MICHAEL FROME

STRANGERS
IN HIGH PLACES

The Story of the Great Smoky Mountains

❧❧

MICHAEL FROME

EXPANDED EDITION

THE UNIVERSITY OF TENNESSEE PRESS
KNOXVILLE

SSCCA

Copyright © 1966 by Michael Frome
Member of the Authors League of America

Copyright © 1980 by The University of Tennessee Press/Knoxville.
All Rights Reserved. Manufactured in the United States of America.
This edition supplemented and reprinted by arrangement with
Doubleday & Company, Inc., Garden City, N.Y.
Cloth: 1st printing, 1980; 2nd printing, 1984; 3rd printing, 1989.
Paper: 1st printing, 1980; 2nd printing, 1984; 3rd printing, 1986;
4th printing, 1989; 5th printing, 1992.
Expanded Edition, 1st printing, 1994.

The paper in this book meets the minimum requirements
of the American National Standard for Permanence of Paper
for Printed Library Materials. ⊗
The binding materials have been chosen
for strength and durability.

Library of Congress Cataloging in Publication Data

Frome, Michael.
    Strangers in high places: the story of the Great Smoky
Mountains / Michael Frome; maps by University of
Tennessee Cartographic Services Laboratory—Expanded ed.
        p.   cm.
    Includes bibliographical references and index.
    ISBN 0-87049-806-1 (pbk. : alk. paper)
    1. Great Smoky Mountains (N.C. and Tenn.) I. Title.
F443.G7F7   1993   93–7122
976.8'89-dc20 CIP

The mountains, John Muir once said, *are fountains,*
not only of rivers and fertile soil,
but of men.
Therefore, shall we feel (as Muir did)
that in some sense we are all mountaineers
and going to the mountains is going home?

Contents

Part One

THE FIRST HALF-BILLION YEARS

Part Two

THE CIVILIZED AGE

Figures

Maps

*To the Natives (by birth and adoption) on the
staff of the Great Smoky Mountains National Park, who
gave it their best for the first quarter-century:*

Miss Mary Ruth Chiles, Carl Davis, Mark Hannah,
Beauford Messer, John Morrell, Frank Oliver, J. Melvin Price,
William T. Rolen, Jake Clyde Smith, Richard A. Stokes,
Arthur Stupka, P. Audley Whaley, and Fred A. Wingeier.

*The wilderness that will endure forever is
your memorial.*

Foreword

Wilma Dykeman

"It was raining in the Smokies."

When I first read that opening sentence of Michael Frome's *Strangers in High Places* in 1966, I knew that this book was going to be all right.

In a single sentence the writer had captured the essential weather that sometimes disgruntles transient visitors even as it nourishes the natural bounty and variety that are these ancient mountains' glory. Without scientific terminology he had introduced readers to a fundamental ecological reality of this place, and with simple, straightforward familiarity he had invited readers to share his discovery of the Great Smokies. It was this marriage of factual information and personal experience, intellect and passion, that set the book apart as a landmark interpretation of the Great Smoky Mountains.

Now it is presented in an expanded edition with a new preface and photographs. Many new readers will find what readers of earlier editions, old friends, welcome again: the history, the scenery, the music and stories, the exploration of wilderness solitudes, accounts of bureaucratic infighting and selfless dedication in establishing and sustaining a national park.

There is inspiration here, in the lives of Cherokees who knew rivers and mountains as part of their own blood and bone, pioneers who had searched and suffered through generations for a place to put down roots, early botanists rejoicing in a plant life of wondrous diversity, explorers, missionaries, writers, philanthropists, conservationists, among the many who brought their own distinctive vision to the Smokies.

There is also challenge here. It is an old challenge of relationships: human nature in relation to nature's laws, people relating to people, the inescapable consequences of past relating to present and present shaping the future. Michael Frome is both specific and eloquent in setting forth these challenges.

I reread *Strangers in High Places* in homes on each side of the Smokies.

One home stands on a hilltop in Eastern Tennessee where my husband grew up and we reared two sons. Along the horizon I see the full sweep of the Great Smoky Mountain range, inviting me, as so many have been invited

Wilma Dykeman is the author of sixteen books and articles in many of the nation's major magazines. She has received awards for her novels, for her histories, and for her writing on subjects of conservation and human relations. A nationally known speaker, she gives some twenty to twenty-five lectures a year. She is a professor of English at the University of Tennessee and a former Guggenheim Fellow and Senior Fellow of the National Endowment for the Humanities.

through the centuries, to accept their beauty, discover their history, share their story.

The other home nestles in a narrow valley in Western North Carolina where I grew up and still find renewal for life and work. In front of this house a stream splashes its way to distant rivers and a pond is fed by the spring guarded by sentinel oaks and poplars. Rhododendron and wild azaleas and laurel are thick cover on the hillside behind this house, and everywhere there are gifts: ferns, galax, rare shortia and familiar birds, lady's slippers in pink and yellow—the list goes on. Here is a smaller, personal kinship with the mountains, a sense of place once described by a poet as "knowledge carried to the heart."

Two homes give me two perspectives on the Great Smokies. Perhaps that is why I recognize and appreciate so fully the dual vision that Michael Frome brings to his story of these mountains and their national park.

From a spacious hilltop view, his exhaustive research on the Smokies provides full and satisfying acquaintance with the strangers and their explorations. From the more intimate view of small wonders and delicate, contained spaces, his familiarity with the wild heart of the Smokies inspires renewed vigor in resisting encroachment at its center or its boundaries.

Years have passed since I decided that *Strangers in High Places* "was going to be all right." Of course, I misjudged. Much that was at best trivial and inadequate, at worst misleading and untrue, had been published about the Great Smokies. I was too reserved about this new volume, which was more than "all right." In fulfilling its title and mission it was "just right."

The Smokies Revisited: A Preface for the Nineties

I Knock on Many Doors

Finding how the park saved Cades Cove—Many now settle for a "leg-stretcher"—Young people are only beginning to see what they missed—"I was sure you was dead"

I knocked on many doors. I felt that was the way to conduct my revisit in the 1990s to the Great Smoky Mountains, the preeminent nature sanctuary in the glorious domain of Southern Appalachia. By asking questions and listening, I hoped to touch the truths the Smoky Mountains hold within them. Although I had returned a number of times since publication of *Strangers in High Places* more than a quarter of a century before, I now sought new understanding of mountains and mountain people, and of others who come to these mountains and of why they do, and of myself as well. I recorded copious notes and later reviewed them, looking to make the pieces fit. I concluded that mystery must always hide beyond the last answer with yet another question, particularly in these ancient mountains, which are composed of far more than reducible substance. But those with whom I talked helped immeasurably by sharing experience and perspective.

When I came to Randolph Shields at his home in Maryville, Tennessee, for example, he clearly was ready. Virtually his first words were, "The last time we met was in 1962, when you came to Roanoke to talk to me about Cades Cove." That indeed was the case. Doctor Shields, then teaching biology at Roanoke College, in Virginia, had been a source of priceless data about life in the mountain valley where he was born and spent his childhood. Now I was back, thirty years later, not in Roanoke but in Maryville, within view of the Smokies, to ask him again about Cades Cove.

Randolph had come home years ago to teach at Maryville College, from which he was now retired. He told me of conducting field classes in the national park, and weekend hikes with students of fifteen to twenty miles, and of studying plant succession over a period of fifty years. He recalled life in the old days before leaving Cades Cove at age thirteen—that was when the park came. There wasn't much entertainment, and church was not a place for recreation. Most weddings were held at home, for nuptials involved too much hilarity to satisfy the Primitive Baptists, and no music was permitted in church. We talked of the depressing curtain of air pollution hanging over the park, and of how Cades Cove is jammed with visitors: On a summer day driving time around the eleven-mile loop is at least two hours. Scores of vans, campers, and cars slow from a crawl to complete stop to view historic cabins, a deer or black bear, yet few visitors at most actually leave their vehicles to touch the ground.

But the most revealing intelligence came when I asked Randolph's assessment of the best thing the national park had brought to the Smokies. "The Park Service saved Cades Cove," he replied forthwith, explaining that a group of Knoxville entrepreneurs had wanted to develop the valley. Several bought land and built cottages. They planned to build a dam for a recreational lake, and a golf course. The advent of the park blocked the development, so that now, all these years later, Randolph could return to scenes he had known in childhood, and which his parents and their parents had known before him.

Days later at the national park visitor center outside Gatlinburg I talked with Glenn Cardwell, whom I have known almost since he started working there in 1961. Glenn was born in the Greenbrier section in 1930; his mother was an Ogle, grandmother a Trentham, old settlers' names in these parts. With the coming of the park, natives moved out of the Greenbrier, but Glen's family stayed close, in Emerts Cove, where he still lived. Glenn mentioned seasonal naturalists of the 1930s, like Stanley Cain and A. J. Sharp, both well-respected University of Tennessee botany professors, working under Arthur Stupka, the first chief naturalist in the park. Cain, in fact, wrote the manual for the first guided walk.

"When I started, tourists came to stay a month," Glenn recalled. "We led all-day hikes to Charlies Bunion and Silers Bald, but by 1964 we had cut back to half-day hikes. Now we have a forty-five-minute 'leg stretcher' that is very popular. The shorter the program the greater the participation. Maybe they're taking the self-guided trails, but visitors seem more oriented to the commercial world. That's the greatest change I've seen."

Local people have changed too. Even after electricity came to the coves in 1947, they preferred agricultural ways with milk cows, smoke houses, and spring houses—until they were drawn into the Gatlinburg labor market, working for cash at motels, restaurants, and trinket shops. The salvation of the cove is that it still lacks city water and sewage, leaving the community out of the commercial loop. When I asked Glenn about the meaning of the park to him, he gave much the same answer as Randolph Shields:

> I took my father back to the Greenbrier on his eighty-fifth birthday. He said, "I fussed and cussed as much as anybody over the park. I regretted most losing my neighbors. It hurt, but now I know it was right." He recognized that the park saved the mountains. It preserved natural beauty. When my forebears came they had an unbroken view of the mountain forests. I have that vision. That is how it should be.

These two interviews gave me a thread to follow, and not simply about the value of the national park. That is too easily defined in terms of numbers of visitors, the amount of money they bring to local communities, the diversity of salamanders, flowering plants and trees, all material and for the most part measurable. The questions I find worth pursuing are the influence of a natural environment on human environment and human dignity, and whether, and how, once the land changes people are likely to change in consequence.

Across the mountains, in Sylva, North Carolina, John Parris, whose family is rooted in the Smokies, gave me further evidence and food for thought. Since 1955 John has been writing a column, "Roaming the Mountains," for the *Asheville Citizen-Times* (which must be some kind of record). Earlier, John was a wire-service correspondent in Europe, who decided he'd rather head home to chronicle the culture of the hills. Now he was seventy-seven, feeling *he* was the oldtimer. John talked about the new culture imported principally from south Florida, bringing with it pretentious, oversized homes and condominiums, golf courses and country clubs, and an upscale crowd hooked on luxury living. The way of the native is hard pressed.

"I grew up when you didn't have radio or television," John said. "You ate three meals in the house. We talked, people would visit, you knew your neighbors and their roots. I knew my grandfather, who was born in 1859 and lived to a hundred. You don't get this today. Storytelling is practically gone. Many people hardly know their parents." For his part, John has been active through the Center of Mountain Living at Western North Carolina University, promoting essay contests and mountain culture retreats for high-school students. "It's tough to get them interested. They're only beginning to see what they missed."

John told of an error I had made in *Strangers in High Places*: Granville Calhoun was not born in Tennessee, as I wrote (on page 146), but at Wayside, on the Little Tennessee River, below the mouth of Hazel Creek, now under the waters of Fontana Lake. John Parris would know, but that was the only error he had found, which I regarded as a considerable compliment.

When I wrote this book nearly thirty years ago I had no idea that it would endure as long as it has, no idea of the meaning it would have for people, or that I would walk into places to be recognized by my name. Once, after delivering a lecture, one man in the audience came up to tell me that his mother gave him a copy to take with him on military service in the Pacific, and when he became homesick he would open the book, read awhile, and feel better. Another time a fellow said, "I had to come talk to you, as I was sure you was dead."

I've been asked many times how I chose to write about the Smokies in the first place and why I keep coming back. The second part is easy: The Great Smoky Mountains are still one of God's special places, even while much of the world, close at hand and far away, goes downhill. Thus the national park becomes more of a treasure with passing years, deserving the same love and care society bestows on magnificent works of art, and likewise for the mountain forests and streams of all of Southern Appalachia.

After various explanations, I now conclude that I didn't choose the Smokies. The Smokies chose me. I was meant to come, to heed and produce this work in 1966, a year of crisis for the national park, and meant to come back now to review and renew the connection. Actually I first saw the Smokies in 1947, soon after working briefly as a young reporter for the *Nashville Tennessean*. I came to Gatlinburg and found it still off the beaten path, a country town, more like it had been in 1940 than what it would become in 1960, certainly with little resemblance to the frenetic Gatlinburg of today. I knew little about conservation or national parks or Southern mountains or mountain people, but when I went to Newfound Gap and saw the bronze plaque marking establishment of the park amidst endless mountain splendor I felt elevated, a sense of something fine.

Then I returned two or three years later as a travel writer living in Washington, D.C., on a writers' tour hosted by the regional promoters. I was introduced to mountain craftspeople—woodcarvers, weavers, makers of pots, dolls, and dulcimers—and to moonshiners, Cherokee Indians, park rangers, and forest rangers. The Biltmore estate in Asheville was magic, with the Vanderbilt mansion, gardens, dairy farm, and weaving seemingly transported whole from some European barony; at Biltmore I learned about Frederick Law Olmsted, Vanderbilt's landscape architect, and Gifford Pinchot, the young forester Olmsted brought along to introduce forestry to America. Tourism was different then, more civic and cultural instead of overblown with commerciality and crowds as it is now. For example, the Spring Wildflower Pilgrimage in Gatlinburg was started to attract visitors. Tourism for the most part was compatible with the natural setting, rather than contradictory to it.

I kept coming back, traveling down the crest of the Blue Ridge, the eastern rampart of the Appalachian Mountains, first on the Skyline Drive in Shenandoah National Park and then the Blue Ridge Parkway, which links Shenandoah and the Smokies. For motoring, I thought there was nothing like it: There were no billboards or high speeds, as on the freeways; I could stop at mountaintop wildflower gardens, restored mills, weathered cabins, and at overlooks facing farms and national forests. I wrote articles about auto touring, even while my instinct told me to move on: to focus on the craftspeople, working at quiet art demanding time and patience, rooted in the world of magic sunsets and misty solitudes, reflecting a time when everything was handhewn and handmade, and on life in the wild parts of Southern Appalachia, so diverse and abundant.

In preparing for this new edition, I decided not to make any changes in the original 1966 or in the Preface and Epilogue I added to the edition of 1980. The text shows the Smoky Mountains as I saw and sensed them at those particular junctures in history. In a way, the book is history too, and I hope this new Preface will add to appreciation of the high places.

When People Count

Jamming the courthouse for Cataloochee—Mark Hannah's haymaking machine—When the Moonshine Maker says, "Have a drink"— Barbara tells of treks with Masa, the tireless trailblazer

I never saw such an outpouring of Smoky Mountain people as on the hot evening of July 25, 1979, in Waynesville, North Carolina, when national park planners conducted a public hearing on the Great Smokies management plan, with particular reference to Cataloochee. I mean the Haywood County courthouse was jampacked with local men and women who one after another rose to tell of the old place where they, or their parents and grandparents, were born and why they disapproved of a paved highway going back in there. It was mountain eloquent and powerful.

Park planning had come a long way, it really had. The draft general management plan discussed in serious professional manner the strategy required to preserve the Great Smoky Mountains unimpaired for the enjoyment of future generations; still, despite appropriate scientific, biological, ecological, and environmental reasons, all presented logically, the plan led to the illogical conclusion that the Cataloochee access road should be built. It was plainly a manifestation of politics above principle—of Park Service leaders delivering to their benefactor in Congress, Representative Roy Taylor, of western North Carolina, the project they assumed he wanted. The people, however, would not stand for it, and the provision for the access road in due course was removed.

People count. Were it not for everyday people who care, the Smoky Mountains likely would be another parcel of real estate, developed and probably overdeveloped. My interest, I daresay, has been in the relationship between mountains and people, how they influence and care for each other. In my early research I met marvelous people and wish now I'd been wise enough to conduct interviews with a tape recorder. I never realized the value of the tape, of how I would love to listen once again to the voices of Granville Calhoun tell about Horace Kephart and about bear hunting, and of Jarrett Blythe, the Cherokee chieftain, talk of his grandfather's talks with him. Showing how little I knew then, Horace Albright, who long ago played a key role in the Smokies as director of the National Park Service, responded to questions I sent him by mail with detailed stories on tape—once transcribed covering forty typewritten pages—yet I foolishly failed to save the tapes.

Incidents and episodes and stories I've never told come to mind as I reflect on those early encounters. Gaining access to an authentic professional moon-shiner, for example, proved more difficult than I had expected. I thought it had all been worked out by a friend with the Internal Revenue Service in Washington. But when I arrived in Asheville, the local IRS agent, Earl Branum, explained the potential contacts were skittish as a consequence of recent raids. Luckily, I remembered that Ted Seeley, district ranger of the Pisgah National Forest at nearby Brevard, was a connoisseur of locally made whiskey. The Forest Service, for that matter, maintained a kind of unwritten field agreement with moonshiners that went like this: "We won't push you if you keep the stills small and quiet and don't burn the woods." So Ted took me out to meet the Moonshine Maker of Chapter XXII. I had my notepad at the ready when this fellow looked me straight in the eye and said, "Have a drink." It was the thing to do. He started talking, but he insisted that I have another, and then another—I heard what he had to say, but that was a boozy afternoon.

This time around I carried a tape recorder. I talked with people with whom I had talked before for their perspectives over time. They themselves are living history, bridging time, filling in gaps, helping to keep the record straight from their own experience.

Arthur Stupka, for instance, came to the Smokies in 1935 as the park's first naturalist, at a time when sixteen or seventeen camps of the Civilian Conservation Corps were building trails and pulling up cross ties of the old logging railroads. He had already been the first naturalist at Acadia National Park in Maine after beginning his national parks career at Yosemite in the summer of 1931 while still a student at Ohio State University, and after beginning his lifetime nature journal in grade school. "I was paid to do what I liked to do. I was lucky, I had my own program, I was my own boss," Stupka told me in 1992. He was well up in his eighties and long retired, living in a modern apartment building, complete with elevators, at the edge of Gatlinburg, to which he was reconciled without enthusiasm. Stupka seemed fragile but keen as ever, as methodical and measured in his speech as when I first heard him conduct the evening naturalist program at the Mountain View Hotel forty-plus years ago. In those days, Stupka, Bart Lieper, of the Gatlinburg visitors bureau, and A. J. Sharp, of the University of Tennessee, started the Spring Wildflower Pilgrimage. It was a simple program that has since grown into a major promotion with eighty-seven separate events attracting at least a thousand pilgrims.

> I remember the first year the park got one million visitors—that was something special. Now the park is pushing ten million, but don't be amazed. It doesn't mean anything, they're staying on the road, rarely get out. Once I was preparing to lead a hike to LeConte. I noticed a young man with one leg. "Are you sure . . . ?" I asked. "I'll be okay," he said, waving one of his two crutches. He did fine; then next day he went to the Chimney Tops. He was determined, that's what it takes.

That's the way to get acquainted with the park. Visitation now is largely superficial.

Stupka himself was still active, leading spring walks and talks from an inn at Bryson City. "Usually I'll have about twenty people, but having three or four is enough reward for me, if they're really interested." Recalling the hike I made with him to Ramsay Cascade (see Chapter XXIV), I wish I could follow the trail once again with this pioneering park naturalist.

He had lately re-read *Strangers* and offered corrections. There are no more than seventy-five trees at the most, even including mountain laurel—not more than a hundred, as I had written. The name of the Big Locust Nature Trail at the base of the Chimneys has been changed to Cove Hardwood Trail. The Chimneys area is not a campground, but a picnic area. The term "unpolluted Smokies" is no longer valid—how sad. In due course I would hike under the pall of poisoned haze and see the great old trees of the high forests on Clingmans Dome and Heintooga Ridge as bare as skeletons, likely weakened by the acid rain, then done in by woolly aphids.

"You know, Carlos Campbell never got the credit due him for his work in behalf of the park," Stupka said. He was right; that was an error of omission. Campbell had been manager of the Knoxville Chamber of Commerce when he turned his lifetime interest to the Smokies. He directed a fund-raising project to bring the entire Tennessee legislature to see the area, leading to purchase of the first large tract of land for the park by the state. He was a founder of the Smoky Mountains Hiking Club and organizer of the Great Smoky Mountains Conservation Association, serving as its secretary until he died in 1978 at the age of eighty-six.

Paul Adams was another person of note in the early days. Growing up sickly in Knoxville, he turned to the outdoors for his health and made his first climb to Mount LeConte as a teenager in 1918. Five years later he wasn't at all sorry to end his freshman career at the University of Tennessee and head for the Smokies. Adams was still in his early twenties when the Great Smoky Mountains Conservation Association hired him as guide and packer on trips to show important visitors the wonders of the Smokies, his guests including worldly members of the federal commission appointed to choose a national park site in the Appalachians (see Chapter XIV). The focal point of interest was the LeConte area, an unlogged fragment of rain forest, a botanist's paradise. Adams established a permanent camp at LeConte; he turned it over in 1926 to Jack Huff, who built the celebrated LeConte Lodge. Over the years until his death in 1985 Paul Adams climbed LeConte more than five hundred times. He was a gentle person who became a weaver on hand looms. Simplicity counted; he felt free of pressure for success as usually measured. "Most of all," he wrote in his later days, "I have enjoyed visiting again the dark forest of spruce and balsams, hearing the call of the veery and winter wren, seeing again the delicate beauty of sand myrtle blossoms, and the red splendor of sunrises and sunsets from Myrtle Point and Clifftop."

Mark Hannah was eighty-six when I came to see him, about the same age as Stupka. Mark was a little creaky, as he confessed, having suffered a stroke, which made him mildly forgetful, and was hard of hearing. But he still had a great sense of humor. "At the last homecoming in Cataloochee I got up and said, 'I'm glad I'm here,' and sat down. They gave me a big hand." Mark was born in Cataloochee Valley in 1906, when it probably looked much as it had fifty years before. After playing football for Cullowhee State Normal (later Western Carolina University) and after the coming of the national park, Mark and his bride, Verda, in 1934 moved out of the home valley to a new rock house in Maggie Valley. He worked for a while as a county warden, then joined the National Park Service as one of the corps of local rangers. So he spent his career tending the home country as public property. When he retired in 1972 he and Verda returned to their old house in Maggie Valley, which is where I came to visit. I was struck by the beautiful photographs of their respective childhood homes, soft and mellow scenes of pastoral paradise lost, which took on the patina of paintings; the pictures were taken about 1915–16 of sturdy country houses built five or ten years before, complete with barn and applehouse, and view of the nearby schoolhouse in Little Cataloochee. These people know their genealogy and who is kin to whom. "Why, everybody you talk to married her cousin," joked Mark, referring to Dolly Parton, the Smoky Mountains country girl who became a superstar in Nashville. But, of course, the Messers *are* related to the Partons, and Verda is a Messer. Be that as it may, Mark gave me a copy of the book he published, *Smoky Mountain Reflections*, a collection of his own poems. With Mark's permission, here is one of them:

A NEW MACHINE AT HAYMAKING TIME
About 1917

Tine Woody said to Dad, "I'll buy a machine,
You and your boys, can furnish the team.
    We'll all work together and stack up the hay,
    To feed our stock, on a cold winter's day."

The mower he bought, was an ideal Deering.
'Twas a horse drawn thing, didn't need any steering.
    Floyd Woody came over to assemble the parts,
    To have it ready, when the hay cutting starts.

When Floyd came over, he was riding a horse,
Falsom was with him, he called her his boss.
    Uncle Tim Woody, was also there,
    Riding Old Maude, that's what he called his mare.

Floyd, Robert, and other boys joined in,
Soon they had assembled, the mowing machine.
   They hooked up the team, started mowing around,
   Uncle Tine said, "God, it's a'shaving the ground!"

Uncle Tine and Robert, were mowing on a hill,
Tine had a mare, that wouldn't stand still.
   She backed the mower wheel up Tine's shin,
   Then it fell down, with a big patch of skin.

When Tine got loose, he opened his knife,
Then threatened to take, Old Maude's life.
   He closed up his knife and rolled down his sock,
   Said to Old Maude, "You're swapping stock."

Bill Rolen was also born in the park before it was a park, in his case at Oconaluftee, when there was a sawmill roughly where the visitor center stands now. His first job in the park, in 1933, was with the CCC, leading to his appointment as a ranger. "I love the Smokies and I loved the work. But I wasn't no outstanding person, I don't think," Bill told me at his home in Bryson City. But he was the only one of the local group who advanced into the professional ranger series. He was placed in charge of the entire North Carolina district and showed me wonderful country with caring insight. After retiring in 1969, Bill was elected a Swain County commissioner on a platform of settling the Fontana road dispute without building the road. Now he was eighty-two, and retired again. "We got close. We went to Washington, trying to work out a settlement for money. But the Democrats lost the election to Reagan and we didn't have anybody to talk to. Swain County needs the money, it doesn't need the road."

I missed people, friends who had helped me, now gone to their reward. I missed especially Carol White, who labored long and hard and selflessly to build the Cherokee Historical Association into a rare successful combination of cultural conservation and tourist promotion (see pages 306–10), while chain-smoking all the way. In Carol's day the Museum of the Cherokee occupied a dinky corner in the old historical association building, which was pretty dinky in itself. Now for the first time I saw the new museum (which opened in 1976)—it was not only comprehensive and impressive in portraying Cherokee history and culture, but included a library and archives complete with a librarian who told me everything is now on computer. There wasn't anything like it twenty-five years ago. It may have been dreamed of, but here it was come true.

"This is *the* place for serious scholarly research," the librarian, Joann Orr, told me. She was a good case study herself, a former school teacher who started as a volunteer, then went back to Western Carolina University when it initiated a graduate program of Cherokee studies. Little wonder, considering the Smoky Mountain Cherokee are as fascinating as the Navajo and as much a part of the mountains as the forest, flowers, and streams. The main street of the town of Cherokee still had its schlock shops trading in trinketry and natives "chiefing," but this time the street scene struck me as more camp than crass, and those gimmicks are strictly for the tourist trade, not for the Cherokee. I was not surprised when Ms. Orr said more and more Cherokee of all ages were coming in to study the old dwellings, language, dress, marriage customs, history. Despite endless predictions of dissolution and assimilation, the tradition and spirit have remained rooted in place. Young Cherokee may go off for education, but they come back to put their learning to use here.

The mountains call us home and build a fraternity to keep the spirit strong across time and distance. That's about how I felt when I called on Barbara Ambler Thorne. She was more than a kindred spirit, but the keeper of the kingdom. The mountain ethos plainly was in her bones and blood, even while she despaired of her recent move to a retirement home in Asheville. She may have been in her upper eighties, but when she spoke of the Smokies her voice was warm, with the lively, lovely lilt of youth to it:

> I'd go by George Masa's office, a little bitty shop in the Arcade Building. I'd say, "Let's go to Guyot," or maybe it was LeConte. "Will you take me?" Or I would say to my friend Jewel King, "Let's go get George!" It didn't matter; he would answer at once, "When do you want to go?" Often we'd get two or three people and start out. We might walk the ridges for hours, or walk where there was no trail. Those trips with George in the early thirties were really pioneering. Jewel and I were the first women. Masa was the most wonderful man. We had to carry his camera, with the heavy tripod of those days, but we were young and it didn't matter.

Her father, Doctor Chase P. Ambler, was a principal figure in the movement for conservation in the mountains, the founder in 1899 of the Appalachian National Park Association (see pages 174–75), but Barbara was an accomplished personality in her own right. She told of the wonderful hikes she made to Guyot, Three Forks, and Mount Sterling, some of the wildest sections of the Smokies, without apprehension about the steep terrain, weather, or mountaineers. She showed photographs on the trail with George Stephens, who was long active in the Carolina Mountain Club; at Cataloochee Ranch, when Tom and Judy Alexander were just starting their camp at the edge of the park, and of herself. "I don't believe I ever carried a heavy pack like that," she exclaimed, but I believed it and the photos gave the evidence.

Mostly she talked about George Masa, the Japanese-born photographer and mountain man who provided pictures to support establishment of the park while neglecting his own business (see pages 110 and 159). She showed a faded clipping from the *Asheville Citizen-Times* of December 13, 1953:

His devotion to the cause of beauty caused him to sleep many nights in the rain so that he might be on hand when the pink fingers of dawn pulled back the purple curtain of night. No sacrifice of personal comfort was too great if he was able to trap a spectacular lighting effect. . . . His camera eye was the eye of the public and he brought the beauty of remote places to magazines and newspapers through his pictures.

Masa frequently pushed a bicycle wheel, to which an accurate measuring device was attached, along mountain trails, carefully recording the distances traveled. Thus there came about a careful measuring of these trails to spots of beauty. Masa and his little wheel were a familiar sight to the people of the mountains and he always had a cheery greeting for those he met.

Barbara had known Benton MacKaye, father of the Appalachian Trail idea, and had corresponded with Harvey Broome, who interested her in the Wilderness Society. She was still zestful, tuned into issues and caring about them. "I've been here [in the retirement home] two months and it's killing me. But the food's good and I don't have to cook it." I wish I could have taken her by the hand and hiked with her to LeConte and Myrtle Point.

Removing Roads Is Progress, Too

Citizens testify, then hike to "Save the Smokies"—They take their case to Washington—Harvey, gentle but determined, sparks the fight— Cain's classic line: "Those who run cannot 'see'"

In 1969 Edward E. C. Clebsch, professor of botany at the University of Tennessee, prepared a paper "concerning the values of science to wilderness." It was no mere academic exercise. Clebsch wrote his paper for presentation to Secretary of the Interior Walter J. Hickel as part of the citizen effort to prevent construction of the proposed transmountain highway across Great Smoky Mountains National Park. Clebsch stated his intent was to show "the ecological consequences of poor stewardship. . . ."

That reference by Clebsch reflected critically on the National Park Service, which I daresay most Americans identify with the absolute ultimate in stewardship. Certainly I identified it that way. For me, in the early phase of my education and evolution, the National Park Service was a strong, trustworthy, principled outfit led by heroes. In the Smoky Mountains, alas, I learned otherwise. I saw the work of weak and ordinary men.

For example, Clebsch in his paper declared the benefits of the proposed transmountain highway to the community of scientists as virtually nonexistent, that the liabilities of such a road far outweighed the benefits—not just to the scientists, but to the population at large as well. He cited reasons the road should not be built: It would split a wilderness in two; alter the chemical constituents of several very fine streams; cause physical changes in the streams by siltation; alter groundwater patterns for an unpredictable distance from the cuts and fills necessary to build the road; require planting exotic species to stabilize the cuts and fills; create a barrier to movement of animal species; provide avenues for the introduction of new pests and pathogens; and serve as a point source for contamination and disturbance of the adjacent wilderness by people and their refuse.

That analysis makes sense. It's almost self-evident, and certainly ought to be to scientists working for a public agency committed to land stewardship. But no such warning of the damages implicit in the transmountain road was provided to the public by National Park Service scientists, nor by anyone in any discipline at any level working for the agency. Personnel either spoke in support of the road or were silent, providing an equal measure of support. "To sin by silence when they should cry out," as Lincoln said, "makes cowards out of men."

Clebsch's paper was presented to Hickel on June 23, 1969, when a delegation of almost one hundred citizen conservationists, representing groups in Tennessee and North Carolina, came to Washington to plead their case. I was there in the huge Interior Department conference room. I watched Hickel walk around the room, looking each person in the eye and shaking hands. "I am impressed by your numbers and the sincerity of your purpose," the secretary declared. I watched George B. Hartzog, Jr., director of the National Park Service. He was there too, though not especially comfortable with the proceedings. For once, he had lost control. The transmountain road was Hartzog's idea and he was a powerhouse, not as a preservationist but as a political wheeler-dealer, a hard driver, heavy drinker, cigar smoker, builder of a bureaucratic empire. Hickel was just as tough as Hartzog and outranked him. Thus the secretary responded to the citizens by assigning the Park Service to review its plan and come back with something different. The new report, issued in January 1971, declared the Smokies comprise "a natural treasure of plant and animal life living in an ecological balance that once destroyed can never be restored," and the transmountain road plan was withdrawn.

Hartzog had worked in the Great Smokies early in his career, but I doubt he ever had the feeling for the place, with its wildness and mystery and limitless future, certainly not in the same sense as Arno B. Cammerer, the director most closely involved with establishment of the park. With the Smokies in mind, Cammerer in a 1938 speech in Washington spoke of potentials: of a new area that might not measure up at a particular present time, but that, fifty or one hundred years hence, with protection, would attain a natural condition comparable to the primitive, and within a thousand years would look as God had made it. Cammerer could envision the future of the earth, while Hartzog dealt with politics of the pragmatic present.

Thus in 1966 Hartzog chose Great Smoky Mountains as the first park for which to propose a new addition to the National Wilderness Preservation System. Under provisions of the 1964 Wilderness Act, the Fish and Wildlife Service, Forest Service, and National Park Service all were required to review potential wilderness under their jurisdiction, to conduct public hearings and submit recommendations for action by Congress. Hartzog evidently thought his old stamping ground, the Smokies, would make an easy beginning. But Hartzog miscalculated, very badly.

> Conservationists the world over are looking to our National Park Service for exemplary leadership in the field of safeguarding the beauty and character of natural landscape and sites. It would be most unfortunate if the Park Service were unable to fulfill this role in the Smokies.

Those words, at the first public hearing on wilderness in the national parks, conducted at Gatlinburg, Tennessee, on June 13, 1966, were spoken by Stewart M. Brandborg, executive director of the Wilderness Society. I felt then, on hearing them in the hall (as I still do now, these years later), that Brandborg touched the heart of the issue with simplicity and directness, denoting a greatness of moment reaching far beyond the hearing itself. For as someone said during the floodtide of feeling and eloquence, "A wrong decision will be severely judged by untold millions still unborn."

Instead of a plan for wilderness, the Park Service offered a design for roads to solve seasonal traffic jams, including the construction of a new transmountain road, that would cross the Appalachian Trail, plus corridors for additional inner loops. What was left over, less than half the park, was offered for inclusion in the National Wilderness Preservation System—in six broken blocks, ranging in size from 110,000 down to 5,000 acres. The wilderness proposal was part of a master plan to accommodate ever increasing numbers with massive campgrounds of two hundred, three hundred, six hundred units.

Hartzog could not possibly have anticipated the public's will to be heard. More than two hundred witnesses presented oral statements at hearings in Gatlinburg and then two days later across the mountains in Bryson City; 5,400 letters were later received for the hearing record. A handful of local politicians and business people supported the Park Service plan, but a parade of preachers and schoolteachers, scholars and scientists, scouts and scout leaders, hikers, trout fishermen, botanists, and birdwatchers spoke for wilderness. They spoke of the joys of wild places, the spiritual exhilaration, the threats of a political road-building boondoggle. They identified with love of land, idealism, a qualitative experience as the essence of our national parks.

The government plan for the Smokies was clearly poorly drawn, designed only to solve short-range pragmatic and political problems. The justification was based on a legal agreement of 1943, when the Tennessee Valley Authority, as part of its program to construct Fontana Dam on the Little Tennessee River, acquired and transferred to the Park Service 44,000 acres of land, in return for which the Park Service pledged to provide a new road on the north shore of Fontana Lake linking the towns of Bryson City and Fontana. (For further details see note 202:3 on page 372.) For a number of years the Park Service sought to convince Swain County, North Carolina, a principal party to the agreement, to accept improvement of Route 129, along the *south* shore of Fontana Lake, outside the park, thus avoiding disturbing the wilderness. But the county said no; it wanted a new tourist route through the park.

Finally, during 1963–64, construction proceeded from Bryson City 2.5 miles into the park, with sheer disaster as consequence—erosion, scars on the landscape, natural beauty destroyed. The project was halted; this stretch has since been known as "the road to nowhere." Then, in September 1965, at a cozy session in Bryson City, Hartzog offered Swain County officials still another alternative: a transmountain route across the Smokies wilderness to Townsend, Tennessee. There had been no advance notice of this proposal, no hearings to determine how the public felt; I doubt the director consulted his own associates. Once it became known, however, complaints poured in. "The Park Service has put forward a road-building project that transgresses the spirit of the Wilderness Act and that would bring heavy automobile traffic streaming through the very area that needs to be protected," editorialized the *New York Times*. "The proposal for this transmountain road reflects weariness rather than foresight and clear thinking."

Editorials in the *New York Times* and other newspapers were part of a marvelous mobilization of public opinion; it was an education to observe, an enrichment to feel as a part of it. In the fall of 1966 I came down to join the "Save-the-Smokies" Hike. Ernie Dickerman, one of the principal organizers, recorded the event (in the *Smoky Mountains Hiking Club Handbook of 1967*) as follows:

> At the Labor Day meeting of the half dozen clubs responsible for maintaining the southern portion of the Appalachian Trail, it was enthusiastically decided to hold a "Save-Our-Smokies Wilderness Hike." On Sunday, October 23, a total of 576 individuals, starting from the Clingmans Dome parking area, walked some portion of the 17-mile route following the Appalachian Trail to Buckeye Gap (where the proposed road would pass over, under or through the crest of the Smokies), thence north to Miry Ridge to Jakes Gap and down to the Elkmont Campground. A total of 234 persons, ranging in age from 5 years old to 81 years old, walked the entire 17 miles. Most of these 234 reached Elkmont between 3 and 6 P.M., though the last half dozen came in around 8:10 P.M. by moonlight. Twenty-two states were represented, 8 national conservation associations and numerous local outdoor groups from far and wide. A total of 260 persons came strictly on their own, with no group affiliation.

Those people turned out to defend the wilderness and to assert that national park policy must transcend local politics and be determined in full public view. Through the research for my book and participating in these activities, I became involved with a new set of mentors. I traipsed around to all the environmental groups in Washington. Of all the leading lights I met, Stewart Brandborg, of the Wilderness Society in Washington, proved the warmest and most patient. I'm certain it was through him that I first met Harvey Broome, who was not only president of the Wilderness Society but an East Tennessean and apostle of the Smoky Mountains, and through Harvey the intrepid Dickerman. On the Save-the-Smokies Hike I met Bill and Liane Russell, who became close friends through the years; I knew them as leaders of the Tennessee Citizens for Wilderness Planning, although in their other lives they were prominent research geneticists at the Oak Ridge Laboratory. I had been impressed at the Gatlinburg wilderness hearing by a courageous young state park naturalist, Mack Prichard, who risked his job by testifying in opposition to the official position of his agency. In due course we became hiking partners, comrades-in-arms; in 1992 he was still on the job, as state naturalist of Tennessee, and still risking it by putting conservation above bureaucracy and politics.

Harvey took me on hikes to the Chimney Tops and Spence Field and took me to his home in Knoxville. I refer to him elsewhere in the book; suffice for the present to say Harvey was a pioneer hiker in the Smokies, who walked sure-footed but lightly on the land; he was gentle, selfless, but thoroughly determined. Harvey gave the spark that fueled the fight to block the transmountain road. Responding to the challenge of providing for more and more visitors, Harvey wrote:

> It must be clear that the demand which now looms over us can never be satisfied. Slow attrition follows development. Almost without exception, wherever there is a road or dug trail or shelter facility in the virgin forest, there is slowly spreading damage. The areas contiguous to developments become littered, eroded or threadbare from heavy use and abuse.
>
> No further development of any character should take place. No more trails; no more shelters; no more roads; no expansions, extensions, or additions to existing facilities. To protect what is left we must learn to live with facilities we now have. The hardest thing will be the decision itself.

That was not how the National Park Service felt, at least not the people who spoke for it. Ross Bender, chief naturalist of Great Smoky Mountains National Park, was an aggressive road boomer. "A cross-mountain road such as proposed is needed to divert the heavy traffic we now experience," Bender wrote to the Student Conservation Association in a statement published in its Spring-Summer 1966 newsletter. "Nearly six million people visited the park in 1965 and if some of these visitors could be diverted to other areas of the park this congestion could be relieved for several years if not forever. Secondly, the proposed route would provide several loop trips, using existing state roads of considerable distance, which we believe visitors would take. Visitors would then be in their cars several hours longer driving and as long as they are in their cars, no damage to the natural features can be done."

I have always found such logic grossly illogical, and particularly inappropriate from a professional naturalist. Stanley A. Cain, of the University of Tennessee, who prepared the pioneering 1937 guide to the Greenbrier-Brushy Mountain Nature Trail, had a much better idea. "This trail can offer little to the sightseeing tourist in a hurry," Cain wrote. "Those who run cannot 'see,' and those for whom hiking is too great an exertion cannot stop to contemplate nature, only to pant."

I could not believe it when a friend on the park staff telephoned to advise that Bender had banned *Strangers in High Places* from being sold in the park. I was furious at such a mean-spirited act of state censorship. Without delay I went to see Hartzog and Clark Stratton, the deputy director of the National Park Service, in Washington. They did not need any persuasion to call the park with orders to sell the book and display it properly. Subsequently I received a letter from George Fry, the park superintendent, explaining that copies of the book simply had not been received from the publisher, poor hogwash on his part. Fry offered to issue a news release announcing the *Strangers* was indeed available for sale, but I was too angry to respond.

Fry, personally affable, was a loyal lieutenant in Hartzog's campaign to gut the Smokies wilderness, though not a hostile foe to citizen conservationists. "None of us is getting younger. In fact, we're all getting older," he was quoted as saying in the *Knoxville News-Sentinel*, November 2, 1966. "So we can't all hike, visit the waterfalls or camp out. We must open roads for visitors who are growing older. Many can't hike anymore." Years later, Fry wrote me (on August 7, 1992) to set the record straight: He had always been a team worker; early in his career he had learned, "If you can't support the boss, or agree with his policies and programs, get out." Maybe so, being a team player is understandable, but Fry made no comment about the effect of the proposed road on the natural character of the park. His only concerns were that his boss, Hartzog, wanted it, and that does not stand the test of principled stewardship. Fry was more of a victim than an enemy, though considerable damage has been done by those who say, "I was only following orders."

It took six years of public pressure, leading to intercession by Secretary of the Interior Hickel, to get Hartzog to throw in the towel on his road plan (before leaving the government in 1972). Park superintendents of recent years have been free, and wise enough, to heed opinions of interested, competent, and responsible scientists and other public parties in facing park problems and challenges, and in planning for preservation and appropriate use. The park to a significant degree has been managed as wilderness or "potential wilderness," even though the old political problems with Swain County still need to be resolved.

Sometimes it takes agencies repeated lessons before they learn. In 1974 the Park Service decided to proceed with construction of a paved highway from Interstate 40 into lovely, fragile Cataloochee Valley (see page 344). Officials tried to keep it quiet, without public review, but a handful of Haywood County (North Carolina) citizens caught wind, hired a lawyer, and obtained an injunction. Then the Committee to Save Cataloochee decided to conduct a protest hike early in August 1974 and invited me to come. The park superintendent, Vincent Ellis, a courtly, silver-haired gentleman, agreed to meet with the group to explain the park's plan. He was following orders, as Fry had done, from the regional and Washington offices, to accommodate the local congressman, Roy Taylor, who held the key post of chairman of the parks subcommittee in the House of Representatives.

Ellis came to the appointed rendezvous with entourage and maps. When he was through explaining things, the superintendent said, "Okay, now let's get in the cars to drive around and see where the new road would go." When members of the group insisted on walking, Ellis was taken aback. "But you won't see *nearly* as much." The citizens hiked anyway, and the Park Service people did too. A reporter covering the event for *The Mountaineer* of Waynesville interviewed me along the way, then recording (in the issue of August 9, 1974): "Frome said he did not think the present gravel road is a safety hazard. 'I think those dirt roads are beautiful,' he said. 'That's what they should have in national parks, if they must have roads.'" Which still makes sense to me. Progress is not in building highways in the Smokies, but in taking them out.

Appalachian Byroads and Backcountry

Appalachia has a unity to it—Our very own rain forests—A source of good as well as wood—Disrupting the bears of Harmon Den—And the snail darters of the Little Tennessee

In the course of research for my book *Whose Woods These Are—The Story of the National Forests*, my first serious conservation work (published in 1962), I spent considerable time in the national forests of Southern Appalachia. After all, the Pisgah National Forest is the "cradle of forestry" where Gifford Pinchot began his career in 1891 (when it was still part of the Biltmore estate of George Washington Vanderbilt) and where the first private land was acquired when national forests came East (following passage of the Weeks act of 1911).

I traveled all around the country exploring forests and interviewing forest people. In those days I respected and admired foresters as professionals serving the public interest. They were my friends and teachers who introduced me through lessons in the field to taxonomy, dendrology, silviculture, hydrology, and wildlife science; they conducted their business as individuals with social conscience, sound science, and vision, while the Forest Service was still proudly pursuing the conservation crusade that Pinchot had started. That was my view.

I called at little places along byroads and in the backcountry of Appalachia from Virginia across West Virginia and the Cumberland Plateau in Kentucky and south through the Carolinas, Tennessee, Georgia, and into Alabama. I loved every bit of it and what the Forest Service had achieved. I saw that Appalachia has a unity to it, comprising a cultural and ecological province, yet each and every hollow is distinctly its own, and so is each creek, creek valley, wooded slope, and ridgetop. Ultimately I concentrated on the Great Smokies, that is true, but the Smokies composition is but one star in the Appalachian heaven from which it cannot be disembodied.

Appalachia is our very own rain forest—no need to look beyond. Everywhere I went in the rich mesophytic (moisture-loving) woodlands I found abundant liverworts, mosses, mussels, salamanders, flowering plants, sometimes flowers even in branches of tall trees, forest life varying with elevation, slope, soil, degree of sun and shade. I recall visiting the Chattahoochee National Forest (deriving its name from the Cherokee word for "Flowering Rock," for the many waterfalls tumbling in the highlands), first in spring, with the beauty of the mountains accented by dogwood, redbud, mountain laurel, azalea and rhododendron, and again in fall, combining southern mildness with color changing of the hardwood trees, and with waters flowing swift and clear, cascading down through creeks into streams and out into rivers, their directions determined by the Blue Ridge Divide, carved through the rocks millions of years ago. I saw wonderful wild gardens wherever I went, scarcely known beyond the local communities.

The Forest Service had given the mountains back their dignity, after many years of poor farming practices and, even worse, poor logging practices of powerful outside companies that extracted profits and then left land and people impoverished. While in the West national forests were formed of land already in public ownership, forests in the East were based on purchase, mostly of land that nobody wanted, with some special primeval tracts here and there. Foresters were community people. Many hadn't been to forestry school so they didn't know the technical jargon that separates professionals from ordinary folk, but they knew their mountains and mountaineers. "We should look at forests as a source of 'good' as well as wood," Arthur Woody, a celebrated ranger in north Georgia, would tell young foresters training under him. Woody in 1925 negotiated the purchase of Sosebee Cove, from a farmer who had held it all his life and then was over seventy-five. Believing it to be the finest stand of unlogged tulip poplar in the state, Woody convinced his superiors to purchase it for ten dollars an acre, the highest price the Forest Service paid in those days. When he died in 1946 funeral services for Woody at a backcountry church cemetery were attended by fifteen hundred persons from all parts of the state.

That doesn't happen anymore, and I haven't met a ranger lately in Woody's class. The major change came in the mid-sixties when the Forest Service leadership proclaimed the old stewardship was out, the new "management" was in, with emphasis clearly on timber-first, timber-foremost. Thus with passage of the Wilderness Act of 1964, only two small (albeit beautiful) areas in the Southeast, Linville Gorge and Shining Rock, in western North Carolina, were included in the new National Wilderness Preservation System. Individuals and groups wanted more saved; they did not want their favorite places cut down and converted from wild forest to tree farm. The Forest Service responded with "interdisciplinary teams," "listening sessions," and "show-me trips," but little more. "The prevailing feeling expressed by those attending the hearings," complained Senator Jennings Randolph of West Virginia in 1972, "is that decisions have already been made and their expressed concerns have only been accepted as an empty polite gesture."

Senator Randolph was referring to the bitter controversy over the management of the Monongahela National Forest in his state. The West Virginia Highlands Conservancy, after studying the Wilderness Act, had proposed designation of three units—Dolly Sods, Otter Creek, and Cranberry Back Country—all as choice as their colorful names suggest. But the Forest Service had responded with plans for logging and road building, approval for coal exploration, and a new use classification, "back country," with logging allowed. So far as the agency was concerned, there wasn't any wilderness in eastern America, and there wasn't going to be any either.

People in Alabama felt otherwise about the Sipsey area of the Bankhead National Forest, a chain of deep gorges threaded with streams and waterfalls, where the southern tip of the Cumberland Plateau meets the coastal plain, and where Chickasaw and Cherokee once roamed in company with panther, bear, and beaver. The Alabama Conservancy surveyed wildlife, plants, geology, speleology, and history, with the foremost authorities in these fields contributing their time and talent. They inventoried deer, squirrels, otters, mink, beavers, and raccoons; fish driven out of major rivers by pollution, siltation, ditching, and damming, found only in remaining natural rivers like the Sipsey and its tributaries, not only popular fishing species, but two kinds of colorful little darters, previously unknown and unnamed; and no less than eighty species of birds, from northern whippoorwill to southern chuck-will's-widow. The conservancy made a strong case, enlisting the endorsement of Governor George C. Wallace, and winning designation of the Sipsey Wilderness in 1974. And one year later Congress passed the Eastern Wilderness Act, assuring more designations to come, with or without Forest Service approval.

I felt let down, disillusioned by the outfit I had trusted. The Forest Service had lost its steam to conserve; I continued to have friends in the ranks, but the agency itself was technocratic, unresponsive to anything but commodity values, and acted progressively only under pressure. It was poorly coordinated internally, with officials giving mindless answers in defense of indefensible decisions. On one hand, in 1971 when a large, choice, privately held tract of fifteen thousand acres in the Snowbirds and Little Buffalo drainage of

Graham County, in western North Carolina, became available for acquisition, the Nantahala National Forest made no effort to acquire it. On the other hand, the chief of the Forest Service, Edward P. Cliff, was publicly stressing the need of major acquisitions in the Appalachians because of the impact of commercial developments upon forest values. Moreover, the area in question, the Bemis tract, embraced prime trout streams and a connecting link on the migration route of the last and largest bear country in North Carolina outside the Smokies. But the forest supervisor, Del W. Thorsen, saw nothing to get excited about: People might build roads and vacation homes on steep slopes, said he, but that didn't mean they would cause any damage to soils and streams, and the damage wouldn't last long anyway.

The Forest Service has not been much concerned with the loss of bear habitat, or trout streams, or rare flora, or watershed damage, or pollution caused by assorted intrusions in the high mountains that always start with road building. Nor have I seen change for the better, no matter how often I've looked. In the fall of 1980 I joined Tom Lustig, of the National Wildlife Federation headquarters staff in Washington, D.C., on a mercy mission hoping to save important bear habitat in the Pisgah National Forest virtually adjacent to Great Smoky Mountains National Park. In the area known as the Twelve Mile Strip we found the Forest Service building what seemed more like a mainstem highway than a logging access road, and construction was headed directly for Harmon Den, a state-designated bear sanctuary.

Tom and I had both come in response to pleas, his from the state wildlife federation, mine from a group of local bearhunters, the Western North Carolina Sportsmen's Association. We had with us a frightening report from the North Carolina Wildlife Resources Commission about the gloomy future of the black bear, citing the urgency of maintaining large roadless tracts in the mountain national forests. Forest Service representatives met us and our local friends at the site for a standard show-me trip. The deputy supervisor and wildlife biologist went through the litany of interdisciplinary team planning. "We don't get everything we want," conceded the biologist, "but all viewpoints are carefully considered. It could have been worse, you know." Those two officials were young men, working in the mountains but not of the mountains, loyal primarily to the organization that gave them sustenance and status in a peer group, looking to their future, their next assignments somewhere else, ever mindful of the "career ladder," and thus ever cautious.

But Charles Hill, a North Carolina state biologist, who had come with us, was an experienced hand in bear country and cared more about bears than about his job. He warned that the new Forest Service roads would only provide a connecting link with the new Interstate 40 and Great Smoky Mountains National Park; the consequence would be increased disturbance and displacement, increased hunting and poaching, and likely increased cub mortality due to abandonment resulting from disturbance. The Forest Service people heard but hardly heeded. I wanted the National Wildlife Federation to bring legal action—it had the resources and clout—but the federation agreed only to send a stern letter to the Forest Service. So life went on, and ten years later University of Tennessee biologists, studying the condition of bears in the national park, expressed their concern about the serious degradation of habitat in Harmon Den.

I had also respected the Tennessee Valley Authority. It was born with promise in the New Deal days to bring electric power to the rural South at rates far below those charged by monopolistic corporate utilities. It was strongly supported by progressive newspapers like the *Nashville Tennessean* and *Chattanooga Times*. It exemplified large-scale regional planning in America for the benefit of the people of the region. "What we are doing there," Franklin D. Roosevelt told a press conference, "is taking a watershed with about three and a half million people in it, almost all of them rural, and we are trying to make a different type of citizen out of them. . . . TVA is primarily intended to change and improve the standard of living of the people of that Valley."

Did it really provide as promised? TVA was neighbor to the Smokies, but in time I discovered all was not well in the neighborhood. As the largest purchaser of coal in the world (to feed its steam plants), TVA's purchasing policies drove the price of coal down to a level at which the cheapest, lowest-quality coal was mined "economically"—that is, profitably—only by strip mining. The agency could readily have required plans for land restoration in advance of mining, as environmentalists urged, but that was not its interest. As a result, many mountainsides in Kentucky, West Virginia, and elsewhere were ruined, and mountain families were driven into cities and ways alien to them; lakes, streams, and rivers were fouled with acid, silt, and sediment.

Over the years I have met environmental educators on the TVA payroll, including unashamed apologists and others believing they actually were raising public awareness of environmental issues. Maybe so, but the Tennessee Valley Authority continued on a destructive course, promoting strip mining, and building tall stacks that spread pollutants widely across the skies, radioactive nuclear facilities, self-authorized dams and pumped storage developments. TVA could do these things, industrializing and polluting the Tennessee Valley, without accounting to the public or public service commissions, thanks to its partnership with politicians and industries.

That was how it came to its "multipurpose development" of the last stretch of the Little Tennessee River left undammed, in free-running condition. I treasure my experiences in floating and fishing on this river before completion of the Tellico Dam. It was a beautiful cold, clear stream rippling over the rocks, close to the Smokies and closely akin to those mountains; with truly progressive regional planning it should have been added to the park. The sad story of the completion of Tellico Dam, even after discovery of the celebrated snail darter, is treated in the final section of this book, "Open Options—An

Epilogue," which I wrote for the 1980 edition. The entire history of the case is detailed in *TVA and the Tellico Dam, 1936–1979*, by two University of Tennessee history professors, William Bruce Wheeler and Michael J. McDonald.

They tell of how Tellico opponents were hounded and harassed, and of how the cards were stacked. One of their academic colleagues, Charles Johnson, for example, wrote President Jimmy Carter urging the project be terminated, but he didn't realize that copies of all such letters were dispatched automatically to TVA's headquarters in Knoxville. Someone there saw it was written on University of Tennessee stationery and forwarded it to the university general counsel, Beauchamp Brogan, a former TVA lawyer, who immediately sent his own letter to Carter, assuring the president that (a) Johnson did not speak for the university; (b) he, Brogan, disagreed strongly with Johnson's view, and (c) the Endangered Species Act was not applicable anyway. Brogan wrote *his* letter on university stationery, sending copies where it would embarrass Johnson. "It was all a little frightening," Johnson wrote later, and this kind of institutional power, whether by TVA, the Forest Service, or any private or public entity, should still be considered frightening.

In 1980, a year after Congress exempted Tellico from terms of the Endangered Species Act, I was in Knoxville again. I met a young woman who had fought to the bitter end. It was now all finished; the dam was complete, the river replaced by a filling reservoir. She had brought with her a yellow T-shirt imprinted with "SAVE THE LITTLE T" and gave it to me—she said she had a whole box of them to give away. My best thoughts at the moment were that for her the Little Tennessee would never die, and that while the snail darter might be gone it would remain as a symbol of humble life in the larger cycle of life. But those coming later will never have known the river or the wild trout or the feel and smell of the little critters in the wild. We may be making "a different type of citizen," as FDR proclaimed, but making a better type of citizen is something else. Roosevelt talked about "standard of living," but protecting and restoring the streams are more appropriate to "quality of life."

A World of Patience and Humility

The Ridge Runner leads the way to Shuckstack Tower—Skies Overcast with "Smaze"—If the park reflects society, society can reflect the park as well—Ernie prescribes for "satisfying, rewarding lives"

I started up the long, steep switchbacks, recognizing it was time to take to the trail and turn to the future. Hiking with Alan Householder gave me the chance to transit generations, and to look at the Smokies through younger eyes. In 1992 Alan was thirty-five, less than half the age of most of the people with whom I had been communing. He was a wiry little guy, toughened by his long-distance hiking, usually with a heavy pack on his back. Alan was the

"Ridge Runner"—that was his official title and job classification, the only one in the Smokies, or anywhere in the country as far as I know—in his third summer of patrolling the seventy-five miles of Appalachian Trail running through the park. He was paid, modestly, with funds provided by the Smoky Mountain Hiking Club, Appalachian Trail Conference, and Smoky Mountain Natural History Association to clear the trail, clean the shelters, pack out trash, and talk with hikers about regulations, backcountry permits, and low-impact camping. There was nothing like that in the days of Barbara Thorne and George Masa, but then there were hardly any trails either.

Campers and hikers were different, too. In the thirties they learned the hard way by doing and from books like Horace Kephart's *Camping and Woodcraft*, which showed how to make do with what they had. Even in my early days the unwritten rule required leaving a camp clean, with a little food as a token of consideration for whoever might follow. Now equipment creates an artificial focus of self-gratification for a breed of tech-weenies. Alan and I had spent the night before at the trail shelter at Fontana Dam with just such a bunch, raucous till the small hours, then probably too hung over to hike.

We headed for Shuckstack Tower, two thousand feet above us, which I had visited thirty years before. It proved a thoroughly peaceful day, in company with bright azaleas in bloom, dark thickets of rhododendron crowding the stream banks, and the characteristic moist, mixed forests. I learned that Alan worked off-season as a waiter, complete with tuxedo, at an upscale restaurant in Asheville, his hometown. In fact, he had started serious solo hiking after a broken romance with a waitress and kept on going until he covered the entire Appalachian Trail and more besides. Certainly out on the trail the Smokies become a different park than the superficial playground ten million motor tourists experience; the trail opens a world of patience, simplicity, and humility, of self-reliance and revelation. I love the story of Bill Irwin, the messenger of glad tidings from Burlington, North Carolina, who in the spring of 1990 started at the southern terminus in Georgia, determined to become the first solo blind hiker to complete the two-thousand-mile Appalachian Trail all the way to Maine; he was guided by his dog Orient and by his conviction that God wanted a pilgrimage as a witness of faith. And he made it, too.

At Shuckstack Tower, where we stopped for lunch, a fair breeze blew. We talked while enjoying the magic vistas. With the exception of Fontana Dam and Reservoir far below and behind us, the mountain forests were unbroken. We were really not far from civilization, but for the present it was happily far removed. Not a building, road, or clearcut in sight. This was all park, all wilderness, all sanctuary. It was Alan's sanctuary, away from a noisy, crowded world. Solo hiking was his release. He deplored the upscale gentrification of western North Carolina (with "condominiums, golf clubs, and art galleries on every block" in parts of Cashiers Valley) and asked many questions about the endless struggle to save the Smokies and where he might fit in.

Presently we became sky-conscious. In all directions conditions were cloudlike but without defined cloud formations, the skycoloring a dirty white. We were witness, Alan said, to an unnatural overload of "smaze"—a combination of ground-borne smoke and haze. Alan and I discussed it coming down the mountain, and then I questioned others. Everyone with whom I talked cited degradation in air quality as the primary problem and the most pressing issue in the Great Smokies. It was by all odds the most significant major change of the quarter century that I could identify, for this was now real smoke and no illusion.

Perhaps this shouldn't have come as a surprise. Each time I visited Chattanooga in recent years the skies above it were increasingly polluted—how could the mountains be far behind? The South has boomed, catching up industrially, while paying a price in toxic emissions from factories, power plants, and automobiles. The South is not much different now from the Northeast and the Ohio Valley, the old urbanized strongholds of industrial pollution.

Inevitably the consequences have become evident throughout the Appalachians. Visibility from overlooks on the Skyline Drive in Virginia that once extended more than eighty miles have diminished to about five miles; sometimes from Clingmans Dome in the Smokies visibility is down to two miles. Within thirty years visibility has been reduced by almost one-third.

For years acid rain, or acid deposition (caused by excessive emissions of nitrogen oxides and sulfur dioxides), has been associated primarily with eastern Canada, New England, and the Adirondacks in upstate New York, but Southern Appalachia is a prime victim too. A victim not only of acid rain, but of ozone pollution (caused by hydrocarbons from tailpipes and smokestacks). While ozone high above the earth provides protection from ultraviolet rays, at ground level it deals a toxic hand to plants, animals, and humans.

I learned that the Uplands Laboratory of the National Park Service at Gatlinburg has found ozone pollution affecting more than eighty plant species in the Smokies. I saw this for myself in the ghost forest of spruce and Fraser fir at Clingmans Dome. It reminded me of the *Sterben Wald*, the tragic "Dead forest," that I had witnessed in Germany. Here in Appalachia the Fraser fir is said to be affected primarily by infestation of the pesky balsam woolly aphid, from which spruce is immune. But with both species dying, the aphid may not be the only problem, or the root of the problem. Air pollution may have weakened the trees, inviting fungi to invade and conquer. More studies may be needed, but in the meantime there is scarcely a living mature tree on the crest of Mount Mitchell; forests of Fraser fir and red spruce on Heintooga, Waterrock Knob and Richland Balsam, high points on the Blue Ridge Parkway, all have suffered dramatic decline. National parks and national forests in the highlands have become catch basins for dirty air, with high levels of ozone and toxic acids. Americans decry destruction of the Amazon rain forest, but the tree loss in the mixed mesophytic forest of Appalachia may be just as serious in the world scale of things.

National parks and wilderness areas theoretically are protected by law from these degrading pollutants: Under terms of the federal Clean Air Act, parks are considered as Class I areas, mandating that conditions be maintained to the highest air quality standards in the nation. On that basis, early in the 1990s superintendents of Shenandoah and Great Smoky Mountains both objected to proposed new power plants. The specific issue in the Smokies was the addition of a large coal-fired boiler by Tennessee Eastman at its Kingsport, Tennessee, plant. Park Superintendent Randall Pope urged Tennessee to deny Eastman its required permit; citing continually worsening air quality, he recommended that states not permit *any* increase in industrial air pollution within a 120-mile zone around the park. But in virtually all such cases industries object, "A lot more research needs to be done to prove the point," to which state regulators add, "Restrictions would impede growth and the economy." So Eastman was granted its permit. In the name of economic progress, Tennessee dumps polluted air from its factories on North Carolina while Carolina dumps polluted water into Tennessee from the Champion International Mill at Canton via the Pigeon River at the edge of the Smokies.

I learned that protecting and preserving the Smoky Mountains doesn't end at the boundaries of the national park. The most difficult challenge may not even be inside the park. Too many roads ring the Smokies: like Interstate 40, the traffic on which probably emits more pollutants in one hour than all the traffic inside the park in a full day, and the new Interstate 26 between Johnson City, Tennessee, and Asheville, North Carolina, and the road between Robbinsville, North Carolina, and Tellico Plains, Tennessee, and the Foothills Parkway, Tennessee's pound of political pork extracted to match federal benefaction to North Carolina for the Blue Ridge Parkway. These roads divide and scar wild country, disrupt wildlife, and silt streams. They may "enhance access," but heavy traffic only creates pressure on fragile areas hitherto protected by lack of access. The new roads and superroads modify natural landscape and human culture, but without improvement to either.

I recognize that the Great Smoky Mountains cannot be uncoupled from the world around them. The condition of the national park reflects the condition of society. I see the reverse as well, society influenced by the good embodied in the park—in the same sense as the moral uplift derived from contemplation in a house of worship. But the park has too many visitors, most of whom spend too little time to get the message of love and caring it cries to give to us. I don't see any limitation on numbers on the existing road system or hear any expression of concern about pollution resulting from auto traffic in the park, but only a chronic rationale in defense of the indefensible.

"The mountains are better off if most people continue to hang close to their cars." So Robert F. Miller, of the park staff, was quoted in the Raleigh *News & Observer*, July 19, 1992. I've heard that line many times before. The article continued:

> The half million hikers a year cause more wear on the park and its wilderness than the eight million people who don't leave the roads, he [Miller] said. Some of the most popular hiking trails are suffering from overuse. Shelters are run down. Litter is a constant problem.
>
> "Do we want to promote more use in the backcountry where most of our problems are already?" Miller asked. "I wouldn't say we're making an active effort to get people out of their cars. I don't think we should require everybody to hike two miles."

It didn't sound right, it doesn't sound right. Hiking, being there, breeds enthusiasm, idealism, love of life, and the hiker champions enlightened use. As Benton MacKaye wrote sixty years ago (in "The Appalachian Trail: A Guide to the Study of Nature," *Scientific Monthly*, April 1932):

> Primeval influence is the opposite of machine influence. It is the antidote for over-rapid mechanization. It is getting feet on the ground with eyes toward the sky—not eyes on the ground with feet on a lever. It is feeling what you touch and seeing what you look at.

The smoke and haze, the death of trees, the smelly traffic jams no different from downtown at rush hour, the huge crowds shuffling through the Sugarlands visitor center too quickly to appreciate that actual mountain people struggled to survive at this very site, the emphasis in park management on catering to crowds rather than caring for wilderness—these detract from the purity of the mountains as God made them, and from the sense of sanctuary the national park is meant to provide.

The surroundings on the Tennessee side detract from it too. Years ago Gatlinburg was endowed with mountain spirit and charm; then it fell apart. Horace Albright in a letter to me dated June 6, 1978, recalled the change this way:

> I well remember that when I was Director [of the National Park Service, from 1929 to 1933], I spent two weeks in the Great Smokies, riding horseback everywhere, and I remember Gatlinburg. On returning to Knoxville, I remember publicly declaring that Gatlinburg was the ideal national park gateway town, and compared its beauty, serenity, good taste, etc., with gateway towns and cities in the West—Estes Park, Colorado, West Yellowstone and Gardiner, Montana, etc. A few years later Gatlinburg had "gone over the dam." I could not say anything good about it. I last saw it in 1961. I feel about it like I do Lake Tahoe—I never want to see it again.

Since 1961, when Horace Albright saw it last, Gatlinburg has gone further "over the dam," its main streets offering a tawdry tourist fare of wax museum, mysterious mansion, haunted house, and over four hundred gift and specialty shops, mostly specializing in trinketry and schlock. And from Gatlinburg the carnival of commerce has spread down the highway to infest Pigeon Forge as well. That is where Dolly Parton, queen of country music, established Dolly-wood, her very own Opryland in the hills; it's impossible to miss, if one simply follows the billboards, pizza parlors, and burger, barbecue, pancake, and ham-and-chicken fast-food chain emporiums that make the old mountain country town look like Anywhere Else USA.

I don't doubt that Dolly's "entertainment capital of the Smokies" is entertaining, or that the adjacent police museum, car museum, helicopter rides, and all the other sideshows are fun, too. I might enjoy them as parts of a circus somewhere or of a carnival in the city. In the foreground to the Great Smoky Mountains, they lack relevance. They create a mood of artificiality, the wrong kind of introduction to a preeminent nature reserve.

Great Smoky Mountains National Park deserves a compatible frontispiece, buffers outside to safeguard the treasures on the inside. It needs understanding of its own rich values that rise above entertainment. The great cove hardwoods, abundant and diverse flowering plants, salamanders, songbirds and flying squirrels, insects and minnows in the streams, tiniest of plants and animals at the base of life in undisturbed soils—they entertain, too, in their own way, and do more besides. They stimulate ecological awareness, of parts connected to each other, and of opportunities to reconnect to make the parts whole.

In late 1991 a group of red wolves, *Canis rufus*, considered the native wolf of the Southeast, was introduced into the park near Cades Cove. It was fitting and appropriate, considering the last known wolf in the area was killed in 1905; but the red wolf, though shy, solitary, and mostly nocturnal, is apt to poke its nose outside and into trouble, unless it is understood. The same is true of the panther, perhaps even more so. Park officials evidently feel they can advocate wolves, since the action here is related to the highly publicized wolf restoration program in Yellowstone, but get skittish about the panther. "There is no proof of the presence of panthers," as superintendent Pope said to me. "There have been sightings, but evidently somebody released a pet. . . . Yes, there have been fairly solid sightings, too. The panther is a native species, but I don't see a program of restoration right now or in the immediate future." This is historic panther country, individual panthers have been sighted (see pages 343–44), and there could be adequate habitat, given proper land use and leadership to enroll public support.

The national park is bordered on three sides by national forests (Cherokee in Tennessee, Nantahala and Pisgah in North Carolina). They ought to be integral to dealing with the region as an ecosystem, with emphasis on protection of wildlife habitat, but this has not been the case. Far from it. In August 1992 the Forest Service announced a draft management plan for the Nantahala and Pisgah national forests; though following a legal challenge by citizen conservationists to an earlier plan (of 1987), the Forest Service still proposed to log steep slopes of old-growth stands at high elevation, with erosive soils, clearly unsuited to timber harvest, but valuable for wildlife, clean water, and scenic beauty.

The direction of the management plan was not surprising. It reflected the agency's consistent emphasis on commodity production, at the expense of beauty and biology. The Wilderness Society has published two commendable reports, "Mountain Treasures at Risk: The Future of the Southern Appalachian National Forests" in 1989 and "North Carolina's Mountain Treasures" in 1992, analyzing these questions in detail. Suffice to say that national forest administrators and planners demonstrate scant sensitivity to ethical or ecological values. Appalachian national forests contain about five thousand miles of permanent Forest Service road, plus state, county, town, and other federal roads. But plans project construction of another thirty-two hundred miles of new road by the year 2030, opening choice wild country to logging, damaging biology, disqualifying the areas for possible review and classification as wilderness.

I recall how in 1969 John M. Reynolds, an Asheville businessman, initiated the campaign for a great new wild park composed of federal, state, and private lands north of Asheville, encompassing Mount Mitchell, the Craggies and Black Brothers range, some of the most picturesque property in the East. That proposal would have been appropriate coming from the Forest Service or the National Park Service. So would Reynolds's statement of warning: "The time is coming fast when there will be no more wild lands to acquire." But neither was heard from.

In 1976 Granville Liles picked up the campaign. He had retired the previous year as a conscientious superintendent of the Blue Ridge Parkway and had served earlier as chief ranger in the Smokies. I knew Granville well and traveled with him in surveying the area; we communicated with Reynolds, still very interested. The boldest concept was for a national park of 50,000 to 100,000 acres centered around Mount Mitchell, straddling the Blue Ridge Parkway and taking in the Great Craggies, Black Mountains, Crabtree Mountain, and westward beyond Celo Knob to Roan Mountain and the Unakas—much of it already in national forest. Harold Warren reported in the *Charlotte Observer* (October 31, 1976) of the enthusiasm of Representative Roy Taylor, who was about to retire from Congress and wanted to bring it off as his last hurrah. Taylor presently succeeded in getting federal funding to conduct a feasibility study. "If the study leads to establishment of the park," wrote Warren, "it could be the biggest step in the Eastern United States since national parks were dedicated in the Great Smokies and the Everglades in the 1940s."

The general reaction was favorable at first, but the Park Service was disinterested and the Forest Service actively opposed. The park campaign fizzled; the "biggest step" was not taken, at least not in that time frame. That was in the

1970s; I hope that in the 1990s a new wave of awareness and concern may still make a difference. History records how decades of unrestrained logging stripped most of the great tree cover that clothed Appalachia. Now recovering forests provide the chance to protect and manage ecologically significant areas. We owe it to the human heritage to rebuild "old growth" in substantial quantity at all elevations, to insure the opportunity of generations unborn to walk again among trees of five-feet diameter.

Prize and precious forests still exist today in the Smokies. The national park safeguards the largest of the undisturbed and least disturbed tracts in Southern Appalachia, with conditions approaching the primeval: trees of all ages, dense canopies of diverse species, and standing snags and downed logs at all ages of decay, feeding micro-flora and micro-fauna in the soil cover of earth. To scientists, these forests provide standards by which to measure human-operated systems. But I see them also providing a model for preservation and restoration of representative forests throughout Appalachia.

That is what makes striving for the ideal in the Great Smoky Mountains a worthy human cause. By defining the issues and working patiently and openly to resolve them, nature in the Smokies will benefit, and so will civilization beyond. The most nagging issue is the long-pending designation of wilderness under terms of the 1964 Wilderness Act—held up by a well-organized and vocal group in Swain County opposing wilderness and demanding completion of the Bryson City-Fontana road on the north shore of Fontana Lake (discussed elsewhere in the book). The group's champion in Washington, Senator Jesse Helms, through the 1970s and 1980s continually blocked congressional action for wilderness in the Smokies, despite the near agreement for resolution by Swain County and the Carter administration (to which Bill Rolen referred during my interview with him). The park fortunately has managed backcountry as wilderness, but full protection under the act is still essential. And Swain County, for its part, needs the $16 million cash settlement offered by the federal government more than it needs the road.

Another issue involves the enclave of nearly fifty resort cabins and the old Wonderland Hotel at Elkmont, the last holdouts of more than six thousand private landowners within park boundaries. The owners first were granted lifetime leases; in 1952 the leases were extended for twenty years, and then for another twenty years. It's been good politics, but bad preservation in a lovely area awaiting natural restoration.

I could cite other problems, impurities, detractions from wholeness. Horses tramping the Appalachian Trail damage the trail, foul water, and disrupt the experience of hikers; the section through the Smokies is the only section of the entire AT on which horses are allowed, yet administrators can only say, "We are conducting studies." The park doesn't have money for the backcountry reservation system, which means the system doesn't work. But, of course, wilderness needs more attention, more emphasis. Alan Householder's Ridge Runner position was initiated and paid for by the hiking club, when it ought to be the park responsibility.

But enough. The ideal is a goal wrapped inside a dream. Happily, my experiences and encounters in the Smokies have shown that a cadre of people, or even a single individual, can make a dream come true. Trying in itself helps to make a person whole and worthy, regardless of the outcome in fact. As Ernie Dickerman, at the age of eighty and still going strong, wrote to me: "It is amazing how political democracy in the United States, despite its deficiencies and innumerable errors, permits so many of us to lead satisfying, rewarding lives."

Acknowledgments 1993

I've been singularly blessed in the Great Smokies with the encouragement, cooperation, and inspiration generously given by a host of classy folks. Connecting with them, and staying connected through the years and across the miles, has enriched my writing and my life.

Mack Prichard, my close friend and tireless traveling partner, heads the list. Mack has never let me down, he always pulls me through in the pinches. Once, in early spring, Mack and I were caught in a freakish blizzard on the way to Mount LeConte. We slid, slipped, and struggled on the icy trail and shivered all night in the shelter on top, but it was basically one more in the endless string of adventures we have shared and survived and later laughed about. Mack's title in the Tennessee Conservation Department is "state naturalist," though he is more properly a state treasure for all the good he has done and the inspiration he spreads wherever he goes.

Bernard Elias, of Asheville, another close friend, has been a member of the Carolina Mountain Club more than fifty years, and has introduced scores of people to the joys of hiking in the Smokies and surroundings. Bernard facilitated my visits and interviews with Barbara Ambler Thorne; Mary Kelly, of the Western North Carolina Alliance; former Congressman Roy Taylor and his wife, Evelyn; former Congressman Jamie Clarke and his wife, Elspeth; Margie Douthit and Barry Hipps, of the Cherokee Historical Association; Joann Orr, of the Museum of the Cherokee; John Parris, the sage of Sylva and columnist for the *Asheville Citizen-Times*; Dan Pitillo, of Western North Carolina University, and Burt Kornegay, of Cullowhee, director of Slick Rock Expeditions, all of whom provided valuable perspective and assistance. I appreciate also the help of Hugh Morton, of Grandfather Mountain, an old friend and sometime sparring partner, lately become an authority on air quality and vigorous protagonist for protecting and improving it.

Liane and Bill Russell, of Oak Ridge and the Tennessee Citizens for Wilderness Planning, have been warm friends and sources of sound counsel since we met on the "Save-the-Smokies" hike of 1966. Leroy Fox and Ray Payne, of Knoxville, in those days were leaders of the Smoky Mountains Hiking Club and still are today; thanks to their initiative, the position of Ridge Runner was established in the park and Alan Householder hired as the first to fill it. Ed Clebsch, of the University of Tennessee, has been involved in the Smokies since student days years ago, befriended and influenced by Harvey Broome, Granville Liles, and Arthur Stupka, the best of mentors. Clebsch is still a key figure in the Spring Wildflower Pilgrimage at Gatlinburg; in addition, he and his wife Meredith operate the Native Gardens, a creative commercial venture at Greenback, accenting native plants in home landscape. I also appreciate the help of Jeannie and Richard Hilten, of Townsend, and of Sam Venable, columnist for the *Knoxville News-Sentinel*, with whom I have traded moonshining stories since we hiked to Slick Rock when he was a young reporter twenty years ago.

I've been privileged to know every superintendent of Great Smoky Mountains National Park since the late John Preston served here in 1950–51 before going to Yosemite. He and Sam Weems, superintendent of the Blue Ridge Parkway, opened my eyes to the wonder of the mountains. Boyd Evison, superintendent from 1978 to 1982, sponsored my election to the board of the Great Smoky Mountains Natural History Association; I never missed a meeting during my three years of tenure and remain proud of the association's work. I appreciate the cooperation provided by Randall R. Pope, superintendent since 1987 and still going strong in 1993, and of park staff members Glenn Cardwell, Annette Evans, Kitty Manscill, and Ed Trout; and of former park personnel, including George Fry, Mark (and Verda) Hannah, Bill (and Lola) Rolen, Randolph Shields, and Arthur Stupka.

A special word about Ernie Dickerman, whom I visited in late summer of 1992, no longer in the Smokies, but still in the mountains, at Buffalo Gap, Virginia, his old family country, and at eighty crusading for wilderness in the national forests close at hand. Dickerman embodies faith and hope, commitment to principle larger than self.

I'm thankful to Peter Kirby, Southeast representative of the Wilderness Society, who has that same spirit. Turning to the book as a product (with feeling, I like to think), thanks to Lisa Friend, for indexing the "The Smokies Revisited," and to Will Fontanez for updating the maps. Finally, my appreciation to Meredith Morgan, Jennifer Siler, all the good people at the University of Tennessee Press who give me cheer and encouragement. Let it be noted that the personnel of the UT Press have adopted and maintain a section of trail in Great Smoky Mountains National Park. I'm certain they treat it with loving care, as we all should.

About the Photographs

Photographers for years have come to the Great Smoky Mountains from all over the world to record flowers, forests, streams, rocks, wildlife, mountain tops, and mountain people. Their works range from the intimate close-up of a raindrop on a leaf to sweeping landscapes reaching for infinity, and no two pictures ever the same.

Photographs have become valuable documents of cultural history, by showing mountain men, women, and children, as well as their houses, fences, roofs, barns, water-powered mills, spinning wheels, and weaving looms, churches, bear traps, and shooting arms.

But photographers have done even more. Pioneers like James E. (Jim) Thompson, of Knoxville, and George Masa, of Asheville, helped to make history by providing powerful visual aids to the park movement of the 1920s and 1930s. Others carry on in their tradition, continuing to provide what Carlos Campbell called "pictorial evidence of the charm and majesty" of the Smoky Mountains.

Thus, in offering the representative selection in this edition of *Strangers in High Places*, I express special appreciation for the cooperation of Thompson Photo Products, founded 1902 and still in the Thompson Family; Dean Stone, of Stonecraft, and longtime editor of the *Maryville Times;* the good folks at Great Smoky Mountains National Park, and Mack Prichard, who helped me sort through hundreds of pictures, including many of his own, to make this selection.

Preface to the Second Edition

Over the course of years since *Strangers in High Places* first appeared I have been asked many times how I came to poke my nose into the Great Smokies to write this book. The answer in itself is relatively simple, as such things go, but there is more to it as part of a continuing adventure which seems fitting to share.

In 1962 Doubleday published *Whose Woods These Are*, a book I had written about the national forests. Within a year, after it had evidently done well, I received a letter from Samuel S. Vaughan, then my editor. A salesman for the firm had recommended consideration of a book about the Smokies as a potential saleable item in his Southern territory. Someone in the editorial department proposed my name as the author. It was all very tentative when Mr. Vaughan invited my reaction.

I was not exactly a stranger in the high places—but no expert either. I had made my first trip to the Smokies in late 1946, after leaving a job as a newspaper reporter in Nashville, just to see what those mountains were like. Then I had been back several times while writing about travel and the outdoors. The book ideas was appealing and I so advised Mr. Vaughan. We corresponded, had one or two personal visits, and agreed to proceed. He sent me off to work with these words of challenge: "You'll have to write 'up' for this one, but if you do, you could have a small classic."

As I studied the various aspects of the region, my concept changed. I did not want to write a travel book at all, as I had originally thought, but rather set forth a definition of values—of the timeless values that make the Great Smoky Mountains worth saving. Under the influence of some of those I met, like Harvey Broome, I wanted more than anything else to contribute a meaningful document to the effort to protect the national park.

Of those I met and interviewed, many are now gone. They were a generation of personalities who bridged the past, the age when the Great Smokies were "the back of beyond," as Horace Kephart would say. I encountered moonshiners and revenuers and bear hunters and a Cherokee conjureman of Big Cove who were closer to Kephart's time than to ours. They would recount what life was like in the days before indoor toilets or lavatory equipment as known in the outside world, when water was hauled from the spring, when the first car came to Gatlinburg—on trails hardly fit for a wagon—and when going to Knoxville was an all-day expedition.

I was privileged to hear Bascom Lamar Lunsford, the music man of the mountains, play the fiddle for me in his living room; Jarrett Blythe, the Cherokee leader, talk in his living room about his fathers and their sensitivity to earth; and Kenneth Chorley, for forty years a lieutenant of John D. Rockefeller, Jr., in his office at Rockefeller Center about the bequest that made the park possible.

Then there was Harvey, champion of high, wild places everywhere, a cheery, gentle spirit but tough when need be. He first went out to the Smokies from Knoxville to build his strength (somewhat like Theodore Roosevelt went to the Dakota Badlands) and from then on experienced the mountains in every season and in every mood. Soon after he died in 1968 a clutch of his close friends made a memorial hike into a section of the Greenbrier that he particularly loved, and it was raining, soft and warm, just like when he took me up the Chimney Tops.

Strangers in High Places appeared in 1966 as the fight over a second transmountain road through the park was reaching fever pitch. That road was part of the first proposal offered by the National Park Service under terms of the 1964 Wilderness Act. It stirred attention all over the country for, as the *New York Times* editorialized, the outcome could prove "critically important for the precedent set for all other areas in the park system."

At hearings held at Gatlinburg and then in Bryson City a national parks official read an opening statement that offered nothing especially new or consequential in wilderness philosophy or protection. It was, rather, more of a road plan for the Smokies intended to solve seasonal traffic jams, more a plan for outlining the location of the trans-mountain highway, plus corridors for additional inner loops. The leftover, of about one-half the park, was offered for inclusion in the National Wilderness Preservation System—but in six broken blocks.

The road proposal had official endorsement from the power structure of the two states, from governors and congressmen down to county commissioners (although Gatlinburgers did not like the idea of traffic being diverted elsewhere), but people came from near and far to testify against it. No road on earth, after all, is important enough to destroy the values inherent in these mountains. And the road never has been built.

I recall encountering Dr. Kelly Bennett, the pharmacist, community leader, and most vigorous proponent of the road, at the public hearing conducted at the federal courthouse in Bryson City, his home town. I had already visited with him a time or two in his drug store, the hot bed of opposition to park bureaucracy headquartered across the mountain in Tennessee. He had been a campaigner for the park as early as the 1920s and was a thoroughly decent man regardless of his position on the issue.

The same could be said of Reuben Robertson, kingpin of the Champion Paper Company, who had fought the establishment of the park in order to save Champion's virgin forests for commercial exploitation. One day in late 1966, I was autographing books at a bookstore in Asheville. I was surprised when a man approached with a list of ten or a dozen people to whom Reuben Robertson wanted to send copies as Christmas gifts. I wrote the appropriate inscription in all of them and the next day the same man returned for two or three more. Sometime later, quite by accident, I met "Mr. Reuben" sitting at the next table at an Asheville restaurant and we had a good talk. I had not made him the villain of the piece and he plainly felt he could share in celebrating preservation of the Smoky Mountain forests.

These personalities out of the past, much alive fifteen years ago, are gone. They played their impermanent roles and moved on. The stage remains, however, for other players.

But for what roles? As history progresses and the land changes, so do people change—apace with their environment. In a thoughtful critique of *Strangers in High Places*, which appeared in the *Richmond News Leader*, Lawrence S. Thompson, professor of classics at the University of Kentucky, wrote as follows: "This reviewer never saw Cadillacs, washing-machines or even radios when he visited Highlands and Bryson City as a boy in the twenties, but the forest of TV antennas today rivals the tall timber of the uncut forests of that bygone day. Today the civilization of the Appalachians is not much different from that of Brooklyn, Toledo, or Oakland."

Harvey Broome made somewhat the same point. He told of overhearing a conversation among a group of Scouts. When an Explorer said the water tasted better on the Tennessee side of the Smokies than on the North Carolina side, Harvey perked up his ears. Then he heard the reason: the preferred Tennessee water came out of a pipe. What a sad and sorry case for society when a Scout feels at home in the woods because he has a metal pipe to drink from.

Happily, in a world where nothing remains static, the Great Smoky Mountains provide the prescription to ward off ills and evils born of super-civilization. A single day spent in the Smokies away from the works of man is therapy to last a year. And with each passing year, the national park grows in value as a model of natural harmony.

For such reasons I feel this new edition appears at a tactical hour. It is quite fitting that the University of Tennessee Press has now assumed the publishing role. I am particularly grateful to Ms. Carol Orr, former director of the U.T. Press, for her cooperation and encouragement.

Part One

THE FIRST HALF-BILLION YEARS

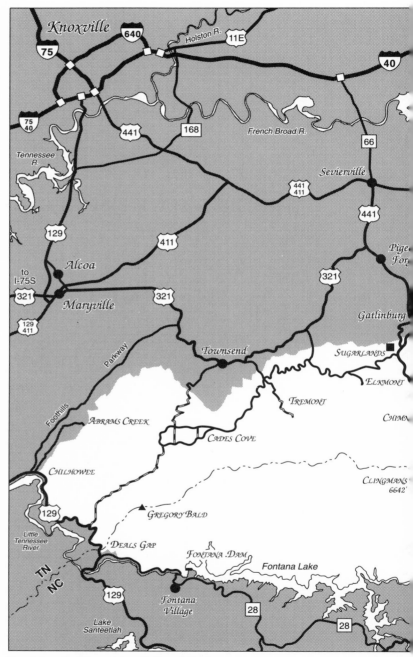

Great Smoky Mountains National Park

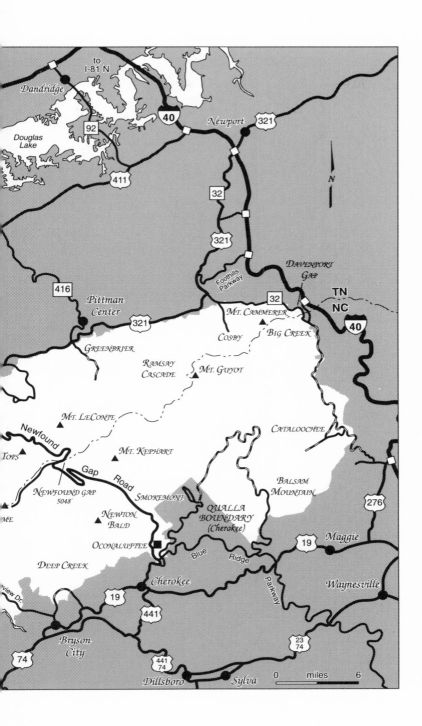

I

Chimney Tops

It was raining in the Smokies.

Above us in the high places the mist formed, watery molecules arriving from distant spheres of the oceans and atmosphere, converging briefly before continuing their long separate journeys. The rain was soft and warm, a summer spray to cloud one's glasses, or roll down the face like a child's teardrop, and mix with the perspiration born of a hard climb. It was the kind of friendly rain to remind you the earth is good, splashing the air with smells of new life in the woods.

To me the image of the Smokies will always begin with rainfall, whether a faint fair drizzle or a drenching downpour. "Rain, rain," I said, "Smoky Mountains is thy name." But Harvey Broome, who had marched in every conceivable mood of the hills, answered with a laugh. "You don't complain about weather in the Smokies," he advised. "You just learn to accept it."

My two companions and I were resting on a narrow, rocky ledge, midway in our climb to the Chimney Tops. It was still early, a cool morning, alternately brightened with sunlight and darkened with the persistent showers. John Morrell and I were puffing. The climb is steep, almost vertical for several hundred feet, hand over hand from one rocky perch to the next, clutching tree roots and raw earth in between; not really a rugged ascent to anyone accustomed to western mountaineering, but the toughest the Smokies have to offer, and tough enough for me. As for Harvey, he had made his first trip of the year to the Chimneys in the quiet cold of January and heaven knows how many more times this grayed eagle would cover this route, or the scores of hiking trails through the forests and atop the main ridge called Smoky.

When we reached the summit between the Chimney Tops, twin craggy pinnacles of rock, it was a world for dreaming on the manifest mysteries, myths, marvels, and meanings of the Great Smoky Mountains. The rains fell no longer. We sat and spread our lunch on a rocky island, surrounded by rolling haze and, at our fingertips, summer-blooming herbs, mosses, and dwarfed rosy-pink Carolina rhododendron, the "deer laurel" that grows high in the southern mountains and nowhere else. Quiet for a time were the three of us, the older eyes perceiving far more than mine. Harvey Broome and John Morrell—scarcely lustrous names in what we normally consider the big scheme of things. But they epitomize a certain breed of Tennesseans and Carolinians who have given their energies to the Smokies and their love to the earth.

These two were high-school classmates in Knoxville. Both became lawyers. John went to work in the early twenties as a land buyer for the Great Smoky Mountains Conservation Association, acquiring parcels of real estate that would comprise the national park, then for the park itself, and has been more intimately associated with its development than any other person. Harvey entered private practice and made good, which was not quite good enough for him, for in due course he took a job as law clerk to a judge with the understanding there would be ample free time to devote to affairs of the Wilderness Society, a national organization of considerable distinction which he and others founded while on a trip in the Smokies, and which he serves as president. And there we were, wordless for a while, finding ourselves in a breeze-swept aerie, watching and listening to the birds.

A towhee flicked her long, rounded tail while flitting upward toward the spruce and fir, where she builds her summer nest. An ensemble of tiny winter wrens, normally reserved, proclaimed their presence with melodious high-pitched trilling and favored us with their rare antiphonal song—as soon as one uttered the last bubbling *crrrrip*, another began, for round after tuneful round. A flock of fifty swifts, high, fast fliers on tireless wings, swirled in circles, feeding on insects while skimming the air, diving occasionally into deep, dark crevices in the rock which must have been their home. What could be more appropriate than swifts nesting in the natural chimney?

The sound of motorcars drifted up to us, a hollow sound, almost unreal, the muted echo of rubber tires rolling through the tunnel on the transmountain highway. It reminded me of how quickly we had removed from our own kind and our own time. As a traveler, I had been acquainted with the Smokies for some years, but merely with their edges, or with the edges of the surface. Harvey Broome, John Morrell, and others were to show me the depths of the Smokies, a distance not readily penetrated. These hills demand time and patience. Entering one must take them on their own terms. They defy the cult of haste, being old and artful and surprising. "There is not a cranny in the rocks of the Great Smokies, not a foot of the wild glen, but harbors something lovable and rare," a man named Horace Kephart once wrote.

From our craggy perch, we looked down on the valley known as the Sugarlands. It became the focus of our attention. It was filled in with growing trees sweeping down toward the mouth of the valley where the park visitors' center and headquarters are clustered. My friends told me how much all this had changed within their recollection. They began coming out from Knoxville as boys, in the teens of the century, when the high places were visited only by herdsmen, bear hunters, and a few venturous hikers who climbed about through brush, briers, and downed timber, often losing their way in torrential rains and heavy fog, without maps, name places, or trails to guide them in many sections. The purple-hazy range was visible from the hills of Knoxville, but barely anyone knew it by name.

In 1913, John Morrell, his father, and two friends came out to camp at the foot of the Chimney Tops. They had first to travel to Sevierville, the county seat, then follow a rough dirt road to Gatlinburg, an inconspicuous mountain village in those days. A guide met them there with a mule to haul their tent and other packs, and up they marched along Fighting Creek and the Sugarlands road, such as it was.

"One morning, while we were camped below," John recollected, "the Chimneys looked so close we started for the top to see if they really had soot in them. Instead, we found a yellow-jacket nest that must have been upset by a bear the night before. We could see the cabins down in the Sugarlands, with their plumes of blue smoke rising over the corn-fields and up between the bright, clear green mountainsides. That place could easily have been called Rocky-lands, for the people who settled there were compelled to stack the rocks before they could plant crops, and then had to dig holes between the rock piles to get dirt for covering the seeds."

Horace Kephart visited the Sugarlands, too. He described it as "Blockaders' Glory," or "Moonshiners' Paradise," a country of ill fame, hidden deep in remote gorges, difficult of access, tenanted by a sparse population who preferred to be a law among themselves. He knew his way around admirably—we will in time cross his trail among moon-shiners, bear hunters, bourbon tipplers, revenuers, and old-time loggers—but Kephart had an imagination which perhaps was too strong in his picture of the Sugarlands.

The average house had one room and a lean-to kitchen. But those mountaineers, for all their reputed furtiveness and suspicion, rarely turned away a stranger, whoever he might be; instead they gave him a meal and a bed to share with the children. When a boy married, his wife's father was likely to furnish him a little shanty on the farm, or he would simply move in with her family. "My wife and I married when we were both fifteen. It was the usual age," one old Sugarlander told me. "We moved into her house directly. We just waited till everybody was asleep and loved in the dark, kids and all in the same room. That was our honeymoon."

Harvey told how he and his uncle would come out from Knoxville through the sawmill town of Townsend to Elkmont, a logging camp with resort hotel, on the other side of Sugarland Mountain. They came aboard the Little River Railroad, covering the fifty-two miles in two hours, fifteen minutes, with the last portion filled with exciting hairpin turns where they could almost reach out and touch the gorge.

All this changed with the coming of the park. Settlements like the Sugarlands were uprooted from the heart of the Smokies. And so, too, the logging camps and logging railroads and herds of cattle grazing on the grassy mountaintops. Hiking the trails, you still find vestiges of the settlement days, rocky foundations of old houses, vine-shrouded bricks, patches of daffodils and daisies in bloom, gaunt and ghostly fruit trees that refuse to die, graveyards still maintained with paper flowers at the headstones to brighten the shadowy woodlands. But mostly the mountains have reverted to their own, as at the Sugarlands, upward through the natural cycle until the cornfield of three decades ago is a young forest of infinite variety, taking its place alongside older, primitive portions that never were cut or cultivated.

It became time for us to start down. Harvey suggested another course, through a trailless jungle of heath thickets. "Goin' up," as the old native used to say, "you can might' nigh stand up straight and bite the ground; goin' down, a man wants hobnails in the seat of his pants." The steep slopes of Sugarland Mountain were dense with masses of dog hobble, or leucothoe, intertwined with trunks and branches of dripping rhododendron and laurel, an almost impenetrable labyrinth with only an occasional patch of sunlight shining on red partridgeberries. We found ourselves following a bear path but about all that I could do, besides sliding, was to envy the old bear who could take it rolling down. It seemed more practical to step over the rocks of the mountain stream, and when rivulets filled my shoes, my only thought was, Let it rain!

Nearing the foot of the mountain, we joined a rough trail, the old Indian Gap Road. Until 1928 it was virtually the only traversable route between the North Carolina and Tennessee sides of the Smokies. Two centuries ago it was a foot trail trod by Cherokee, connecting their great Warpath down the Valley of East Tennessee with the trail network of North Carolina. It became a route for settlers crossing the divide from Carolina in wagons and on muleback, sometimes in deep snow and cold. It was, in its time, the slim thread of human movement through the hills, but now it was weed-grown, shadowy, lost unless you looked for it.

Suddenly we emerged into the foreground, out of the past, out of wilderness. Cars rolled along the transmountain road, very slowly, this being the height of the now bright Sunday afternoon. Along the West Fork of the Little Pigeon River, many people had parked their cars and taken to the water. A pair of young lovers held hands on a rock. A father dipped the bare toes of a child into the splashing stream and made him laugh. If a man likes the human race, he would have warmed to the scene.

The Smoky Mountains are the laughter of children and the romance of the young and the music of birds in flight. The Smoky Mountains are the rock that was old when natural life first appeared in the recess of geologic past and the trees, plants, and flowers that sheath almost every cliff and the rain-born streams that flow without end down from the heights in torrents and trickles. The Smoky Mountains are the peaked and spurred ridges, the knifelike edges, the plunging valleys, the splendid solitudes. The Smoky Mountains are the stories of the Eastern Cherokee, whose soul has never died, and of the back-country settlers, who live on the brink of yesterday and tomorrow. The Smoky Mountains are the national park that came into being as a testament of man's faith, and not without sacrifice and struggle. The Smoky Mountains are a composition of endless themes and variations, changing with every season, with every month, in every cove and hollow, on every summit, with every pair of eyes that sees them.

Here is a place where forests bloom and regenerate themselves, where the natural creatures belong, and are wanted. They are no strangers in high places: the modest herbs that flower in spring and by summer have withered and vanished, the woody giants that survive for centuries; the red-cheeked salamander and millepede, the bear, the night-prowling bobcat, the flying-squirrel, and the two hundred kinds of birds that serenade the woods. All of these, the sturdy, the graceful, the exquisite, the puny and humble, the least and lowest. When one enters the hills, as I said, one must take them on their terms.

But also, of course, there is rain. When we came off the mountain from our Sunday climb and drove past park headquarters toward Gatlinburg, the skies clouded anew and showers fell. It was the natural blessing.

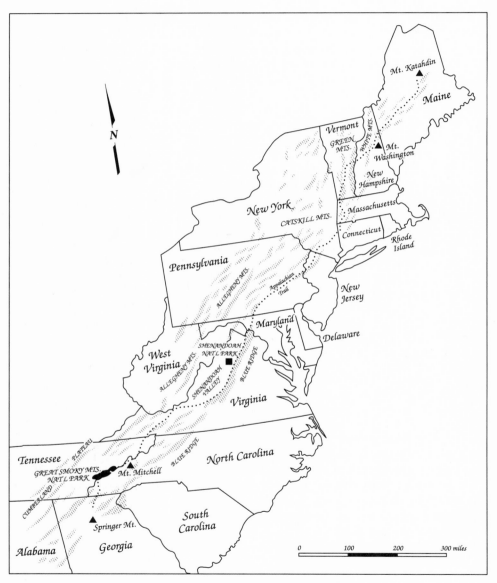

Appalachian Range, showing Appalachian Trail and relationship
of the Smokies to other eastern mountain groups.

II

Approach to Soco Gap

The Great Smoky Mountains spill over both sides of the high frontier shared by Tennessee and North Carolina, roughly one hour's drive from either Knoxville or Asheville. The entire mountain range is embraced by the national park and the abutting Cherokee Indian Reservation. These mountains represent the climax, or summation, of the natural truths inherent in Appalachia.

From a high vantage point facing the mountains, vistas unfold of waves of green forested peaks, shrouded here and there by a deep-bluish mist rising from the valleys. Such is the unpolluted smokiness from which the Smokies derive their traditional name. Moving in closer, one approaches the park's boundary which safeguards eight hundred square miles, much of it an unspoiled wilderness of singing mountain streams feeding their clear waters democratically to a fantastic variety of flowering shrubs, small herbs, and tall trees. If one must justify the word "Great" to go with "Smokies," these creations of earth's fertility should suffice.

Entering the national park is a simple matter, perhaps too simple. A certain conditioning, or orientation, is in order. For instance, in arriving at the eastern portal to the Cherokee country, after traveling the long way south through the Appalachians, it is fruitful to linger thoughtfully at the roadside. The slender passageway between forested crests is ancient, a route discovered and trod by the aboriginals. Here the Cherokee were accustomed to posting a lookout to warn of approaching enemies. However, on withdrawing finally into sanctuary behind the gap, they left only the name Sa-gwa-hi, "one place," to be corrupted by the whites into Socah, and subsequently Soco.

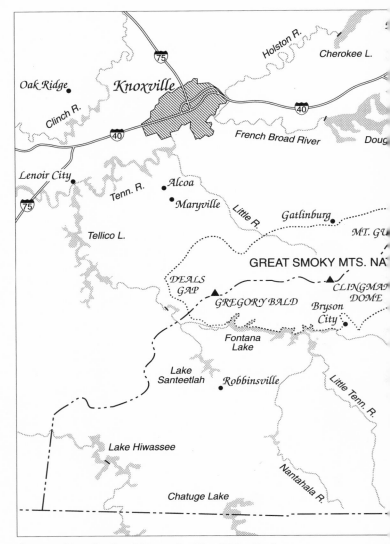

Approaching the Smokies on the Blue Ridge Parkway
through the heart of the mountains.

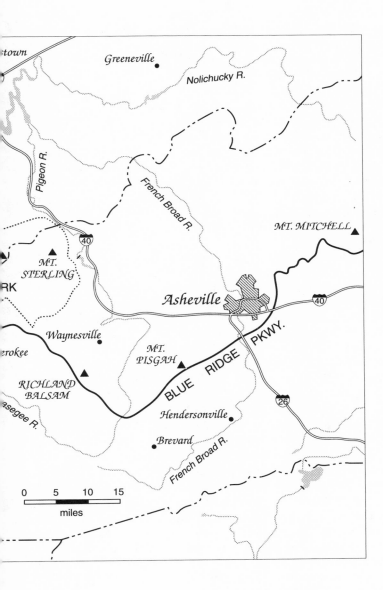

town

Greeneville •

Nolichucky R.

Pigeon R.

French Broad R.

MT. MITCHELL ▲

40

▲

MT.
STERLING ▲

RK

Asheville

I-40

40

Waynesville •

MT.
PISGAH ▲

BLUE RIDGE PKWY.

erokee

RICHLAND
BALSAM ▲

I-26

26

asegee R.

Hendersonville •

Brevard •

French Broad R.

0   5   10   15

miles

The mysteries and histories, the movement of people in times past, somehow demand the pause at Soco Gap. Unfortunately, only a small metal marker suggests the meaning of the gap, and that scantily. It reveals this point as the gateway to the Qualla Reservation, where the Eastern Cherokee survive in the remnant of their forces. But few motorists will see it as they start descending in spiral curves into Soco Valley. Signboards on the route from Asheville must be of large size and distinctive color to be observed. A tawdry army of signs marches along, patrolling the roadside and proclaiming the presence of caged bears, snake pits, amusement parks of a low order, hillbilly entertainments that purport to reflect the mountaineer way, and "genuine" craft shops without a single craft item. All these debase and vilify the glory of the hills; they call to mind the words of Horace Kephart quoting a lumberman's confession in a moment of frankness, "All we want here is to get the most we can out of this country, as quick as we can, and then get out."

But there is another route to reach Soco Gap, over the Blue Ridge Parkway through the sister mountains of the Smokies. It is more in keeping with the spirit of the mountains, more evocative of the old isolation that visitors try to capture. This parkway is a long corridor in a gallery, its alcoves alive with art, treasures that prepare the viewer to properly comprehend and absorb the masterpiece of the Smokies at the end. One cannot rush onward; he must allow his eye, senses, and intellect time for seasoning, for deepening perception. (Approaches to the Park from the central and eastern United States and a detailed map showing the area adjacent to the Park will be found in the Appendix.)

Thus, in almost five hundred miles of parkway, from Shenandoah to Smoky, the Appalachians unfold a story, these mountains that are older by millions of years than the Rockies, Cascades, and Sierras. Sometimes they are spoken of as extending a thousand miles in length from New York to Alabama, relating them geologically to earth formations continuing upward through New England to Newfoundland.

The Blue Ridge, the eastern rampart of the mountain system, seldom rises higher in New Jersey and Pennsylvania than 1500 or 2000 feet, but in Virginia it begins to assume the proportions of a major range.

West of the Blue Ridge, and parallel to it, lies the Great Appalachian Valley, a broad, broken succession of inner valleys, blocked from each other by crossing ridges—the Lehigh, Lebanon, and Cumberland valleys in Pennsylvania, Shenandoah in Virginia, the Valley of East Tennessee, continuing southward across portions of Georgia and Alabama.

Beyond the Great Valley, the Alleghenies swing southwestward from the Catskills in New York, across Pennsylvania reaching their fullest heights, up to 4500 feet, along the line between Virginia, West Virginia, and Kentucky. And beyond them lie the roughs of West Virginia and Kentucky leading to the Cumberland Plateau, a tableland rising above the Valley of Tennessee. These are the mountain companions of the Great Smokies.

In southwestern Virginia, the Blue Ridge becomes loftier, more massive, seeming to coalesce with the Alleghenies, forming a 150-mile-wide girth. Here is the beginning of the southern Blue Ridge province, stretching through parts of eight states from Virginia to Alabama, covering an area of land as large as the Alps. And this is Appalachia, a cultural, social unit, the "Back of Beyond" sparsely settled and little visited until its discovery near the end of the last century by lumbermen and miners, who joined the hillside farmers in stripping the soil of its treasures and the streams of their sweet waters. No section of this country offered to the white man greater gifts of nature; no section was accorded in turn greater abuse and less appreciation.

These parallel ranges connected by cross ranges and by tumbled mountains and hills—how long have they stood this way? The deepest mystery of the Appalachians is contained within their rocks. Their structure is complicated, imperfectly known by geologists; the landscape has undergone profound, endless change through countless ages; the broken ribbon of mountains, which once probably was more continuous in its form, has been worn away under the erosive chiseling of the elements, rain, wind, frost, heat, even long before the arrival of any man.

Geology is the heart-science of the hills. The rock types in many ways are different, but share the ancient age, the Archean, or oldest known, when the first seedbed of life was laid underwater on the floor of a shallow sea. South of Roanoke, the rocks are characteristically grayish, compressed into bands or wavy layers. The banded rock, gneiss, is among the oldest known on earth. The wavy layer, schist, sometimes catches the sparkle of the sun on shiny flakes of mica which aid in giving the rock its good cleavage. In places, coarse-grained granite is visible, an igneous rock solidified from molten lava and cooled far below the surface before being exposed by the erosive removal of thousands of feet of overlaid rock. On this basement of schist, granitic, and gneissic rocks, other strata of mud, sand, and gravel were deposited. Among these strata were the Ocoee series, which prevails in the Smoky Mountains. It accumulated, compacted, and cemented into rock underwater through interminable ages of the later Pre-Cambrian period, growing into thicknesses of 25,000 feet or more. The Ocoee rocks, formed of quartz and feldspar pebbles, are so old—more than 500 or 600 million years, according to best geological judgment—they contain no trace of plant or animal fossils, being created before life was abundant on the earth.

In that age, when the Ocoee series was being formed, mountain ranges may have risen as high as the Alps, but forces of erosion cut them down to an even, rolling surface. Then began the Paleozoic era, 300 million years ago, when amphibians began crawling out of the sea and the earth's first forests began to grow; the low-lying land of eastern America was bent downward, toward Newfoundland, inviting the sea to deposit new sand and coarse gravel, including masses of quartz, sandstone, and conglomerate rock. In the Ordovician period, widespread seas spread limestone, the fossilized remains of primitive shellfish, which underlies the Great Appalachian Valley and characterizes the Smoky Mountain coves. The accumulation of sediments extended over long periods in geologic time, woven together in geologic history with subterranean mountain-building upheavals. Often from the roadside or parking overlook along the parkway, one can see how the rocks are tilted, warped into huge arcs, or synclines, folded downward, evidence of tremendous pressures causing earthquakes ages ago.

Roughly 200 million years ago the violence of geologic forces erupted into a major disturbance in the earth's crust called the Appalachian Revolution. The result of stresses built up over long periods between huge masses of subterranean rocks and by lateral pressures from the sides of the basin, it caused formations to buckle into folds, to crack, or "fault," in many places, and to form "thrust faults" of one rock mass atop another. In this great epoch of eastern mountain building, 125 million years before the Rockies were born, rock weathering and stream erosion began to carve the valleys. This happened not once but several times, the Appalachian region being reduced to a plain, then being followed by an uplift of the geologic revolution, and the gouging of the high ridges into valleys—a massive, marvelous process that removed far more material than in the canyons of the West, including the Grand Canyon.

In western North Carolina and East Tennessee the Blue Ridge widens into a complex belt, rising more than 3000 feet above the sea and in its highest peaks, Grandfather, to 5964 feet; Pinnacle, to 5665 feet, and Standing Indian, to 5562 feet. But about fifty miles west of the Blue Ridge, near the border of Tennessee, Virginia, and Kentucky, the range that corresponds to the Alleghenies of Virginia now proceeds to dwarf all others in the entire Appalachian system. This is the massive Unaka, with eighteen peaks rising above 5000 feet, sculptured by rivers —the Nolichucky, French Broad, Pigeon, Little Tennessee, and Hiwassee—that rise on the western flanks of the Blue Ridge and flow through wild, deep gorges into the Tennessee and beyond to the drainage net of the Mississippi. The segments of the Unakas between these river clefts are the Northern Unaka, Bald, Great Smokies, and Unicoi.

Connecting the Blue Ridge and Unakas are transverse or cross ranges, vestigial bridges of land that rise above the Blue Ridge. Some, like the Blacks, dominated by 6684-foot-high Mount Mitchell, the tallest mountain in eastern America, are short but massive, bulking even above the Smokies. Others, like the Roan, 6285 feet, are crowned with rounded domes, covered only with grass or rhododendron. The cross ranges are separated by valleys, river basins, while rising on their slopes are smaller creeks, tributaries which flow down the flanks carving small valleys of their own that feed into the main valleys. And between the subvalleys are ridges running off the main crests, with tributary coves opening into the subsidiary valleys, and each cove with its own creek or branch or fork, and between these smaller streams, spurs descending from the ridges.

Such is the composition of the mountains of Appalachia. Water shapes are indivisible with the land. Water leads the unending march toward dissolution of the land. The moist atmosphere is conducive to rock decay; the pulsations of freezing and thawing crack loose the surfaces, the underground waters and organic acids erode and disintegrate the masses below the surface. The flowing water carves the groove in which it flows, fashions the depth, the cross section, the longitudinal profile, the areal configuration. Each stream has a wonderfully timeless history of its own, an evolution in many respects analogous to the evolution of a biological species. An existing river is inherited from an earlier one, which in turn derived from an earlier progenitor, extending backward to the time when the continental area was under the ocean. It changed with the changes in climate, the changes in elevation, the concomitant changes in vegetation. These streams are the means and the route by which the products of continental weathering are carried to the sea; washing soil, crushing rocks, uprooting boulders, obstructions, and seemingly insurmountable barriers, until most of the original lofty ranges have worn away.

The parkway veers away from the Blue Ridge just before it reaches the Blacks at Pinnacle. From this junction, it skirts the Blacks, crosses the Craggies into the Asheville vicinity, climbing through bolder mountains and widening vistas. It approaches the culminating Smokies by passing the towering, pyramid-shaped Pisgah Ledge, over a mile high, and entering into the heart of the Balsams, a mighty range in its own right that extends forty-five miles to join the Smokies at Mount Guyot.

The Balsams and Smokies are interwoven. The views from the Balsams embrace all the Smoky Mountain themes: the ancestral heartland of the Cherokee, the wars with advancing whites, the bear hunting, logging, exploration. The parkway rises over 6000 feet to become the highest motor road in eastern America, sometimes coursing through wispy clouds, and between spires of Fraser fir and red spruce, remnants of the "Canadian" forest that once covered the higher Appalachians, and still survive in the Smokies, Pisgahs, Balsams, and Blacks.

The most sweeping view of all unfolds from the open crest of Waterrock Knob, a superb 360-degree vista over the main ranges of southern Appalachia. The 6292-foot summit is the junction of the Great Balsams and Plott Balsams, named for the Plott family, old master bear hunters and breeders of prized bear dogs. To the northeast rise the Newfound Mountains and beyond them the Blacks and Craggies. Southeast, beyond Tennessee Ridge and Pisgah Ledge, the misty Blue Ridge outlines its route into Georgia. Nearer at hand in this same direction are the long rows of the Cowees, where one can follow the trail of William Bartram, the first naturalist into this country, and the more distant Nantahalas, the scene of his classic encounter with the chief of the Cherokee.

And northwestward, the Smokies rise upward from the Pigeon River, where it courses through the Unakas after collecting a hundred tributaries. The mountain wall extends southwestward seventy miles to the Little Tennessee, the greatest height and mass in all the Appalachians, with sixteen peaks above 6000 feet; for almost thirty-four miles the crest does not dip below 5000 feet, nor is it crossed by a single stream.

The mountaintops are green, their slopes are contoured, in contrast with the sharp peaks and saw-tooth ridges of the Alps and Rockies and the rock exposure of the New England peaks. This is because the Appalachians were never glaciated by the ice sheets that flowed down over North America during the Pleistocene age of a million years ago. But as all life is affected by climate shifts and geologic actions in near and distant places, these southern mountains played their role in the glacial periods, and still show the evidences.

Ages earlier, when the Appalachians were four or five times higher than now, a true alpine vegetation probably existed above timber line. In the course of 100 million years the mountains wore away and the vegetation changed. In the Cretaceous period, roughly 95 million years ago, the angiosperm, the complex flowering plant, originated and spread out (though no one really knows where on the earth angiosperms first appeared), displacing ferns and the ancient conifers. The climate of the succeeding Tertiary was favorable over much of the earth, equable and mild; many species of deciduous trees had a continuous distribution from North America across Europe to temperate Asia. The forests were nearly homogeneous. Then came the glaciers, in at least four distinct epochs, each lasting hundreds of thousands of years, coming as near the Appalachians as the Ohio Valley, frigid tongues of ice over-riding mountains, destroying life in their path, driving plants and animals south in search of survival.

This they found in the Appalachians. The mountains became a haven for northern life forms, who shared the refuge with southerly species. And when the raw earth warmed, the visitors remained while some of their number returned to revegetate their old homes. But in Western Europe, most of the hardwoods were driven out forever—only the primeval conifers would survive in the arid climate. In Europe, the retreat of the species during the Ice Age was blocked by mountains and the sea. They were doomed. The hardwood species were reduced to fewer than exist in the Smokies today. And in the Smokies, above all other places, the mixed hardwood forest endures as a living fragment of universality, the forest that once covered much of the earth. The primitive crest visible from Waterrock Knob is the finest example of similar forests that once covered thousands of square miles in the Appalachians.

The parkway dips to Soco Gap, the eastern portal. In the valley below live the Cherokee, who in summer are on display to amuse and enter-tain, with beads, baskets, feathers, drums, and pots. Yet the spiraling road following the old Indian trail passes unmarked, unheeded scenes of their greatness: the grounds of the council house of heroic chiefs, Yonaguska and Junaluska; the site of the trading store on Soco Creek, where Yonaguska met Will Thomas and adopted him into the Nation. It does not serve comfort to recall the heritage, for the prevalent policy of the whites ever since the first encounter has been to degrade, de-ceive, and confuse the red man.

The traveler who rushes onward through Soco Gap will not be troubled with the tragedies and heroisms. Nor will he learn the an-cestral passion of these people for the earth, the acceptance of them-selves as partners in the web of life of the Great Smokies.

Luckily, a man need not rush onward, but can pause to absorb the misty sky lines converging at Soco Gap. As William Bartram, lover of earth and Cherokee, once said, the mountains themselves are embodied with transience in the movement of the green crests where they join the clouds. Here is the place to feel the spirit of Bartram and the an-cient Cherokee and the truth of the hills in the waterfalls tumbling from the heights into rivulets down V-shaped valleys; the waters above and beneath calling to each other, and all to the ocean, their home.

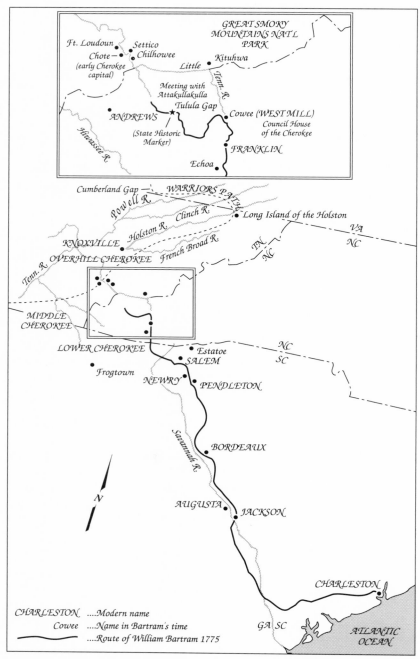

Bartram's route from the seacoast to his encounter with the Cherokee.

III

Bartram

An Irishman is the kind of fellow who can turn up any place on earth
and feel at home. Galahan of Cowee, an ancient and honorable Hiber-
nian, was thus content beyond the edge of white man's civilization. He
was a trader but one of the handful the Cherokee trusted. In 1775,
most traders were despised for their duplicity, dishonesty, and violence.
With bloodshed on the frontier, their goods were confiscated, they were
driven out or slain. Not so, old Galahan. He continued to live in Cowee
undisturbed, protected by its people.

We know of Galahan from the writings of William Bartram, the
singular explorer who searched out the true adventure of the hills. "It
was the botanist who discovered this Eden for us," said Kephart. "Far
back in the eighteenth century, when this was still Cherokee country, inhabited by no whites but a few Indian traders, William Bartram
of Philadelphia came plant-hunting into the mountains of western
North Carolina, and spread their fame to the world."

The Cherokee country into which Bartram entered as a stranger to
encounter old Galahan once covered 40,000 square miles. In the Stone
Age, before the coming of the white man, their lands and hunting
grounds embraced portions of the present Virginia, North Carolina,
South Carolina, Tennessee, and Alabama. Their population numbered
10,000 to 20,000 in some forty to sixty settlements clustered along the
streams. They ranged in freedom from the Ohio and Kanawha rivers
in the north to the southernmost reaches of the Tennessee, while their
hunting parties would foray into Kentucky, the magic place among Indians, uninhabited, fertile, with vast herds of buffalo, deer, and small

game, where they clashed with the Shawnee and other tribes from north of the Ohio.

The only sign remaining of Bartram's trail is located in the Nantahala National Forest, south of the Smokies. The Nantahalas have a glory of their own. They were a favorite Cherokee hunting ground and are still popular for boar, bear, and deer. The rugged mountains are forested with oak, tulip-poplar, pine, basswood, many species of shrubs and trees and include sixty miles of the Appalachian Trail following the crest of the Cheoah and Nantahala ranges. The Joyce Kilmer Memorial Forest embraces a remnant of the original Appalachian forest within its 3800 acres.

On the upper rim of Nantahala Gorge, near Beechertown, I crossed Bartram's trail. The gorge was surrounded by mile-high peaks, its slopes forested with hemlock. The sun still shone late in the morning only, therefore the place was worthy of the old name given by the Indians, "land of the middle sun." A historical marker read:

WILLIAM BARTRAM

Philadelphia Naturalist, Author,
exploring this area met a Cherokee
band led by their Chief Attakullakulla,
in May 1775, near this spot.

Bartram has recorded that he arrived here after leaving trader Galahan and Cowee, visiting Indian villages, botanizing in a wide arc, crossing the Little Tennessee and climbing either Wayah or Wine Spring Bald, well over 5000 feet, to look upon a world of mountains piled upon mountains, the Smokies included. Being May, the flood of flowers had burst into the fullness of their bloom. At night he slept surrounded by towering cucumber trees, listening to the shrill, social cries of the nighthawk, then awakening to the song of the mockingbird at the hour when the sun was at the tops of the hills.

What brought Bartram here? What happened when he met the chief? Where were they going? And with what outcome and meaning? To fully understand, one must trace him back to the stone house on the Schuylkill River in Philadelphia, where he was born and died. His father, John, had enlarged the house, originally a little cottage built by Swedish settlers in 1685, into an ample dwelling of gray stone, performing the work with his own hands. John Bartram was the plainest of men, a plowman, who taught himself to become a natural scientist, a scholar, and the principal figure of the botanical discovery of America underway in his age. He was the first great botanist born in the New World, the master naturalist of his time, ranging and collecting in the far wildernesses of the Great Lakes, Canada, and Florida for wealthy patrons abroad, including the King of England.

William Bartram, however, spent his youth in floundering and failure. He tried to earn his living as a merchant, farmer, trader on the North Carolina seacoast, as a rice and indigo planter in Florida. As a business-man he encountered wretched disaster, being forced to flee to escape creditors, and for times his whereabouts were unknown.

The fact was that since a frail childhood his sole interests were to follow his father through the woods, to hunt plants, to paint and draw the natural creatures. But John gave no encouragement; he thought the boy helpless and hopeless and probably did not even like his son. At last, after he was thirty-five, William turned his back on the past and proceeded to his life's work, inspired by the lines of Alexander Pope which his father had inscribed in stone above the seedhouse on the Schuylkill—

> Slave to no sect, who takes no private road,
> But looks through Nature up to Nature's God.

One of his father's patrons in England, Dr. John Fothergill, who knew William through his drawings, gave Bartram the encouragement he needed. "It is a pity that such a genius should sink under distress," wrote Dr. Fothergill, the leading physician of London, and, like the Bartrams, a Quaker. Thus he commissioned William, or Billy, as his father and his father's eminent friends called him, to explore the South in order to "collect and send me all the curious plants and seeds and other natural productions." To Bartram, in 1773, at the age of thirty-six, this was the beginning of the climactic experience of his lifetime, four years of scientific, literary, and religious probing of the Carolinas, Georgia, Alabama, Florida, to the Gulf of Mexico and as far west as the Mississippi. Occasionally he would emerge at a trading post or seaport in order to send specimens or letters of report to Dr. Fothergill, to obtain provisions (though he always traveled light) or letters of introduction. But for months on end he was out of touch with his civilization, visiting and befriending the Cherokee, Creek, Seminole (who called him Puc Puggy, "Flower Hunter"), Chickasaw, and Choctaw. Mostly he was alone, a wandering Robinson Crusoe, at home in the wilds, in harmony at last with his universe, collecting the source materials for his classic work, now called *The Travels of William Bartram*, living in his own style of "primeval simplicity and honesty," as one scientist later described it. He was totally unlike the image of a hardy adventurer, being of medium height, possibly a little smaller, benign in appearance, far from robust or strong. But in the company of nature his endurance and self-reliance matched that of the hardiest frontiersman or Indian.

After coming up from Florida and Georgia, he began his march into the highlands quite naturally at Charleston. It was the greatest city of the South, prospering on shipping, rice, indigo, and the Indian trade. As early as 1700, only thirty years after its settlement, the English had extended their trade channels from Charleston far to the west, beyond the Mississippi. Barter for pelts of beaver and deerskin was not only profitable, but sound diplomacy, particularly among the Cherokee. They comprised the largest nation bordering the English colonies, abutting the French lands to the west, the Spanish to the south. The English reckoned that if they treated the Cherokee fairly—at least reasonably fairly—they would serve as allies and a useful buffer. Thus, from the wharves and warehouses of Charleston, traders set forth into the mountains, each leading a string of pack horses loaded with commodities the Indians found useful: coarse cloth, axes, hoes, guns, blankets, and the commodity they did not want and resisted, whiskey. They bore something else unwanted, too; by Bartram's day, smallpox and yellow fever had ridden the trading paths in at least half a dozen waves.

Bartram went to see Captain John Stuart, superintendent of Indian Affairs in the southern colonies, who knew the Cherokee and their country as well as any white man of his time. Stuart, a romantic figure, had begun his service to the English cause in America as a campaigner under Oglethorpe in Georgia in 1733, and later rose through the ranks to become second in command at Fort Loudoun in the shadow of the Smokies. He was perhaps the most talented Indian negotiator the English ever had in the South, highly regarded by the Cherokee for his honesty, handsome appearance, and thick shock of red hair (for which they called him "Bushyhead"). He was beloved especially by Attakullakulla, leader of the Cherokee Nation, who had plucked Stuart from death in the bloody frontier massacre of 1760.

When Bartram called on Stuart, the old soldier and diplomat was over seventy. They had met ten years earlier when Bartram accompanied his father in exploring the South. Now the young naturalist sought guidance for his own trip into the high country of the Cherokee. The range that would later, much later, be called the Great Smokies was unknown to him; it was simply a portion of the southwestern wilderness, a mass of interwoven hills and swooping valleys, called the Appalachians or the Cherokee Mountains. But Stuart during his long military service had supervised the making of some of the most valuable maps of the colonial period and had prepared at least one of his own of the Indian lands.

Stuart warned his visitor that it was not a choice time, the spring of 1775, to go adventuring in the mountains. The territory beyond the eastern rampart, the Blue Ridge Divide, was in the Cherokee Nation.

The only white men allowed across the divide were the traders located in almost every village under permits issued by the Crown. Settlers were excluded, though they encroached increasingly in violation of the law. Hatred and bloodshed were rising between Indians and white frontiersmen. Strangers were not welcome. Bartram, however, never thought of himself as a stranger; all peoples were his brethren, the most ferocious animals of the wilderness his friends and teachers. As a Quaker he had no appetite for violence or destruction, but he yearned to know the Cherokee in their elemental surroundings. So he proceeded up the trading route, bearing the good wishes, advice, and introductions to traders from John Stuart. The date he departed Charleston on the northwest trail was April 22, 1775, three days after the opening shots of the American Revolution at Lexington and Concord, that would not only be heard around the world but felt, surprisingly, in the dim recesses of the Smokies.

Billy Bartram stopped at towns and trading posts between roving the swamps and woodlands, collecting plant specimens, and setting down notes. By mid May he had reached Fort Prince George, an outpost in the South Carolina foothills, on the site of the old Cherokee village of Keowee, one of the "Lower" towns, which had been destroyed fifteen years earlier in the War of 1760. A few miles south on the Keowee River was the new Cherokee town of Seneca, a respectable settlement of five hundred; but it lay too close to the spreading white world and would not survive much beyond the time of Bartram's visit.

What lay ahead in the high country? Only danger. Not a single frontiersman would agree to join him as a guide. He advanced alone into springtime in the Appalachians, discovering the Eden to which Kephart alluded; Kephart who himself would say, "These flowers that spring up from under the dense forests are such as defy cultivation. They exist nowhere but in the untouched wildwood, which has been left to itself these many thousands of years." In this primeval manner, Bartram found the pent-up forest teeming with fresh color after its thaw of early spring. In deep shade were scatterings of wild snow trillium, the pale white flower of the Trinity, bearing three green leaflets, three green sepals, and three petals. In dark, moist places, the dwarf mountain iris glowed in purple flower among sword-shaped leaves. The red and yellow columbine, with buttercuplike leaves, moved in a soft breeze, awaiting the ruby-throated hummingbird. Dogwood spread its blossoms like a milky way—chalky white or as pink as a cloud—surrounding the true flowers, a small bouquet of greenish white or yellow. He observed and recorded the lively little lily of the valley, with perfumed white bell-shaped flowers; blushing rosebay; sweet syringa, with creamy-white flowers in terminal clusters of five or seven; and the sky-robed delphinium, or larkspur, with fine, threadlike leaves and blue, purple, or white flowers, its nectary shaped like the spur of a lark's foot. And the exciting flame azalea, spreading across the ascending hillsides, which evoked from Bartram one of the loveliest, and renowned, botanical descriptions: "The epithet fiery I annex to this celebrated species of Azalea, as being expressive of the appearance in flower." It seemed to him that the clusters of the blossoms cover the shrubs in such incredible profusion on the hillsides, "that suddenly opening to view from dark shades, we are alarmed with the apprehension of the hills being set on fire. This is certainly the most gay and brilliant flowering shrub yet known."

In this virginal woodland, which continues to endure in the Great Smokies, he recognized trees common to his native Pennsylvania, or New York, or even to Canada: the white pine, monarch of the eastern forest; the long-lived sugar maple scattered through the moist bottom lands; the beech, with smooth bluish-gray bark; the graceful birch, with cinnamon-colored bark, on the shores of ponds and riverbanks; yellow birch, with silvery-yellow bark peeling in paper-thin curls; and the white ash, with bronze bark, its rich green foliage shaped into a pyramidal crown eighty feet above him.

Bartram perceived the remarkable quality of the Appalachian forest in the mixture of its species. Here was the native vine Carolina jessamine, or wild woodbine, which he knew could not survive the slightest frost of Pennsylvania, in company with Canadian vegetables and "roving with them in perfect bloom and gaiety." The Stewartia, a small tree or tall shrub, normally restricted to the South, shared the scene with the diminutive silver-bell, or snowdrop, tree, a Carolina species which does bear the hard frosts of Pennsylvania. On the same mountainside was the red spruce of the Canadian forest thriving above the Fraser magnolia, or cucumber tree, the giant of magnolias, a breed normally of the humid climate, blossoming contentedly with long creamy-white flowers.

On his lonesome pilgrimage into the steep rocky hills he would come upon a cascade of clear water, rolling and leaping off the rocks, spreading into a sheet of crystal, the waters trembling, then gliding swiftly on their way to the sea. Bartram seated himself, under the shade of hemlock and rhododendron, to join the "charming circle of vegetable beauties." To this poetic romancer, every living thing had personality, purpose, beauty. He was admirer even of the rattlesnake, whom he considered a generous creature, who is "never known to strike until he is first assaulted or fears himself in danger, and then always gives the earliest warning by the rattles at the extremity of his tail." But he believed the essence of divinity to be embodied in the plant, a humbler, simpler creature, therefore closer to the heart of God. Or, as Bartram would say, "Perhaps there is not any part of creation, within reach of our observations, which exhibits a more glorious display of the Almighty hand than the vegetable world."

As a pantheist, he saw a soul in each of these. He endeavored to prove this with pitcher plants, whose insect-eating habits he was the first to describe. "See the incarnate lobes expanding," he wrote of the Venus flytrap, "how gay and ludicrous they appear! ready on the spring to intrap incautious deluded insects, what artifice! there behold one of the leaves just closed upon a struggling fly, another has got a worm, its hold is sure, its prey can never escape—carnivorous vegetable! Can we after viewing this object hesitate a moment to confess the vegetable beings are endued with some sensible faculties or attributes, similar to those that dignify animal nature; they are organical, living and self-moving bodies, for we see here, in this plant, motion and volition."

In these beliefs he was like the Cherokee. Probably he derived source and inspiration from them while in their midst; as in the case of the pitcher plant, *Ugwili*, which some Cherokee still employ symbolically to attract fish and game, women, and tourists. Living in this land of luxuriant flora, from the giant trees of the coves to the wild fruits along running streams, they incorporated vegetables into their ceremonies, myths, and medicines. They believed the plant world friendly to them, even at their service, willing to co-operate with their medicine men in counteracting the jealousy and hostility of the animals. They showed their keen observation by the names which they gave to plants. Mistletoe, which fixes its roots in the bark of a supporting tree or shrub, from which it draws sustenance, was called *uda'li*, "it is married." Bear grass was "greensnake," because of its long slender leaves; black-eyed Susan, the "deer-eye," and lady's-slipper, "partridge moccasin." Ginseng, the "mountain climber," was addressed by priests, or shamans, as "little man, most powerful magician." This sacred term had its origin, like the Chinese, in the frequent resemblance of the root shape of this member of the English ivy family to the human form. The root, radishlike, is a spindle with semblance of head, arms, and legs, manlike or womanlike. Though for almost two hundred years it has been uprooted mercilessly for the Chinese trade, the Cherokee of Bartram's day were extremely considerate of the plant. They used it for medicinal purposes, but their medicine man spoke of it as a sentient being. In hunting for it in the hills, he would pass over the first three, ask permission of the fourth to cut a small piece of its flesh.

Whenever skies permitted, Bartram observed the expansive, magnificent landscape, but thick gray clouds, tumbling, boiling masses, often filled the heavens. The weather grew warm, sultry; the days were wet. He rode through misty clouds, fording rivers with difficulty, his horse forced to swim, rather than walk, across the rocky bottoms. He was alone for days. While he met some of his own kind in the Indian villages, white traders who were friendly and hospitable, their manners and customs were so different from his that they seemed like strangers. On a lucky night in the wilds he might find lodgings in a deserted Indian hunting cabin, where he would dry his soggy clothes and converse with bats and whippoorwills taking refuge from a violent storm. The weight of solitude turned his mood; he thought of man's predilection for the company of his fellows, he yearned for the polite Charleston society. Instead, he could only compare his circumstances with that of Nebuchadnezzar, constrained to roam the mountains and wilderness, to feed with wild beasts of the forest.

Then he passed through the first of the Cherokee "Middle" towns, Echoa and sacred Nequassee (on the site of the present Franklin, North Carolina) and Watauga, a larger town, where the chief welcomed Bartram to his house, fed him, and cheered his spirits. At last he entered the Cowee Mountains, where he followed a valley into the village of Cowee (at the site of the present Wests Mill, between Franklin and Bryson City), the principal settlement of the Middle towns. It was here that he met Galahan, very likely on the basis of a letter from Captain Stuart. The old trader took the wanderer into his home.

At Cowee, he rested and reconnoitered, observing the sheer hills rising from the clear waters of the Little Tennessee. He was already across the Blue Ridge in one of the transverse ranges connecting with the Unakas. He had no way of knowing that the Cowees were barely one long step from the Smokies, joined by the link of the Alarka Mountain (west of Bryson City), and further related by the meeting of their waters. He could have followed a trail to the villages on the Tuckasegee and Oconaluftee and found himself heading for the summit of Smoky. But his eye was on the Nantahalas, which lay astride the main trail to the Overhill towns and the capital of the Cherokee Nation. Mistakenly, he thought the Nantahala Range contained the highest peak in the Appalachians.

Would Galahan guide him into the Overhill country? The Irishman, who knew well his time and place, refused. Such an expedition was unsafe. Almost all the traders across the mountains had packed and cleared out. He tried to dissuade Bartram from an unpromising undertaking. The foolhardy or fearless innocent pleaded that he must, at all events, cross the Jore Mountain, or the Nantahalas, the rooftop of America.

Galahan conceded to lead him down the trading path and get him started. They rode into the hills, Bartram and his "worthy old friend," passing through an Indian village, where he noted a grove of cassine yaupon, or holly, far from its coastal range. He knew it from the Creek and the old maritime tribes who called it the "beloved tree"; they kept it pruned and cultivated and drank a strong infusion of the leaves, buds, and branches celebrated as the "black drink." Here too, apparently, did the Cherokee.

After fifteen miles they reached the parting of the ways. Galahan returned to Cowee. Bartram went on alone, apprehensive. When he stopped for lunch, of biscuit, cheese, and meat, a stout young Indian approached armed with rifle and two dogs attending. They fell to friendship, though neither understood the other's language, and Bartram presented his guest with a passel of choice tobacco. After they parted in cheerfulness, Bartram proceeded to botanize in a wide arc, diverting from the trading path, absorbing the world of mountains piled upon mountains—the most "sublimely awful" scene of power and magnificence he had ever seen.

The next day, after riding through spacious high forests and flowery meadows, he arrived at Nantahala Gorge. In the distance ahead, descending from the heights, he saw a band of Indians. They were riding rapidly toward him. Traveling alone, beyond the pale of safety, he could not have had the least idea of how they would greet him.

In his favor was the uncanny sense of encountering Indians with friendship under any circumstances. And without fear. It was the same inborn gift shared with his contemporary, Daniel Boone, which might have derived from their Quaker training. Once Boone was hunting alone on the Tennessee side of the Smokies, near the present Jonesboro. He was rudely awakened in the night as he lay under a snow-covered blanket. A Cherokee party had surrounded his camp and one brave was in the act of pulling back the blanket to see who was under it. He recognized Boone, who awoke in time to hear the red man say, "Ah, Wide Mouth, have I got you now?" Boone sat straight up, with a friendly smile. He shook hands with the Indian, then with all the others gathered round him. They exchanged bits of wilderness news and gossip and treated him kindly. Next morning Boone broke camp early and lost no time high-tailing for distant parts.

As for Bartram, his most classic Indian encounter, excluding the one that now awaited, occurred one evening farther south, when he was marching beyond a frontier settlement under calm skies. Suddenly a wild-eyed Indian blocked his path with a loaded rifle. Bartram prepared to meet his end, tranquilizing his mind with a Quaker prayer. He, like Boone, smiled, then extended his arm in greeting and spoke the one word that came from his soul to all men, "Brother." The Indian halted in his tracks, confused and befuddled, and slowly gave his arm in response. Then he directed Bartram to the nearest trading post on his route. The traders told him the Indian was a noted murderer, outlawed by his own tribe, whom they had driven off the night before. But Bartram's sympathy, quite typically, lay with the Indian.

The chief riding at the head of the procession was Attakullakulla, or Leaning Wood, also called Little Carpenter. In his youth he had been known as Oukou-Naco, or Ookoo-naka, the White Owl. Now he was old, over seventy, slender, small of stature, delicately built. His ears were cut and banded with silver, which, in the notion of the Indians, was a mark of distinction. He and his followers had come from Echota, also called Chota or Chote, the acknowledged capital of the Nation, in the Overhill country. They were traveling on the path through the present Robbinsville and Andrews to Charleston, which he had visited many times in the preceding fifty years and where he was known variously as "the wily savage" and "the Indian capable of enthusiasm for good and evil."

Bartram has furnished a description of their encounter. As a token of respect, he gave ground, yielding the trail to the chief. Attakullakulla and his entourage halted. The chief smiled cheerfully and clapped his hand on his breast, then leaned over his horse to extend his hand. They shook as friends.

"I am Attakullakulla," the chief introduced himself. "Do you know of my name?"

"Yes," Bartram replied. "The Good Spirit who goes before me spoke to me, and said that this is the great Attakullakulla." Then he added quickly that he was a Quaker. "I am of the tribe of white men, of Pennsylvania, who esteem themselves brothers and friends to the red men, but particularly so to the Cherokee. Notwithstanding that we dwell at so great a distance we are united in love and friendship, and the name of Attakullakulla is dear to his white brothers of Pennsylvania."

The chief smiled. Though spokesman and chief diplomat for the Cherokee Nation, he was pleased to hear of such regard far afield. "Are you come lately from Charleston?" he asked. "Is John Stuart well? I am going to see him."

"Yes, I am come lately from Charleston on a friendly visit to the Cherokee. I have the honor of a personal acquaintance with the superintendent, the beloved man, whom I saw well but the day before I set off. The beloved man by letters to the principal white men in the Nation recommended me the friendship and protection of the Cherokee."

"You are welcome in our country as friend and brother," the great chief answered respectfully. They shook hands heartily anew. But the Cherokee were pressed to resume their long journey. The chief bid Bartram farewell, while his followers, the lesser chieftains and warriors, raised their voices as one, in assent with his.

"My name is Bartram," the white man called as Attakullakulla began to ride. "Please give my compliments to the superintendent."

They went their separate ways, neither to fare well. Bartram rode for a time through a botanical wonderland in the glory of its bloom till loneliness and depression overcame him. The next Indian party might not be friendly. In the valley of Junaluska Creek, near Andrews, he wheeled his horse around, turning back to the companionship of Galahan and the comforts of Cowee.

Attakullakulla rode through a crumbling world. It was then barely six weeks after the events of Concord and Lexington, the opening of the war for freedom. The white Americans sought freedom to rule themselves, freedom for shipping merchants and manufacturers; freedom, also, to cross the mountains and colonize new lands for their children. The shreds of freedom that once belonged to the Cherokee, Attakullakulla held in his hands and heart. His people had surrendered almost all their ancient territorial claims; they were reduced virtually to their home settlements in the high valleys. Now he was going to counsel with his old friend and adopted brother, Captain John Stuart, Loyalist, and organizer of Indians and Tories against the Revolution. When Attakullakulla reached the coast, he would hear that Stuart's activities had been exposed and even he was forced to defend himself by fleeing to Florida.

IV

The World Is a Ballroom

After his encounter with Attakullakulla, Bartram returned to Cowee to observe the Cherokee way of life. The Cherokee formed the largest single tribe in the South and one of the largest of all tribes north of Mexico. The people were the mountaineers of their race, dwelling among the blue-topped ridges and lofty peaks. They were already touched but not yet crushed by the civilizing hand, crossing the bridge of change, in psychology and social structure, after centuries of slow evolution.

Cowee, like most Cherokee villages, was located in a fertile bottom. Along Cowee Creek the Indians grew corn, potatoes, squash, beans, pumpkins, and melons. They kept horses, hogs, and poultry. Apple orchards surrounded the town at the foot of the mountains.

About one hundred houses formed the settlement, almost all being one-story cabins of logs, stripped of bark and notched at the ends. The typical dwelling was plastered with tempered clay or dried grass, then roofed with the bark of a chestnut tree or with long, broad shingles. It was partitioned to form two or three rooms, while outside, opposite the door, was a little conical lodging, excavated to a slight depth and covered with dirt, called the winter house or hothouse—the sleeping quarters in cold weather.

The focal point of the community was the council house, or town house, a large rotunda accommodating several hundred persons, where festivals were held almost every week, and sometimes every night, for spiritual ritual was inherent in Cherokee life. The council house was located near the stream so people could take the prescribed plunges during or after ceremonies.

Bartram observed that the Cherokee were intelligent, tenacious of the liberties and natural rights of men, "secret, deliberate, and determined in their councils; ready always to sacrifice every pleasure and gratification, even their blood, and life itself, to defend their territory and defend their rights."

They were eloquent people, who would in time produce a series of eminent national spokesmen to plead their cause before the whites. Their language, as all Indian languages, was rhetorical, figurative, stressing style and figures of speech; enunciated with primitive theatrical vanity, turning or bending of the head, with every part of the body that added to eloquence and persuasion. It was as though the world was a ballroom, and all the men and women dancers, each with his entrances and exits, in reflecting the deep cycles and rhythms of life. "If there is anything written clear across the almost infinite diversity of primitive society," John Collier wrote, "it is that the group molds its members toward emotion, toward the experience of crises of realization and of conscience, and toward a profoundly romantic world-view which includes a profoundly romantic view of man in the world." Thus, everything had its theatricality. The tribe was divided into seven clans, Wolf, Deer, Bird, Red Paint, Blue, Wild Potato, and Twister. Clan members were regarded as descendants of one and the same family and each clan member owed fealty to all others; it was the violence of the drama that when a Cherokee was killed, his clan was required to exact blood for blood, regardless of circumstance.

The Cherokee tribal organization in the eighteenth century was loose. There were four principal groups of villages, including many clustered on the southern and western flanks of the Great Smoky Mountains. The Overhill towns centered around what was known popularly as "Chote the metropolis," on the lower reaches of the Little Tennessee, with a few on the Tellico and middle portion of the Hiwassee River. Separated from them by rough mountain country were the powerful Middle settlements on the headwaters of the Little Tennessee and Tuckasegee rivers. The Valley towns were located near the present Robbinsville and Murphy, in the southwest corner of North Carolina, and the Lower towns centered around Keowee, on the headwaters of the Savannah River in South Carolina and the Tugaloo River in Georgia.

Each village went its separate way, which contributed to the ultimate undoing of the Cherokee. Three different dialects were spoken. When there were no wars to fight against other tribes, they warred against each other. Some chieftains were friendly to the English cause in America, others to the French; some urged war to the bloody bitter end against all whites and denounced Attakullakulla for advocating peace with any. The Cherokee were torn by dissent, jealousy, and confusion within their tribes, generously stirred further by European intrigue.

As aboriginals, the Cherokee were accustomed to small, loosely formed societies. "This practice," explained Thomas Jefferson (who studied the Cherokee among his many fields of interest during his term as governor of Virginia), "results from the circumstance of their never having submitted themselves to any laws, any coercive power, any shadow of government. Their only controls are their manners, and that moral sense of right and wrong which, like the sense of taste and feeling, in every man makes part of his nature. An offense against these is punished by contempt, by exclusion from society, or, where the case is serious, as that of murder, by the individuals whom it concerns."

These serious offenses were, in fact, adjudicated on the old Mosaic principle of blood for blood. One crime was to marry within the clan. Another was murder. Often the penalty was simple and direct: the guilty party would be pushed out front in battle to face certain death. Or, he would be taken to the top of a cliff, where his feet would be drawn up and tied, his elbows tied behind, and then pushed over. One or more towns, including ancient Chote, were designated as places of refuge, though sometimes a clan would force a criminal to leave, then execute him elsewhere.

There were no laws against adultery. It was up to clan and friends to restore a man's honor. The punishment for adultery in many southern tribes was the feared cropping, whereby the ears of the delinquent, whether male or female, were sheared close to the head. Yet, true to simple aboriginal morality, dishonor never was cast upon the children.

In one recorded incident, a number of warriors, belonging to the family of the husband, learned that his wife loved a great many men. Justice told them her yearnings should be gratified—and thoroughly. Late one day they followed her into the woods, waiting till she was a little way from town, as decency would fairly demand. They encouraged her to assume a fitting position on the grass, then tied her hands and feet to stakes. One by one, the young Cherokee, fifty in number, took their turns in satiating her desire.

But, observed Jefferson, though such species of coercion appear imperfect, crimes were rare among the Cherokee. He then asked, Does the absence of law, as among the savage Americans, or the presence of too much law, as among the civilized Europeans, submit man to the greatest evil? One who has studied both conditions, he reasoned in rhetorical response, would pronounce it to be the latter; that the sheep are happier of themselves than under the care of the wolves.

The Indian, explained Jefferson, is brave when an enterprise depends upon bravery, being trained that the point of honor consists in destroying an enemy by stratagem while preserving himself free of injury. He would defend himself against a host of foes, always choosing to be killed rather than to surrender, meeting torture or death with firmness and religious deliberation. His sensibility was so keen and family ties so strong, that the bravest warrior wept at the loss of one of his children.

And while the white man's affections weaken, noted Jefferson, from circle to circle as they recede outward from the central core of blood ties, the Indian's friendship remains unbroken to the outer extreme. In demonstrating this point, he cited a well-known episode involving Attakullakulla. It occurred when William Byrd and Peter Randolph were dispatched from Virginia to Chote to discuss a proposed treaty. They were negotiating peaceably in the council house when a runner arrived with the frightful intelligence that frontiersmen had attacked and slain a family of Indians; worst of all, while the Indians were their hosts and serving them food. The council was thrown into an uproar. Attakullakulla, realizing the danger to Byrd and Randolph, warned the Virginia commissioners to keep closely within their tent and delegated Saloue, a young chief of Estatoe, to their guard. Saloue on a former occasion had developed a friendship with Colonel Byrd and vowed to defend him. When it was determined that Byrd should die and warriors arrived to perform the execution, Saloue threw himself between them and the Virginian. "This man is my friend," he cried. "Before you get at him, you must first kill me."

The Cherokee were finely trained fighters. They dreaded the fierce raiding forays of the Iroquois and Shawnee from the North. They were the foes of the Creeks, a great and ancient people who forged a confederacy in the Southeast; the long enmity worsened when the Cherokee usurped the lands on the headwaters of the Coosa, Chattahoochee, and Savannah rivers. They fought the Congaree, Yamassee, Yuchi, and Cheraw. But warfare had deep reason in tribal being, as though reflecting the violence and struggle for survival of all creatures in the primordial community. Treading the warpath was the ambition of every young man, and a source of exaltation. Even romance was intertwined with war. If a youth were to discover fondness for women before he had been to battle, he would become the object of contempt by men, of scorn and ridicule by women. Or, if he were to indulge himself with a captive taken in war or, even worse, gratify his lust with violence, he would incur indelible disgrace. However, the celebrated warrior more often was courted than he had occasion to court—and this was the vantage for which the youthful Cherokee aspired.

Kituhwa, an ancient settlement, was regarded by the Cherokee as the mother town, or one of the seven mother towns of the Nation. Located on the Tuckasegee River, in the shadow of the Smokies, it extended from above the junction with the Oconaluftee, at the foot of Thomas Divide, down nearly to the present Bryson City. The people of this village and others nearby were known as Ani-Kituhwagi, the people of Kituhwa, or Yunwiya, "Principal People." The word Cherokee itself has no meaning in the Indian language. It may have had its origin in the time of the De Soto expedition with the word Achelaque, modified in stages to spell Cherokee, until not even their name remained to them.

The Cherokee beginning is as much a mystery as the geologic story of the Smokies. Ancient burial or ceremonial mounds still remain on the banks of the Oconaluftee, though neglected and grazed over. The ancient people followed the rivers and streams of Appalachia, here and there building a settlement of lean-tos of wooden poles in a fertile river bottom, broad enough to provide arable land, secure from sudden invasion by the mountains, yet convenient to them to pursue game.

But how long have the Cherokee been in these mountains? When and from where did they come? The definitive answer has remained a mystery. In the Old World, human history has been traced to its beginnings, and, even earlier, to fossil remains which suggest the evolutionary sources of animal development preceding man. But in the Western Hemisphere, no such remains have been located. The prevalent theory judges the American Indian by his Mongoloid physical characteristics—the color of his skin, the prominent cheekbones, straight dark hair, dark eyes—as a migrant from Asia, though the possibility is recognized that some features may have been acquired elsewhere.

Whatever the circumstance, whatever the hour in history, man has been the wanderer for the entire span of his existence, the stranger crossing the face of the earth, following the lead of the high stars from one ocean shore to another, tracing the streams over the land, exploring his own dreams in the endless search for his place in the universe. For the Indians, or their predecessors, the journey from Asia across the Bering Strait presumably began somewhere between 15,000 to 20,000 years ago; but, as all of time and space are joined together, the journey traces back further to the start of the Ice Age, when glaciers spread across the northern continents. The seas yielded their moistures to the expanding ice; the ocean levels lowered, and in the shallow draft of the Bering Strait a dry land passage emerged. Animal herds crossed first, followed by the Wandering Hunters, advancing during long periods of time down the dry central plain of Alaska, south along the eastern slope of the raw young Rockies. The climatic swings of the Pleistocene epoch were natural pulsations, like the beating of a pump, the heaving of a sea, the throbbing of a heart, stirring life within thousands of miles of shifting ice fronts, driving life southward with icy winds, drawing it north as cold and dampness were replaced by warmth and drought.

The primitive peoples felt the natural rhythms, the cycles, the continuum that bound their past and present with the unknown future. They had few impersonal, artificial instruments to cloud their view of natural forces. They could feel the relationship between the hours of their lives and the centuries of time. Somewhere in the course of their migrations their early rituals developed: the ritual of fasting to reflect the time of starvation and want in wintertime when game was scarce and the future problematical; the dances, lustrations, ceremonial hunts, new-fire making, new-moon feasts—primitive art expressions that tie the generations together were born.

Gradually the Wandering Hunters spread across the continent, their journeys and diffusions continuing until the entire Western Hemisphere was traversed and occupied. It was at least 15,000 years ago, when the Ice Age still held the world in its frozen grasp, that human beings first came into the valley of the Tennessee River and the highlands above, small bands of nomadic hunters venturing into the untrodden wilderness, leaving fluted spear points, cutting and scraping tools as the signs of their presence. Other migrations and movements followed through the subsequent Stone Ages. The races developed their arts and crafts, using native materials like steatite, found in the Appalachian hills, for their pottery; they cultivated maize, or Indian corn, and built towns and ceremonial mounds. In some distant period the people who became the Cherokee entered the hills. Because their language bears similarity to the language of the Iroquois, many ethnologists believe they derive from the broad Iroquoian stock, driven south to form a salient into groups of different and hostile stocks—the Shawnee and Catawba of the Algonquian, and the Creek of the Muskhogean. Yet evidence has also been unearthed indicating their possible origin as a subtype of the Muskhogeans of the lower Mississippi.

Bartram was able to observe elements of the ancient ceremonialism in the culture of the Cowee people. Religion was the controlling force, that natural religion in which every animal, stone, and tree was believed to have its spirit and a particular reason for being.

The priest, or shaman, was a person of tribal consequence, employing a combination of superstition, magic, and theatricality. The people believed he had communion with powerful invisible spirits, who shared in ruling human affairs as well as the elements. His influence was so great in predicting the outcome of expeditions that a gloomy forecast might cause an armed force to turn back after marching several hundred miles. He would foretell rain or drought, sometimes presuming to bring rain and to exercise the power of directing thunder and lightning. As medicine man, he would frighten away sickness and death by use of secret formulas and herbal remedies, dancing around his patients with incantations, rattling gourds filled with pebbles or beans. Witchcraft, but powerful medicine.

Women occupied a high place in Cherokee life. As Attakullakulla once said to the British colonial governor, Lyttelton, when he brought a group of women to bear witness to their mistreatment by the notorious trader Elliott, "It is customary among the red men to admit women to their councils. As the white people, as well as the red, are born of women, is it not the custom among them, also?" The family ties of the wife were more important than those of the husband, for land was inherited and kinship traced through her family. Early custom usually demanded that during marriage plans a young man send to his betrothed a ham of venison, as a pledge of ample food supply, while she tendered to him an ear of corn, her promise the fields would be tended and food prepared. After the wedding, he would take residence with the clan of his wife, while his children became property of the mother and members of her clan.

On one occasion Bartram went to the council house with his friend and mentor, trader Galahan, to witness the ceremony preceding the ball-play of the next day. The council house was the essence of the worldly ballroom, where the Cherokee staged a variety of dances, all of which were like exhibitions or plays. They were martial, comic, tragic, sometimes lascivious. Men exercised in a variety of gesticulations and capers. Women, however, as Bartram put it, conducted themselves with restraint; when their responses conveyed surrender, they veiled themselves and consented with a blush. Some ceremonies were brief. Others were lengthy spectacles. The Green Corn Dance, *Selutsungitisti*, in the seventh moon, lasted two weeks, a thanksgiving celebration held when the first corn ripened and became fit to eat. Enemies were forgiven, fires extinguished, and new fire kindled by the conjurer, or *Adawehi*, then fires were lit on each family hearth. The first fruits were deposited in the council house for the poor, who might otherwise have no corn for winter. On the main day no voices were heard until nightfall, when the whole town assembled to hear the shaman sacrifice the new fruit, express thanks for the sweet beneficence of earth, and pray for the spirits to bless the corn and meat during the year. Then all would eat, repair to the river to bathe, and return to the council house for a religious dance.

Now Bartram entered, along with the people of Cowee. The council house was a seven-sided structure, reflecting the Cherokee belief in seven as the sacred number. Around the walls of the interior were three tiers of benches, elevated as in an amphitheater, with seven sections, one for each clan. Near the great pillar in the center a fire cast a glow across the musicians sitting around it.

The program opened with an oration by an aged and honorable chieftain. He spoke long and he was spirited, exhorting the young men for the ball-play of the morrow, recounting the many victories, the brilliant and memorable victories, that Cowee had scored over other villages in the Nation. Nor did he overlook his own exploits, or those of the other aged men present, in their youthful days.

His talk was the prologue. The musicians began to play their melancholy, discordant music on flutelike instruments, made of a joint of reed, or the tibia of a deer's leg. A company of young girls entered, hand in hand, singing in gentle, low voices, accompanied by skin drum and gourd rattle, a "pathetic harmony" that has ever characterized Cherokee song. The girls, ornamented with beads, bracelets, and colored ribbons, formed a semicircular line in two ranks, one facing the spectators, the other facing the musicians around the fire. They moved slowly round and round.

Suddenly, a loud shrill whoop! Young men's voices. A band of fellows marched in briskly, forming a semicircle in front of the girls. They were painted and ornamented, wearing silver bracelets around their wrists, gorgets and wampum at their throats, high waving plumes in their hair. The girls formed a parallel single rank, raising their voices in response to the men's. The semicircles moved around continually in a complex, weaving ensemble executed with incredible alertness, revealing to the spectators a grandly universal movement. The men would strike their hands with the open hand; the girls would clap their hands. And when the men gave a war whoop, the girls raised shrill voices in response.

Attending this ceremony was the last of Bartram's experiences in the Smoky Mountain country. Next morning he turned southward to Keowee, there to wait for Galahan who was to accompany him to Seneca, in the Lower towns. In due course, the publication of his masterpiece in 1791 furnished a list and location of forty-three Cherokee towns and villages, together with a picture of natural and human life in the primeval mountains of the eighteenth century. "I remember when it was much the custom to ridicule Mr. Bartram, and to doubt the truth of many of his relations," wrote Major John Eatton Le Conte in 1854. (He was a member of the distinguished family of Georgia scientists that included Professor Joseph Le Conte, for whom the third highest peak in the Smokies later would be named.) "For my own part I must say, that having travelled in his track I have tested his accuracy, and can bear testimony to the absolute correctness of all his statements. . . . Mr. Bartram was a man of unimpeached integrity and veracity, of primeval simplicity of manner and honesty unsuited to these times, when such virtues are not appreciated."

Bartram lived until the age of eighty-five, managing modestly and peaceably the wonderful botanical garden on the Schuylkill which his father had started, but exercising wide influence in the natural sciences, guided to the last by the old code of looking through nature to nature's God.

V

Little Carpenter

Attakullakulla was a highly civilized, practical statesman. He served the Cherokee Nation for almost half a century, through painful and trying years, holding his people together and giving them hope through one defeat after another. He was the first of the eloquent English-speaking Cherokee orators, but much less remembered than others who followed. Though of primitive source, he moved with grace among the circles of white leadership, whether on the frontier with Daniel Boone, or in Charleston with a colonial governor and his council, or in London before the King.

He was called by the whites the Little Carpenter, a name he liked and used in referring to himself. It was intended to imply that, as a carpenter must bring the notches of wood to fit in place, Attakullakulla could maneuver artfully to bring various conflicting minds together in the political framework of his nation. This was not simple, for other leaders considered him a tool of his ally, the British. But the Crown was his long-time tool, as well, furnishing the Cherokee protection against the French, Spanish, and Indian tribal enemies, restraining the encroachment of frontier settlers, and coercing the many village chieftains to set aside their differences and stand together, which was their critical need for survival.

Attakullakulla derived his authority as head of one prong of the Nation, the peace, civil, or White, organization. White represented the color of peace; in almost every important town the peace chief, or high priest, the *Uku*, the "highest," would sit in the council house on a white deerskin, clothed in a white costume.

When war threatened, however, the Red organization would take command. In Attakullakulla's day the war chief of the Nation was Oconostota (Groundhog-Sausage), known as Great Warrior. He was widely traveled and respected, a member of St. Andrew's Society of Charleston in company with prominent men of the colony. In his youth he had been a strong supporter of the British, even visiting the Virginia governor at Williamsburg, but harsh experience turned him to bitterness. Oconostota was a brave mountain man candid enough to admit that he never ran from an enemy but "once walked fast up a branch." As the war chief, called Kalanu, or Raven, he presided with red-painted war club, the emblem of battle, and in his scalp lock wore eagle feathers with red stripes. Among his entourage were the war women, called Pretty Women, old and honored matrons who decided the fate of captives.

Attakullakulla was related by blood to principal and distinguished figures in the Cherokee drama. He succeeded as peace chief his uncle, Kana-gatoga (Standing Turkey) of Chote, called Old Hop because he was lame. His half-sister was Nancy Ward, who achieved fame during the Creek War of 1755 in Georgia when she saw her husband slain, and took up his gun and fought in his place. She was awarded the title of Ghigau, or Agiyagustu, Beloved Woman, whose special duties included preparing the "black drink" for warriors going to battle. But Nancy Ward had strong ties with the whites, particularly John Sevier, to whom she sent warnings of attack. A son of Attakullakulla was Dragging Canoe, a great leader in his own right, who headed the Chickamaugas during the American Revolution, rallying many tribes to fight on against the whites. After the Carpenter's death in 1777, the chieftainship passed to his nephew (through the female side), named Old Tassel, who ultimately was murdered by Sevier's marauding bushwhackers. The fiery Doublehead and Pumpkin Boy were Old Tassel's brothers. One sister of these three, Wurteh, married Nathaniel Gist, trader and emissary to the red men, and is generally regarded as the mother of Sequoyah, the genius who created the written Cherokee language. Another sister was the mother of Chief John Watts, rousing leader of the Chickamaugas after his uncle, Dragging Canoe. Watts and Sequoyah lived as boys in the Overhill town of Tuskegee, near Echota, on the Little Tennessee River.

Attakullakulla was born about the turn of the eighteenth century, the end of an old era and the beginning of a new one. It was approximately at this hour in history that guns were introduced to the Cherokee. It was also about the same time as the outbreak of the European struggle known as Queen Anne's War, reflected in the New World with the English fighting the French in the North and the Spaniards in the South. The Cherokee were not involved directly, but this proved the first of a sequence of related wars during Attakullakulla's lifetime, each of which penetrated farther inland, steadily engulfing the Indians, finally swirling around and through the wilderness of the Smokies.

The mission of the first recorded white expedition into these mountains had been one of "lofty" purpose. In 1540 Hernando De Soto, the intrepid governor of Cuba and *adelantado* of Florida, having served as second in command under Pizarro in the sacking of Peru, proposed to locate treasures of gold on his own. His itinerary has been obscured and his influence unlasting, but he led six hundred to one thousand men, armed with swords and muskets, and two hundred horses, north from Florida through the Creek country in Georgia and up the Savannah River past the farms and villages of the Lower Cherokee. It was a remarkable expedition for a force of that size, considering the difficulties of unknown mountain terrain. According to "the Gentleman of Elvas," his companion and chronicler, in *The Narrative of the Expedition of De Soto*, a beautiful Creek princess received the conqueror with ceremony and gifts and promptly was kidnaped as hostage and guide. He kidnaped headmen or chiefs, burned villages, dragged Indians with him in chains as carriers. His route was circuitous and sometimes he was lost; there is a vague possibility that he visited the Smokies. But he found no gold and pressed westward to the Mississippi. Other Spaniards followed, including Juan Pardo, who led an expedition to the mountains in 1566–67; traces remain near Franklin of diggings believed made by the Spaniards in this period. But the Spaniards moved on, leaving the mountain Indians to their own ways.

At the turn of the eighteenth century the Cherokee were still a Stone Age people, whose weapons were the ball-headed war club, spear, and bow and arrow. They hunted with darts and blow guns, while children sharpened their eyes and aim on grasshoppers. They were artisans of pottery and basketweaving. The man wore a shirt of buckskin hanging to the knees, which became known among whites as the "Cherokee hunting shirt." As an undergarment he wore a loincloth, or "flap," of animal skin, and sometimes it was his outer garment as well.

The Cherokee were superb travelers, as were most Indians, acquainted with ancient boulevards and byroads, capable of swiftness afoot and long hard marches. They traveled for many reasons, for barter, commerce, hunting, fighting, and friendship. The most famous of their routes was the Great Indian Warpath, or Warriors' Path, one of the oldest trails on earth, associated with prehistoric migrations, and even earlier with the movements of endless herds of buffalo, pounding hard and wide and deep into the soil. It extended from the Creek country in Alabama and Georgia north through the eastern Tennessee

Cherokee settlements and up to the Long Island of the Holston River, at the present Kingsport, just below the Kentucky boundary. There it divided into several branches, the most celebrated of which followed the elusive, mysterious passage across the mountain barrier into southeastern Kentucky at Cumberland Gap.

In the vicinity of the Smokies, the Warpath passed through the Overhill towns of Hiwassee, Tellico, and Chote to the mouth of the Tellico River, then by the present Maryville and along Little River to Boyd's Creek near Sevierville, proceeding north across the French Broad River. There were several cross-mountain routes as well, including the one across Indian Gap, descending the west fork of Oconaluftee River to the Tuckasegee, then dividing, one fork following the basin to ancient Cowee, the other continuing through Soco Gap to the Blue Ridge Mountains. On the east flank of the mountains, the famous Estatoe Trail led from the village of Estatoe in South Carolina to the mineral-rich Toe River Valley, between the Black Mountains and Roan Valley; from great distances, Indians came to travel this route in order to dig for mica, the glossy, sheetlike material, which they cut into ornaments or sprinkled as glistening dust over the graves of their departed.

No sooner was Queen Anne's War ended than the Yamassee War began, in 1715, with awakening of the shattered coastal tribes in revolt against abuses of the English trading system. It derived its name from the Yamassee, or Yemassee, tribe, which was fated to disappear, although leadership in rallying the tribes was furnished by the Creek, and their able chieftain, Brim. The Indians fought so well that at one point the whole South Carolina colony faced extermination and Charleston was flooded with refugees from outlying plantations. For the first time some Cherokee villages appear to have raised their hand against the British, though most of the Nation was friendly, doubtless preferring to watch the power of the Creek broken.

The Cherokee foresaw the British as protectors against their enemies. They welcomed trade. It provided guns and knives to repel invaders, clothing, and farm implements to make their lives easier. They did not resist the invitation to sign a treaty in 1721, by which trading methods would be regulated and the first boundary line defined between their lands and those of the English. The only trouble was that it reduced the Cherokee from a free people, ranging where their pleasures led, to dependent vassals with bounds fixed by a colonial governor, a people who in less than a century would be forced to sign away their whole original territory.

They did not resist the lures of English civilization. When the Scottish adventurer Sir Alexander Cuming suggested sending a delegation to England to meet the white King, seven chiefs agreed to make the journey for the Nation. Among them was the young White Owl, later to be the Little Carpenter. From Charleston they sailed in the spring of 1730 aboard the man-o'-war *Fox*, accompanied by Eleazar Wiggan, a trader known as the Old Rabbit, as their interpreter. During their four months in London they were the toast of the town, presenting His Majesty four scalps and five eagle tails; going to the theater and inspecting ships, and delighting the English public with their painted faces and feathers in their hair. They posed for a portrait by William Hogarth, for some curious reason wearing court costumes for the sitting. And at one end of the group stood the smallest of all, Attakullakulla, the young savage from the Little Tennessee, a dark-haired cherubic court messenger, an openhearted smile on his lips, and a slender dagger hanging down the side of his knee breeches. He liked the British then and thereafter; they were the friends of his people, friends with strength that he felt could never wane. In September a treaty was signed. The English pledged their friendship "as long as the mountains and rivers last, and the sun shines," a sweet sentiment which they almost intended to be genuine, and vowed to punish any of their countrymen who killed a Cherokee. The Indians spoke through Oukou-Ulah, who said, "We look upon King George as the sun, and our father, and upon ourselves as his children; for though you are white and we are red, our hands and hearts are joined together."

Thereupon the trade gates opened wide. Laden caravans rolled out from Charleston up to the new settlement at Augusta, then over the trading path marked by the Cherokee into the high country. Traders were stationed throughout the Nation under strict regulation. But traders varied. Some married Indians, raised Indian children, and became Indians, running naked except for the breechclout. Some were the best ambassadors their country could have sent to the wilderness. Others deceived and exploited the Indians. The Indians insisted that no whiskey be sold, for the only liquors that they had known were the waters of the clear streams; but rum, whiskey, and brandy were forced into their villages in appalling amounts. One of the worst of the traders was John Elliott, who operated a store at Fort Loudoun near Chote. He was notorious for charging women customers exorbitant prices and treating them uncivilly. On one occasion he loaded one hundred kegs of rum on pack horses at Charleston and set out for the Overhill country, until he was intercepted by Captain Raymond Demere, a brave officer destined for a grisly fate, who seized the rum, denounced Elliott as a "crack-brained fellow who does not know or care what he does," and threatened to revoke his trader's license.

The Little Carpenter developed a taste for whiskey that might easily have proved his undoing. In 1756, while at Fort Prince George, near

Keowee, he got to craving a drink. He met Captain Demere, who was then en route to construct the new Fort Loudoun. "Governor Glen," he said sourly, "has told me a great many lies. I now believe you to be as great a liar as the governor. When you first came here, I took you for a great warrior, but now take you for a little boy."

Demere was taken aback by such talk from a chief who professed friendship with England. Why, he asked, this change in attitude?

"You should know," the Carpenter replied. "Governor Glen promised me two kegs of rum, which you were bringing with you."

The captain knew nothing of such a promise, if ever there had been one. But he pledged to deliver a keg to be shared equally by the Carpenter and his uncle, Old Hop. Later that day he did so. The Carpenter, however, had no intention of waiting until reaching Chote before he sampled the contents. Next morning he appeared in the fort with rolling eyeballs. Demere took him in stride until the Carpenter tried to crown him king with a bottle. Then several Indians of Keowee were summoned to carry off their fumbling, struggling, warring peace chief.

Next day Attakullakulla returned, recovering from a hangover. "I hope you will forget the whole of it," he apologized meekly, "for there were three of us when the thing happened. Demere was the first, the Little Carpenter the second, and Rum the third. The people of Keowee have scratched me this morning, to make me remember it, and to make my blood good."

As whiskey affected the Little Carpenter in this instance, so the introduction of European materials transformed the Cherokee in many ways. "I can slay more deer," thought the Indian. "There is no need to make an arrowhead of flint." A musket cost him twenty-five skins; bullets were forty to the skin. During Attakullakulla's lifetime stone tools vanished, flint chipping fell to a lost art. Since furs were the commodity the Europeans sought most from the Indians, hunting was carried to an excess in a massive slaughter of wildlife; the Indians began to deplete their own hunting grounds for, as that archprimitive William Bartram observed, "the white people have dazzled their senses with foreign superfluities."

The price the red men had to pay for their new appliances was high, and there has been no end to the payments. First came disease, waves of smallpox, strange, unknown, unremediable by the strongest medicine, in plagues so horrible that many Cherokee men killed their wives and children and then committed suicide. Half the Nation perished. Then came the settlers, a different species from those who lived along the coast, different from traders and soldiers. They were land-famished and freedom-craving, drawn by virgin soil and fertile valleys. They saw woods filled with wild peas to fatten hogs; streams that ran clear, overrun with fish; game that was plentiful, and wild turkey everywhere. The living wasn't easy, but it was free for those with fortitude to settle the land, fight to hold it, against the Indian, against the British Crown, if need be.

In 1754, the Cherokee were swept full scale into the series of eighteenth-century European wars, which now became a conflict to decide whether the future of North America would belong to the French or British. The French claimed all the land drained by the rivers they had explored, from the St. Lawrence to the Great Lakes and south along the Mississippi. The British claimed all the land inland from their colonies, which lay in a narrow strip along the coast. Thus the area between the Appalachians and the Mississippi was claimed by both. In gaining support and alliance from Indians, the French had the advantage, for their diplomacy was based on trade without the burden of settlement. But George Washington, the young Virginia militiaman, who had been to the disputed territory at the forks of the Ohio, warned his royal governor, "Without Indians to oppose Indians, we shall have little hope of success."

The Cherokee were divided. Under pressure of French threats to send an army against them, some Overhill settlements wavered and were ready to give them their allegiance. The British, in turn, accelerated their activities, through propaganda by their traders and the entertainment of Oconostota and other chiefs in the Virginia capital at Williamsburg. In the summer of 1755, Governor Glen of Carolina invited the Cherokee to a council at Saluda, near the present Columbia, South Carolina. It was attended by five hundred Indians and lasted seven days. As the price for their support, the Cherokee asked for arms and for the construction of a British fort in the Overhill country to protect them from the French and their Indian allies.

No sooner said than done, Governor Glen replied willingly, providing the Cherokee ceded more land and agreed to send their warriors to join the English battles in the North.

It was a hopeless situation. Whatever choice the Cherokee made would have proved wrong. Attakullakulla, spokesman for his people, believed their security lay with the British.

The treaty of Saluda opened the way for the first intrusion of the British across the Appalachians. Near the meeting of the Tellico and Little Tennessee rivers, only five miles from the Cherokee capital at Chote, a force under Captain Demere proceeded to erect the palisaded-log Fort Loudoun during the winter and spring of 1756–57. It was the southwestern outpost of the French and Indian War, strategically significant in guarding the southern frontier and in holding the friendship of the Cherokee. The second in command, the red-haired, bushy-headed Captain John Stuart, did his part toward this end, siring a Cherokee family since well known by the name of Bushyhead.

But relations between red men and white deteriorated. Their soldiers quarreled on the fighting fields of the Ohio Valley and were more inclined to do each other in than to concentrate on the French. The French provoked the Indians further. While warriors were away, settlers encroached their lands. Contempt was mutual.

The main war became forgotten. Time was nearing for the slaughter known as the Cherokee War, now little more than a footnote, but it turned the mountains into the setting for one of the bloodiest years in the history of this continent. First there were scattered "frontier outrages." Indians scalped and murdered whites. For horse stealing, the Cherokee were tomahawked, their bodies mutilated, their scalps sold in settlements. William Henry Lyttelton, now governor of Carolina, worsened the issue by advancing to the frontier and tactlessly demanding the surrender for execution of a number of Indians known to have killed colonists, specifically the chiefs of Citico and Tellico. The Nation responded by sending a delegation of prominent men, variously reported as between twenty-five and thirty-two, headed by Oconostota, to plead for peace. Lyttelton ordered the entire delegation seized and imprisoned at Fort Prince George, in a room not large enough for half their number. Despite time-honored rules of both savage and sophisticated warfare that the persons of ambassadors are sacred, Lyttelton decided they should be held as hostages until an equal number of Cherokee were surrendered to be executed for murders committed against his people. This brought Attakullakulla, the old negotiator, who succeeded in obtaining the release of three or four chiefs, including Oconostota and Saloue of Estatoe.

Oconostota washed the hands of his disgrace in white man's blood. He laid siege to Fort Prince George in the dead of winter, when help from Charleston would be impossible, and ended it dramatically. In February 1760, he summoned the commanding officer from the stockade for a parley, then signaled hidden warriors to shoot the man down. The soldiers within retaliated by murdering every one of the remaining imprisoned chiefs.

The whole frontier was now embroiled. Trader John Elliott was one of the first to die in the Cherokee outburst. On the other hand, from Fort Ninety-Six, on the Saluda River, the commander sent Governor Lyttelton a message that he had lately scalped five Indians, adding the heart-warming postscript that, "We have the pleasure to fatten our dogs upon their carcasses, and to display their scalps, neatly ornamented, on our bastions." A British force of 1600, having relieved Fort Prince George, proceeded to annihilate the Lower towns with fire and sword, then advanced for the first time through sacred Nequassee to the Middle towns of North Carolina. But they were repulsed in the hills by an ambush of war-whooping Cherokee.

Meanwhile, across the mountains, Oconostota had attacked and laid siege to isolated Fort Loudoun. The troops were reduced to eating horses and dogs, except when their Indian women, truer to white husbands and sweethearts than to their own color, brought them food. In August Demere capitulated, on condition that his two hundred men be permitted to retreat in safety to the lines of their countrymen. After one day's march of fifteen miles, however, where Cane Creek empties into the Tellico River, the Indians struck anew. Demere was scalped alive. His arms and legs were cut from his body. "You want land. We will give it to you!" the Indians shouted while stuffing dirt in his mouth. Another man's body was burned, his head set atop a stake as a spectacle of wrath and vengeance. A prominent chief, Judd's Friend, also known as Outacity, or Man Killer, went among the warriors pleading with them to stop the massacre, without success. About twenty-five whites were slain, according to one report, the others taken prisoner; later the Indians would say the number was in retaliation for Fort Prince George —a scalp for a scalp.

Yet there was the Carpenter, true to his British loyalty, who compassionately plucked from death the second in command, Captain Stuart. "I have given you one proof of friendship," he said while leading Stuart from the bloody arena, "and I propose to give you another." For nine days they wandered together, following dark trails north through the wilderness, until they arrived in the vicinity of Fort Patrick Henry, the Virginia outpost at the Long Island of the Holston. Before leaving Stuart, Attakullakulla solemnly named him "eldest brother," with the promise of enduring friendship—which these two held strong until each died in the defeat of his cause.

By the following spring, the campaign in Canada had ended. The French were crushed. It became time to deal properly with the Cherokee. On the order of Lord Jeffrey Amherst, governor-general of British North America, a mighty force of two thousand, including old Indian foes of the Cherokee, advanced toward the mountains. Their commander was Lieutenant Colonel James Grant, a veteran of Fort Duquesne, who had recommended against this expedition as unnecessary. Among those in the ranks were Henry Laurens, William Moultrie, Francis Marion, and the infantry company of Indian fighters called Rogers' Rangers.

When the army arrived at Fort Prince George, the Little Carpenter was waiting, hoping to blunt the bloody edge with conciliation. "I am and always have been a friend to the English," he reminded Colonel

Grant, "although I am called an old woman by the warriors. The conduct of my people has filled me with shame, but I would interpose in their behalf and bring about peace."

The hour was too late, his pleadings were in vain. The imminent war was senseless and unnecessary, but had to be fought. The massacre at Fort Loudoun had been the first instance in which the King's troops surrendered to Indians, a disgrace that demanded retribution—the same kind that Oconostota had demanded for his insult and imprisonment.

But would the whites claim their vengeance in more civilized fashion? The army swept north, establishing itself at Cowee, then marching across the mountains at night to strike the Middle towns. It was the first time these villages felt the bloody touch and fiery sword. Within five days not a single cabin was left standing, nor a stalk of corn.

Francis Marion, the young Huguenot lieutenant, was overcome with the cruelty and futility of his role. He wept with shame. Everywhere he let his eyes follow the footsteps of children where they had lately played under the shade of rustling corn. He heard none of their laughter, nor could he see any of their faces. "When we are gone," he thought, "they will return and, peeping through the weeds with tearful eyes, will mark the ghastly ruin where they had so often played. 'Who did this?' they will ask their mothers, and the reply will be, 'The white people did it,—the Christians did it.'"

For the Christian soldiers, the command was onward, onward. Uprooting peas and beans, slashing stalks of corn, demolishing everything edible, destroying everything habitable on the east side of the mountains. The soldiers fulfilled their mission so well they were footsore, lame, and sick. Fifteen villages were in ashes, their fields were wasteland. Five thousand savages, having been taught their lesson, were starving, or living on grubs and roots, in the recesses of the Smokies, the Balsams, the Cowees and Nantahalas.

In all directions, for the Cherokee, their old enemies the Iroquois and Shawnee, and for all tribes, it was a hard year of defeat and retreat. Some of them believed their salvation rested with fighting, yielding land inch by inch, drenching it with blood. Attakullakulla believed that if his people surrendered land peacefully, they would spare themselves and still preserve sufficient of their dominions for breathing space. In September he and the other chiefs went to meet Governor William Bull at Ashley Hall, or Ashley's Ferry, a one-room brick house outside Charleston. The Carpenter had despised Lyttelton for his arrogance, broken promises, and ill treatment of Oconostota; it was no disappointment when Lyttelton was transferred to governor of Jamaica. But Bull he esteemed wise and true. Moreover, Bull appreciated the graveness and complexity of Indian diplomacy.

"You live in waterside and are in light," the Carpenter told the Governor in behalf of the assembled chiefs. Solemnly he smoked the pipe, then passed it to Bull and to each member of the council. "I am come to you as a messenger from the whole Nation. I have seen you, smoked with you, and hope that we shall live as brothers together." He delivered a string of wampum from each of the Cherokee towns, signifying their desires for peace. "The Great Father above made all people and there is not a day but some are coming into, and some going out of, the world. I hope that the path, as the Great King told me, will never be crooked, but straight and open for all to pass."

In winter, soon before the white man's Christmas, he traveled again to confer with the Governor, presenting the tail of an eagle and a string of wampum to bind the Cherokee pledge to spill no more blood. "I have suffered great hardships going about continually, often naked and starved, to convince my people of their error in falling out with the English," he said, in the summation of his entire life. "They are now convinced of their folly, and hope the Governor and his beloved men will not remember what is past, seeing that it has been so ordered by the Great Man above."

In this manner, the Cherokee War ended, the only way it could have ended. The people were fugitives in the bitter cold mountains, without cover, eating their horses, fighting the bear for berries. The best of the warriors were dead. Smallpox had struck again to worsen the miseries. But now at least there was peace; they would sign treaties, surrendering ancient territorial claims and much of their best hunting range north of the Tennessee line and east of the Blue Ridge, yet Attakullakulla had brought the blessing of peace, and of time to rebuild the shattered towns, time in which to rebuild the old relationships with the British.

The Cherokee needed the British. The activities of traders and royal agents were more tolerable to them than the pressures of frontier settlers, the "borderers." At the end of the French and Indian War in 1763, King George had defined the Blue Ridge Divide as the boundary for settlement, ordering that all squatters beyond return to the white frontier. Yet they poured down upon the mountains and into the valleys, hating the Crown and the aristocrats of the coastal plain, craving and claiming freedom and space.

In March 1775, Attakullakulla and the other chiefs presided over the last major cession of land, the Henderson Purchase, that preceded the American Revolution. It was the temper of the times for enterprising men of the colonies, even the most virtuous, including the Father of his Country, to turn to land speculation. Then, as always, there were riches to be made in claiming, buying, selling American soil. Has it ever really been regarded as more of a treasure than a commodity?

None was more aggressive or hopeful of turning land into wealth than Richard Henderson, a youthful Carolina lawyer and former judge. He organized the Transylvania Company with the intent of purchasing twenty million acres from the Indians and establishing a fourteenth colony; the King's prohibitions of settlement west of the mountains and Indian treaties with private individuals he considered unenforceable technicalities. Under Henderson's plan, he and his partners would retain large tracts for their own estates, sell the remainder to settlers while charging a perpetual quit-rent for every acre, and hold special rights in the government for themselves. It was the proprietor system, a form of royal land grant under which some of the early colonies had been settled—now it was the native Americans venturing into imperialism in their own land!

The expanse of central and western Kaintuckee, southwestern Virginia, northern and northwestern Tennessee was the goal of the Transylvanians. Henderson wisely engaged as his principal agent Daniel Boone, the master of wilderness, who proceeded to journey about the forests, as a tub-thumping advance man, urging the Indians to attend Henderson's council at the Sycamore Shoals on the Watauga River. The Indians regarded Boone as a fair man. He was a rough Indian fighter, but not an Indian hater. He dressed as they did, in hunting shirt, moccasins, leggings, and breechclout, his long hair clubbed in the frontier manner.

They responded to his call. One thousand Cherokee rallied along the banks of the clear Watauga, where the stream widened and bubbled, murmuring over boulders tumbled down by the freshets of thousands of centuries. They were led by their great chiefs, the Little Carpenter and Oconostota, both aged and withered, Dragging Canoe, distrustful, eloquent, the lean fighter, and Oskuah, or Abram of Chilhowee, a Smoky Mountain man. Many whites were present, too, among them the youthful, handsome John Sevier, who had migrated to the Watauga settlement the year before. Abram might have marked Sevier well; they would know each other in the struggle for the western lands and one would cause the death of the other.

The Transylvanians offered goods valued at 10,000 pounds sterling in return for Cherokee agreement to relinquish their claims. The truth is, the Cherokee had at best a shadowy or fighting title to the Kentucky land, while the impressive goods filled a house. Nevertheless, Oconostota, long disillusioned and revolted by the white man's consuming desire for land, opposed the sale. Dragging Canoe did likewise. "You have bought a fair land, but there is a cloud hanging over it," warned the son of Attakullakulla in vehement prophecy. "You will find it dark and bloody."

As for the Little Carpenter, who had seen the Indian world tumbled and crumbled in his lifetime, who could recall the magic days, the world before, filled as it was with game herds and only the other primitives to contest for them, who had lived the three score and ten while his people perished as victims of the white diseases and the white man's wars, who had watched frontiersmen like Boone become more knowing of wilderness than the Indian himself, for him the best way was the peaceful way, to transact with Henderson. His people now were cut off from the Ohio River and the Kentucky hunting grounds; they had surrendered everything east of the Blue Ridge and the Savannah River. Attakullakulla was tired, his people were tired. The spirit-conscience of the people would never die, but the future of the land no longer was theirs.

VI

The Early Settlers

Once the streams of settlement started to flow into the southern mountains, there was no stopping them, not by the Indians, nor by the laws of England or of the new republic. The defeat of the Cherokee in 1761 and the end of the French and Indian War two years later opened the gate to a hardy trickle, if not quite a flood. The French were eliminated, the Iroquois ceded their claims in 1768. The land boom began, with every businessman in the thirteen colonies dreaming of wealth in real estate. Daniel Boone spurred their prospects when he and five companions blazed the way from North Carolina through Watauga River Valley and Cumberland Gap into the fertile fields of Kentucky.

The early settlers of the mountain valleys have been glorified and romanticized, but certainly they were a breed who loved their roving room, room to breathe, to hunt, to wander at will; who were democratic by nature, resenting implications of social superiority and resisting interference in their affairs by any force; and who adapted themselves to the struggle for survival. The first comers took up the bottom lands, where the soil was generous. At a suitable spot the pioneer camped to erect his cabin, usually of one or two rooms. He felled the forest, but the trees were so wide that no man could cut them down. He had to girdle them, hacking through the bark into the life force, the cambium layer, then burning the dead trees to clear the way for cabin and farm. He contended with deep snows of winter, floods of spring, heat and drought of summer, with gnats, snakes, wolves, panthers, Indians. He was strong-willed, an individualist, a crack horseman and rifleman, who sometimes brought down a ton of bear. Since he could only get one shot at a time, his eye and hand had to be firm and steady.

The settlers did not suddenly drop into the hollows and coves from the English islands, as some of our present writers suggest, to "preserve their quaint Elizabethan speech without change." The principal breeding ground for the successions of generations that settled Appalachia was the frontier at the foot of the mountains in Pennsylvania. A number of Germans and Quakers moved south as early as 1735 into the Valley of Virginia. By 1750, more and more families, hungry for land and space, headed down the long valleys, flowing beyond Virginia into the "Southwest," or North Carolina. They traveled along the flank of dark mountains which blocked the westward path. There was nary a trail over hills except the mysterious Warriors' Path, which ran through an unknown gap and then vanished. Nevertheless, the spring of 1750 was an active season for going places. On a bright March morning, Dr. Thomas Walker, physician and land surveyor of Albemarle County, Virginia, struck out to locate the natural break in the mountain barrier —and one month later walked through the Cumberland Gap into Kentucky. Though his discovery was to play a major role in the channels of settlement, for the present travel continued solely down the east side of the Blue Ridge.

Symbolically enough, that same spring the family of sixteen-year-old Daniel Boone departed Berks County, Pennsylvania, for Carlisle, then swung down the Cumberland Valley into Maryland and Virginia. The Boones evidently lingered en route, possibly to visit their old neighbors, the Lincolns, who made their home in Virginia until Abraham, grandfather of the President, moved to Kentucky. In late 1751, or early 1752, the Boones reached their chosen land, the Yadkin River Valley in North Carolina. Those were great days for Daniel. Game was everywhere, even a few buffalo wandering across the mountain in winter. In the beginning he could take thirty deer without leaving the valley. In his deerskin moccasins, he roamed the Yadkin, Clinch, Holston, and Watauga valleys, east and west of the Blue Ridge, preparing for the day when he would cross to stay.

The stocks that settled Appalachia derived from several sources. One was the Palatinate German community of Pennsylvania. Another movement, which reached the mountains in later years, began in tidewater Virginia and Maryland, among the former indentured servants and yeomen farmers, who lost their place with the introduction of slavery. In the early years the coastal settlements had been dominated by industrious, freedom-minded farmers, but when Britain directed that all tobacco crops be marketed through English ports and there taxed, it became evident that only by employing the cheapest kind of labor—the African slave—could a profit be turned. In this manner, the new feudal plantation aristocracy was born and the yeomen farmers driven out of competition; they and the servants who had earned their freedom drifted into the piney backwoods and southern lowlands, "filing off," as William Byrd II put it derisively, in order to escape their debts, many of them later crossing the Piedmont to the mountains.

But the first ripple of the main tide toward the southern Appalachians fretted the surface of the British Isles long before actual settlement began. In 1607, the same year as the landing at Jamestown, a horde of Scottish lowlanders crossed the Irish Sea to occupy the forfeited estates of the rebellious earls of Northern Ireland. They were a mixed people, as all peoples have been mixed at one time or another, despite preferences to speak of "purity" of stock; mostly Scottish, with some English and French-Huguenot, who now became the Scotch-Irish. They were highly independent, quick-tempered Presbyterians, despising both the Church of Rome and the Church of England, but they found little peace in Ireland. It was off to America for them, along with the undernourished Irish and Welsh.

The Scotch-Irish came to America in two streams, the larger leading to Philadelphia, greatest city in the Empire outside London, which many found too crowded for their tastes and left for the westward frontier, and the lesser to Charleston, in the Carolina colony. These two streams would meet again, at the foot of the mountains, in the years after the American Revolution.

The Scotch-Irish, Germans, Huguenots, and English began crossing from the Valley of Virginia into the northeast corner of Tennessee in 1769, bringing their few essentials with them—saw and ax, auger bit, hunting knife, blankets and coverlets, pots and pans, gourd of salt, and that indispensable implement, the Pennsylvania rifle. William Bean, blacksmith-gunsmith, built his house on Bean's Creek, in which was born the first white child west of the mountains. In 1770, William Cobb built his two-story log house, Rocky Mount, which twenty years later would become capitol of the Southwest Territory. In 1771, a group crossed from North Carolina, a wagon train of twelve familes led by James Robertson, blazing a transmountain route, the Yellow Mountain Road, between Marion and Spruce Pine. They had been part of the force called the Regulators, back-country farmers who fought and lost a grim struggle against the rule of Governor William Tryon in the battle of Alamance. From the cluster of homes on the Watauga River, the settlers spread into other valleys, along the Holston, Clinch, Powell, south on the Nolichucky, and ultimately to the French Broad. They were all on backwater land—west of the Blue Ridge Divide where streams drained "back" to the Tennessee and out to the Gulf, rather than "forward" to the Atlantic.

The man was armed protector and provider, the wife his housekeeper and child bearer. They married young and had large families, all living in one-room cabins. There was little money; barter, of beaver, buckskin, bear, wildcat, fox, coon and mink, was the common exchange. A ham of deer could be either marketed or smoked for eating at home. Deerskin, like buckskin, could be dressed and cut into plowlines, bridles, and traces. Deer horns served for spoons and buttons, the antlers for coat racks and the rifle rack. The settler learned to master the forest resources, choosing poplar or chestnut for his cabin as wood that would not decay, shingling his roof with oak because it split straight and thin, building the butt of his rifle with hard maple or walnut, and the cradle of peeled hickory bark. All he needed to import were iron, powder, and reading matter. He and his wife made soap from ashes and fats, dyes from the bark of trees, baskets of withes split from oak trees, and their own buckets and barrels.

He borrowed from the Indian. Each cabin, for instance, had a hominy block, a large block of wood with a hole burned in the top, as a mortar, in which a wooden pestle was worked. Even the red man, who despised the white intruder, was obliged to respect his adaptability to the wilderness.

He grew to be like the Indian, yet differed basically. The pioneer's Christ was a less appreciative symbol than the savage's Master of Life. Though his faith lay in the Bible, he did not adore the beauties of nature, or look up to nature's God; he lacked the intuition the Indian had developed over the centuries; he was determined and destined to conquer his surroundings, but thought these resources were so plentiful they would last forever, though in time he would virtually decimate the woods and wildlife. He learned to scalp the Indian, but never to pray for him as a brother-child of God.

The forces of law were dim and distant. He considered himself capable of resolving his own problems and, though primarily a settler, always kept his rifle near the plow. But he had also to consider the problems of his neighbors, with whom he joined to do what each could not do alone. They shared protection against attack and made forays against the Indians to preclude attack. There were log rollings, house raisings, corn shuckings, and quiltings, which in the simple society were both social functions and practical mutual assistance.

The year 1772 was a time of decisive co-operation for the "Men of Western Waters." They were Virginians but no longer a part of the Virginia frontier. They were on the Carolina border and North Carolina was unable to protect them from Indians. Thus, for their protection they organized their own government, the Watauga Association, and wrote a constitution, the first west of the mountains. When Virginia signed a new treaty with the Cherokee and ordered them to withdraw east of the Blue Ridge, they refused. "Have we not gained our own sovereignty," they demanded, "by having established our own militia, in which each man serves at his own expense and furnishes his own uniform?"

They further asserted their lawful right through negotiation with the Cherokee, leasing Indian lands for an eight-year period in return for six thousand dollars' worth of blankets, paint, and muskets. Come what may, they were ready, under the leadership of energetic, ambitious men like James Robertson, later the founder of Nashville, John Donelson, of Maryland, and John Sevier, trader and land speculator, the fiercest of all frontier fighters. When the American Revolution began, they may not have been trained soldiers in the ranks, but they were warriors to reckon with. And the environs of the Smokies would again become a bloody battlefield, the bloodiest field of meeting between frontiersman and Indian.

The Cherokee, together with virtually every other Indian nation, stood with the British. They welcomed the war as their Armageddon, the ultimate conflict between the forces of good and evil, the outcome of which must be either victory or honor in total defeat.

Though Oconostota still lived and nominally remained as war chief, Dragging Canoe had become key figure in the Nation. It was he who presided early in 1776 when Cornstalk, the great Shawnee chief, and a delegation representing the Iroquois, Mohawk, Delaware, Nantuca, and Shawnee nations came to the council house at Chote. While Oconostota and Attakullakulla sat silent and dejected, one leader after another presented to the Cherokee the war belt of his tribe. After a thousand years of conflict among themselves, they prepared for unity in the common cause. Cornstalk, who two years before had led the Indians to a heroic standoff against the Virginians at Point Pleasant on the Ohio River, spoke for all.

"The lands where the Shawnee have lately hunted are covered with forts and armed men," he said. "When a fort appears, you may depend upon it there will soon be towns and settlements of white men. It is plain that the white people intend to exterminate the Indians. It is better to die like warriors than to diminish away by inches. The cause of the red men is just, and I hope that the Great Spirit who governs everything will favor us.

"Now is the time to begin. No time should be lost. If we fight like men, we may hope to enlarge our bounds. The Cherokee have a hatchet that was brought to you six years ago. Your brothers, the Shawnee, hope that you will take it and use it immediately. If any nation shall refuse us now, we shall hereafter consider them the common enemy of all red men. When affairs with the white people are settled, we shall fall upon such nations and destroy them."

The Indians were provided hatchets, guns, and ammunition from the revived French in Canada and from the British, including the old friend of the Cherokee, Captain John Stuart, now operating from Florida. In the same July when the signing of the Declaration of Independence was being hailed throughout the colonies, Dragging Canoe unloosed his forces. They swooped down upon the Catawba settlements in North Carolina. Together with Tories, sometimes dressed as Indians, they ravaged the South Carolina and Georgia borders. Cattle and horses were driven off, cabins burned, men, women, and children terrified or massacred. On the Overhill side the blow was lessened when Nancy Ward sent a warning message through Isaac Thomas, a trader in the area of the present Sevierville, to the Watauga and Holston settlements. The militia rallied to meet the Indians and defeated them near the Long Island of the Holston, though wide damage was inflicted all the way into southwestern Virginia.

The border states rallied for swift reprisal, dispatching four expeditions against the Indians. The largest force, of more than 2000 North Carolinians under General Griffith Rutherford, marched down the Swannanoa River, crossing Swannanoa Gap east of Asheville, and then Balsam Gap into the heart of the Cherokee country. They struck and destroyed all the Tuckasegee and Oconaluftee settlements, trampling crops and killing cattle and any Indians caught in their path. They swept through the Cowees into the Nantahalas. At Wayah Gap the Cherokee rallied for a final stand, but most of their number had already fled to the mountain wilderness or to the Overhill towns, and the attempt proved futile. They found little surcease, for shortly 1800 Virginia and Tennessee militiamen, under Colonel William Christian, advanced from the Long Island of the Holston to the Little Tennessee, guided by Isaac Thomas, burning Tellico, Chilhowee, and Citico, though sparing Chote, for the present, in respect for Nancy Ward.

In this swift tableau, barbarism was common on both sides. A prisoner taken by Abram of Chilhowee was tortured and burned at the stake at Tuskegee. A Georgia militia officer was found tied to a tree with scalp and ears removed and twelve arrows embedded in his chest; a gun barrel, which evidently had been red-hot, was thrust into his body. The whites killed women as well as men; they killed the wounded, and apparently preferred to kill rather than capture any who tried to surrender.

The difference between white and red barbarism, it was said, was that the Indians were well known to be savages to the root of their being, while the Americans marched behind the banners of Christendom. As in all wars, it helped to have present a messenger of the Lord. Near Abingdon, Virginia, in those fearful days, a party of white soldiers returned to their fort with eleven scalps and the precious religious books which their minister had left behind in his cabin at the instant of his flight. Thus it was fitting that he should conduct a prayer of thanksgiving, a prayer of hope, a fervent prayer for divine guidance and future successes, all of which were made more the tribute to the Heavenly Father by hanging the scalps to the gate of the fort.

With such supplications, the outcome was inevitable. The Cherokee lot now was to become prisoners and sold into slavery, to flee to haven with the British in Florida, to die of starvation, to flee with women and children into the high hiding places, where they built little huts and little warming fires, while the mountains heaved and wept with blood flowing in the streams and flowering the rocks. Old Attakullakulla was to be spared the last bitter chapter. In the spring or early summer of 1777, he departed to a rendezvous of peace with the Great Spirit. He was a singular American and an honorable one, who once had said, in referring to the duplicities of his own people, "I speak not with two tongues, and am ashamed of those who do." Even so, it is difficult to identify, among the many treaties signed with the Cherokee, one which the Indians violated, or one which the whites honored.

After these bitter defeats, it was time anew to cede land. Dragging Canoe left the mountains in disgust, leading many of his people to settle farther down the Tennessee River as a new tribe, the Chickamaugas, and to continue the fight. In May, the Cherokee surrendered everything in South Carolina except a narrow western strip. In July, the chiefs came to the old treaty ground at the Long Island of the Holston to surrender portions of western North Carolina and East Tennessee north of the Nolichucky. In this treaty for the first time the term Great Iron Mountains was used to designate the Smokies, "being the same which divides the hunting grounds of the Overhill Cherokee from the hunting grounds of the Middle settlements."

As the war proceeded, the settlers tended largely to their own affairs and protected the frontier from Indian harassment. But the redcoats reconquered Georgia and South Carolina during 1779 and '80 and prepared to invade North Carolina en route to what they hoped would be victory in Virginia. They rode a rising tide, bolstering and emboldening the Tories. In this advance, Colonel Patrick Ferguson was ordered to stamp out hope in western North Carolina. He marched to the foot of the mountains, doing well in burning houses and impressing or hanging Revolutionary sympathizers. Then he blundered. He might have proved the hero of the war had he overlooked the backwater settlers. Instead, he sent a message demanding they desist in their opposition and in harboring refugees, threatening to hang their leaders and lay their country waste with fire and sword.

Poor Ferguson had no way of knowing that coercion is the worst way of convincing a mountaineer and the best way of stirring his quiet temper. To this day the best laws and law enforcers have not dissuaded game poachers and moonshiners from their chosen undertakings. As the story is recorded, Ferguson's words of greeting were brought to John Sevier, colonel in the North Carolina militia, the prototype of the mountain man, while he was in the midst of a festive day of barbecue, horse racing, and shooting contests. Sevier was thirty-five, tall, blue-eyed, brown-haired, known as the most handsome man and best Indian fighter in the Southwest. Born in the Shenandoah Valley, he had lived all his life on the frontier, variously as farmer, hunter, trader, storekeeper, land profiteer, and sire of a houseful of children. To the Indians he was Tsan-usdi, Little John. He lived a charmed life, never once wounded in thirty-five engagements, while his closest friends and family were slain. "Come on, boys!" was the battle cry his adoring followers loved to hear from his lips. He was the master of a blood-curdling war whoop. Or, as one Englishman confessed after the affray at King's Mountain, "We could stand your fighting, but your cursed hallooing confused us. We thought you had regiments instead of companies." Sevier was a man of destiny, a first-class frontier politician and opportunist, defier of authority, rallier of mountain men—who called him "Chucky Jack" and would follow him anywhere.

Swiftness was his way, and the way of the settlers. Their response to Ferguson's invitation to take protection under his banner was to assemble 600 men at Sycamore Shoals. On September 26, 1780, under command of the seasoned Colonel Arthur Campbell, with Sevier as one of the seconds-in-command, they began the march. On the old narrow Indian trail, the man in the ranks rode in snow above his bootstraps, wearing buckskin hunting shirt, breeches and gaiters of home-dyed cloth, and wide-brimmed hat, adorned with a bucktail or sprig of evergreen, covering his hair tied in a queue. He was equipped with knapsack, blanket, tomahawk, scalping knife, and hunting rifle—the strictly American rifle, designed by Swiss and German gunsmiths of Lancaster and York in Pennsylvania, which was light in weight, graceful in line, economical in use of powder and lead, fatally precise for the long distance its lead would fly.

On the east side of the mountains the force was joined by another 300, bringing their total to more than 900. They picked up the trail of Ferguson's army, of 1100, below the North Carolina line soon before he chose the summit of King's Mountain as the most favorable arena to make his stand. The King's Mountain encounter reads like fiction, except that the place is real. And so, too, are the footsteps of the unorganized mountain men chased into the woods by British swords and drawn bayonets; then regrouping and fighting Indian style, the rebels darted from tree to tree, shouting their war whoops and following their commanders up the slopes. The British smooth-bore musket, the "Brown Bess," was no match for their rifles. Within an hour they gained the crest and pierced Ferguson with at least a dozen bullets. Three hundred Englishmen were slain or wounded, the remainder surrendered; American casualties numbered less than one hundred. The stunning hunting-rifle victory shattered the dark pall over the American cause in the South; it fired the colonial spirit and slowed the advance of Cornwallis, contributing to his ultimate surrender at Yorktown the following year.

But in the meanwhile, when Sevier returned home to the Nolichucky, he found the Cherokee had made the most of his absence, plundering, murdering, and stealing horses. Rallying the militia again, he advanced down the Warpath and across the French Broad to defeat an Indian force at Boyd's Creek, near the present Sevierville. On December 22, Colonel Campbell arrived with 400 Virginians and their combined force continued to Tellico, Chote, and Hiwassee, destroying 1000 cabins and 50,000 bushels of corn. One must wonder how much pounding and punishment these Indians could absorb, even though such was their continuing fate. But Sevier was not finished. In late winter he led his horsemen in another swift stroke, possibly through the heart of the Smokies, to burn the Tuckasegee and other Middle towns, capturing women and children to be sold in slavery, and climaxing the season by burning Cowee to ashes.

With the Cherokee disposed of—for the present—some settlers joined the American forces in the East. Sevier himself enlisted with Francis Marion in his guerilla campaign through the South Carolina swamps.

In November 1785, the Government of the United States entered into its first treaty with the Cherokee Nation at Hopewell, South Carolina, on the Keowee River. George Washington and the Federal Government tried for a degree of fairness in defining boundaries. Georgia and North Carolina protested against interference—little wonder, considering they were parceling the western land to Revolutionary veterans in lieu of payment. The authority of the states was limited, too, for the settlers wrote their own rules. "Has not all America," demanded Judge David Campbell, a friend of Sevier, "extended its back settlements in opposition to laws and proclamations?"

West of the mountains, the settlers had one year earlier split away from North Carolina. Having wearied of being the neglected stepchild called Washington County, they decided to organize their own state, Franklin, and thereupon established the capital at thriving little Jonesboro. It was happily linked with Abingdon by a wagon road. This was a country with a future; before long, John Crockett, father of Davy, would open a six-room tavern near Morristown, farther southwest along the Holston, to provide food and shelter for drovers taking livestock to the Virginia markets.

John Sevier was elected governor of the new state, which promptly opened its own land office for settlement south of the French Broad, forcing the Cherokee boundary to a point below Boyd's Creek. Though settlers encroached on lands reserved to the Indians under the Treaty of Hopewell, and though Old Tassel petitioned for their removal, their champion, Sevier, defied the Government. "It is unthinkable," he said, "to put these people to such inconvenience [as withdrawing] on account of a few miserable savages who would not be noticed but for their cruelties practiced upon our people."

But Sevier developed problems of his own. The state of Franklin couldn't enforce its laws, collect taxes, or gain recognition by the Federal Government. Sevier's arch rival, John Tipton, headed a popular movement to rejoin North Carolina. When the state began to collapse, Sevier endeavored to stir frontier political hysteria against the Indians as a last hope; but after four turbulent years the state of Franklin died an unmourned death.

At the age of forty-three Sevier was a man with a ruined career, which proceeded to follow strange turns. He organized an adventurous bushwhacking campaign against the Indians, defying Federal efforts to control these affairs. The worst of it was the brutal tomahawk murder by his henchmen of the respected chiefs Old Tassel and Abram; the deed was done under a flag of truce at Abram's house at Chilhowee, on the bank of the Little Tennessee. "I fear," said the Governor of North Carolina, in revulsion, "that we shall have no peace in the western counties until this robber and freebooter is checked."

But Chucky Jack lived a charmed life, then and to the end of his days. Though apprehended on a charge of treason, he not only escaped punishment but became the first governor of Tennessee, serving six terms, then was elected to Congress. He survived land fraud charges brought against him by Andrew Jackson. In Washington he never quit arguing for advancement of the frontier and extirpation of the Indians. In 1812, nearing the end of his time but combative as ever, Sevier rose on the House floor to urge "fire and sword" to the Creek country—and probably his greatest regret was that he was too old to lead the way. In 1815 he died, happily no doubt, for at the time he was in Alabama running a line through newly ceded Indian lands.

The fighting continued through the 1780s and '90s, but the focal point shifted from the mountains southward on the Tennessee River and westward toward Nashborough, later to become Nashville. Old warriors like Dragging Canoe were hard to convince. There was vengeance left aplenty, as when Doublehead, scourge of the frontier, brother of the martyred Old Tassel, scalped two white men, drank their whiskey, then stripped the flesh from their bones, cooked and ate it. It was not so much to satisfy his appetite as to demonstrate a clear insult to the whites; more the insult when he complained later that white man's meat tasted "too salty."

But the die was cast. In 1789 the Federal Government formed the Territory South of the River Ohio. And a new term appeared to define a part of the boundary, which extended to "the Painted Rock on French Broad River; thence along the highest ridge of said mountain to the place where it is called the Great Iron or Smoky Mountains. . . ." It was the first official use of the name Smoky, though exactly when and by whom the name was coined is not known. William Blount arrived from North Carolina to assume his duties as governor. He selected William Cobb's home, Rocky Mount, north of Johnson City in the Watauga settlement, for his headquarters and for the next eighteen months it was capitol of the first recognized English-speaking government west of the mountains.

He had no intention of limiting Territory affairs to this corner, however, and chose the place known as White's Fort as the new capital, renaming it Knoxville for General Henry Knox, Washington's Secretary of War. In 1791, he summoned forty-one of the principal chiefs to sign the Treaty of Holston; they wept with grief while ceding a northeast portion of the Smoky Mountains hunting ground and agreeing to settlement north of the Little Tennessee and between the forks of the French Broad and Holston. Maryville, even closer to the mountains, was named for the Governor's wife, Mary, while Sevierville, honoring the lusty hero himself, was established as a county seat in the forks of the Little Pigeon River. By 1795, Tennessee numbered a population of 77,632, more than sufficient to call a constitutional convention for statehood, and shortly the Territory became the sixteenth state of the Union. Sevier was elected governor, Blount one of the two United States senators, and Andrew Jackson, an up-and-coming expansionist politician, a member of the House of Representatives. Sevier and Jackson despised each other, while Blount soon became the first and only member impeached by the Senate.

Blount, an old land speculator and slave trader before moving west from North Carolina, proved to be one of President Washington's special mistakes. He was a frontier opportunist with little humanitarian approach toward the Indians, who despised him as an avaricious land-seeker and bestowed upon him the title of the Dirt Captain. At a time when the Federal Government was endeavoring to right its course with the Indians, he recommended that "the Creeks must be scourged and well, too, and the Cherokees deserve it." He had barely taken his seat in the Senate when his abortive conspiracy to seize the lower Mississippi from Spain, with the aid of Great Britain, was uncovered. President John Adams called for his expulsion from Congress, but proceedings were dismissed because of lack of jurisdiction. In Tennessee, however, he was regarded as a martyr, worthy of reward by selection as speaker of the state Senate, which post he filled until his death in 1800.

Across the mountains, Asheville, formerly a part of the Cherokee hunting ground, was incorporated in 1795 and named for North Carolina's governor, William Ashe. The state having generously awarded Indian lands to Revolutionary veterans, settlement was already under-way westward along the Pigeon River. Colonel Robert Love reversed the usual pattern of migration by moving from the old Washington County, now Tennessee, to establish Waynesville and acquire one of the largest estates in the mountains. Known as the "Love Speculation," the lands in the possession of his family totaled 375,000 acres by 1865 and undoubtedly included portions of the present national park. Will Thomas, the white chief of the Cherokee, and other Love in-laws also controlled substantial holdings. On one occasion, in 1788, Andrew Jackson denounced the Loves as a band of land pirates. Colonel Love replied softly by calling Jackson a "damned long gangling sorrel-topped soap stick."

The 1790s opened the way to settlement, land grabbing, and specu-lation. Choice lands were taken along the Oconaluftee River, pressing into the hills past the Raven Fork to the Bradley Fork, where the river flows down from Laurel Top. At the mouth of a fast-flowing creek, John Jacob Mingus built his home and later a mill. Felix Walker, one of those adventurous, restless Virginians who had been with Daniel Boone in blazing the trail through Cumberland Gap in 1775, had two abutting grants totaling five square miles, one extending over a mile up the Raven Fork. Both were marked at one corner by a poplar tree, which became known as the Boundary Tree, or Poplar Corner Tree, and long remained as the marker between Indian and white settlers. Walker was lawyer, merchant, farmer, and politician, who operated three trading stores, including one at Quallatown in Soco Valley. After running for clerk of court and losing to Colonel Love, he was elected to Congress in 1817 and served till 1823, during which time he was called "Old Oil Jug" and contributed the term "Buncombe" to lexicography. But, like Daniel Boone and Davy Crockett, he was destined to wander westward, to Tennessee, then south to Mississippi.

As to the Cherokee, they had still more treaties to sign before the eighteenth century yielded to the nineteenth. The Treaty of Tellico included cession of a southern portion of the Smokies. Chote was gone from their hands. They were obliged to move their ancient capital to northern Georgia, a site which they would name with hope New Echota. They gradually took over the white man's culture, trusting that acceptance of civilization might insure their survival. Hardly a warrior could be found on the Warriors' Path; yet deep in the mountains, shut in from the outside, women were still potters and basketmakers as their mothers' mothers had been, and the old beliefs were far from gone.

The mass migration began in earnest. The main stream went to Kentucky, where the fertile fields and rolling savannas were firmly held. In England extraordinary tales were circulated about the fabulous Kentucky, where a man was not a subject but a citizen, where taxes were ridiculously low. Between 1792, when Kentucky became a state, and the turn of the century, its population soared from 100,000 to 220,000—far too many for Daniel Boone and his restless kind. Others found their way into the valleys bordering the Smokies. Virginians and Pennsylvanians followed the Valley of the Holston into East Tennessee; from eastern North Carolina, families crossed Swannanoa and other low gaps in the Blue Ridge, and from Charleston, the Scotch-Irish came up through Cashiers Valley to meet their old brethren, the Pennsylvanians.

At first they settled the fair valleys and generous coves, prosperous for tillage. The high places were still uninhabited. The settlers were too occupied in finding to become lost.

VII

Lonely Cathedrals

"Live or die, I must ride," said the Prophet of the Long Road, Francis Asbury, Bishop of the Methodist Church in America, greatest of the circuit riders. "Those who wish to know how rough is this way may tread in my path, over rocks, ridges, hills, stones, and streams."

The Bishop might readily have had in mind his arduous journey in the Smokies in 1810, when the mountains were sparsely settled and barely known, visited by occasional peddlers, game hunters, preachers, livestock drivers, and surveyors charting the boundary line between North Carolina and Tennessee and revising again—and again—the boundary with the Cherokee. It was the time of transition from the culture of the red mountaineer to the culture of the white mountaineer. The years before the Civil War, before the villages and long before the sawmills and railroads, were the age of solitudes and self-sufficiency derived from the riches of the earth.

Settlers came slowly. From Sevierville, often called Forks of Little Pigeon, on the Tennessee side, they advanced through the low gaps looking for greener pastures, and finding them in the chain of secluded coves, each five to six miles long and one to two miles wide, with fertile bottom land and meadows, ideal for hay and grass. They went from Wears Cove, named for Colonel Samuel Wear, the old lieutenant of John Sevier, into Tuckaleechee Cove, and over the high mountains into Cades Cove, possibly named for Kate, the wife of Abram of Chilhowee, sheltered and fertile, from which they could lead their cattle to summer pasture on the grassy crests of Smoky; or through Tuckaleechee and Miller Cove to Happy Valley, flanked by the Chilhowee Mountains and Abrams Creek, leading to the Little Tennessee at the site of Abram's old village, Chilhowee. They began the migration before the turn of the century, hazardously penetrating the Indian camping and hunting grounds, until the settlement of Tuckaleechee was spurred by the first Treaty of Tellico in 1798. Cades Cove had been pre-empted before entry was legalized by the Treaty of 1819; when John Oliver arrived with his family, and William Tipton, a Revolutionary veteran known as Fighting Billy, forebear of the Tiptons who still live in the coves.

Not everyone stayed. Some settlers discovered and were delighted by lush crannies overlooked in the general migration from East and North, but many felt hemmed in by the mountains. The feeling was that this country would never be heavily populated or immensely prosperous. Like Davy Crockett, of northeast Tennessee, they moved across the state, searching greater promise; after the Cherokee removal of the 1830s, there was a general migration from the coves into the newly opened lands of northern Georgia. But others came to take their places in oxen-drawn wagons over the mountains from the Carolinas and down the valleys from Virginia, stopping because of sickness or broken wagon axle and then moving on, or remaining because they liked the country, or were too poor or wanting in energy to continue.

On the North Carolina side, they came across Soco Mountain through Cherokee following the broad valley of the Oconaluftee past the Mingus and Enloe farms, settling the interior basin. About 1805 Jim Spillcorn had a grant on the present Mingus Creek, which became known as Spillcorn Creek. Most of those who had first choice of land in the flat river bottoms took pains in building their houses, squaring the logs like bridge timbers, joining and notching them closely, smoothing puncheons as if they were planed, using mortar instead of clay in laying chimney and hearth. With plenty of pasture available, they built commodious barns to shelter large herds.

In those days, as the saying went, the first sound in the wilderness was the ring of the settler's ax and second the greeting of the traveling preacher, the circuit rider, at his front door. Principally Baptists and Methodists, circuit riders followed the frontiersmen in the westward march, determined to rescue their scattered flocks from savagery and whiskey-drinking with words of Christ. As Bishop Asbury recorded in his journal, after visiting Rutherfordton, at the foot of the Blue Ridge on the edge of the Piedmont Plateau, in 1784, "The country improves in cultivation, wickedness, stills, and mills." He and others carried Bible, hymnal, news of the outside world, and messages against intemperance, at the same time establishing churches and schools, often in the same building. The work of the early preachers was so extensive that when the "Great Revival" swept the frontier in the fall of 1800, camp meetings were attended by the thousands, culminating the following summer with services in Bourbon County, Kentucky, drawing 20,000 hosanna-singing worshipers every day for a week.

Francis Asbury was the master of them all. In forty-five years, from his arrival in America in 1771, he covered an estimated 275,000 miles, averaging at least one sermon a day, more often sleeping on a bed of boughs at night than on a bed indoors. He was the first of the circuit riders, establishing the itinerant system which enabled the preachers to keep up with the migrating multitudes; or as he wrote soon after preaching his first sermon in Philadelphia, "My brethren seem unwilling to leave the cities, but I think I will show them the way."

From the time of his first journey west of the Appalachians in 1788, he crossed and recrossed the mountains at least sixty times. The Bishop traveled armed with rifle as well as Bible, for he did not share the tranquillity of his contemporary, William Bartram in the prospect of encountering an Indian, nor was he of missionary bent to civilize the red man. "I do not fear; we go armed," he wrote. "If God suffer Satan to drive the Indian on us, if it be His will, we will teach our hands to war, and our fingers to fight and conquer."

In late autumn 1810, when he was sixty-five, he and three other prominent preachers of the wide fields (Bishop William McKendree, German-speaking Reverend Henry Boehm, and the Reverend John McGee) approached the Smokies, having traveled through Kentucky to Nashville and the Holston country of East Tennessee. Two years earlier he had preached at Shiloh Church near Sevierville. The frail Bishop was still able to ride a horse, but not long after had to rely on a chaise for transportation and on his last journey, in 1816, was so ill that he couldn't stand and had to be lifted bodily from chaise to preaching place. He knew the over-mountain routes, having sometimes crossed via the present Hot Springs and Marshall along the French Broad River to Buncombe Court House, or Asheville; or from East Tennessee over the Blue Ridge at Elk Park, between Grandfather and Roan mountains, to Morganton. Hot Springs, known in the early days as Warm Springs, was not one of his most pleasant memories. In 1800 he had endured a hazardous journey over the Newfound Mountains to the watering place. "After we had crossed the Small and Great Paint Mountain," he wrote of this experience, "and had passed about 30 yards beyond the Paint Rock, my roan horse led by Mr. O'Haven reeled and fell over, taking the chaise with him; I was called back, when I beheld the poor beast and the carriage, bottom up, lodged and wedged against a sapling, which alone prevented them both being precipitated into the river." Perhaps it was this recollection that inspired him and his comrades to try a new route being developed over the Cataloochee

Trail, or Cattalucha Track, in the valley of the Pigeon River, part of the ancient Indian network.

From the home of Mitchell Porter, three miles south of Sevierville, they traveled thirty circuitous miles to a toll gate near Cosby and stopped the night of November 29 with the toll keeper. Next day must have been grim, as well as cold and long. They passed through Daveport Gap and advanced between Mount Sterling and Scottish Mountain. When they came into Cataloochee Valley, the Bishop was in no way constrained to appreciate the beauty of its steeply rising wooded slopes. As he recorded in his famous journal, the foaming, roaring stream marked the beginning of their troubles. While he and the other two balanced their way over the stream on a log, the Reverend McGee drove their horses through the water. On the bank of the creek they rested and asked a blessing on a spartan meal of bread. "But O, the mountain," recorded the Bishop, "height after height, and five miles over!" Now and then they were lost, following ancient paths that ran straight up the hilltops, splitting one way and then the other, passing Indian "flats," stones marking abandoned settlements or stopping places, before reaching the eastern foot of the mountain and the settlements on Richland Creek and the Pigeon River. At 9 P.M., long after dark, they reached Jacob Shook's house near Clyde, with the Bishop concluding, "What an awful day!"

Shook, a Revolutionary soldier and son of a Dutch immigrant, maintained a room in his house for preaching by Asbury and other circuit riders. He also gave a parcel of land, known as Shook's Campground, where camp meetings were held in summer or fall, an American institution of its time that provided back-country people with a combination of jubilee week, county fair, and diversion from their narrow corners. They must have been awesome spectacles, filled with emotional fervor from sunup until past dark. About daylight the first trumpet would sound as a signal for the people to rise and prepare for worship. In about half an hour, the second trumpet summoned them to family prayer in their tents. At Shook's, the tents numbered about forty, some of which were neatly framed and weatherboarded, with scaffolds built as beds and dirt floors carpeted with straw. The third trumpet was the signal for public prayer under the big tent, wherein the tenters covered the ground with fresh cut wheat or oat straw so they could kneel without soiling their clothes. From then on, preaching was scheduled at 8 A.M., 11 A.M., 3 P.M., and at candlelight. The camp meeting was considered a more advanced form of worship than the primitive rituals of the Indians, but could not have been totally dissimilar, with fires and candles reflecting light in the branches of trees towering over the widely ranged tents, and illuminating the faces of hundreds of people moving about in varying stages of emotional fervor, while the praying, preaching, and shouting gushed from the ground.

They were a blessed people. Even in loneliness and austerity, their dwelling place in the mountains was spacious, nature-rich, and beautiful.

There was the blessing of beauty in the clouds gathering over the crest of Smoky, presaging a storm by their deep purplish undercoating, accompanied by a chorus of dark voices in the sky. And then the beauty of the streams running full, rising suddenly and shouting, rushing downward through laurel and rhododendron to strike and revolve the wooden turbine of the tub mill with a splickety-splat, grinding the corn, and splashing a hazy silvery spray over the flume.

The streams overflowed with the blessing of fish, and the woods with the blessing of game—bear, squirrel, white-tail deer, coon and wild turkey, the great wary bird of the hills, and in the mountaintops the sleek panther (or "painter" in the vernacular), piercing the wilderness night with its own song, was the source of "painter bacon" from hams and shoulders.

There were blessings and beauties of the trees. They gave plentiful, choice timbers for building homes, furniture, and fences; bark for tanning; barks and berries for dyeing; hazelnuts and chestnuts to be gathered and saved for winter feeding.

And the handy beauty of the moon, as the source of folk belief to work by. To split rails, shingles, and shakes when the moon was dark, which prevented warping or cracking. To rive in the dark of the moon, too, to keep shakes from warping. To build and lay fence rails when the moon was light, to prevent rotting. To lay boards and shingles when the horn of the moon pointed down, to prevent cupping and twisting. To make soap on a waning moon, in order to prevent it from boiling over.

There was beauty in the way the mountain family lived—self-sufficient to a large extent, self-contained—and in the way they built their houses. The chimney was formed of massive stone from the ground up and where stones were scarce of sticks and clay—gray, tan, yellow, brown, rose, black, and red, woven together in a contrast of color against the gray log walls. The roof was made of stout pin oak logs, split and quartered with maul and wedge, then rived into two-foot shakes or shingles. The walls, made of matched logs by the proud early mountain man, were hewn on two sides and notched at the ends to fit and hold the corners steady. The puncheon floors, cut from the towering yellow poplar, or tulip tree, were three feet or more wide.

Inside, the fireplace was the heartbeat of the house, serving both as cookstove and furnace, although it sometimes smoked for want of vent and contributed to unhealthiness in the healthiest of climates. The woman cooked in a black pot hanging on a hook over the flames, baked in a covered iron pan or oven which sat in hot ashes, and in the flickering firelight she worked on her coverlet, or "kiverlid." From the darkened beams overhead hung bright strings of field corn, popcorn, leather britches, red and yellow pepper, and fingers of light showed that every bit of space in the house was used. There were as many as five or six double beds, plus a trundle bed, in a one-room cabin; and, since there were no closets, clothing hung on wooden pegs above the beds, while apples were stored under them. A family could hardly be more closely knit; and by the fire parents and children could sit together and view through the lookout, cut in the logs next to the chimney, the starry sky of a broad universe they had come to call "over the mountain."

The woman was bound to the house by children and chores. She dried beans, corn, apples, peaches, and pumpkins and stored them, as well as kraut, hog, and squirrel meat, for use in winter. She made her own soap from a boiled mixture of the lye of hickory ashes and grease, and her own candles or else used a "slut," a saucer filled with fat around a string of cotton cloth that served as a wick. In the day before cottons appeared at crossroads stores, to be bartered for eggs, nuts, honey, herbs, or a poke of water-ground meal, she was obliged to manufacture the family clothing. She started by shearing the sheep, then picking, washing, carding, and spinning wool, linsey for underwear or dresses, jeans cloth for men's clothing (with chain of cotton, filling of wool). Dyes were derived from materials of forest, field, and garden: indigo for deep blue; madder root for red; maple bark for purple, if the material was cotton. She also used the hulls, roots, and barks of walnut, or "warnut," sumac berries and laurel leaves. Roots and sprouts were best gotten on the new of the moon. They were skinned, boiled three hours, then boiled together with the wool, outdoors to let odor free, after which the wool was hung in the sun to dry and darken further. Weaving with heddles and treadles was serious, creative work, a quiet art demanding time and patience. And if any time was still left to her, she might help to plant, hoe, and gather fodder, or to plow and split rails.

The mountain man, who in the early days was likely to be his own smith, cooper, cobbler, and carpenter, worked seriously but slowly. He prided himself on brandy made from apples and peaches and on whiskey from corn. While the sun blazed in summer passion and the air was still and sultry, he could be cultivating or hoeing his cornfield or laying by his crop. To show his attitude toward time, the yarn is told of a stranger once coming along and finding a mountain man holding a razorback shoat in his arms, lifting the animal so that it could feed on ripe persimmons hanging on a tree. It was one of those coarsely and variously colored razorbacks, long in body, legs, tusks, and squeal. "You may get that hog fat," observed the stranger, "but it's going to take a mighty long while." The mountaineer, barely heeding, replied, "What's time to a derned hawg?"

Every man owned a rifle, as the means of food, safety, and sport, a single-shot muzzle-loader, sometimes an ancient flintlock altered to caps. It had a long, heavy octagonal barrel and slim, curving curly maple or walnut stock, fitted with brass box for bullet patches. Unlike most American rifles, adorned with silver inlay, tooled and engraved trigger guard and patch box, the Smoky Mountain rifle was simple, straight-forward, and unostentatious—but efficient, sighted at sixty yards and formidable up to two hundred. A man wanted to say, "I can shoot the eye out of a squirrel in the tallest tree," and then prove it. Shooting matches were regular functions with cows offered as prizes; a substantial attraction, considering that pork, not beef, was the standard fare.

Those who settled early had room on their lands for ample barns and surrounding buildings: the spring house, where crocks of milk and butter were refrigerated in the cooling trough over a mountain spring; the bear-proof pig pen, where choice razorbacks (which mostly roamed free in the mountains, identified by their notched ears) were fed on corn to "harden the fat" before killing time in autumn; the chicken house, skunk- and weasel-proof, and protected from all "varments"; the tub mill, where the tub, or wooden turbine, powered by water, in turn revolved the upper millstone to grind the corn; the tool shed, with wooden "A" harrow, slide, three-foot plow, "lay-off" plow, almost always homemade gear; and the bee gum stand, so named because the hollow boles of mature gum trees often were used for cylindrical honey-producing beehives—though sourwood honey has always been a choice item for sweetening.

In the course of slow community growth, artisans and tradesmen developed. One became a specialist at chairmaking and carpentering; another at pottery, making churns, crocks, bake pots, and dishes, a third at shingle cracking, deftly riving several hundred shingles a day. People came from miles to the blacksmith to have tools mended and horses shod, and to pick up hinges and other items fashioned from worn horseshoes and mule shoes. In due time a tub mill operated in every community, running on certain days of the week to grind meal, with the miller getting a "toddick," or small measure as a toll. By 1834, a settler named Couch operated a powder mill at the mouth of Couches' Creek on the Oconaluftee, selling and bartering his products. Barter would long continue as the common exchange, with items like beeswax, wool, hides, herbs, and nuts among the stock in trade; later, wool would be an exchange for finished cloth.

Cades Cove showed considerable progress. It was so rich and fertile that by 1825 the price of corn had dropped to six and a half cents a bushel, and it became more profitable to feed grain to cattle and sell the cattle. About one year later Daniel Davis Foute established the Cades Cove Bloomery Forge on Forge Creek, which produced wrought-iron "blooms" direct from ore mixed with limestone and charcoal, and kettles, wagon tires, hoes, and plowpoints to make the settlers' lives easier. Amerine's Forge in Miller Cove later became the most productive ironworks in the area, producing twelve tons of bar iron a year by 1854.

Scattered residual masses of iron do occur in the foothills between the Smokies and the Great Tennessee Valley, and the early name of the range, Great Iron Mountain, probably indicates the value placed on the metal by the pioneer highlanders. In the 1830s, after the gold discovery in northern Georgia, the prospecting fever spread into the Carolina and Tennessee hills as well. Among those arriving in the Smokies hoping to strike it rich was one Bobby McCampbell, who entered the land later acquired by the Little River Lumber Company. He found some "colors," therefore sank shafts and built a smelter at a place appropriately called El Dorado, on the lower slopes of Rich Mountain. But the amount of gold hardly proved worth the effort and Bobby moved across the mountains into the wilderness of Hazel-nut and Eagle creeks, where he reportedly discovered something quite different—copper ore. He later was connected with the opening of mines at Copperhill, Tennessee.

The coves on the Tennessee side of the Smokies were not entirely isolated, certainly not as much as later settlements would be. They were linked with the world, receiving mail service weekly from Sevierville and Maryville by the 1830s. From both sides of the mountain, settlers and traders looked upward to the crest and the ancient Indian Gap trail and thought it time to open contact between them. In 1831 the General Assembly of North Carolina authorized the formation of the Ocona-lufty Turnpike Company to build a wagon road from the top of the Smoky Mountain down the Oconaluftee River as far as John Beck's house near Quallatown. One of those involved was Abraham Enloe, who lived in the interior Lufty Basin. Another was Will Thomas, who was building his shaky financial empire on land speculation, trading stores, turnpikes, mining, and cattle. Thomas, who ran a fleet of freight wagons to trading centers in Georgia and South Carolina, contracted to build the road and evidently operated it for a while. Work proceeded slowly, for in June 1839, Thomas wrote James Porter at Sevierville, urg-

ing him to try to get the Tennessee portion finished by fall. Nevertheless, the road was sufficient for John Jacob Mingus and others to
organize the Epsom Salts Manufacturing Company and endeavor to
mine and market the minerals of Alum Cave Bluff, on the flank of
Mount Le Conte, though without great success.

The toll keeper on the Oconalufty Turnpike was Robert Collins, who
lived at the foot of the main ridge on the North Carolina side and in
years hence would figure as guide in the first truly significant scientific
exploration of the Smokies. According to the charter, he was to collect
tolls at the rate of 75 cents for a four-wheeled carriage of pleasure; 37½
cents for gig or sulky; 75 cents, six-horse wagon; 50 cents, five-horse
wagon; 37½ cents, three- and two-horse wagons; 25 cents, one-horse
wagon or cart; 6¼ cents, each traveler on horseback; 2½ cents, one
horse without rider; 2 cents, one head of cattle; 1 cent per hog or sheep.
But the principal traffic consisted of livestock ambling over the course
from Whittier to Indian Gap, then down the west prong of the Little
Pigeon River to Sevierville. In the movement of cattle herds from
grazing lands to markets in the East, drivers would stop at regular intervals one day's journey apart, at taverns or private residences, where
meals and lodgings were provided, and livestock were fed and bedded
down in barns.

It did not take long for the white man's culture in the hills to become
slow of pace, gradually losing contact with the mainstream. The process
of deterioration began as families grew in size, in the second and third
generations, pressing against the limits of subsistence, retreating from
the generous low valleys into the subvalleys, along creek branches and
up the steep hillsides to scrabble for a hard living. There was nothing
approaching sanitation. Shoes were little worn around the home. People would suffer diet deficiency, hookworm, typhoid, and tuberculosis,
queer diseases for mountain men who lived in the environs of God's
cleanest air. They had no choice but to prescribe their own medications,
for while tradesmen came into the hills, doctors did not. Bloodroot was
considered a good tonic to make the blood run in spring. Sassafras tea
also thinned the blood. Buckeye was prescribed for rheumatism, also
for tea to cure cramps, or to carry in one's pocket for good luck. Spignet
root did for kidney ailments; so did the resin from the blisters gathered
on balsam trees. These dwellers had to become their own pharmacists,
too. Some pills were made of black walnut bark boiled down to an ooze.
A combination of "sowbugs," found under the hearth rocks in the
chimney, and 'lasses was prescribed for yellow jaundice, or "yaller jan-
ders." And sometimes these home-brewed remedies worked; the people
were close to the earth of the Smokies, which has yielded herbs and
roots to the most distant pharmaceutical houses.

In 1833, the Cataloochee Turnpike was chartered. The circuit rider of that year traveling the old trail of Bishop Asbury would have done so in slightly improved circumstances. He might have tarried in the narrow Cataloochee Valley, the old Indian Gadalu'-tsi, to absorb the early rising splendor of clouds entangled with the upper thickets, and to hear the ruffled surge of the creek, a music that no organ has ever matched. Mark Hannah, the national park ranger in Catalooch', told me that his great-grandfather came into the valley as a wandering game hunter in the 1830s and stayed to become one of the first settlers. He and the others grazed cattle on the upland steep as a mule's face, raised corn in the bottom land for winter feed—and Cataloochee was not unknown for its whiskey. In such a place they were lost to time, but the earth was theirs.

VIII

Genius of the Species

The Cherokee, meanwhile, did not want to die. They wanted to live, as do other natural species in the unending struggle to survive against more powerful forces. Curiously, throughout the long history of the earth, only one species, the human, has ever successfully perpetrated the total destruction of another, and then of lower forms, like the passenger pigeon, that once darkened the skies over the Great Smokies. But could one race of man exterminate another?

The Cherokee did not believe it would be their fate to perish. They decided to accept the hand of hope held out to them by the Government of the United States. They would place their trust in this Government, forsaking the warpath and aboriginal hunting ways, living not in the forest but on the farm, applying themselves to the use of plows, hoes, spinning wheels, and looms which were distributed among them.

How well could they meet the test of peacefulness and practicality? This is the story of the first thirty years of the nineteenth century and, indeed, provides an important key to understanding the Smoky Mountains Cherokee down to this day. Whether it was a test based solely upon civilized rules is another question. As a historian, Theodore Roosevelt observed the Cherokee were "a bright, intelligent race, better fitted to follow the 'white man's road' than any other Indians," a statement which he intended as a compliment. But essentially Roosevelt was a chronicler of expansionism, to whom the frontier days were best defined as "the winning of the west" by heroic pioneers specially chosen "to conquer the wilderness and hold it against all comers." Like almost all others, he regarded the Indians as strangers, intruders in the path of national destiny.

The Cherokee, however, hung on and adapted their ways. Having already signed the first Treaty of Tellico in 1798, surrendering a portion of their lands on the Government's pledge that it would "guarantee the remainder of their country forever," they were willing to concede the short span of "forever" in the second and third Treaties of Tellico in 1804 and '05. More important to them was to progress. They welcomed schools and missions; they professed the Christian faith, generally conducting themselves by its tenets. In 1808 they adopted a written legal code and established their own form of police, a system of patrols to "suppress horse stealing and robbery." Two years later the National Council abolished the custom of clan revenge, the primeval Indian order of justice. Before long they would write a remarkable constitution and adopt a legislative form of government based on that of the United States; they would achieve a written language, and the publication of a national newspaper in their own tongue. In the measurement of human advancement, it is quite possible that no nation has ever made more sizable forward strides in so short a span of time.

By the 1830s, when elected representatives were conducting the affairs of a republican government, most Cherokee dwelled on farms, in homes ranging from log cabins to plantation mansions, and wore the frontier costume. Some of the mixed-blood offspring prospered, owned slaves, and were well educated. But while the center of the new Cherokee culture had shifted to northern Georgia, the tribal remnants in the high hills of Tennessee and North Carolina, shut in from the outside world, clung to the older conservative beliefs; and only in the primitive hills would the Cherokee find the spark of their survival. Many volumes have been written about this period; the story here is designed to relate the principal events to the ultimate climax in the Smokies.

The Cherokee in the early nineteenth century were endowed with a rare quality of national leadership and with representation from Washington that genuinely endeavored to serve their interests—also a rare quality. Colonel Return Jonathan Meigs, who arrived in 1801 at Tellico blockhouse as Indian agent for the Cherokee and would suffer with them for twenty-two years, faced the trying, contradictory assignments of guiding the Cherokee to become civilized while at the same time encouraging them to surrender additional land and to move to the vacant West. Unfortunately, he was not above employing the secret weapon in Indian negotiations, the "silent consideration," or the bribery of chiefs. But Colonel Meigs distributed farming implements and household utensils while it seemed this course would help them protect their country; he went with them to Washington, defending their rights at treaty conferences; he encouraged them in the establishment of their republic, and protected their land from invasion by troublesome whites while it was still possible to do so. Today the proposal is often made that Indians should be accorded the "full rights of citizenship" through the dissolution of their reservations, but in 1820, when the Cherokee were nearing the peak of their greatness, agent Meigs learned through his own experience the fate of such a suggestion. When he proposed that, since the Cherokee were so far advanced that further Government aid was unnecessary, their lands be allotted to individual Indians and they be invested with citizenship, the generous states of North Carolina, Tennessee, and Georgia responded with vehemence—no Indian was welcome to live within their boundaries under any circumstance.

It was difficult for a white man on the frontier to be a friend of the Cherokee. Young Sam Houston, however, was one who could. Born in the Shenandoah Valley in 1793, he moved as a boy to Tennessee with his widowed mother, eight brothers and sisters, opposite the Cherokee territory on the Tennessee River. When he was sixteen, he crossed over to join the Cherokee and was adopted by Chief Oolooteka, or John Jolly. For three years he lived the Indian life, spoke the language, wore the dress, and bore the honored name Ka'lanu, the Raven. When he returned to civilization in 1812, he looked for a job in Maryville, near the Smokies, and became master of a log schoolhouse, an "old field school," where he was ridiculed at first as a graduate of the "Indian University." He charged eight dollars for a semester's tuition, one third cash, one third in corn, and one third in bright-colored calico for his shirts. The semester began in May, after corn planting, and ended in autumn, before the gathering and cold weather. Next spring he left Maryville to join the army and fight in the Creek War. But his heart would always be with the Cherokee. In 1829, after walking out on his unhappy marriage in Nashville and the governorship of Tennessee, he returned to his foster father, John Jolly, then living in Oklahoma, and married the chief's niece. In 1832 he served on a Cherokee delegation to Washington, dressed as an Indian, and remained one of the few political figures of his time who dared to fight for the Indian cause at the risk of his own popularity.

Despite local encroachment and abuse, the Cherokee continued to place their trust in the Government. During the War of 1812, they gave valuable support when hostile Indians went on the warpath in the British cause. The nearest to them were the Upper Creeks, who had been stirred by the eloquent Shawnee chief, Tecumseh, and his idea of an Indian confederacy to save the lands west of the Ohio River. From tribe to tribe, Tecumseh traveled to forge the confederacy, aided by his brother, Tenkswatawa, the Prophet, who filled a particularly important role with his "revelations" that the Indians must return to tribalism in order to preserve their existence. The Upper Creeks, responding with religious fervor, accepted Tecumseh as the leader who would restore the old life. There was much enthusiasm among the Cherokee as well, though when and where the message was brought to them is subject to conjecture. According to Smoky Mountain tradition, Tecumseh met an assemblage at the Soco town house, below Soco Gap, where his eloquence was well received until Junaluska, an influential patriarch, insisted that his people remain neutral. It is more likely the key decision was made at Ustanali, or New Echota, in Georgia, under persuasion from agent Meigs, and from Cherokee progressives led by John Lowery and The Ridge (later called Major Ridge), who warned that to join the attacking Creeks would invite destruction of the Cherokee by the United States.

Instead, the Cherokee sent hundreds of warriors into the field behind General Andrew Jackson, while those at home collected provisions for the American troops. In the final crucial encounter, the bloody battle of Horseshoe Bend, fought March 27, 1814, on the banks of the Tallapoosa River, Alabama, the Cherokee proved their value under fire. After Jackson was held at bay and no force could approach the Creek fortress without being exposed to cross fire, a group of Cherokee under Junaluska silently swam the river to the enemy's rear, captured a flotilla of Creek canoes, and used them to establish a beachhead. Sam Houston, young lieutenant of the Tennessee mountains and brother of the Cherokee, was among the first in the ensuing attack over the breastwork. When the day was done an estimated one thousand Creek warriors had been killed.

It was a high-water mark for the Cherokee in their relationship with the United States. They were credited with turning the tide. Among those in the ranks was Young Dragging Canoe, son of the fiery foe of Americans, and grandson of Attakullakulla. Others were Major Ridge, who had been instrumental in enlisting the Cherokee to join the war, and John Ross, of northern Georgia, who though one eighth Cherokee and seven eighths Scot would become the Principal Chief and the greatest figure of the Nation in the nineteenth century.

The time of travail called for great figures. Despite their efforts at peacefulness, the Cherokee were beset by the insatiable appetite of borderers for their land; and, in reward for their troubles at Horseshoe Bend, they returned to find their homes ravaged and despoiled by white troops; roads were built across their lands and five new treaties forced upon them by 1820. The Tennesseans, in particular, were anxious to be rid of them altogether. The Government pressed them to remove beyond the Mississippi; where earlier it had sent farm implements so they could follow the white man's path, it now told them of good hunting grounds and offered rifles if they would go.

But most Indians wanted to remain in the ancient homeland. They wanted to feel their trust was not misplaced in the Government. They wanted to taste the sweet American fruits of liberty that already had been transplanted to distant soils. So in 1819 they yielded nearly six thousand square miles, or one fourth of the land that still remained to them; they offered to accentuate the process of civilization to prove they were indeed worthy of remaining in the East.

By terms of the Treaty of 1819, they relinquished claim to the heart of the Smoky Mountains. The boundary line became the Little Tennessee. They had to move south and west of the boundary, which extended along the Little Tennessee to the mouth of the Nantahala River, then along the divide between the two rivers—the mountain crest our old friend Bartram had crossed—in a southerly direction to the South Carolina line.

But an odd circumstance was attached to the treaty. Yonaguska stayed. He stayed a short distance above the present Bryson City, near the confluence of the Tuckasegee and Oconaluftee, the site of the ancient Kituhwa. He stayed on 640 acres, or one square mile, which was the amount of land agent Meigs had succeeded in establishing as the size of an "individual reservation" within the ceded territory. Such tracts were available to a few Indians who were "believed to be persons of industry and capable of managing their property with discretion," and who had made considerable improvements on the lands reserved. So Yonaguska and a few others stayed, while the rest of the Indians retired west of the Nantahalas, though they continued to visit and trade on Soco Creek.

Yonaguska, or Ya'nu-gun'ski, Drowning Bear, is a key figure in the Smoky Mountains story. Others in Georgia played much larger roles in the history of the Nation, but none meant more to the isolated mountain Cherokee. He is described as a handsome, tall man of six foot three, a powerful orator, and a prophet. It was he who supervised the erection of the council house on Soco, which was the focal point of his existence until the hour of his death in 1839. At the time of the Treaty of 1819, when he was about sixty, he was felled by a severe sickness, during which his people mourned him as dead. It is not impossible to surmise that the incident was related to a whiskey hangover, for until then he had been a formidable drinking man, but never again. At the end of twenty-four hours he awoke with a revelation that he had visited the spirit world, talking with old friends and with God, who had sent him back with a message to his people. On the recommendation of his young white friend, Will Thomas—who evidently bore a relationship to him somewhat comparable to that of Sam Houston and John Jolly—he swore off whiskey and led his people in taking the pledge. Thus, during Yonaguska's lifetime the Smoky Mountain Cherokee were free of the historic cursed plague inflicted upon them from without. Since early days, traders had found it profitable to haul in liquor, legally or otherwise. Sometimes treaty commissioners weakened Indian opposition with doses of firewater. Its dangers were of grave concern to Cherokee leaders, who enacted strict laws regulating the sale of whiskey, which the whites persistently and successfully evaded. In the Smokies, however, after Thomas convinced Yonaguska that whiskey was ruining him and his people, temperance apparently prevailed.

Drowning Bear's principal influence, however, was in holding his people to the mountains and to the old religion of the mountains. He did not succumb to Christian missionaries, but after listening to one or two chapters of the Bible, remarked, "It seems to be a good book—strange that the white people are not better, after having had it so long." And despite pressures and persuasions that he lead his people in removing to the West, he insisted that they would be safer dwelling among their own rocks and mountains, that the Cherokee could be happy only in the country where nature had planted him.

As to the mainstream of events centered in Georgia, the Cherokee proceeded with their forward strides. In 1820 they adopted a republican form of government, headed by a president, or Principal Chief. The Nation was divided into eight districts, each represented in the bicameral legislature; the upper house, of which John Ross was president, was called the National Committee; the lower house, of which Major Ridge was speaker, was the National Council. A system of district and circuit courts was established, and in 1822 the National Superior Court, later called the "Supreme Court of the Cherokee Nation." Laws were enacted for collection of taxes and debts, support of schools, road repair, for licenses to white persons doing business in the Nation, for the regulation of liquor traffic and the conduct of Negro slaves. To negotiate the sale of lands to whites without consent of the National Council was defined as the most serious of crimes, treason, punishable by death. In 1827 the establishment of the republic was climaxed with adoption of a constitution. John Ross, chairman of the constitutional convention and a principal author of the new document, was a student and admirer of Thomas Jefferson. The preamble reads:

"We, the representatives of the people of the Cherokee Nation in convention assembled, in order to establish justice, ensure tranquility, promote our common welfare, and secure to ourselves and our posterity the blessing of liberty; acknowledging with humility the goodness of the sovereign Ruler of the Universe, in offering us an opportunity so favorable to the design, and imploring his aid and direction in its accomplishment, do ordain and establish this Constitution for the Government of the Cherokee Nation."

The constitution, though intended to safeguard individual liberties and rights, in keeping with the American spirit, was poorly received in the surrounding Southland. To many of their neighbors the civilizing process, promulgated by the Federal Government, had gone too far. The Cherokee in their improved state were even more obnoxious than as savages.

But the pressures for survival evoke the genius of the natural species. The Cherokee not only adapted themselves to the white form of government but produced their own written language, an invention the more remarkable considering the status and character of the inventor, Sequoyah. He was not of the educated Cherokee, nor did he ever learn to read, write, or speak in English. Though now much idealized, he never abandoned the native religion for Christianity; nor did he invent the written language as the means of civilizing the Indian with white ways, but rather as the means of saving the Indian ways. He was a mountain Cherokee, probably born about 1760 in the Overhill town of Tuskegee, outside Fort Loudoun, who lived in maturity at Willstown, Alabama. His name was Sikwa'yi, whose mother is generally believed to have been Wurteh, the niece of Attakullakulla and sister of Old Tassel; his father may have been Nathaniel Gist, the white trader (or possibly a soldier of the Fort Loudoun garrison). In his youth he was a hunter, trader, and silver worker, known among the whites as George Gist, or Guess; and from the whites he became intrigued with the ability to communicate thought through marks on paper.

Between 1809 and 1821 he tried many approaches, including pictographs, single signs for complete sentences, then signs for whole words. Finally, he hit upon the idea of breaking words into syllables. After analyzing thousands of words of the spoken language, he discovered they could be classified into roughly one hundred syllables and subsequently devised eighty-six signs, one for each syllable, sufficient to render all the sound combinations in the Cherokee language. He used characters in an old English spelling book, which he could not read, German printed characters and letters out of a Bible, placing them right side up, upside down, adding a few strokes, curlicues, and symbols of his own invention. Friends thought him unhinged but harmless, while Cherokee neighbors around Willstown complained he was a "witch" who should be put to death.

The accomplishment of Sequoyah belongs to the Nation as much as to the man. When he announced his invention of the alphabet, or more properly the syllabary, the National Council gave him a hearing, with the critical Alabama Cherokee sending a delegation to listen and be convinced. The acceptance of the national language syllabary had an immediate effect—within months almost all the savage people became literate, teaching each other the system of the "talking leaves," in cabins and along the roads.

The national leadership realized that in Sequoyan print they held an instrument with which to crystallize their institutions and culture. The proposed constitution and laws could be read by every Cherokee. They established a national newspaper, the *Cherokee Phoenix*, printed at New Echota with hand press and type shipped from Boston by water to Augusta, then two hundred miles overland by wagon.

How feverishly these people worked! Sequoyah had presented his syllabary in 1821 and less than seven years later, February 21, 1828, the *Phoenix* appeared, printed in English and Cherokee, with editor Elias Boudinot explaining the title:

"We would now commit our feeble efforts to the good will and indulgence of the public, praying that God will attend to them with his blessings, and hoping for that happy period, when all the Indian tribes of America shall rise, Phoenix-like, from their ashes, and when the terms 'Indian depredations,' 'war whoop,' 'scalping knife,' and the like shall become obsolete and forever be buried deep in the ground."

They were believers in God and the syllabary was used in translating the Bible and hymn books. It was right that this should happen, for the most devoted missionary among them, the Reverend Samuel A. Worcester, was a moving spirit in advancing literacy and the publication of the *Phoenix*. Strangely and secretly, however, the new written word was seized upon by the old order, the conservative medicine men and conjurers, as the means of preserving ancient rituals and witchcraft formulas, which previously had been passed down only by word of mouth.

Unfortunately, God's message is variously received by His children. The missionaries taught the Cherokee the message of love. As forest primitives for centuries, they had already learned to know God in nature. On the other hand, God's word was not unspoken in the states of Alabama, Georgia, Tennessee, and North Carolina, nor in the Federal City, where the Houses of Congress opened their sessions with the customary daily prayer. But His image differed.

In 1828, Andrew Jackson, expansionist politician, Indian fighter, and Indian hater, was elected President of the United States, marking the beginning of the end of the Cherokee Nation in its hour of finest promise. Immediately he put through Congress the Indian Removal Act, placing in his hands the task of leading or driving all Indian tribes west of the Mississippi. His policy clearly understood, the sovereign state of Georgia advanced to claim first honors in persecution of the Cherokee.

Georgia had substantial reason for its course. In this same period gold was discovered in the mountain country. It is truly a beautiful parcel of this earth, the Georgia mountains, drained by the Chattahoochee River, which derives its name from the Cherokee word for "flowering rock," denoting the many tumbling waterfalls in the Appalachian highlands. It was considered much too good for Indians, better suited for 10,000 gold-fevered men, including many driven to lust and lawlessness, who gorged themselves until lured West by better diggings in California. And those who remained would slaughter the wildlife until, after three quarters of a century, the last deer was dead.

So Georgia proceeded to pass an act confiscating all Cherokee lands; it declared all laws of the Cherokee Nation null and void, forbade Indians to testify in any state court against white men, to dig for gold on their own land, to hold councils or to assemble for any public purpose; it distributed their lands to whites by lottery, and unloosed a bloody reign of terror by armed bands who brought plunder, torch, and terror. From the White House, Old Hickory cheered the proceedings. He favored leaving the "poor deluded Cherokees to their fate, and their annihilation," and denounced Reverend Worcester and the other missionaries as "wicked advisers."

He helped further by pushing through Congress the Removal Act of 1830, providing "for an exchange of lands with the Indians residing in any of the states or territories, and for their removal west of the Mississippi." The vote was close in both houses. A storm of protest was stirred by speakers and writers throughout the country. There was far more public appreciation and debate of the Indian plight then than now, when the survivors of the Cherokee and other Indian tribes have been reduced to the status of historical curiosities, with scant awareness of their problems in the contemporary world.

Because the Cherokee were helpless, the missionaries prepared to sacrifice themselves in their behalf. When Georgia demanded they either leave the state or take an oath of allegiance to its laws, eleven of them refused. Worcester was the strongest holdout; he insisted that he was a citizen of Vermont, living among the Cherokee with their consent and the consent of the Indian agent. He and Elizur Butler were sentenced to four years of hard labor in the penitentiary. Subsequently, the case of Worcester vs. Georgia was heard before the Supreme Court of the United States. To the joy of the Cherokee and their supporters, the Court finally ruled in their favor. The decision was based on the time-honored principle of the sanctity and sovereignty of small nations, a principle which the United States has since held aloft many times in circumstances relating to distant continents. The Indian tribes or nations, declared the Court, had "always been considered as distinct, independent, political communities, retaining their original natural rights, . . . and the settled doctrine of the law of nations is that a weaker power does not surrender its independence—its right to self-government—by associating with a stronger, and taking its protection.

"The Cherokee Nation, then," concluded the Court, "is a distinct community, occupying its own territory, with boundaries accurately described, in which the laws of Georgia have no right to enter, but with the assent of the Cherokees themselves, or in conformity with treaties, and with the acts of Congress."

The Cherokee rejoicing was short-lived. Georgia defied the Court. The Reverend Worcester languished in jail almost another year at the Governor's pleasure. President Jackson interpreted the decision as part of an effort by his enemies to embarrass him during an election year. The classic remark attributed to the man of the people was, "John Marshall has made his decision; now let him enforce it."

The rush of thousands of whites into Cherokee territory heightened the turmoil and confusion. The Cherokee were nearly spent by constant battle. In May 1834, the *Cherokee Phoenix* breathed its last. On a glowing note of faith in God and in tomorrow's inevitable dawning, the editor signed off:

"To our Cherokee readers, we would say, DON'T GIVE UP THE SHIP; although our enemies are numerous, we are yet in the land of the living, and of our clearly recognized right. Improve your children, in morality and religion, and say to intemperance now growing at our doors, depart ye cursed, and the JUDGE of all the earth will impart means for the salvation of our suffering nation."

By 1835 some Indians, headed by Major Ridge, came to the realization their troubles must end with removal and that the best they could do was to hope for favorable financial terms. The majority, however, supported the national party of John Ross and were determined to fight for home and national existence. They clung to the trust in the Federal Government, presenting memorials and petitions to Congress, and appeals to the White House. Up until the very end it appeared that favorable action might forthcome from Washington, so vigorous were the efforts of Ross and so intensely was the Cherokee removal question debated. The Jackson Administration played the trump card by dispatching to the Cherokee no ordinary emissary but a clergyman, the Reverend J. F. Schermerhorn, of New York, who extorted the infamous 1835 Treaty of New Echota by deceiving both the majority and minority and gaining acceptance by a handful of the people. Neither President Ross nor any officer of the Nation was present or represented at the signing. By this document, written on the darkest day of American diplomacy, the Cherokee were to receive $5,000,000 for their seven million acres in return for lands in the West, plus allowances for the cost of removal. When the Senate ratified the fictional treaty, it did so with a pledge of perpetual peace and friendship, guaranteeing, of course, the western lands to the Cherokee Nation "forever."

The Cherokee did not want to go. They were hard to budge, despite a wave of brutality in Georgia, which saw them flogged with cowhides, hickories, and clubs, the women as well as the men stripped and whipped without law or mercy. Councils were held in protest all over their Nation; resolutions were adopted declaring the treaty null and void and denouncing the methods used to obtain it. Three years passed, they were still on their land, while in Congress Henry Clay, Daniel Webster, and the old Tennessee frontiersman, Davy Crockett, fought for their right to remain. Colonel Crockett risked the fates by denouncing the treatment to which the Cherokee were being subjected as "unjust, dishonest, cruel, and short-sighted in the extreme." He had been threatened to support removal or face the finish of his public career; after this interlude, Jackson's influence led to Crockett's political undoing.

By May 1838, the expiration of the time fixed for departure, only about 2000 of the 17,000 Indians had removed, despite all the pressures brought against them. Here and there efforts were exerted locally in their behalf. In 1837 a memorial to Governor Edward B. Dudley of North Carolina from twenty-four citizens of Haywood County stated the belief that Cherokee neighbors were "fast improving in Civilization, knowledge of the arts and agriculture, for sobriety not surpassed by the same number of whites in any part of the state." The memorial pleaded that the Indians were qualified to make useful citizens, since they had lived in peace and friendship. Except for the signatures, this document was in the handwriting of Will Thomas. Nevertheless, the following year General Winfield Scott was dispatched to force their eviction with infantry, artillery, cavalry, and eager local volunteers, totaling 7000 in number. A chain of twelve stockaded concentration camps was erected throughout the Cherokee country. There were five in North Carolina; the closest to the Smokies, Fort Lindsay, could hardly have been closer, being on the south side of Little Tennessee River at the junction with the Nantahala (now under the waters of Fontana Lake). There were five concentration camps in Georgia, one in Tennessee (Fort Cass, at Calhoun, on the Hiwassee River), and one in Alabama.

Cherokee men, women, and children were seized at bayonet point wherever found and without notice removed to the concentration camps. Livestock, household goods, and farm implements went to the white camp followers, who burned the homes and dug the Indian graves for silver pendants and other valuables. In the stockades, hundreds died. Hundreds of others waited their chance and escaped. Within the stockade walls they set up preaching places. Native ministers like the Reverend Jesse Bushyhead and the Reverend Stephen Foreman preached constantly and baptized children.

In October 1838, the main procession of exile began, the old, the young, the sick, and the small, 14,000 of them; having stowed blankets, cook pots, and trifling remembrances in their six hundred wagons, they bid adieu to their ancestral land, and marched across the Tennessee, across the Ohio, across the Mississippi in the dead of winter, averaging ten miles a day over the frozen earth, stopping to bury their dead who perished of disease, starvation, and exhaustion and to conduct Sabbath worship to the Great Spirit, an army of strangers advancing over the Trail of Tears, while the new President, Martin Van Buren, advised Congress before Christmas that all had gone well, the Indians having moved to their new homes unreluctantly. The whole movement was having the happiest effects, he so reported with sincere pleasure.

Out West, an early order of business among the Cherokee was the dispensation of justice. Major Ridge was done in by bullets. His son, John, and Elias Boudinot, who had shared with him sponsorship of the Treaty of New Echota, were dispatched by tomahawk, the more honorable ancient reward, perhaps because they were less guilty of violating the law that land can be ceded only by the general council of the Nation.

The Cherokee did not fare well in the West. During the Civil War they were bruised and bloodied by both sides, driven to wander from Oklahoma into Kansas, their lands pillaged and their homes sacked in an episode that may even pale the torment they had already endured in the Southeast, and they suffered further from the ferocities of internal dissension. After the Civil War, the wonderful West was opened to the progress and profits of railroads and the trampling hoofs of millions of cattle and the inevitability of white settlement. It was the same old story, the incursion into the Oklahoma territory guaranteed to the Five Civilized Tribes—Cherokee, Choctaw, Chickasaw, Creek, and Seminole—followed by their piecemeal destruction: abolition of their courts, abolition of tribal taxes, impoundment of funds, denial of access to their public buildings, leading to the appointment of a Congressional commission in 1893 to execute the "extinguishment of tribal titles to any lands" in Oklahoma. And then came the coup de grace, the "final act" liquidating tribal holdings, passed by Congress in 1906, although looting of Indians in eastern Oklahoma continued openly long past that date.

The annihilation of the conquered nation was virtually completed. The ashes of desolation were heaped into a mound, a mountain of suffocated spirit that has smothered aspiration to this day, and thwarted the birth and training of leadership of the like of Drowning Bear, Junaluska, or John Ross and of creative genius to compare with Sequoyah's. As to the intellectual competence and energetic capacity of the Cherokee, these were demonstrated to the world and to history during the first thirty years of the nineteenth century. The consequences of their defeat have been largely hopelessness and frustration.

The spark of the race, however, flickered in the ashes, struggled for air, and would not die. Not all the Cherokee allowed themselves to be driven West. Hundreds eluded the soldiers or escaped the stockades or fled the Trail of Tears, hiding themselves in scattered pockets of safety in the homeland. The principal group of these were the mountain Cherokee, the pure-blood, conservative, the most primitive, who had no possible way of knowing the words in the final resolution adopted by the National Council before the removal: "The title of the Cherokee people to their lands is the most ancient, pure, and absolute known to man; its date is beyond the reach of human record; its validity confirmed by possession and enjoyment antecedent to all pretense of claim by any portion of the human race." But in the spirit of these learned, eloquent expressions, several hundred, perhaps one thousand, of the unlearned picked their way to the head of Lufty and of Deep Creek, to the domes along the crest of Smoky and the caves below them, defying every effort at capture, suffering starvation and exposure, subsisting on roots and wild berries, enduring as fugitives and aliens. But they were drawn to the bosom of the mountain from whence they had come, the warm, generous mountain-mother, shrine and sanctuary of all forms of life, where they could kindle the spark and nourish the species.

IX

Professor Guyot Charts the Hills

The Smokies were as quiet as quiet could be in the summer of 1859, when Robert Collins, the mountain man, cut a trail to the highest summit and the wandering geographer, Arnold Henry Guyot, rode a horse behind him.

Guyot was a mountain man, too, but born of very distant mountains. He was of medium height, lean, with deep-set brown eyes and spectacles, a scholarly, professorial type who looked as if made more for thinking than acting. He was a tireless climber, zestful, energetic, always ready to press onward, and a good companion on the trail. He enjoyed building the morning fire, brewing tea, and cutting boughs for beds at nightfall.

They made a curious combination that summer, barely able to understand each other, Collins speaking the mountain dialect of English, and Guyot, the Swiss, fracturing the language that was not his own, while they struggled through the dense evergreen thickets known as woolly heads, crawled over narrow bear trails, and shivered together under rocky ledges to escape the storms. But both, the outlandish professor and the sure-footed mountaineer guide, are immortalized in place names of the Smokies, and with valid reason.

In that year, the parade of national progress had long bypassed the southern Appalachians. Except for a few copper mines being worked in the ridge between Cullowhee Valley and the main Tuckasegee, the principal commerce was in cattle, which grazed the high forests and by far outnumbered the human population. In the Tuckasegee Basin, East La Porte and Cullowhee had been occupied since the 1820s, but Webster, the county seat of Jackson County, was a cluster of half a dozen houses around courthouse and store. Waynesville was an inconsiderable village at best. In the Little Tennessee Valley, Hazelnut (now called Hazel) and Eagle creeks were wild and unsettled. So was the Nantahala Valley, the narrow, precipitous gorge then still clothed with the virgin forest. Only the valleys descending from the Cheoah into the Little Tennessee were populated, and even among them the nightly prowling and growling of bears and beasts disturbed the settlers.

The eastern portion of the Smoky Range, between the Pigeon River and Indian Gap, covered with dense heath thickets and tall trees, was wild and well shunned. West of the gap, however, though the mountains rose higher to the climax of Clingman's Dome, the crest grew less rugged; portions of it, in fact, were used by Tennesseans for grazing cattle, with numerous trails running up the slopes.

The only road across the mountains was the mule path, or cattle trail, that had begun as the Oconalufty Turnpike, with Bobby Collins as toll keeper, from Webster over Indian Gap to Sevierville. But a new turnpike now extended from Asheville to Waynesville and Webster, then through Franklin and Murphy, crossing the transverse ranges to Ducktown, Tennessee. Another wagon road from Asheville followed the valley of the French Broad through the gap in the mountains at Hot Springs, splitting into two branches, one keeping to the river into Newport, the other bearing north to Greenville.

Professor Guyot trod all these routes and more, the trails and the trailless. The Appalachians were his. And he was theirs, their geographic discoverer and definer. They were his work and romance and, though the second highest peak in the Smokies bears his name, the full measure of his accomplishment in these parts is still scarcely recognized or appreciated.

He arrived at a time when the Smoky Mountains were essentially unknown, when maps that professed to show any details were vague and erroneous, when the mountain chains of southern Appalachia appeared to extend in all directions with equal prominence, defying reduction to orderly classification or schematic outline, and when Mount Washington, in New Hampshire, was accepted as the highest point east of the Mississippi. It remained for Guyot to chart virtually the entire Appalachian chain, from north to south, to determine and describe its major geographic features and to make the first accurate scientific measurements of elevation.

It was Guyot who developed the first comprehensive system of nomenclature for the principal peaks of the Smokies. Only few of his designated names remain in use, but naming was incidental to his total study and its meaning. In perspective, the Princeton professor gave the reason for selecting the Smoky Range as a national park almost one century after his visit, through his discovery of the Balsams and Smokies as "the culminating region of the whole Appalachian system" and his revelation that Smoky alone, "by the general elevation both of its peaks and its crests, by its perfect continuity, its great roughness and difficulty of approach, may be called the master chain of the Appalachian system."

Guyot's passion for the Appalachians had begun eleven years before, in the cool September of 1848, barely a fortnight after his arrival in America. His beloved friend and countryman, Louis Agassiz, in whose house he was living at Cambridge, Massachusetts, had taken him to a scientific meeting in Philadelphia. It proved to be a fateful session. First, he encountered Dr. Joseph Henry, Secretary of the Smithsonian Institution, with whom he began at once to plan the beginning of a meteorological reporting system in the United States, which later evolved into the Weather Bureau. Then, he headed into the Appalachians, spending a week on the prowl in western Pennsylvania, though he spoke no English. On this preliminary skirmish, he discovered the woeful inadequacy of American geography—for some of the highest peaks were not shown on maps, while others were inaccurately measured. Thus he began thirty-five years of deep involvement in mapping and measuring the mountains of the East.

But Guyot's genius and clarity of judgment derived from more than his technical training as a geographer. He was a total being, a scholar of nature and the universe, and of man's role in them. Born in 1807, he spent his boyhood at Hauterive, outside Neuchâtel, where he had before him the inspiring vista of the Alps. As he wrote of Agassiz, his friend, collaborator, and neighbor of the village of Môtiers, "From his very home he could see looming before his eyes the snowy heights of the Bernese Oberland; the Jungfrau, with its immaculate white robe; the Schreckhorn and Finsteraarhorn with their dark, jagged peaks too steep to retain the snow; both Eigers, with their sharply defined forms, together with scores of peaks. Who can doubt," asked Guyot, "the influence of these magnificent scenes upon the impressible mind of young Agassiz in awakening, developing, and directing his innate love of nature?" Or, upon his own impressible mind as well?

In the classrooms and fields of Neuchâtel he studied almost everything, insects, plants, Latin, Greek, philosophy. For their higher studies he and Agassiz went to Germany, where their minds were opened to new views of embryology, botany, and zoology. At the University of Berlin, Guyot studied under the masters of the day, Hegel, Dove, von Humboldt, and Ritter. For a time he considered the ministry; it was for this reason that he had gone to Berlin. But under the influence of Carl Ritter, the eminent geographer, his love of nature-science gained possession of him—perhaps, more properly, we should say that he determined to search the core of religious truth through nature-science. "It is a strong faith that our globe, like the totality of creation, is a great organism," he would write later, "the work of an all-wise Divine Intelligence, an admirable structure, all the parts of which are purposely shaped and arranged and mutually independent, and, like organs, fulfill, by the will of the Maker, specific functions which combine themselves into a common life. But"—as Ritter had taught him—"that organism of the globe comprises not nature only; it includes man, and with man, the moral and intellectual life."

Both Agassiz and Guyot were driven almost to the point of obsession by religion, the concept of the life system as the expression of God's thought and power. In time it proved their weakness, causing them to resist the theory of evolution. But it was also their strength, impelling them into relentless scientific investigation in diverse fields. In the spring of 1838, Agassiz came to Paris to see his friend, who was teaching between explorations all over Western Europe. The year before Agassiz had read his startling paper on the "Universal Glacial Era," expounding a theory that was to sweep away grotesque, antiquated, and unscientific notions of topographic formation being caused by floods (including the ancient biblical flood), or by icebergs moving across an ancient hypothetical sea. He invited Guyot to join with him in solving the puzzle of continental glaciation, in proving the glacial age as a period in the earth's history.

So Guyot spent six weeks that summer in the Central Alps, subjecting the theories of Agassiz to severe tests, climbing upward through forests of dark evergreen and larch, and slopes of hardy moss studded with tiny wildflowers, above the treetops and stunted dwarf pine into the snowy mists, crossing crevasses, cols, and crags, through forests and cathedrals of ice, and the ancient glacial rivers of the Aar, Rhone, Gries, and Brenva. How unlike the Smokies! Yet how much this experience must have prepared him, in many ways, for the unknown adventure in the southern Appalachians of two decades hence. In this six-week period he studied the moraines, glacial motion and the laminated or ribboned stratification called "blue bands," all of which advanced glacial theory and understanding.

The following year Guyot, at the age of thirty-two, joined Agassiz on the faculty of the Academy of Neuchâtel. He was, above all, a teacher, much loved, a fact forgotten in the flood of his other activities. But he was consumed with intellectual energy. Besides lecturing and instructing, he did all he could of outside work. He organized a system of uniform weather stations throughout Switzerland—which very likely became known to Dr. Henry in the United States, where he was trying to accomplish the same. He undertook a hydrographic survey of the lovely Lake Neuchâtel, making no less than eleven hundred soundings, preparing to study the annual temperature variation in all Swiss lakes. But his chief research was with Agassiz, endeavoring to prove that the plain of Switzerland had once been overlaid by a sheet of ice half a mile thick, and, from that foundation of knowledge, to furnish Agassiz with the picture on a gigantic scale, of continents laboring under millions of square miles of life-extinguishing glaciers at the end of the Tertiary age.

While Agassiz led a group of companions in measuring the main force of glaciers, Guyot worked alone on the study of boulders, or erratics, spread throughout Switzerland. It occupied him from 1840 to 1847, "singlehanded, seven laborious summers," tracing the path of boulders which had been torn from the mountainsides and carried downward by creeping ice. He covered an area 190 miles by 310 miles, not only in the Swiss Alps but the Juras along the French border and into the slopes of Italy, examining glacial markings on the ridges and peaks; collecting and carrying with him between five and six thousand rock specimens, making thousands of barometric measurements while determining the heights along the lines and limits from plain to mountain peak. He identified the eight erratic basins of Switzerland which left him "no alternative but to admit the ancient existence of mighty glaciers as vast as the erratic basins themselves, and having a thickness over two thousand feet."

In 1846, Agassiz was called to Harvard University, where he was destined to become one of its immortals, and soon after urged his friend to follow. Guyot did not want to leave his friends, family, and country, the scene of his many current investigations, but in 1848 the Academy of Neuchâtel was closed in the course of the Swiss revolution against Prussian rule. He packed his baggage (including his trusted barometer and the five thousand glacial stones) and departed for the unknown without the vaguest prospect of employment.

Once at Cambridge the calamity that had befallen him commenced to prove itself a blessing. He fell in love with America, the land of the future, where he could join the "geographical march of history." Not only did he go with Agassiz to Philadelphia, where he was welcomed with open arms by Dr. Henry of the Smithsonian, and then find new mountains to conquer, but soon after he was invited to deliver a series of lectures at the Lowell Institute in Boston, later published under the title, *Earth and Man*.

These lectures, even though delivered in French, made his American reputation and thrust him into a commanding place among American geographers. A natural scientist, he declared, must be a philosopher as well; and his philosophy derived from the concept of the unity of earth, in time and space, of all history resulting from actions, reactions, and interactions of differences or unlike conditions, co-ordinated or subjected to evoke a sequence of "harmonic units," of organic and inorganic nature, of continents and human societies, all fulfilling their purposes by preparing for and producing other developments beyond them.

From Agassiz's home, the fields of Guyot's acquaintance broadened. Shortly he was appointed by Massachusetts to deliver lectures on geographic education—which really were an extension of his philosophy—in which field the Guyot methods would become universally adopted in America in his lifetime. Atlases, maps, and teaching techniques in use when he arrived were dry, dull, and uninspiring. He urged normal schools and teachers institutes to start with nature, reproduce its reality in a manner so that topographic features are "described in their mutual interactions with the living tribes of the waters and the land, that thereby the activities of the earth and their varied consequences might be understood, and also the influence thence arising that bear on man and human history."

Then there was his meteorology work with the Smithsonian. The distinguished Dr. Henry had been elected Secretary of the Institution in December 1846 and soon after proposed to organize a system of weather observations for solving the problem of American storms. With Guyot's arrival the system came into being. In 1849 he designed a set of instruments, rejecting the old barometers in favor of the cistern barometer with improvements of his own (subsequently known as the Smithsonian barometer), plus thermometer, hydrometer, wind vane, and snow and rain gauge. He also prepared directions for meteorological observations, published by the Institution in 1850, and a volume of meteorological and physical tables, issued in 1852.

As part of these labors, he set out to locate and establish stations modeled after those he had organized in Switzerland. In 1849 and '50 he traveled over New York State, in the depths of winter, establishing almost fifty widely scattered stations and instructing observers in use of the instruments. He also mapped the high plateaus and valleys, employing the background of experience in the "thousands of barometric measurements in the Alps." The national plan of weather observation and recording envisioned by Dr. Henry was not immediately inaugurated, but the Smithsonian conducted and broadened the program begun by Guyot until it initiated the United States Signal Service Bureau, later to be the Weather Bureau, in 1870.

But meteorology occupied only part of Guyot's time. In his "leisure" weeks during the summer and fall of 1849 he began the monumental project of mapping the mountains of the East, which ultimately would bring him to the Smokies. To the everlasting credit of Dr. Henry and the Smithsonian, Guyot received both encouragement and financial support. The project would continue until 1881, when he was seventy-four; in the later years it would fill only his vacation periods, but mountains were the heart and soul of his research.

Guyot started with the White Mountain system (where Mount Guyot, 4589 feet, in the Pemigewasset Range is named for him) and in the first five years covered the mountains of New Hampshire, the Green Mountains of Vermont, the Adirondacks, and other parts of New York —the most important northern ranges with the exception of those in Maine. Meanwhile, in 1854 he was appointed professor of physical geography and geology at Princeton, where in time the first graduate work in geography was given under his direction. He was respected and admired by his students, a few of whom he would take along on his summer excursions to assist in hypsometric observations, but they understood his fractured English with difficulty. For example, when he would say, "The yox were devil-upped," they were supposed to fathom that the rocks were developed. He brought with him to Princeton his five thousand neatly labeled rock specimens, comprising a display on "the extent, thickness, limits, and courses of the great ice-mass that once covered all Switzerland," which served as the nucleus of the Natural History Museum, which he established. The Museum is presently located in Guyot Hall on the Princeton campus (but the University somehow permitted the collection of stones to disappear).

After his five years in the northern mountains, he continued south to Virginia and North Carolina. In the summer of 1856 he arrived in the Black Mountains, measuring twelve peaks and finding them all higher than Mount Washington. He returned in the summers of 1858, 1859, and 1860. The summer of 1859 he spent in his "most laborious experiences," a pioneer hiker on the Appalachian Trail long before it bore the name, from the Pigeon River to the Little Tennessee—a distinguished man in the Smokies and drenched in many a downpour, like the rest.

Before Guyot, geographic exploration and the process of naming the mountains had proceeded very slowly. Until the American Revolution the general term Appalachian Mountains, or Cherokee Mountains, had been applied to the highlands of the South, without separate names for their segments. Perhaps the first distinct name given to the Smokies was the Great Iron Mountain, a designation employed in the Act of 1777 by which the General Assembly of North Carolina established Washington County, the wide spaces extending to the Mississippi River and including the present state of Tennessee. The first use of Smoky as an alternate title appears in the Act of 1789, when North Carolina offered to cede Washington County to the Federal Government to form the "Territory of the United States South of the River Ohio," bounded by the "Great Iron or Smoaky Mountain, thence along the extreme height of the said mountain, to the place where it is called Unicoy, or Unaka Mountain, between the Indian towns of Cowee and Old Chota, thence along the main ridge of the said mountain, to the southern boundary of this State."

Determination of the boundaries between the two states and between them and the Indians was the principal purpose of early geographic demarcation—such as it was. After negotiating the Holston Treaty of 1791, Governor William Blount reported to the War Department, "As the geography of the country cannot be known to you, there being no correct map of it, I think it necessary to inform you that the country to the east, or rather southeast of the Chilhowie mountains, through which the line reported upon, if continued beyond it, will pass, for fifty or sixty miles, is an entire bed, or ledge after ledge, of mountains . . . near which no settlement can be formed, hence I conclude it will not be essential to extend it."

But the country was surveyed in 1797 by Colonel Benjamin Hawkins, for whom the Hawkins Line between Indians and whites was named, and again following the Treaties of Tellico by Colonel Return Jonathan Meigs. After the Cherokee surrendered the Smokies in 1819, the two states undertook seriously to delineate the boundary between them, establishing a commission of three members from each state. William Davenport, surveyor for North Carolina, in his field notes mentioned the range once as the "main Smoky or Iron Mountain," twice as "Smokey Mountains" and once as "Big Smokies Mountain." But apparently the peaks themselves still remained unnamed.

Then came the explorers of the 1850s who set the stage for Guyot. The first was Thomas Lanier Clingman, for whom the highest peak in the Smokies is named, and not without good reason. Clingman, a mining prospector, politician, United States senator, and Civil War general, was a tub-thumper, a booster par excellence of western North Carolina. He extolled its mineral wealth, timber treasures, and health resort qualities. "Even the climate of Switzerland is not equal to this region," he boasted in a letter to a New York businessman. "No country is more healthy, being alike free from the diseases of miasmatic regions, as well as those common in rigorous or damp climates."

Clingman labored to attract attention to the mountain wilderness by disputing the general impression that the White Mountains in New

Hampshire were unexceeded in height east of the Mississippi. His personality and psychology were perhaps best summarized by Dr. F. A. Sondley in the *History of Buncombe County.* "He was an intrepid man," wrote Dr. Sondley, "of most arrogant and aggressive character, greatest self-confidence, unlimited assurance, prodigious conceit, stupendous aspiration, immense claims, more than common ability, no considerable attainments or culture, great boastfulness, and much curiosity. His scientific knowledge was not large, yet he rendered public service by arousing interest in western North Carolina, in local mineralogy and geography." The pre-Civil War exploration period found him at the height of his power and influence, but in later years he would embark on a variety of adventures, such as the manufacture of "Clingman's Tobacco Remedies," prescribed for a variety of ailments, before his death, in homeless impoverishment, at Morganton in 1897.

Clingman's pride, ambition, and contentiousness help to explain his celebrated dispute with Dr. Elisha Mitchell, for whom Mount Mitchell in the Black Mountains is named. Dr. Mitchell, a Connecticut Yankee, came to the University of North Carolina in 1824 as a professor of science. As early as 1835 he climbed the mighty Black Mountains and, by means of barometer readings on several high points, determined that they, rather than Mount Washington, represented the highest elevation in the East. Again, in 1844, Mitchell returned to make further, more precise measurements, aided by Big Tom Wilson, local bear hunter and guide. But in the same year Clingman also explored the Blacks and shortly published a claim that he had discovered a higher peak than the one measured by Dr. Mitchell. They became intense rivals, each with a coterie of supporters. The issue was not whether Clingman had measured the highest point—everyone agreed that he had—but whether Mitchell had done so first.

In 1857, Mitchell set out from Morganton to verify his measurements, intending to stop at the home of Big Tom to enlist his aid. But, unfortunately, he fell to his death in a pool bordering a cascade now called Mitchell's Falls. Clingman and his supporters thereupon accepted the course of moral rectitude and yielded to Mitchell's name the highest peak east of the Mississippi (elevation 6684 feet). Clingman, who may very well have deserved the honor, settled for a nearby mountain (Clingmans Peak, elevation 6520 feet).

Clingman continued to explore the Blacks, Balsams, and the Great Smokies. The following year, 1858, found him on a trip from Waynesville in a party of six heading over Soco Gap, through Cherokee and along the Lufty River, then climbing up the high mountains, through the spruce and fir, to the peak known as Smoky Dome, which was to bear his name. One of the party was Dr. Samuel L. Love, prominent physician and political figure, but essentially this was a scientific expedition. The principal figure was Samuel B. Buckley, a well-known natural scientist of the day. Buckley had already traveled extensively through the southern mountains; in 1856 he had explored in company with Guyot, whom he respected highly and who, in turn, respected him. It has often been stated that Professor Joseph Le Conte was posted as observer at a stationary barometer in Waynesville. This is not likely, according to Professor Le Conte's own account of his affairs, although Buckley or Guyot gave his name to the third highest peak of the Smokies.

On this trip, Buckley made barometric measurements, not wholly accurate, and prepared a list of names, some of which remain in use—including Mount Le Conte and Mount Guyot—though a number of his peaks later could not be identified. He also published a description that must have cheered General Clingman's heart. "The scenery of the mountains, especially in the Smoky Range," he wrote, "abounds in precipices and deep chasms surpassing anything we have seen among the White Mountains of New Hampshire. Such prospects pay the explorer for his toil, their remembrance is sweet."

And now, Guyot came. Clingman welcomed him and aided in arrangements, including the assignment of Robert Collins as his guide. Paul M. Fink, of Jonesboro, Tennessee, devoted twentieth-century scholar of the Smokies, has written this summary of Guyot's expedition:

"Much of Guyot's interest was centered in the ascertaining of the precise altitudes of the various mountains. He had neither the time nor the facilities to run a line of levels to all these points, so he was forced to content himself with a barometric survey, a method that is always susceptible to much error. To guard against this, he enlisted the services of other interested persons as observers at his stationary instruments, while he, in the field, never relied upon a single reading, but took a series at each spot. The convenient and compact aneroid barometer was not in use in his day, only the much larger and more delicate mercurial instrument.

"To one who has pushed his way through the jungle-thick vegetation of the more remote parts of the Smokies, even in this late day (1938) when trails of a sort exist, there can be no more striking illustration of the zeal that actuated this great explorer than a mental picture of him, with but a single companion, struggling up the steep, trackless, laurel-tangled slopes of Smoky, burdened with supplies for a week or more, and handicapped still further by a bulky, fragile barometer, that must be carefully protected from any rude contact that might wreck beyond repair its delicate mechanism. But though laboring under such difficulties, so painstaking was Guyot with his observations and subsequent calculations that the figures he cites for the various points in the Smokies seldom vary from as much as a score of feet from the latest altitudes announced by the United States Geological Survey."

Guyot plowed through dense, shadowy forests and tangled thickets of tough, interwoven stems. His measurements were often interrupted by storms which he said characterized "the remarkable rainy season" between late June and early August. He observed that, while not a drop of rain fell in the Great Valley of Tennessee or in the eastern lowlands, he was being drenched in the hills. Night and early morning were deceptive, with clear skies—then, toward 11 A.M., or noon, thick clouds arose, gathering around the highest peaks, and thunderstorms and copious rains followed for an hour or two; by 4 P.M., or a little later, the sky was clear again, the night cloudless, and misleading for the morrow. Nevertheless, as he wrote that fall, "I camped out twenty nights, spending a night at every one of the highest summits, so as to have observations at the most favorable hours. The ridge of the Smoky Mountains I ran over from beginning to end, viz: to the great gap through which the Little Tennessee comes out of the mountains."

It was not only the geography that overwhelmed him, but the vegetation that makes the Smokies a supreme harmonic wilderness. There was nothing to compare with it in New England, or in Switzerland, or anywhere else. "The forests," he wrote, "which, with the exception of a few spots, cover almost the totality of that mountain region, are truly magnificent, especially near the foot of the hills [referring to the hardwood coves] where humus has been accumulated by action of the water. The trees there are from 80 feet and upwards, and 8 to 11 nay 12 feet in diameter are no great rarity. The Oak, the Chestnut, the tulip-tree, the wild cherry, over 60 ft. high, with beautiful straight stems, the Magnolias and the Hickory compose the bulk of these immense forests, and cloth with a foliage of perfect beauty the Mountain slopes up to 5,000 and 6,000 ft. Beyond 6,000 ft. the dark Balsam fir or its allied species the Fraser pine [now known as Fraser fir] crown with black caps all the summits which rise beyond that limit." He admired, but did not try to explain, the lush verdure on the strange high balds which provided summer pasture for cattle and horses, "covered with grass a foot thick and interspersed with bright-colored flowers, and an abundance of ripe strawberries."

Guyot found few established English names in the mountains, few Indian names either, though many have been ascribed to them and variously interpreted. Indians were not intent on naming places, certainly not on memorializing individuals. Often the titles they gave referred to the shape of landmarks in reference to the natural scene. But these were awkward to the whites and not understood. Egwanul'ti, which meant "by the river," became corrupted to Oconaluftee, or Lufty. The double peak known as Chimney Tops was Duni'skwa'lgun'i, or forked antler, indicating the antler is attached in place, as though the deer itself were concealed below. The name of the river Tuckasegee derived from Tsiksi'tsi, which may have had no meaning at all, except for the sound of the waters splashing over the rocks (though the word has also been interpreted as meaning "slow-moving"). The abandonment of Indian names of euphony and beauty and their substitution by others that grated harshly on Cherokee ears was regretted and deplored by the noted Tennessee historian James G. M. Ramsey. But many places had no names at all, or two names, which complicated life for the geographer Guyot almost as much as the dense thickets through which he was forced to travel.

If nomenclature was difficult to unravel in Guyot's day, it remained so long after. For instance, the 5025-foot peak at the eastern edge of the range now named Mount Cammerer, for Arno B. Cammerer, Director of the National Park Service who played a major role in establishing the park, formerly was called White Rock by the Tennesseans, Sharp Top by the Carolinians. Collins Gap was recognized by that name on the Carolina side, where Bobby Collins lived, but the Tennesseans knew it as Wears Gap, or just plain Grassy Gap.

Guyot was anything but capricious or arbitrary in his choice of place names. "When more than one name has been given to the same point," he explained, "as happens when it is seen from the valleys on two different sides of the mountain, it seems proper for the observer to adopt the name which appears most natural or more euphonic. When the choice lies between the name of a man and that of a name which is descriptive and characteristic, I should choose the latter. In regard to points without established names, but recently named by scientific observers, and not by residents of the country, the right of priority ought to be respected, provided the identity of the points can be sufficiently established, a matter by no means easy, unless the positions have been determined by instruments, or otherwise with considerable care. But it is evident that popular usage will decide in the last resort and that the name universally adopted will, in time, become that which geography ought to accept."

He emphasized the importance of local option in a letter to the *Asheville News*, published July 18, 1860. "As a matter of course, it is for the people of the surrounding country to choose the one that they prefer. That one the geographer will adopt. As to the Smoky range and the mountains of Haywood County, wherever I do not find any name current among the people living in and about the mountain, I preserve the one attached to it by Mr. S. B. Buckley in the publication of his meritorious measurements made in September 1858, provided, however, that the points can be identified."

Nevertheless, he denied to Buckley the privilege of naming the highest peak for himself (as he had done) and insisted that it be given to Clingman. "I must remark that in the whole valley of the Tuckasegee and Oconaluftee," he wrote in his letter to the *Asheville News*, "I heard of but one name applied to the highest point, and it is that of Mount Clingman." Instead, he assigned a knob on the west of the Dome the name Mount Buckley. To another knob he assigned the name of Mount Love, in tribute to Colonel Robert G. A. Love, who had loaned him the horse on which he rode when Bobby Collins cut the six-mile path to the summit. Guyot believed it was the first time a horse had reached the top.

Few names shown on Guyot's map and in his reports were destined to last. Near Mount Guyot itself, his Mount Henry (for Joseph Henry of the Smithsonian) became Old Black, from its cover of black-green spruce; his Mount Alexander (probably for his Princeton colleague, Professor Stephen Alexander) became Inadu Knob, from a Cherokee word meaning snake, suggested by the snake dens on its sides. When he reached the top of Balsam Mountain (via the Straight Fork of the Oconaluftee) he named the sharp peak the Pillar, which is now known as Lufty Knob. An accident to his thermometer presumably accounted for his title to the next point, Thermometer Knob, now Mount Yonaguska. His Mount Safford (for James Safford, distinguished geologist of Vanderbilt University, author of *Geology of Tennessee*, 1869) later became Myrtle Point, named for the Allegheny sand myrtle which once grew in profusion until trampled under the feet of visitors.

His Road Gap, logically named since it was the low point on the route of the transmountain wagon trail, became Indian Gap, through more frequent use. And his Indian Gap became Dry Sluice Gap. What he called the Central Peak of Great Bald became Gregory Bald, for the early settler Russell Gregory. South Peak became Parson Bald, named either for one Mr. Parson or for outdoor preaching where a parson held forth—in all likelihood the latter, considering two nearby streams are named Bible Creek and Testament Branch.

Some of his names were too logical to be lost. One is the Tricorner Knob, for the massive junction of the Balsams and the Smoky crest; another, the Sawteeth, for the "sharp, rocky, deeply indented" section west along the crest. It was he who gave the basis of the name of Newfound Gap, which he called New Gap, or Righthand Gap, being on the right side of the better-known Indian Gap on the climb from North

Carolina. But this nomenclature was confused when the road ultimately was built through Newfound and first called Indian Gap Highway.

Paul Fink has recorded the diverse sources in lore of many Smoky names. Among these, Blanket Mountain supposedly was named after Return J. Meigs had hung a bright-hued blanket at the 4609-foot mountain above Elkmont in order to have a plain target for his compass. The likelihood is supported by the name of a nearby lower point as Meigs Mountain. Then there is the story of how Bote Mountain, farther west, got its name. In the 1850s a road was built from Cades Cove to the Spence Field on Thunderhead. Since there were no engineers to lay out the route, it was left to the decision of the builders, some of whom were Cherokee, as to which ridge the road should follow. As each Indian was asked his opinion, he reportedly pointed to the westernmost ridge and said "Bote" to indicate how he voted. There being no V sound in the Cherokee language, "Bote" was as near as they could frame the word; thereafter it was Bote Mountain, while the other ridge, the loser, became Defeat Ridge.

More easily demonstrable are the names given to Bone Valley and Bone Valley Creek, marking the scene of a sudden blizzard of the 1880s, when scores of grazing cattle succumbed to the cold, their bleached bones remaining scattered along the valley for years afterward.

But there is little doubt about the origin of names like Polecat Mountain, Turkeypen Ridge, Scratch Britches, Indian Grave Flats, Dripping Spring Mountain, Bearpen Gap, and Augerhole Gap, which are found not only in the Smokies but repeated throughout Appalachia. They may not have quite the euphony as the old Indian names, but they are born of the functional culture in the hills. The geographer, as Guyot conceded willingly, could not improve on them.

In the late 1880s and early '90s, the United States Geological Survey charted anew the southern Appalachians, publishing a series of topographic maps, on a scale of two miles to the inch, that supplanted Guyot's work and remained standard until the coming of the park. But the Survey found that many of the names given the peaks and passes by Buckley and Guyot had been displaced or discarded. So it compounded the confusion by a new set of nomenclature and by simply leaving some points unnamed.

This geographic perplexity was not limited to the Smokies. All over the country there were people who knew where they lived, but were not sure of their addresses—and neither was the Post Office Department. In due course the Government established a body called the United States Geographic Board with the power and duty of settling, once and for all, absolutely and unalterably, disputed points of nomenclature in the United States and its possessions. And furthermore, the

Board was authorized to give new names to natural features that needed them.

Thus it happened that admirers of Horace Kephart, on the North Carolina side, decided that Guyot's Mount Collins was a needy natural feature. What it needed, they told the United States Geographic Board, was the name of Mount Kephart. Seldom is a man honored in this manner during his own lifetime, but the Board agreed. Kephart presented a very special case because of his exceptional identification with the Smokies, in his writing and in himself. On October 3, 1928, the Board published its decision that the mountain two and a quarter miles northeast of Clingman's Dome henceforth would be known as Mount Kephart.

This caused a disturbance on the Tennessee side. There it was claimed that the mountain's name had been fixed by long usage as Mount Collins—at least on their side. And the Tennesseans objected to displacing an "ancient landmark" with the name of a living Carolinian. This stirred Kephart, who was normally a mild fellow and uncontentious.

He wrote a letter of particulars to Verne Rhoades, chairman of the Committee on Nomenclature of the North Carolina Park Commission (of which he was also a member) declaring that, while Guyot had named the mountain for Collins on his map, the Geological Survey had given it no name at all, but instead shifted the name of Mount Collins "to the high peak on the state line that connects with Myrtle Point of Le Conte, in Tennessee, and is the nearest to the old home of the Collins family in Carolina." Thus he was referring to the great mountain presently called Mount Kephart. But he preferred the other peak to be named for him and explained why in his letter to Mr. Rhoades:

"Mount Kephart is at the head of the Deep Creek watershed, on the North Carolina side. It is easily accessible from that side, owing to the comparatively easy slope; but it is difficult to ascend from the Tennessee side and very rarely climbed there. Consequently this mountain has always been better known by North Carolinians than Tennesseans, being frequently visited from the south by hunters, herdsmen, and others. Nevertheless it has never had a name of its own among the Carolinians. By them it was simply known as 'the main high top where the Fork Ridge tops out on Smoky.' Long ago I myself lived for two years in the last house up Deep Creek, and I knew personally nearly every resident within a radius of ten miles of it on the Carolina side. None of them knew the peak by any name.

"It is said that Mount Kephart was known on the Tennessee side as Mount Collins by some, and as Meigs Post by others. If so, the Carolinians did not know it. As for Meigs Post, it is not the name of a mountain, but of an important survey corner set up on the top of the peak in question, at which the Hawkins line of 1797 ended on the east and was subsequently joined by the Pickens and Butler lines. It derived its name from the fact that in 1802 Return J. Meigs, United States commissioner, ran from this point of intersection the Meigs and Freeman line. Meigs erected on the summit of Mount Kephart a post as a survey monument, and this was ever afterwards called Meigs Post."

Kephart was obviously upset and unhappy, but he concluded, "I assure you that to me personally the whole matter is a bore, and I hope to have no more of it." But the mountain that ultimately was named for him is no bore but is a splendid peak, lying astride the Appalachian Trail east of Newfound Gap. More accident than design went into the selection of Clingman's Dome, Mount Guyot, and Mount Kephart. If the place namers were to start afresh, they could not choose more wisely.

Kephart was a namer himself, of the curious place with the curious name of Charlie's Bunion, which lies not far east of Mount Kephart on the jagged ridge of the Sawteeth. I hiked out there one day, beyond the Appalachian Trail shelter at Ice Water Spring, beyond the steep Jump-off that connects with the Boulevard trail from the main ridge to Mount Le Conte, to the Bunion, an outcrop of bare rock, one of the few mountain cliffs in the entire Smokies where the vertebrae of the earth is exposed. Nearby an ancient conifer, polished by the wind, clung to a rocky hold. Two hawks dove a thousand feet in seconds, plunging over the silent ridges and wild forest.

The Bunion was stripped of its cover when fire swept over four hundred acres in 1925. But how did the Bunion get its name? Charlie Conner, who was the inspiration for it, told me the story. At Pigeon Forge I visited him, a strong, slender old gentleman of over seventy, who was raised at Smokemont, in the heart of the park, ranged cattle as a boy, worked in the logging mill, and became a guide. I suspect that Robert Collins was not unlike Charlie Conner.

In 1929 he was out with Horace Kephart and three or four others, including George Masa, the Japanese photographer of Asheville, who was one of the Smoky Mountain personalities, to look over the damage caused by a monstrous cloudburst. The Oconaluftee was swollen, and full of silt and logs; tons of vegetation, soil, and rock had been swept from the high places into the ravines. When they reached the Bunion —which had no name at the time—they observed the scene and sat a while.

"But did you really have a bunion, the way the story is told?" I asked Mr. Conner.

Not really, he admitted with an honest smile. In fact, he couldn't quite recollect whether he had been afflicted with an ingrown toenail, a turned ankle, or a sore foot. It must have been one of those three because he had removed his shoe, whereupon Kephart, gifted with imagination, volunteered, "I'm going to get this put on a Government map for you." And that's how places are named—or names are placed —in the Great Smokies.

In 1860 and '61 Professor Guyot published summaries of his findings. A new map of the whole Appalachian chain, made under his direction by his nephew, Ernest Sandoz, appeared first in Switzerland, then with revisions in the United States, to illustrate his paper, "On the Physical Structure of the Appalachian System of Mountains." This paper outlined the geography of the eastern mountains and included over three hundred altitudes he had measured with such remarkable accuracy.

The main body of his work, however, did not appear in his lifetime. It was lost for three quarters of a century, until 1929, when Myron H. Avery, chairman of the Appalachian Trail Conference, discovered in the forgotten archives of the United States Coast and Geodetic Survey an 86-page manuscript which Guyot had dictated to a Government stenographer in 1863. Together with Kenneth S. Boardman, Mr. Avery edited and published as an article and then as a booklet the "Notes on Geography of the Mountain District of Western North Carolina," which constitutes Guyot's major contribution to southern Appalachian geography.

Guyot was deterred from more extensive reporting on the mountains by his teaching duties at Princeton and his involvement in geographic education. The "Guyot system" became widespread in classrooms all over America. Between 1861 and 1875, with the aid of his nephew, Sandoz, he published a series of six school geography textbooks; wall maps which he believed must be the starting point of geographic learning; map drawing cards for grade-school pupils to use at their desks and blackboards; and classical maps of Greece and the Roman Empire for history classes. His maps and books forced publishers of older texts and maps either to fall by the wayside or to follow his modern techniques.

In 1871, he visited the Rocky Mountains and the Coast Range of California. Mostly, however, his "vacation work" continued to focus on the mountains of the East, particularly the Catskills, a "plateau of piled-up strata owing its mountain forms chiefly to sculpturing waters." Despite being near New York City and the Hudson River, and frequented by thousands of tourists, large portions remain untracked forests. Sometimes his only chance for making triangulations was by climbing to the tops of the highest trees—and then he would likely encounter difficulty in identifying distant, featureless, nameless summits. Yet he pursued this work until the close of the summer of 1879, when he was seventy-two, discovering during the course of his exploration nineteen summits that were higher than the highest previously known.

Thus, as he began in America, so did he near his end, roaming the high places, measuring the summits, discovering and describing the truths of geography. Of all his interests, his first and last scientific field was mountain work; as Professor James D. Dana, of Yale, observed before the National Academy of Sciences, Guyot made more numerous and more accurate barometric measurements than anyone else before or during his time.

In December 1883, six weeks before his death at Princeton, Professor Guyot wrote a note to M. Coulon, president of the Society of Natural Sciences in Neuchâtel, the town with which he never lost touch, congratulating that venerable Swiss for keeping up his walks even though he was eighty. "Even last year," wrote Guyot, "I could have told you of my seventy-six years and my ability still to climb our mountains, but unhappily it is not so now." As for his religion, it remained the reason for his being; his last work, a book published posthumously, was titled, *Creation, or the Biblical Cosmogony in the Light of Modern Science.*

His fervent religion was the search into natural phenomena for divine law and purpose. Truth in nature was the core of his belief which he brought to the Smokies, "that ardent, devoted, disinterested love of nature"—as he wrote of Humboldt—"which seemed, like a breath of life, to pervade all his acts; that deep feeling of reverence for truth so manifest in him which leaves no room for selfish motives in the pursuit of knowledge, and finds its highest reward in the possession of truth itself."

X

Rise and Fall of Little Will

When he was twelve, in 1817, little Will Thomas, an undersized father-less lad, left his mother and home on Raccoon Creek at Waynesville. He crossed the mountain into Soco Valley, perhaps on foot or on mule-back or by hitching a ride on a wagon, and took up his duties at the frontier Walker store. It was a branch of the main store at Waynesville owned by Felix Walker, Revolutionary veteran and landowner, who that year took his seat in Congress, representing western North Carolina, and left management of the business to his son, Felix Hampton Walker.

Little Will learned a great deal during his three years in the Walker employ, about trading, politics, land, law, and Indians, the Cherokee being his principal customers and neighbors, and all these lessons served in good stead during his rise as the tycoon of the hills. Unfortunately, he learned little about money matters or how to keep his accounts straight, and in later years, after he had saved the Indians, this weakness very nearly destroyed them and certainly brought torment and destruction to him. But trade was all in barter—ginseng, herbs, and animal skins in return for dry goods, hardware, gunpowder, and whiskey. Besides, Hampton Walker was too preoccupied with studying the law to concentrate on accounting himself. In three years the Waynesville store was closed for debt and, though Will was to receive one hundred dollars and expenses for his services during that time, Hampton paid him instead with a set of secondhand law books.

It was a period of exodus from North Carolina. Though the state had virtually the highest birth rate in the nation, it dropped in population from fourth place among the states in 1790 to seventh place in 1840.

Hampton Walker was among those who departed for opportunity beyond the mountains (to be followed in a few years by his father). Being fond of little Will, he hoped the boy would join him. "I don't want you to embark in any business that will detain you," he wrote Thomas from Tennessee in 1821, "because when I settle myself if I should ever be so fortunate, it is my wish for you to come and study the law or anything else that will be best adapted to your talents."

But Will saw all the opportunity in the world in the shadow of the Smokies. With the Treaty of 1819, the state acquired the Indian lands and was selling them at prices from five cents to twelve and a half cents an acre. His mother, Temperance Thomas, purchased fifty acres of "third-class" land on the west side of the Oconaluftee opposite the mouth of Soco Creek so she and her son could live together again. A neighbor was Yonaguska, Drowning Bear, one of the few Indians who remained after the treaty, living on an "individual reservation" at Governor's Island, the confluence of the Tuckasegee and Oconaluftee. Yonaguska was much more than a neighbor; soon after Thomas had come to work at the Walker store, the old chieftain had adopted him as his own son, giving him the name of Wil-Usdi', or Little Will. Thomas not only had this advantage in trading with Indians, but he had already learned their language as well as any white man could learn it.

Thus, in 1821, Thomas, still a teen-ager, opened his first store and began to build his empire. His principal business was with the Indians who had moved west of the Nantahalas but still visited and traded on Soco. They brought him hides of deer, cow, and hog; skins of bear, panther, wildcat, rabbit, raccoon, mink, muskrat, otter, fox, and rat; hams of pork and venison; ginseng for the China trade; pinkroot and snakeroot. His profits he translated into land. Nobody knows how much real estate he acquired, but at his peak, holdings in his name totaled substantially over 100,000 acres in North Carolina, plus additional properties in Tennessee, Georgia, and Louisiana. He took some land as payment for debts; he purchased other land at sheriff's sales for unpaid taxes. Whatever no one else wanted he bought, paying two and a half cents an acre for rugged mountain slopes as well as twenty cents and higher for fertile bottoms. Soon after the Removal of 1838, he acquired Stekoa, or the Stekoa Field Farm, on the bank of the Tuckasegee near Whittier, which either he or a former occupant named for the ancient Indian village destroyed by Rutherford's forces during the Revolutionary War. The old stone house with an old stone chimney still survived well into the twentieth century, surrounded by sycamore, hemlock, aged and dying maple trees, facing into the heart of the Smokies, where Thomas Divide and Thomas Ridge rise toward Newfound Gap.

By the early 1830s he was a man to reckon with, expanding in all directions, growing in influence, though much of his financial dealing was built on paper over a foundation of sand. His business was credit, borrow and loan, dun and be dunned. But it scarcely showed or mattered while he was still young, vigorous, and in control of his mental faculties. From trading he went into transportation, including construction of the road through Indian Gap in the Smokies and running the Cheoah Turnpike in Cherokee County. Before 1832 he really stepped up in the world, entering into partnership with James R. Love and William Welch, two of the leading lights of the Waynesville mountain community. James Love, later Thomas' father-in-law, was the son of Colonel Robert Love, founder of the immense land estate known as the "Love Speculation." Welch had married one of the Colonel's seven daughters and, when she died, thoughtfully married another. At the time of their partnership with Thomas, James Love was a member of the state House of Representatives and Welch of the state Senate. The three partners were to operate a store on the farm of John B. Love, on Scott's Creek, near Webster, but for some reason Thomas bought out the other two and proceeded alone. For seventeen years he also ran the Scott's Creek Turnpike. In due course he plunged into one business venture and then another, operating a fleet of wagons to markets in Georgia and South Carolina, a wagon-making shop, grist mill, tanyard, grazing cattle herds, trying his luck at mining, expanding his stores to number at least seven.

Then there were the Indians. With the passage of time, his role among the Cherokee has been glamorized to a fault. He is pictured as the savior of the Eastern Cherokee, which is undoubtedly true; as the white chief who dwelt among them, which is not exactly so, though his Stekoa farm was at the edge of their land; and as the selfless, consecrated altruist, which could not be the full story, even though it makes a good one. The Indians were a phase of his business at first; as their lawyer and friend and leader, he fought for their just rights, but in the later years he needed their money to rectify his accounts and save his own property, and only through the intervention of other forces, including the Federal Government, were the Indians rescued from his mishandling and mistakes.

In 1831 the Indians under Yonaguska appointed Thomas as their attorney, business agent, and clerk. It was the time of the intense coercion against the Cherokee, leading toward the Treaty of New Echota and the forced Removal. Though centered in Georgia, the pressure against the Cherokee extended into North Carolina as well; only two years before a Federal commission had unsuccessfully endeavored to persuade the Carolina Indians to sell their remaining lands and head

West. Unlike John Ross and other Georgia mixed-breed leaders of the Nation, who were their own eloquent advocates, Yonaguska and his mountain people understood little English. They needed Thomas, who was versed in law and literate in language, theirs as well as his own, and even though a Cherokee law forbade whites from holding office, these remote Oconaluftee Indians were virtually outside the Nation. They were not a party to the efforts of Ross before Congress and the Supreme Court in Washington, nor to the schism between Ross and the Treaty Party of Major Ridge, but after the New Echota Treaty Yonaguska sent Thomas to Washington in order to determine what its provisions meant to those who wanted to remain in their native country.

It was a confusing, complicated, and ambiguous document that ultimately would require endless years of litigation to unravel. As the treaty had first been signed in 1835, it provided not only for the five-million-dollar lump payment for lands ceded, but an additional compensation for improvements the Indians were forced to abandon, plus per capita allowance to cover the cost of removal and subsistence for one year in the new country; in addition, articles 12 and 13 provided that families that did not want to leave and were "qualified to take care of themselves and their property" could become citizens of the states where they resided with pre-emption right of 160 acres—plus their share of personal benefits for claims, improvements, and per capita. But before the treaty was ratified on May 23, 1836, President Jackson double-crossed his own treaty commissioners as well as the Indians. He declared his determination "not to allow any pre-emptions or reservations, his desire being that the whole Cherokee people should remove together." Therefore, the provisions of articles 12 and 13 were nullified before ratification, and supplementary articles substituted with some additional compensation offered as soothing balm in place of the promised pre-emptions and the cancellation of all individual reservations granted under previous treaties. "Every Cherokee," as James D. Mooney recorded, "was thus made a landless alien in his original country."

So, for twenty-four years, from 1836 until 1860, Thomas was not only involved with the Cherokee as they lived their lives in North Carolina, but was their lobbyist in Washington, making repeated trips to the capital, including one continuous stay of three years, endeavoring to obtain, first, permission for his people to remain, and second, their share of the money from the "removal and subsistence fund."

But his role during the Removal was a curious one. Serving the Oconaluftee Cherokee was not his only activity. He apparently worked on all sides. He knew the Reverend J. F. Schermerhorn, who had extorted the treaty at New Echota, and joined with him in a land speculation in the mountains of Macon County three days before the treaty was ratified; also loaned the Reverend two hundred dollars. Evidently he was appointed a disbursing agent by the Commissioner of Indian Affairs, at five dollars a day, to divide and distribute funds among Indians before they headed West, as provided under article 15 of the treaty. He also set up his trading stores adjacent to concentration camps at which the Indians were herded during the roundup, including Fort Cass, the main headquarters, merchandising his wares to prisoners and guards alike, and evoking complaints from officers in charge that he was a nuisance.

Was he, in fact, some sort of double agent? There is the possibility. Consider the two versions of the celebrated incident of the capture of Tsali. According to the account furnished by Mooney, the eminent and honorable ethnologist, historian, and reporter, which has since become the basis for many romantic fables and fantasies, the Tsali affair was a "remarkable incident that revealed Thomas' great character." He related it in this manner:

In late 1838, during the brutal roundup directed by General Winfield Scott, one old man, Tsali, or "Charley," was seized with his wife, his brother, his three sons, and their families. When his wife was prodded with bayonets to hasten her step, Tsali became exasperated and urged the other men to join him in a dash for freedom. Each Cherokee sprang upon the soldier nearest him and in the sudden scuffle one soldier was killed. This small group of Indians fled to the Smokies, along with hundreds of others. Many of these refugees placed themselves under the leadership of an Indian named U'tsala, or Euchella, and later were referred to in official documents as "Oochella's band." Realizing that it was impossible to track down all the fugitives, Scott seized this incident as an opportunity for compromise. He engaged the services of Thomas, dispatching him to Euchella with a promise that if he would bring in Tsali's party the pursuit would be called off, all others permitted to stay unmolested, while an effort was made to secure some permanent reprieve from the Government. Thomas made his way over secret paths to Euchella's hiding place at the head of Oconaluftee and offered the proposition. Euchella thought it over, deciding at last that it would be better to sacrifice a few in order to save the many.

Then, after so reporting to General Scott, and knowing that Tsali was hiding in a cave at the head of Deep Creek, where he could not possibly be taken without bloodshed, Thomas determined to go to him alone, without escort, in order to persuade the fugitive to come in and surrender. So it evolved. "I will come in," Tsali told Thomas at their meeting. "I don't want to be hunted down by my own people." Sacrificing themselves for the good of all mountain Cherokee, Tsali, his brother, and the two older sons were shot near the mouth of the Tuckasegee, a detachment of Cherokee being compelled to serve as the execution squad in order to impress upon the Indians their utter futility. Only Wasituna, the smallest son, was spared.

Now consider the War Department version. According to reports written by Lieutenant Andrew Jackson Smith, Colonel W. S. Foster, and General Winfield Scott, Thomas was among those present at the original Tsali episode, having volunteered the first week in November to help capture the groups under Tsali and Euchella. But as they headed from the hills toward Fort Cass, the Indians became unwilling to move. A scuffle ensued, in which two soldiers were killed (one with an ax) and a third wounded. General Scott, writing to the War Department on November 6, advised of the course he would follow:

"Indians, to be pursued, are mere outlaws. They have obstinately separated themselves from their tribe, and refuse all obedience and entreaties of its chiefs. Nevertheless, they shall again be summoned to deliver themselves up with a promise of kind treatment to all except the murderers. Every Cherokee in this neighborhood who has heard of the recent outrage has expressed the utmost indignation and regret, and it would be very easy to obtain from the emigrants on the road any number of warriors to march with the troops against the outlaws. I shall, however, only accept the services of a few runners, to bear invitations of kindness, deeming it against the honor of the United States to employ, in hostilities, one part of a tribe against another.

"Col. Foster will also have the aid, as runners, guides, and interpreters some of Mr. Thomas' Oconalufty Indians, as well as the personal services of Mr. Thomas himself, who takes a lively interest in the expedition."

As to the honor of the United States, it is questionable whether restraints were effected on employing one part of a tribe against another. It is a matter of record, as Colonel Foster should have known, that nine years earlier in the Cherokee country the Secretary of War authorized the expenditure of two thousand dollars for use by secret agents to purchase the influence of chiefs in favor of removal. Nor was this the sole occasion of its kind.

In any event, the Colonel advised that on November 12 Euchella came down from the hills to the council house in Quallatown, there joining the volunteer company to capture Tsali and his family. "They captured thirteen Indians," the Colonel reported, "including Tsali, who were tried by Euchella and his group, shot by the warriors in the manner of the tribe, requiring life for life, and buried a short distance above the graves of the soldiers they had murdered on the banks of the Little

In this historic turn-of-the-century memorandum drafted by Dr. Chase P. Ambler, fourteen North Carolinians pledged to underwrite a delegation to Washington on behalf of the Appalachian National Park Association. From 1889 to 1905 Dr. Ambler led an intensive campaign to establish a national park covering twelve thousand square miles extending from the mountains of Virginia down through North Carolina, Tennessee, South Carolina, and Georgia. The association later switched gears to become the Appalachian National Forest Reserve Association, playing a role in passage of the Weeks Law of 1911, which brought national forests to the East. Courtesy Barbara Ambler Thorne.

Harrison Moore, Tennessee mountain man, circa 1910–20, brought home the
bear with an old-fashioned small-bore rifle. National Park Service.

Wiley Oakley, legendary "roaming man of the mountains," and guide, with child, about 1920, early in Oakley's career. He charmed Henry Ford when the motor mogul visited Gatlinburg in 1926. National Park Service.

George Masa at work in the mountains he loved. Though slight of build, he often toted equipment weighing more than half his weight, for which he compensated by carrying little food. When Masa died of tuberculosis in 1933 his funeral was held under an enormous white pine in the woods he had said were his church. Courtesy Barbara Ambler Thorne.

A hiking party of the 1930s takes a break at a cabin near Andrews Bald in the Smokies. Barbara Ambler Thorne, then twenty-seven or twenty-eight, is third from right (in beret). Courtesy Barbara Ambler Thorne.

The Mountain View Hotel, shown about 1930, likely began as a rooming house for loggers, then, under the Huff family, grew into the center of activity in Gatlinburg. John D. Rockefeller, Jr., was among prominent visitors who stayed here. National Park Service.

In front of Huff's Hotel, or Mountain View, guests prepare to saddle up. In pre-park days riding was a popular means of seeing the mountains, but has largely given way with roads, hiking trails, and time. National Park Service.

At the 1927 Gatlinburg Fair, girls evidently favored bonnets, boys caps, and most wore shoes. Tennessee children like these chipped in their nickels, dimes, and quarters to help purchase land for the national park. Laura Thornborough, courtesy National Park Service.

Tennessee." Foster stated there were five murderers, but that one was so young he was retained as a prisoner; this was Wasituna.

Foster took the families of the murderers to the Cherokee agency at Fort Cass, Tennessee, leaving the day before the execution. "The honor of the nation," he announced to General Scott, "has been fully cared for, as well as the honor of the regiment to which I belong. At and over the graves of our murdered comrades, funeral honors were paid."

And in tribute to his collaborator, the Colonel added, "I should do my feeling great injustice were I to omit to you and through you to the Government, Mr. Wm. H. Thomas, in the most favorable light, and as an individual, deserving the confidence and patronage of the country, both for himself and the O-co-nee-lufty Indians, over whom he appears to exercise unbounded influence for good purposes." Foster also expressed the hope that Euchella's band would be permitted to remain with Thomas and the Lufty Indians.

Perhaps this plea by Foster was actually inspired by Thomas. As T. Hartley Crawford, Commissioner of Indian Affairs, wrote later (in 1844) of the Indians' conduct, "Another portion of them called Oochella's band, from the part they took in arresting the murderers of some soldiers, induced the white citizens to request the military commander (Colonel Foster) to remain East, which was granted." This, too, indicates intervention by Thomas for the Indians, although at variance with the manner described by Mooney.

The military commander, Foster, also entered a special word for Yonaguska. "The conduct of the Drowning Bear, the aged chief of the Oco-nee Lufty," he wrote, "was honorable to himself and useful to me, and I ask that it be remembered in his and their favor." Thus, the pressure against the North Carolina Cherokee to remove was diminished. Soon after, in 1839, Yonaguska died. As the end neared, according to the record written by Mooney, he directed that he be carried into the town house at Soco. He made a last talk to his people, warning them against ever leaving the mountains and urging them to accept Thomas as their new chief. Then, wrapping his blanket around him, he lay back and died, to be buried nearby, with a mound of stones marking the spot.

As combination chief-agent, Thomas was virtually the only law and leader the Indians knew. He met with them in council and attended their dances; he promoted temperance, made available a translation of the Scriptures, and arranged for a mission school. Between 1836 and 1839 he had advanced to them goods and supplies worth $1200, against their later settlement. In 1840 he paid $1200 for 33,208 acres of land, including portions of the present Qualla Boundary (and perhaps he now was settling the Indians on lands once owned by his former employer, Felix Walker). In such purchases through the years he used money from the Indians, his own money, and borrowed money with liens as security. He laid off these lands into five districts, or towns, which he named Bird Town, Paint Town, Wolf Town, Yellow Hill, and Big Cove, which even now continue as the structure of the reservation; and he drew up a simple form of government. He went to Washington to argue the Cherokee case for their share in personal benefits provided in the 1835 treaty. Though their right to the money was not denied, it was withheld, conditional upon their removal to the West. The Government's attitude in general was stated in reply to Thomas' request for aid in education so the Indians could learn "the habits and arts of civilization." "The Cherokee have ample provision for school purposes in their country west of the Mississippi River, and if those in North Carolina want greater facilitation in this respect than they enjoy in their present location, then they can obtain them by removing among their own people in that country." Besides, the Western Cherokee opposed dividing the money with the Eastern remnants, contending they had forfeited their right to participation (and later that the number qualified was exaggerated).

But Thomas was persistent and forceful in Washington, arguing that "each individual of the tribe has a vested right in the fund, no difference where he now resides, and the Cherokee nation has no power to divest his interest, and the United States are bound to the individuals." Of his group of Indians, he wrote, in his self-trained legal style: "A larger portion of them can read and write than is found among the white population, in a majority of the States of the Union. Their lands are situated at the base of the Great Iron or Smokey Mountain, which furnishes rich pasturage for their cattle, both winter and summer, and where game is plenty. Their lands are productive, their orchards supply them with fruit; springs and brooks of the purest water from the sides and base of the mountain; and the atmosphere is one of the healthiest on the globe. No local causes for disease; no chills and fever which are so prevalent in the South. And that country is endeared to those Indians by the graves and sacred relics of their ancestors—the bones of their children, sisters, brothers, fathers, and mothers lie there; they say we cannot leave them; let us alone in the land of our fathers."

For all his protestations in behalf of the Indians he was also anxious to collect his commissions and fees. As he wrote the Attorney General, "When an attorney has performed an important service, collected the evidence, and been instrumental in securing a claim which might otherwise have been lost, and where this has been done under the stipulation or with a bona-fide understanding that he was to receive the amount to which he was entitled directly from the United States, he has an interest in the fund which the principal himself could not revoke and which the Department is bound to recognize."

At last, following Congressional action in 1848, some of the money began to see the light of day in North Carolina. It was an extremely complicated arrangement. Amounts of $41,367.31 and $156,167.19 were appropriated for distribution among 2133 Indians, but a stipulation was added that North Carolina must first give assurance the Cherokee would be permitted to remain permanently in the state. Since this would not be granted until 1866, certain portions of the money were not distributed. As for sums that were distributed, the Indians saw little of them either. Thomas received the money. As their authorized agent and trustee under the Government, he purchased lands for their legal settlement upon the Oconaluftee and Soco, and detached tracts in the western corner of the state; but since North Carolina refused to recognize Indians as landowners, he held the deeds in his own name.

By the early 1850s his business activities were far-flung and involved, yet he continued to expand, joining the copper boom in southwest North Carolina, and entering full scale into politics. He engaged James W. Terrell, then in his early twenties, as employee, junior partner, and assistant chief of the Cherokee. Terrell ran the Quallatown store, taught at Quallatown Academy, assisted as special United States agent in the disbursement of payments to the Indians, conducted the semi-monthly Cherokee council, built and ran the tanyard, and later served a term in the legislature. He lived until 1908 and became a prime source of information to Mooney and others on Thomas. Even though Thomas fell behind now and then in paying his wages—as with other employees—Terrell was loyal to the end.

Meanwhile, Thomas, being a man of wealth and influence and having already served as justice of the peace, had been elected to the state Senate in 1848. He served until the outbreak of the Civil War, spending part of every second year in Raleigh, gaining in fame if not in fortune. In 1852, the year he was a presidential elector, the press mentioned him as a possibility for governor. His principal influence was in road building, as chairman of the Committee on Internal Improvements. The two decades before the Civil War were the age of the plank road, otherwise known as the "farmer's railroad," built of parallel rows of heavy timber covered with crosswise timbers, when the 129-mile Fayetteville and Western, the "Appian Way of North Carolina," became known as the longest plank road in the world. Thomas sponsored road improvements for the mountain district and hard surfacing. By the mid-fifties, when it became plain that the plank roads were doomed—by worn-out planks, rising costs, and inability to serve long-haul transportation—he became a champion of the railroad. It was felt the iron horse would work wonders for the mountains, connecting them with distant markets and opening an era of undreamed-of prosperity. Moreover, as the *North Carolina Argus*, of Fayetteville, explained, railroads would rescue mountain people from "bad habits naturally engendered by a life of idleness." In its issue of January 20, 1855, the *Argus* expressed this editorial judgment:

"We have frequently heard temperance lecturers proclaim that in almost every ravine and mountain gorge of western North Carolina you will find a still house and an apple mill, placed there for the purpose of turning the healthy grains and fruits of the earth into a maddening and killing beverage. The fact they will tell you; but if they know the cause they keep it from the public. The cause is this:—the people in those regions where still houses abound have scarcely any other way of converting the produce of their farms and the fruits of their beautiful orchards into a marketable commodity than by distilling them into whiskey and brandy. That is the only way in which they will bear hauling to market. We are thoroughly acquainted with the mountain region of North Carolina, and know we are giving the circumstances of the case in their true light. Run improvements through these sections alluded to, so that the people can get remunerating prices for their fruits in the natural and healthy state in which a kind Providence gives these products to man, and our word for it our temperance lecturers will soon quit holding up the mountain region of our state to their eastern brethren as a land abounding in still houses and apple mills; while we of the east will get from the up-country good fruit instead of fiery brandy, and good and sound grain and flour instead of mean corn whiskey."

On this popular wave, Thomas fathered the Western North Carolina Railroad, later part of the Southern Railway system; he also was president, chief promoter, and stock salesman of the Tennessee River Railroad, chartered to run from the Tennessee border along the river to the Georgia border at Rabun Gap, as part of a great rail network from the coast at Charleston to Knoxville and Cincinnati, but only a few miles of track were laid on this line.

The larger his empire and influence extended, the deeper he went into debt. Between 1853 and 1856, at the height of his power, judgments against him in Jackson County alone amounted to $16,000. He borrowed from James R. Love, his old partner and leading light of Waynesville, giving a deed of trust on Stekoa. He borrowed heavily from William Johnston (husband of Lucinda Gudger, granddaughter of the late Colonel Love) and was sued by him; Johnston became his largest creditor and will be heard from in the resolution of the Cherokee lands.

In this set of circumstances, Thomas was now courting Sarah Jane

Burney Love, the eldest daughter of James Love. Though he was well acquainted with lady friends from the Carolina hills to Washington, D.C., he plighted a romantic troth. "I presume that it will be with you as it will be with me," he wrote his beloved on January 4, 1857, "your friends will be my friends, be they rich or poor, and mine will be thine even the poor oppressed Indians. I look forward to the time when we will ride through their settlement on our way to our mountain home when you will witness the affection of these people for their 'so-called chief.'" And so in June 1858, they were wed, he being fifty-three and his bride twenty-six.

With the outbreak of the Civil War, Thomas continued to play the central role in the Smokies, a remote region out of the mainstream of action but nonetheless involved. At first North Carolina remained aloof from the secession; it took no part in organizing the Confederacy in February 1861. Union sentiment was strong in a democratic state much less dominated by the landed aristocracy than neighboring Virginia and South Carolina. But with the firing on Fort Sumter and Lincoln's call for troops to "suppress the insurrection," North Carolina threw in its colors with the Confederacy—Thomas was among the 120 delegates attending the secession convention at Raleigh on May 20. To him, the war would be the making of the mountain country. It was in the middle of the Confederacy and could hardly avoid becoming the center of learning and industry, maybe even the capital of the new nation. "It will become connected with every part of the South by railroad," he predicted to his wife in a letter on June 17. "It will then become the center of manufacturing for the southern markets. The place where the southern people will spend their summers, spend their money, educate their children, and very probably make laws for the nation." And so it has always been with the hopeful promoters of the highlands, men of that day like Will Thomas and his contemporary, Thomas L. Clingman, and with others in days thereafter, foreseeing some turn in human events, be it the coming of the railroad, the coming of the war, the coming of the lumber industry, the coming of the national park, to transcend the natural course and usher in a marvelous age of prosperity.

The mountaineers actually had little stake in the war; many remained independent and unconcerned. Those who fought served well. Western North Carolinians were involved on all fronts until the end came at Appomattox, while the state gave to the Confederacy its greatest supply of manpower, despite protestations over "the rich man's war and the poor man's fight." Across the mountains, East Tennessee was overwhelmingly loyal to the Federal Government. Sevier County was said to have sent more volunteers to the Union Army than the county had voters. Radford Gatlin, the shopkeeper at the crossroads settlement of

White Oak Flats, which became known as Gatlinburg, was a Confederate sympathizer and therefore encouraged to depart for a friendlier environment.

The Smoky Mountains and surroundings were variously invaded by Confederate and Yankee troops in need of supplies. Union forces at times occupied Wears Valley, Pigeon Forge, and Tuckaleechee Cove. But mostly the country became an arena for deserters, bushwhackers, and guerillas owing allegiance to neither side, who looted, burned, and pillaged. On one occasion, when such raiders came calling at Tuckaleechee, Frederic Emert buried his rifle for safety's sake and declared truthfully he didn't "have a gun on top side of the green earth." The Cherokee land was preyed upon, too, and when nearly all able-bodied warriors followed Thomas into the Army, many wives and children lived on weeds and bark, or went south in search of bread. Food in general was scarce, particularly since speculators held their produce until they forced prices up or shipped their supplies to more profitable markets.

From the beginning of the war Thomas was a military enthusiast. First, he mustered two hundred Cherokee into state service under the name of the Junaluska Zouaves, and proposed a full Indian battalion to guard the mountain gaps. When North Carolina rejected the proposal, he enrolled in the Confederate Army. It was April 1862; he was then fifty-seven, and authorized to recruit a regiment. This unit was mustered into service at Knoxville with at least 2000 men, mostly Carolinians, a few Tennesseans, and four companies of Cherokee Indians, officially called the 69th North Carolina, but known as Thomas' Legion of Indians and Highlanders, or simply the Thomas Legion. Colonel Thomas was joined on his staff by Major (later Lieutenant-Colonel) William Williams Stringfield, who became further allied with him after the war as a son-in-law of James R. Love. James W. Terrell commanded Company A, before being promoted to regimental quartermaster. Joseph A. Collins, one of the sons of Robert Collins, the mountain guide, later joined the 69th as a first lieutenant.

At first the Thomas Legion was assigned to help defend the eastern portions of Tennessee and Kentucky, scattered along the railroad from Bristol to Chattanooga, but shortly the main body of the regiment was dispatched into hard fighting on the Virginia front lines, while Thomas and a small force returned to the Smokies. Possibly this occurred in order to fortify the mountains and so prevent the Union from splitting the South in two. Or because Thomas hoped to keep the Indians close to their homes. Or as the result of his first—but not last—brush with higher military authority. Being a prolific letter writer, he extended advice to President Jefferson Davis and Governor Zebulon Vance of

North Carolina and expressed disagreement with his superior, General Alfred E. Jackson, known as "Mudwall" among the troops. His reward was to be arrested on Jackson's orders and given a stiff reprimand.

Back in the hills, the Thomas force set to work widening and improving the old route through the Smokies, which Professor Guyot had described as the "only one tolerable road, or rather mule path, connecting Sevierville with Webster." The project was undertaken either to provide a usable military avenue or in order to tap the mineral supplies of Alum Cave (alum, saltpeter, copperas, and magnesia) on the slope of Mount Le Conte for use in making munitions. Whatever the precise purpose, the 300 to 400 Indians, with white officers and overseers, were camped near the present Chimneys Campground on the Tennessee side, where they erected earthworks and posted guard. The spot was named Fort Harry, for some Harry since forgotten, and the nearby river crossing known as Fort Harry Ford. Thomas is said to have set his Indians to work digging in the alum bluffs and carrying the materials down a steep trail to a point where they were loaded for transport into North Carolina. Remains of the trail, plus timber and rocks piled in a manner suggesting a Confederate earthworks, were found early in the twentieth century, tending to lend substance to the account.

All such activities, however, were thwarted and terminated in the fall of 1863 when General Ambrose Everett Burnside overran most of East Tennessee and Union troops from Knoxville brought the war into the mountains. The focal point for both sides was Chattanooga, the gateway through the Cumberlands to the heart of the Confederacy, but nevertheless General Robert B. Vance, commander of the Western District of North Carolina, and brother of the Governor, determined to make a show of strength through the Smokies. In early November he wrote Thomas: "Keep in view the operations of our army in East Tennessee so that if an effort is made to dislodge the enemy from that important country we can assist. You could move your force across Smoky, and I down by the Warm Springs, and hook on to the troops either from below or above. It is very important to arrest every Deserter in the country, and you will give especial attention to that. . . . Deserters soon become our worst enemies & they ought to be attended to at once."

Thus, the night of December 9 found Thomas and his troops encamped on the Tennessee side, with log huts and frame buildings erected on the steep wooded slope commanding both roads into Gatlinburg. A number of squaws had reached the site and the plan apparently was to spend the winter in Gatlinburg. Or so deduced Colonel William J. Palmer, of the 15th Pennsylvania Cavalry, whose scouts surveyed the scene in advance of a morning attack. Palmer estimated the force at around 200, including 150 Indians. They were good fighters, the Indians, and a credit to the cause, as Colonel Stringfield recorded. Only once, he said, did they go in for scalping. This was during an encounter in the Baptist Gap of Cumberland Mountains, Tennessee, September 15, 1862, when Lieutenant Astu'gata'ga, or Astoogastoga, said to be a grandson of Junaluska, was killed in a charge, which so incensed his men "that they dashed forward with their war-whoop and battle-cry and before they could be restrained they had scalped several of the wounded." Before starting to the front, every man consulted an oracle stone to learn whether he could expect to return in safety. A grand old-time war dance was celebrated at the Soco town house, and the same dance repeated at frequent intervals thereafter, the Indians being "painted and feathered in good old style," with Thomas himself presiding. Alas, there were no such demonstrations that night in Gatlinburg and bright the next morning Colonel Palmer deployed his troops and attacked. Firing lasted an hour; the Thomas Indians continued to shoot while withdrawing into the hills. Palmer concluded that Thomas had been taken by complete surprise—his hat was left behind in his headquarters. The Union troops destroyed the huts and frame buildings, and returned most of the Confederates' horses to their owners.

The next month, in the dead of January, General Vance arrived to take charge himself. Though he fared even more disastrously, the crossing of the mountain appears to have been a heroic episode. Having marched from Asheville with a force of 100 infantry, 375 cavalry, and one section of artillery, to Quallatown, where he picked up Thomas and 150 Indians, Vance advanced into the Smokies. Getting wagons and cannon up the North Carolina side over the Thomas Road to the crest was managed without complication. But moving down the rougher Tennessee side was well nigh impossible. Wheels and axles were taken apart from wagons, carried down, and then reassembled. Cannon, too, were dismantled, an operation recalling Napoleon's grand crossing of the Alps—but where the Frenchmen tied guns to hollow logs, the Carolinians dragged theirs over bare rocks and steep mountain slopes. And to add to the problem, the weather was colder than usual for January.

Once on the Tennessee side, Vance charted his course. He would proceed to Sevierville with 180 cavalrymen, leaving Thomas and Lieutenant-Colonel James L. Henry with the remainder of the troops at Gatlinburg, and Henry would rendezvous with him later, with cavalry and artillery, on Cosby Creek. On January 13 Vance met good fortune, capturing a train of seventeen wagons and twenty-three Union soldiers. Heading toward Newport, he stopped to rest at Schultz's Mill on Cosby Creek. Colonel Henry was nowhere about, having decided to fall back with Thomas at Gatlinburg, but Vance presumed himself out of danger and did not post pickets. Nor did he reckon with the redoubtable Colonel Palmer, of the 15th Pennsylvania, who charged the mill on January 14 with less than 200 men, in columns of four, routed the Confederates, retook the wagon train, captured General Vance, fifty-one men, 150 horses, plus an ambulance with medical stores and food. In consequence of the disaster, Colonels Henry and Thomas were ordered by General Joseph E. Johnston to appear for court-martial in Asheville on February 23, though it does not seem this trial took place.

For in the meantime General S. D. Sturgis dispatched the 14th Illinois Cavalry, under Major Francis M. Davidson, from Tuckaleechee Cove to strike Thomas on his own ground. The engagement took place February 2 near the fork of the Little Tennessee and Tuckasegee, following which Major Davidson claimed a clean victory. "The enemy," he wrote, "were 250 strong. Of these, 22 Indians and 32 whites were captured, including some officers. It is reported that not less than 50 made their escape, the remainder being either killed or wounded . . . nearly 200 of them having been killed." But Thomas' version differed. He conceded, in his account of February 28, that on "the second instant they advanced up the Little Tennessee to the mouth of Deep Creek, when the Indians under my command arrested their progress. The enemy lost about twelve killed or wounded, the Indians five. I am informed the northern forces boast of killing 200."

Thomas did admit the capture of between 20 and 30 Indians and whites. The Indian prisoners were taken to Knoxville where—according to the *Daily Confederate*, published in Raleigh (on May 17, 1864)—they were promised their liberty plus $5000 in gold dollars if they would bring in the scalp of Colonel Thomas. The *Daily Confederate* said they agreed and returned to the mountains, giving a full report to their chief and taking up the warpath, after Yankee scalps. This, however, was not true of all of them. Several deserted to the Union and served with the 3rd North Carolina Mounted Volunteer Infantry in the same region until the close of the war; when they returned home their tribes were so bitter that for some time their lives were in danger.

Undoubtedly Thomas protected the mountains from Federal raiders. The enemy noted that action was required to suppress him and his followers as "a terror to the Union people of East Tennessee and the borders of North Carolina from the atrocities they were daily perpetrating." But he was regarded in this period as a nuisance on his own side, as well. In May 1864, he was charged with receiving into his command twenty-one deserters of the 65th North Carolina Regiment and near the end of the year Governor Vance wrote, of the situation in western North Carolina, "There are troops enough there to afford ample protection both against the enemies and the tories and deserters, who throng the mountains murdering and robbing the citizens, if under proper control and management. Col. Thomas is worse than useless, he is a positive injury to that country. His command is a favorite resort for deserters, numbers of them I learn are on his rolls, who do no service, he is disobedient of orders and invariably avoids the enemy when he advances."

Vance and others, however, may not have realized that Thomas had already begun to travel another journey, all alone, into the dark craggy corners of his mind. He was no longer quite the same person they had known before, the sure and steady businessman, promoter, politician. It was in 1864, while his hopes were going down with the Confederacy, that his brother-in-law, Dr. W. L. Hilliard, noticed that at intervals he was "laboring under some peculiar mental excitement—that his mind was a little out of balance."

But the war was not quite done for the Smokies. In one of the final encounters, five weeks before Appomattox, Colonel George W. Kirk, with a regiment of more than 600 East Tennessee partisans and regulars, came through the mountains via Newport, Mount Sterling, and Cataloochee. Kirk, an early defector from the Confederate cause, was feared and hated as the leader of underground guerilla forces operating from mountain refuges in Madison County, north of the Smokies. His band, which often skirmished with Confederate troops and struck against helpless communities, now turned aside a Confederate company at Cataloochee, pushed into Waynesville, where he burned the home of the late Colonel Robert Love, liberated prisoners from the jail and then burned it. After skirmishing with local troops in the Balsams, Kirk retreated over the Maggie road into Soco Valley and fought a battle with the Carolinians on March 6. Jarrett Blythe, the chief of the Cherokee, whose grandfather, Nimrod Jarrett Smith, as first sergeant in the Thomas Legion, was probably among those present, once showed me the setting of the action, above the Macedonia Baptist Church; he said both sides shot at each other most of the day, and somebody killed a horse. Kirk withdrew over the Smokies but soon came back to renew raiding and horse stealing.

As for Will Thomas, the nearer to the end of the war the more his mind craved action. The rumor of Lee's surrender at Appomattox was received in the mountains on May 9, but discounted. That night the last Confederate stalwarts camped on the mountains surrounding Waynesville, while a New York regiment of 1000, commanded by Colonel Thomas Bartlett, occupied the town. Thomas showed he had no intention of surrendering by having his 300 Indians build bonfires and war-whoop through the night. Next morning Bartlett sent out a flag of truce and asked for a parley. Along with other officers, Thomas came into town, but he brought along twenty or twenty-five of his warriors painted, feathered in fighting style, and stripped to the waist. "Colonel Thomas," according to Stringfield, "who was usually very cool and discreet, became quite boisterous," demanding Bartlett's surrender and threatening to have him and his men scalped. But the powwow simmered into a discussion of truce terms.

The war finished Thomas and very nearly the Cherokee. Their harvest was one of death, misery, and civil feud. Smallpox struck in 1866, and despite the efforts of Thomas, who brought a doctor from Tennessee, more than one hundred died. He, meanwhile, became increasingly irrational. His affairs were totally and hopelessly muddled, opening the way to pressures from other whites to renew the age-old effort to acquire Indian land. "This would not have happened," as Stringfield summed it simply, "but for the unfortunate illness of their much loved chief, who was stricken in mind and body when his services were most needed. Rival claims for the chieftainship arose, and great confusion ensued. The younger generation growing up 'knew not Joseph,' and were the easy prey of designing men."

In March 1867, Little Will was declared *non compos mentis* and committed to the state asylum, then located at Raleigh, beginning a series of journeys back and forth. His wife, Sarah, secured his release the following summer and clung to him at Stekoa, though at times he was violent. The Love family fortune was dissolving too, and she had not received nearly enough from her father's estate to cover her husband's mistakes. As he had bought land now it went to others, at sheriff's sales. Everything Thomas owned passed into the hands of creditors, the principal creditor being William Johnston, husband of Sarah's cousin. In 1869 he obtained deeds for all the Indian lands under judgments against Thomas totaling $33,887.11.

Terrell still felt there was hope of redemption through settlement of the Indian claims money; he was also concerned over his own account as disbursing agent. He went to Washington with an appeal to the Commissioner of Indian Affairs. The Cherokee, he declared, had been "permitted to remain in North Carolina on certain conditions with domiciliary rights, but the treaty left them landless. William H. Thomas, their acknowledged chief and business agent, purchased for them the lands they now live on, partly with his own funds, and I think partly with theirs and in part with funds which he borrowed on his private credit. In all cases he took the deeds or titles in his own name and deposited with the Indians a bond on himself for a title to the nation East at large as soon as they completed to him the payments for the land. The Indians have occupied the lands free of rent but have not yet completed the payments for them. A few, however, in accordance with a provision of the bond have deeds for the tracts they live on but Mr. Thomas yet holds the legal title to the greater part of the Indian lands and he certainly has an equitable interest in them till paid for."

At long last the Federal Government took note of the Eastern Cherokee in their impoverishment and acknowledged its responsibility. In 1868 it recognized them as a separate tribe, under the title of Eastern or North Carolina Cherokee, but, consistent with the long inconsistencies, failed to provide any funds for administration or guidance. In December of that year a general council of the Eastern Cherokee convened at Cheoah as the preliminary step toward adopting a regular form of tribal government.

In the effort to unravel the jumbled status of the lands, and to enable the Indians to gain title, Congress authorized the Indians to institute legal proceedings, which became known as "Eastern Band of the Cherokee Indians vs. William H. Thomas, et al." They alleged they had been "greatly and grossly wronged" by Thomas. The other defendant, William Johnston, was charged with taking sheriff's deeds for the land though knowing of the Indians' existing equity. And in a separate suit, Terrell was accused of failing to account properly for money he had received from the Government for the Cherokee. Terrell was so grieved and provoked that he confessed to feeling that the sooner "manifest destiny" overtook the Indians, the better for everyone. Poor Terrell, for all his efforts, as he said, "to save Thomas' reputation as well as my own," would be sued again in the unending litigation by the Thomas heirs for "fraud and misuse of funds."

The award in the case of the Indians vs. Thomas, delivered in 1874, found the Indians were still indeed indebted to Thomas for $18,250, less deductions they had paid to Johnston—and whatever was left went to Johnston, anyway. The land itself, however, was denied him; he was allowed to hold it only as security for the balance due him until paid. And out of the ashes of the tragedy, Congress finally paid to the Cherokee the remainder of the "removal and subsistence fund" for the purpose of securing full title and cost of litigation. It would hardly be the end of intrigue, fraudulent claims, and dissension, which have continued to this day, but at least the Indians were given some degree of protection by declaring their lands inalienable except by assent of their council with approval of the President.

In 1875 an agent arrived from Washington to supervise their affairs. He found the Cherokee destitute and discouraged, without stock, farming tools, or school, although nearly all could read and write their own language. Just as he was getting started the next year, the agency was discontinued.

Thomas, meanwhile, languished in confusion. Directly after the death of his wife in 1877 he grew so deranged that he had to be returned to the hospital at Raleigh. For much of the remaining fourteen years of his life, he lived in the shadow-world beyond the brink of rationality, ranging in mood from excitability to deep melancholia, worrying for fear he would starve to death, writing letters all over the country about Indians, railroads, and his health.

Yet when Mooney visited him in the new state hospital at Morganton before the final hour in 1893, he observed occasions when Thomas would flash the old spirit, with an exact memory and the clear-cut statement of a man of affairs. From interviews in the lucid hours, Mooney concluded that, "To Colonel William Holland Thomas the East Cherokee of today owe their existence as a people."

Then he would lapse into periods when the Cherokee language dwelt more strongly in his mind than his mother tongue. He was again Little Will, Yonaguska's favorite, who found the whole world waiting for him in the Smokies and for a little while held the world in his hand.

XI

Mooney as More than Footnote

James D. Mooney came to the Smokies for the first time in 1887 in order to collect plants. His purpose was not the same, however, as that of the naturalist William Bartram a century before him. Mooney had been sent out by his mentor and chief, James Wesley Powell, Director of the Bureau of American Ethnology, to study the flora of the hills as employed by the Indians for their food and medicines.

Mooney did this, learning plant names, uses, methods of preparation, collecting and labeling over five hundred specimens, which now repose in the herbarium of the Smithsonian Institution. But he determined on this trip, and others the following two summers, that medicine was the subordinate part of an ageless ritual, the totality of which was closely guarded, known only by the medicine men, or shamans, also called conjurers or "conjuremen." He unlocked the door to the secret store-house of prayers, sacred songs, and formulas relating not solely to medical treatment but to all of human existence, love and war, hunting and fishing, self-protection, witchcraft, and the ancient ball-play. His discovery Major Powell considered unique in the history of scientific investigation, "forming a complete exposition of an aboriginal religion as set forth by its priests in their own language."

As a pragmatist and passionate democrat (who was really a misplaced Irish Revolutionary), Mooney accomplished more than this. He stands as one of the two most significant personalities sent to the Smokies by the Government in Washington, the other being Arno B. Cammerer, of the National Park Service. Above all other men, red or white, Mooney secured for the Cherokee their place of dignity in the books of history. With his classic work, called "Myths of the Cherokee," a 548-page segment of the *Nineteenth Annual Report of the Bureau of American Ethnology,* published in 1900, he became—and still remains—the foremost biographer of the Indian nation. Despite the title, he covered, in addition to mythology, the full span of Cherokee history in a bold and literary fashion that one hardly expects to find contained in an official report. This work is the standard reliable reference, accounting for thousands of footnotes in all other major books dealing with the Cherokee and their relationships with whites.

Mooney was born to his life's career. He was an Irishman, not a Scotch-Irish, but the son of parents who emigrated from Meath, capital of the ancient Tara, land of paganism and druids and clans, to Richmond, Indiana. An Irishman he was always, who studied Gaelic, organized a chapter of the Land League in Indiana when he was eighteen, and was the first president of Gaelic Society of Washington when it was founded in 1907—two years after the Sinn Fein in the old land. He also had the passion, stubbornness, and sentimentality of an Irishman. "When once he reached a conclusion he maintained it with unfaltering courage," wrote Dr. John Swanton, of the Bureau of American Ethnology, following Mooney's death in 1921, "and clung to it with a tenacity which not infrequently seemed to his friends to be carried to extremes." Nevertheless, added Dr. Swanton, "Beneath all was an intense emotional attitude which was part of himself and was the secret both of his success as an ethnologist and his influence as a man. As for his seeming extremism, or obduracy, it was oftenest in evidence in defense of a subjugated race or an oppressed class, for which the circumstances of his ancestry were no doubt largely responsible."

As a Hoosier boy of nineteen in 1880, having been through school, and a teacher for two semesters, Mooney joined the local newspaper, the *Richmond Paladium,* as printer and reporter. But his main energies were given to reading about Indians and to self-training in ethnology; even in this time he began compiling a detailed list of all Indian tribal names, which later figured in the preparation of the well-known *Handbook of American Indians.*

The truth is that Mooney was dreaming of a voyage to the Amazon and Brazil to study the aboriginals of the deep jungles, but in 1885 he encountered Major Powell in Washington; Powell, that formidable American geologist-explorer, who had led the exciting expedition down the waters of the Green and Colorado rivers in 1869, and then came East to establish the Bureau of Ethnology as a unit of the Smithsonian. They were mutually impressed. Said Powell to Mooney: Why study the primitives of South America when we know so little about our own, whose ancient fabrics are daily disappearing? Thus Mooney began his monumental work of thirty-six years until his death, titled only as

"Ethnologist." He would become the leading authority not only on the Cherokee, but the Kiowa and the entire Plains area, would range the Southwest, exploring pueblo ruins and the living tribes, follow the course of shattered Mexican tribes across the border into Mexico, observe and interpret the Tarahumari Indians in the mountain fastness of Chihuahua performing ceremonial rites with the narcotic peyote. When he died he was recognized by his colleagues at the Smithsonian as the greatest in the field, in a resolution of mourning and tribute that declared his research "unsurpassed, if equaled, by that of any other scholar."

Before him, Charles C. Royce, while working on a historical atlas of Indian affairs, had produced a study, "The Cherokee Nation of Indians," which appeared as part of the Bureau's *Fifth Annual Report* in 1887. Royce detailed all treaties and cessions of land from the colonial period down through the Removal and covered the legal case of the Indians *vs.* Thomas, accompanying the text with substantial maps to illustrate the course of history down to 1884. Mooney went on from that point, with his passion for research, reporting, and for the oppressed peoples, talking with survivors of the Civil War and the Thomas Legion, of the Removal; talking with patriarchs like John Ax, born about 1800, who spoke no English but remembered the stories of his fathers. From the Smokies he traveled to Cheoah in Graham County, into Georgia, South Carolina, Tennessee, and Alabama, interviewing old traders and old settlers, locating burial mounds, peaks, coves, and river bends, all the while piecing together the Cherokee story in the Appalachians.

Through good fortune he made his quarters in Cherokee at the home of Nimrod Jarrett Smith, Tsa'ladihi', a veteran of the Thomas Legion and chief of the Eastern Band; his principal interpreter was Smith's son-in-law, James Blythe, Diskwa'ni, or Chestnut-bread, a graduate of Maryville College, across the mountain in Tennessee, and the father of Jarrett Blythe, who in the twentieth century was elected to serve as chief longer than any predecessor. Curiously, although Jarrett himself has done much to keep the old language alive by encouraging its use in services and Sunday school at the Macedonia Baptist Church, he once told me his father forbade him to speak Cherokee at home as a child.

In Mooney's time Indian medicine was strongly relied on. Their pharmacopoeia included roots, leaves, herbs, barks of various trees, animal dung, and occasionally human urine (for the strong urea content). Many of the herbs have found a place in the white man's formulary and dispensatory, though not necessarily for the same purposes as the

Indians used them; Mooney, in fact, believed their medical and botanical knowledge had been overrated. There was much symbolism in the cure and treatment of disease, in the use and search of botanical materials. For instance, the venerable Big-witch, or Tsil-e'gwa, the oldest man of the tribe, who died during a grippe epidemic in 1897, would hunt for plants barefoot and when the snow was deep. The Cherokee had faith in his cure for rheumatism, particularly with the use of medicine from the fern, whose tightly coiled young fronds unroll and straighten as the plant develops to full size—suggesting the stimulus for a hunched rheumatic to stand erect. Old and deformed plants, a tree struck by lightning, a plant grotesquely formed with parasitic growth also were believed to hold curative powers. The rattlesnake plantain, a little orchid with net-veined leaves, looked enough like a rattlesnake skin to suggest the name of "rattlesnake master," source of the cure for snakebite. Black cohosh served a similar purpose because its spike of buttonlike leaves resembles an uplifted rattlesnake tail. The tight-sticking burr of certain wild plants provided a signature for love potion boiled from the root—to make the lover remain true to his sweetheart (and may still be administered by some women to their husbands to stimulate manhood). Some plants were eaten by mothers to keep their breasts full for suckling children.

It is now recognized that the power of Indian medicine is primarily psychosomatic, derived from its direction at the entire man, his mind, body, and faith; the natural remedies being enhanced by varied paraphernalia and ritual, which make him believe in the efficacy of the cure and the authority of the practitioner, the shaman, who enters as intermediary between the afflicted patient and the supernatural world, toting with him his medicine or healing bundle, the equivalent of the doctor's little black bag.

So Mooney perceived that medical treatment was always accompanied by certain rituals and words, which were guarded jealously by the shamans even from the tribesmen. These medicine men were like the Celtic druids of old; in their training the candidate for the priesthood had to cultivate a long memory; no formula would be repeated twice for his benefit—he who failed after the first reading was considered unworthy of this high profession. And none would reveal the secrets to Mooney. When one young woman volunteered to write the words used in her prescriptions, the shamans learned and opposed it, and she changed her mind.

Then Mooney met Swimmer, or A'yu'ini, priest, doctor, guardian of tradition, a recognized authority who officiated at the Green Corn Dance, ball-play, and other tribal functions. He was over fifty, a veteran of the Thomas Legion, who spoke no English, though his mind was a storehouse of Indian tradition and the ancient system, and he wore moccasins and turban, carrying a gourd rattle, his badge of authority. Mooney was enchanted with his voice, a pleasure in itself, a recital even to one who understood not a word of the language, but a plaintive recital, which is characteristic of all Cherokee singing, whether the native songs or the Christian hymns. And Mooney hopefully arranged to pay Swimmer for his services—consulting services, as it were—in matters of history, mythology, medicine, and botany.

They began by parrying. Mooney wrote that he was testing Swimmer. Jarrett Blythe told me the same. One day, he said, Mooney and Swimmer were in a room together. The ethnologist announced he would hide a quarter in the room next door and see if Swimmer was able to divine its location. Later, after deep thought, Swimmer shook his head —the coin wasn't in the next room, he said. "Boy has it." Mooney checked the hiding place. The coin was gone, the boy did have it. Apparently Swimmer was testing Mooney, too, leading him on with one little story, then another. After several days, in the presence of several Indians, the shaman related the myth of the Origin of the Bear. The bears, he said, formerly were part of the Cherokee tribe, who decided to leave their kindred and take up their abode in the forest. Their friends followed, trying to persuade them to remain; but the bears, or Ani-Tsa, kahi, were determined. Before parting at the edge of the forest, they turned to their old relatives and said, "It is better for you that we should go; but we will teach you songs, and some day, when you are in want of food, come out to the woods, and sing these songs. We shall appear and give you meat." Their friends, after learning several songs, started back to their homes. They turned for one last look but saw only a number of bears disappearing into the woodland. The songs which they learned, concluded Swimmer, are sung yet to attract the bears.

"Do you know these songs?" asked Mooney, through his interpreter.

"Yes," replied Swimmer. But he made an excuse not to sing them and fell silent. The interpreter asked again. Swimmer demurred. It was useless, the interpreter told Mooney, to press further in the presence of others. They could try another day.

Now that Mooney had the sense of his objective, he tried another approach at the next meeting. He appealed to Swimmer's fairness. It was unfair to furnish incomplete information when he was being paid to tell all he knew; if this continued, Mooney would have to employ someone else.

"I am willing to tell anything in regard to stories and customs," conceded Swimmer, "but these songs are part of my secret knowledge. They command a high price from the hunters. Sometimes they pay as much as five dollars for a single song, because you can't kill bear or deer without them."

Mooney, who regarded Swimmer as a true and honorable aboriginal antiquarian, turned to his Cherokee patriotism. "The only object in asking about the songs," he explained, "is to put them on record to preserve them. When you and the half dozen old men of the tribe are dead, the world will be unaware of how much the Cherokee knew."

Swimmer was reflective. "A great many similar songs have been sent to Washington by medicine men of other tribes," Mooney added—it was the blow that struck the shaman's vanity.

"I know as many as any of them. I will give all the information in my possession, so that others may judge who knew the most. But these secret matters must be heard by no one else but the interpreter, and should not be discussed when other Indians are present."

His fellow medicine men suspected or learned, or divined, of Swimmer's intention to divulge the secrets. They tried to dissuade him. That failing, they denounced him with charges of dishonesty and peddling inaccurate information. They warned other Indians that Swimmer would surrender treasured secrets to be locked up in Washington, where the Cherokee no longer would have access to them.

Swimmer grew restive under the insinuations of his rivals. Above all, his sensibility was hurt at the suggestion of fraud and one day he came to Mooney, producing a book from under his ragged jacket; a small notebook, of about 240 pages, originally obtained from a white man. It was about half filled with writing in the Cherokee characters. "Look at that now," he crowed, "and see if I don't know something."

The little book was the answer to Mooney's prayer. It was a combination of songbook-ceremonial-and-pharmacopoeia. In its pages were prescriptions for chills, rheumatism, frostbite, wounds, bad dreams. Here too were love charms to gain the affection of a woman; also to cause her to hate a detested rival. Prayers to make the corn grow; to frighten away storms. Black magic to drive off witches. Prayers for long life, for safety among strangers, for acquiring influence in council, success in the ball-play. Prayers to the Long Man, the Ancient White, the Great Whirlwind, Yellow Rattlesnake, to a hundred other gods of the Cherokee pantheon.

Mooney was overcome, so astonished at the fullness of the revelation that it took several minutes for him to recover. "Do other shamans have such books?" he asked.

"Yes, we all have them."

A new bargain was struck. Mooney was to purchase the original— now in the files of the Bureau of American Ethnology—and Swimmer would be given another in which to copy the formulas for himself. This breakthrough represented only the beginning; it now became possible for Mooney to collect papers from others. Some had been written so long ago that the ink was almost faded from the paper. Some were in pencil, the characters blurred, almost illegible, or on scraps of paper of all sizes and shapes. Some consisted simply of the prayers, with no headings to show their purpose. All told, as Major Powell later reported, Mooney acquired all the material in the possession of the tribe, formulas numbering about six hundred, prayers and sacred songs, myths of cosmogony, birds, animals, insects, explanations of ceremonies, directions for medical treatment and the underlying theories. It was the religion of the Cherokee as it existed before contamination by contact with the whites, and yet preserved through the invention of the Sequoyah written language. Mooney engaged an alert nineteen-year-old, Will West Long (later a patriarch of the tribe), who was acquainted with English; together they set down the formulas and songs in English.

Mooney returned the following summer, collecting new linguistic materials, observing the ceremonies associated with dancing, conjuring, scratching of the body for purification of the spirit, using a camera to picture the ball-play. This ancient game, once used by entire villages to settle clan arguments, as he saw it, consisted of two teams playing with a walnut-sized ball and wooden rackets, the object being to carry or throw the ball between the goal a dozen times, without time limit, time out, or substitutions. The rule was that anything goes—biting, choking, banging each other on the head with the rackets—while spectators bet feverishly, their clothing, horses, money, sometimes everything they owned.

Jarrett Blythe told me that Mooney behaved as though he believed in the ancient religion, recalling his fervor during a visit in 1914 in the course of "going to water" (being ritually washed in a flowing stream) before the ball-play. This could be. Mooney was not only respectful of the Indian cultural forms, but defended the Indians from the belief they had no religion save meaningless mummeries of the medicine man. He identified the Cherokee as a polytheist, showing that Bartram must have been wrong when he spoke of the single Great Spirit. The Cherokee had no Great Spirit, no happy hunting ground, no heaven, no hell. Consequently, death held no terror; he awaited the inevitable end without anxiety over the future.

"The Indian is essentially religious and contemplative," concluded Mooney. "It might almost be said that every act of his life is determined by his religious belief. It matters not that some may call this superstition. The difference is only relative. The religion of today has developed from the cruder superstitions of yesterday, and Christianity itself is but an outgrowth and enlargement of the beliefs and ceremonials which have been preserved by the Indians in their more ancient form. When we are willing to admit that the Indian has a religion which he holds sacred, even though it be different from our own, then we can admire the consistency of the theory, the particularity of the ceremonial, and the beauty of the expression. So far from being a jumble of crudities, there is a wonderful completeness about the whole system which is not surpassed even by the ceremonial religions of the East."

Mooney wrote at the turn of the century that the Indian day was nearly spent, though older people still clung to the ancient rites and sacred traditions. A stranger could rarely distinguish an Indian's cabin or cove farm from that of a white mountaineer. The old crafts appeared to be vanishing; with the death of the aged woman Wadi'yahi, Mooney said the art of making double-walled baskets was gone; Kata'lsta, the daughter of Yonaguska, he called the last conservator of the potter's art.

Yet, these many years later, one must wonder. The double-weave basketry did not die. In recent years a slender, soft-spoken, but extremely determined Indian named Lottie Stamper struggled to master the craft, then undertook to teach it to others, showing them how to collect their own materials—river cane, split oak, and honeysuckle vine, gathered early in the year before the snakes awake in the woods—and how to use roots and leaves for dyes. As part of the program of the local Indian Service homemaking department, the use of old native vegetable dyes was revived. Consequently, Cherokee women once again make fine double-weave baskets as did their mothers' mothers. Nor did the potter's art perish. Old patterns have been reborn, based on researches at the University of Tennessee and a private collection at Asheville. In the same period, hand spinning and weaving, which had almost been abandoned, were revived through the interest of progressive reservation superintendents, notably Joe Jennings.

"Predictions as to the future complete dissolution of the Cherokee tradition may have been premature." So wrote Dr. William H. Gilbert, Jr., of the Library of Congress, in 1956. A first-class scholar on the Cherokee, who approached his subject with the same depth of appreciation as Mooney, Dr. Gilbert cited in particular the semi-isolated section known as Big Cove, which lies under the high Smoky peaks on the Raven Fork, above the confluence with the Straight Fork of the Lufty River.

Half a dozen years after Dr. Gilbert's report, I made my own way into Big Cove. The beliefs or practices relating to medicine still endured. So did conjuring—although one would-be "conjureman" disgraced his ancient art by hauling more moonshine than medicine in his little black bag.

But John Swaney, seventy-eight years of age, the oldest man in the Cove, part Irish and part Indian, who was a boy when Mooney came to the reservation, told me simply, "The Indian doctor takes up where the white doctor leaves off." He recalled a story of forty years ago, when his mother was paralyzed with a stroke. An Indian Service doctor came to see her, and so did one from the Ravensford Logging Company. Both gave up. "She will fly before she will walk," said the lumber company doctor. John went to consult an Indian medicine man. He performed a ceremony called "rolling the beads" to determine if he could help. He could not; then he rolled the beads, or stones, again to divine if another doctor could treat the patient. He sent John to a medicine man in Soco. This one went to a stream and conjured alone for half an hour. "It will be slow," he said at last in Cherokee. "If you had come at the start, it would have been easier. But she will get well." Then he came to the little frame house in Big Cove to see John's mother. He sent everyone else out of the room and stayed with the lady a long time. Within one month she was able to sit up in bed; in three months she walked. The white doctor who had said she would fly first returned and said, "I would give anything to know how the Indian did it."

John's wife Nellie showed me bear oil she had canned, on prescription, for ear aches and tea from the bark of a tree ordered by an Indian doctor to cure her eleven-year-old child's bed wetting—despite the admonition from a white physician to serve "nothing to drink after supper."

Late one night, after much groundwork and negotiation, a young man took me into his little house in Big Cove to tell me of conjuring, which he was endeavoring to master. It was Sunday night, after the Christian church services. These people were earnest goers, followers of two religions as well as two medicines. First, he said, he had to perfect his knowledge of the language, which is fast disappearing among the young. As John Swaney had put it, "I talk to the children in Cherokee, they answer in English." Then my host produced his little notebook, in which he was recording formulas as he learned them.

"Conjuring is a long, long way from dead," he said. "It is different from herbal medicine, which deals with the treatment of physical ills. The Indian goes to the conjureman when he has a psychological or mental problem, or wants the help of witchery in solving some family affair. A young man may go to the conjureman before the ball-play, though he doesn't follow the old taboo of not sleeping with his wife seven days before the game.

"The conjureman rolls the beads, uses rattlesnake fangs, bear claws, and mock turtle claws. The beads are colored, representing points of the compass. The color black stands for the West, and for death. Practices are not as mean as in the old days, when one member of a family standing death watch over another would prolong his own life by killing the dying person through witchery.

"The native wild tobacco, or 'old tobacco,' when fixed by a conjureman in a little black cloth is like a little witch. Tobacco has always been used for driving off evil spirits. 'Putting a man on the road' means breaking up a husband and wife. 'Somebody is trying to witch you' is another expression. If the right sayings are made and you hear a hoot owl screech in winter, this means you got him. Or, when the proper words are said, and four stakes placed at the corners of a new house, if one stake is gone the next morning, this means you got him. The sound of a whippoorwill has meaning, too.

"The conjureman can find lost objects. First, he performs a ceremony over a small stone. Then he asks questions to get a yea or nay. Through trial and error, continually asking questions, he finally determines the location. It works.

"*Ugwili*, the pitcher plant, which draws bugs and insects, is treated by the conjureman and carried and used in many ways: by the chiefing Indians to attract tourists, by young men to attract women, by hunters and fishermen to attract game."

Mooney bore witness to the efficacy of this last use. "The root of the rare plant known as Venus flytrap (*Dionoea*)," he wrote, "which has the remarkable property of catching and digesting insects which alight upon it, is chewed by the fisherman and spit upon the bait that no fish may escape him, and the plant is tied upon the fish trap for the same purpose."

What it all means is that, as Dr. Gilbert wrote, a people firmly rooted in the soil and in their own traditions will never be extirpated but will persist and grow in spite of an adversity which may seem to undermine their existence. I hope that I have not overstated the sinister qualities of black magic. Certainly the white civilization had produced evils of its own, some of the worst of which have been manifest in fomenting the Cherokee adversity. And if I appear to dwell upon the Indian, it is because he is part of the natural blossom arising from the soil of the Smokies, and of all the plants and flowers that Mooney found in the hills he recognized the true glory of the human flower and its part in the environment of creation.

Part Two

THE CIVILIZED AGE

XII

Horace Kephart

So priketh hem Nature in his coráges,—
Thanne longen folk to goon on pilgrimages,
And palmeres for to seeken straunge strondes.
—*Chaucer in the* CANTERBURY TALES

Corks are in bottles and easy to pull,
And that's why little Horace is always full.
—*Kephart in Townsend, Tennessee*
(*on a lodging house wall*)

One day in 1904 Granville Calhoun, the young squire of Hazel Creek, came down from the hills to the railroad depot at Bushnell, a town in the valley of the Little Tennessee River, to meet a fellow named Horace Kephart whom he had never seen before.

Granville told me the story almost a half century later, on an evening after supper while we sat in my room at the Calhoun House, a modest hotel in Bryson City run by his son and daughter. He was, at the age of eighty-seven, a man with a sparkle in his eye and a flood of mountain stories rolling from his lips. Granville was a famous bear hunter of his time (who continued to hunt until he was over eighty) and a credit to the mountain breed in every way.

In 1904 Granville lived at Medlin, a settlement far up Hazel Creek on the Sugar Fork, consisting of his own house and three others, each one a few hundred yards from the next. He ran a little store, mostly on barter, for neighbors scattered through the woods (and bought dried ginseng for the China trade); he also ran the post office, and looked after the nearby mining property under dispute of ownership. He was not born in the Smokies but he was meant for them. The day after his parents brought him from Tennessee to the virgin forests of Hazel Creek late in the winter of 1886 it snowed fourteen inches, but he was out on the creek banks catching fish a foot long, and longer. It was the kind of wonderful world where a boy could bring in one hundred native square-tail trout before breakfast—and that was exactly Granville's idea of boyhood. His father, Joshua, raised bees, grazed cattle, and preached on Sundays, in the "churchhouse" at Bone Valley and once a month in Cades Cove, riding muleback. Joshua's old mule was so gentle and well trained he could mount it from a log. The mule, being sure-footed and smart, is a highly regarded constituent of any mountain community.

Granville waited at the depot with a pair of mules for the stranger Kephart, who was coming out on the train from Sylva. He knew nothing of the man, but had received word from a friend, a mining official, that Kephart wanted to get as far back into the hills as he could. Granville had been requested to show the newcomer around. He had planned to carry the stranger to Hazel Creek in a one-horse rig, but was forced at the last instant to borrow the mules instead.

The train arrived on schedule from Asheville through Waynesville, Sylva, (or "Sylvy"), and Bryson City. Bushnell itself, now under the waters of Fontana Lake, was a hamlet. Granville watched a dozen or so passengers dismount and go their way. Finally only one remained, lounging idly at the end of the depot.

"I'm the man who came to meet you," Granville said to him.

"Oh, I was sort of thinking about getting back on the train," Kephart replied strangely. He was puzzling both in appearance and behavior. He was of medium height—"average flesh, medium all over," as Granville described him—but pale and weak looking, like a very sick man, afflicted with tuberculosis, transfixed with some distant image.

"Can you ride a mule?" Granville asked.

"I'll try anything in the way of horseflesh," Kephart answered; but after struggling into the saddle all he could manage was to clutch the horn, riding with scarcely any control. Granville didn't know what to make of the fellow. Soon, he didn't know how to get him home.

"Pick it up!" he ordered sharply. "Sixteen miles to go!" It did no good at all. Finally Granville stopped; he tied the reins of Kephart's mule to the saddle horn, letting Kephart hang on as best he could, then climbed back on his own mount. With a hickory switch in one hand he kept the other mule moving ahead on the rocky trail, now and then leaning forward and grabbing its tail with the other hand.

When they arrived at the house it was dark. Kephart sat slumped and motionless on the mule. Granville had to carry him and thought he had a dead man on his hands. It was a five-room house Granville occupied with his wife and three small children, much larger than the usual one-room cabin of the mountaineer family. He offered the stranger supper, but all that he would eat was a cracker, with sugar and water. Granville undressed him and put him in bed, then offered a glass of milk. Kephart closed his eyes and turned away.

"You need a stimulant," said Granville, pouring a half glass of wild strawberry wine mixed with a little sugar. Now Smoky Mountain wine is reputed to awaken the dead and delight the angels; besides, Kephart's nostrils were attuned to the smell of such medicine, and stronger. His hand shook reaching for the glass. "If it helps, I'll give ye a little more," said Granville encouragingly and hopefully. Kephart downed the wine in three gulps and held out the glass. His eyes brightened; for the first time he seemed more alive than dead; then he fell away to sleep.

In an hour Granville woke him with a glass of milk, but Kephart pointed a finger beyond the milk, silently pleading for more wine. "No, you try this sweet milk," insisted Granville.

So it went for three weeks, Granville spoon-feeding Kephart, first milk, then bread and butter and fish from the stream, while Kephart arose very slowly from his torpor and tremens, the long hangover, the flight away from himself and the world he knew before.

Then he entered a new world where he found his place, on the Little Fork of Sugar Fork of Hazel Creek, where his life became the life of the mountain people and he their chronicler as no one before or since. Curiously, he arrived in the same period as the loggers and when the movement for a national park was getting underway. He devoted himself unselfishly to preserving this wilderness where he exercised the freedom of his soul, and to the cause of the park. He became a famous writer in his day, sometimes called the "Dean of American Campers" or the "Grand Old Man of the Campfire and Long Trail". When he died he was mourned by outdoor enthusiasts all over America. His classic *Camping and Woodcraft* still stands unchallenged for guidance on how to live and travel far from the beaten path and haunts of men.

Horace Souers Kephart, a lonely creature of this earth, was cut from much the same cloth as Francis Parkman. He was inspired and influenced by Parkman; and when that frontier historian died in 1893, Kephart was deeply engaged in building a collection of western Americana at the St. Louis Mercantile Library, the oldest library west of the Mississippi. He knew Parkman's breath-taking description of man against nature on the Oregon Trail at mid-century. Parkman, the Boston Brahmin, son of a clergyman, was devoted to the cult of contact and combat with nature. Kephart, too, was the son of a clergyman, keen for history and the wilderness, but where Parkman had to fight physical ills, near blindness and neurosis, Kephart had to fight addiction to the bottle.

Kephart, the librarian, in the course of tracing diaries and other records of participants in the saga of the West, was saddened to discover that hardly any of them wrote well. There was only one Parkman, who could clothe the bones of history with the flesh of vital description. "With the exception of his *Oregon Trail*," wrote Kephart, "it is most unfortunate that there exists in American literature no intimate and vivid account of the western hunters and trappers by one who has shared their camps and accompanied them on trail and warpath. It is one thing to describe events; it is another to make the actors in those events live and speak in the reader's presence."

He was anxious to pick up the thread of history and historical writing from Parkman and Theodore Roosevelt and pursue "the winning of the West" on to the last frontier. In the 1890s he was already an authority on early American rifles, contributing articles to the *Magazine of American History* and *Shooting and Fishing*. He was the editor of *Hunting in the Yellowstone*, a new edition of *The Great Divide: Travels in the Upper Yellowstone in the Summer of 1874*, by the Earl of Dunraven. He owned a Deckhard rifle, known for its precision and distance of firing range, the kind that most of the backwoods soldiers had carried in the Revolutionary victory at King's Mountain, and also a Hawken, the most noted pre-Civil War muzzle-loading single shot, the rifle of the old mountain men, trappers, explorers, and Indian fighters.

Kephart reflected much later that his special passion for mountains may have been inherited from Swiss ancestors, who were among the early pre-Revolutionary settlers west of the Susquehanna River. He was born at East Salem, Pennsylvania, in 1862, but five years later his father, the Reverend Isaiah Lafayette Kephart of the United Brethren Church, took the family to Jefferson, Iowa, a frontier village set in a prairie wilderness. The elk and buffalo had left, but their bleached skulls and antlers were strewn over the sea of grass. Indians often passed the Kephart house, not always in a friendly mood. Game birds of every description swarmed overhead in myriads and Kephart even as a small boy became a crack shot.

In 1876 the family returned to Pennsylvania and Kephart began his training for scholarship. He was graduated from Lebanon Valley College (1879), then moved to Boston University for a year, and to Cornell for three years, followed by travels with his professor, Willard Fiske, in Europe. From 1886 to 1890, before going to St. Louis, he was an assistant in the Yale University Library, while studying and researching frontier history and beginning to write for magazines. In 1887 he married an Ithaca sweetheart, Laura White Mack; they had two sons and four daughters, all of whom attended Cornell, under trying circumstances, considering they were deserted by their father.

As a parent he had his good points. On Sundays in St. Louis he would take the family to the German *Schützenverein* rifle range, shooting heavy rifles from sand-bag sights and for his children rigging a telescopic sight on a little .22 caliber rifle. He would bring home Indian headdresses, war clubs, and buffalo-hide shields, elements of the collection on the Plains Indians he was developing at the Mercantile Library. Once he found his son George playing with ancient bow and arrows; but instead of scolding the boy he patiently explained the historic value of the pieces.

But he couldn't stand confinement or the responsibility of raising a family. He was too self-centered, too difficult to live with, poring over maps and dreaming of the frontier. He preferred solitary camping in the Ozarks, where he could spend his time working on tents and camping devices. "She despised me to go on camping trips or to go shooting. She gave me hail-come for not wanting to go to hen clubs," was how Granville Calhoun told me Kephart had expressed his differences with his wife.

Then in 1904, he was caught on the street in the midst of the St. Louis hurricane, a traumatic experience during which he clung for his life to a lamppost while people and debris were blown past him. Together with his drinking, the hurricane shattered his strength and his nerves. And so he came to the Smokies, as sometimes has been stated, "to recuperate his health and to enjoy the thrills of singlehanded adventure in a wild country."

"Knowing nobody who had ever been here," wrote Kephart later, "I took a topographic map and picked out on it, by means of the contour lines and the blank spaces showing no settlement, what seemed to be the wildest part of this region; and there I went." He arrived by train at Sylva, where he stayed at a hotel and met the mining man who contacted Granville Calhoun in his behalf.

Kephart, in *Our Southern Highlanders*, wrote that before his departure from St. Louis, "The most diligent research failed to discover so much as a magazine article, written within this generation, that described the land and its people. Nay, there was not even a novel or a story that showed intimate local knowledge. Had I been going to Teneriffe or Timbuctu, the libraries would have furnished information a-plenty; but about this housetop of eastern America they were strangely silent; it was *terra incognita*."

He was endowed with an imaginative touch and therefore may be excused, or at least understood, for overdrawing the picture. As a librarian, he probably was acquainted with the stories of Constance Fenimore Woolson, who described the mountain people she met around Asheville and on her wagon journey through the Smokies, and surely with the novels of Charles Egbert Craddock—the pen name of Mary N. Murfree—including *In the Tennessee Mountains* and *The Prophet of the Great Smoky Mountains*. Miss Murfree in some respects was the precursor of Kephart; she was drawn to the mountain folk when she heard others ridicule their outlandish manner of speech and their barbarous ways, and some of her fictional characters—moonshiner, revenue spy, preacher, hunter, farmer with bull-tongued plow—were described by him as the real people among whom he lived.

Besides, he also had knowledge of the momentous document published in 1902 by the Federal Government, a 200-page book opening with a message from President Theodore Roosevelt and followed by a report of the Secretary of Agriculture on the forests, rivers, and mountains of southern Appalachia. This document was the keystone in the conservation movement in the East, affording the philosophy and factual foundation for the Weeks Law of 1911, under which national forests were established in the eastern mountains, and delineating the value of the Great Smokies. Kephart did comment, "In the dustiest of rooms of a great library where 'pub. docs.' are stored, I unearthed a Government report on forestry that gave, at last, a clear idea of the lay of the land."

For the first three years, after he left Granville's place, Kephart lived on the site of an unworked copper mine, the Adams Mine, on the Little Fork of Sugar Fork. His home was a log house, fourteen feet square, formerly occupied by a blacksmith, with a tent attached to the side, handily located for experimentation. At first Granville went to see him every few days; then Kephart became well enough to walk down to the post office and take his place in the community. The first three years he was drunk only once, though half a dozen 200-gallon stills were in walking distance and the price was only $2.00 a gallon—$1.50 if you collected the merchandise at the still.

It was a strange environment, the frontier of time for which he'd been looking, where old legends were daily realities of the pioneer farmers, herdsmen and hunters, trappers and traders, preachers, outlaws and Indians. As he wrote, it was almost as though he had been carried back, asleep, and had awakened in the eighteenth century, to meet Daniel Boone and his kith in flesh and blood. The degree to which he was reverting to the primitive came home one day when a mountain dowager, finding Will Tahlahlah giving him a lesson in Cherokee, remarked sourly, "You needn't teach him anything; he's more an Indian than you are."

He came as a "furriner" but made himself useful and welcome in the mountain community. Now and again he was pressed into service as the nearest thing to a doctor. In the group that gathered at mail time at Granville's store (the mail came up daily by rider, serving four other settlements along the way) he gave out the news, deciphered letters for men who couldn't read, and when Granville was away registered letters for himself or anyone else. Once, while walking the two miles down to the post office for a check he'd been expecting, a hen crossed his trail and he shot it for supper. Next day he encountered a small boy in the same place looking for a stray hen. "Here," said Kephart, extending some change to the lad, "go buy a new hen."

Throughout summer and autumn he cooked outdoors; he did his own washing, of course. Later on some of his cronies or a crank or two would say, "Kep wrote a book on woods cookin' but nobody ever caught him cookin'." But anyone who had been with him—and I have talked with those who have—vow that he was indeed the maestro of the camp-fire. His days in those early years were full, particularly as he went deep into mountain research. He took photographs of the churchhouse, schoolhouse, post office, the people. He loved to listen to mountain yarns and would tell a joke to get them started. In a soapbox in his cabin he constructed a library and filled it with loose-leaf notebooks—"indexing," as Granville said, on mountain life, the mountain vernacular, plants and animals, rifles, descriptions of Deep Creek, Hazel Creek, and Bryson City. Later he would take his studies as far as the Historical Commission archives in Raleigh and the Library of Congress in Washington. Unfortunately, he degraded himself and his talent in his more drunken times with sloppy work for so-called adventure magazines, but at his best he was a genuine scholar, worthy of his past studies at the universities and of his subjects in the hills.

In those three years in the forest, though days seldom were lonesome, the nights were another matter. When supper was over and darkness closed over his hermitage, and the owls called to the night creatures, and the trees creaked, and all sounds, whether the dry leaves rustling in the wind or a pine cone falling on a dead log, were magnified, and even the stillness was heard, he asked himself why he had deserted his family and fled so far.

More to his credit, he exercised with writing: about camping and woodcraft, of course, which became the title of a series in *Field and Stream*, and of his first book, published in 1906. Other articles appearing later in *Sports Afield, Recreation, Forest and Stream* (which later merged with *Field and Stream*), and *Outing* were incorporated in subsequent editions. Inside of ten years the little book went through seven editions, grew to 900 pages, and was recognized as the standard work on the subject. It would endure long after Kephart's passing—with its twentieth printing in 1960. That was when the publishing house approached his heirs, the six children, who were still drawing a small royalty from the sales, with a proposition to engage a new writer to revise and update the text. Certainly it had grown old-fashioned in the age of snazzy sleeping bags, instant campfires, powdered dinners, and lightweight tenting gear. A revision of *Camping and Woodcraft* undoubtedly would have appealed to an entirely new market and brought the Kepharts more money. They decided, however, it was the writing style of their father as well as the substance that made the book; they hadn't lived with him since 1908 (when he came to Ithaca for a few months of trial reconciliation that didn't take); but they probably understood him better than he did himself, never bore him ill will, and appreciated the letters he would write two or three times a year. In declining the publisher's offer they saved the book as their father had written it, an American classic on the outdoors.

Camping and Woodcraft is filled with adventure; historical references to Jim Bridger, Kit Carson, Lewis and Clark; the tepee-building techniques of the Indians; personal recollections of the author's experiences; good humor about the whiskey- and gin-drinking habits of mosquitoes; good writing about cave exploring, bee hunting, and skunks in the woods; and practical guidance about living off the land. It was the camper's bible, and the expression of his philosophy and way of life.

"First, and above all," he instructed, "be plain in the woods. In a far way you are emulating those grim heroes of the past who made the white man's trail across this continent. We seek the woods to escape civilization for a time, and all that suggests it. Let us sometimes broil our venison on a sharpened stick and serve it on a sheet of bark. It tastes better. It gets us closer to Nature, and closer to those good old times when every American was considered 'a man for a' that' if he proved it in a manful way. . . . It is one of the blessings of wilderness life that it shows us how few things we need in order to be perfectly happy.

"Let me not be misunderstood as counseling anybody to 'rough it' by sleeping on the bare ground and eating nothing but hardtack and bacon. Only a tenderfoot will parade a scorn of comfort and a taste for useless hardships. As 'Nessmuk' says: 'We do not go to the woods to rough it; we go to smooth it—we get it rough enough in town. But let us live the simple, natural life in the woods, and leave all the frills behind.'"

Although the forest, streams, and mountains had attracted him at first, he became increasingly absorbed in the study of his human associates, the southern highlanders. He traveled in other parts of the Appalachians, eastern Kentucky, Tennessee, and northern Georgia, and studied statistics of the mountain counties. "The typical southern highlanders," he concluded, "were not the relatively few townsmen and prosperous valley farmers of the Appalachian region, but the great multitude of little farmers living up the branches and on the steep hillsides, back from the main highways, and generally far from railroads. These, the real mountaineers, were what interested me; and so I wrote them up."

Thus, in 1913 *Our Southern Highlanders* appeared and sold 10,000 copies in the first edition. It has since gone through revisions of Kephart's own doing and seven printings by 1957. His book was peopled not with hillbilly caricatures, but the originals themselves—whom he collected and "indexed," yet happily without reducing them to clinical specimens. For instance, he often went hunting with Granville and others, not necessarily to hunt but to observe and listen. Mostly he would stay in camp, usually drinking tea rather than whiskey. Granville told me he carried the makings of black Japanese tea. Once he offered some to a hunting companion, poured it in a cup, and passed it around the fire. The man sipped, smacked his lips, and sipped again.

"How do you like it?" asked Kephart.

"Not much," the hunter answered, "it tastes yaller."

Around such a campfire, after the inevitable tall talk of bear dogs had run its course, the group discovered there was a musical talent, of a sort, in Little John Cable. He cut a pigeonwing, wrote Kephart in *Highlanders*, twirled around with an imaginary banjo, and sang in a quaint minor:

> Did you *ever* see the devil,
> With his *pitchfork* and ladle,
> And his *old* iron shovel,
> And his old gourd head?
> O, I *will* go to meetin',
> And I *will* go to meetin',
> Yes, I *will* go to meetin'.

"Other songs followed with utter irrelevance—mere snatches from 'ballets' composed, mainly, by the mountaineers themselves, though some dated back to a long-forgotten age when the British ancestors of these Carolina woodsmen were battling with lance and long-bow."

His ear was tuned to the mountain vernacular, a vigorous, colorful, and expressive dialect, spanning a remarkable range for people who could barely read or write. Much has been made of words or expressions carried over from old English, undoubtedly with some justification—as in *ax* for ask, as found in Chaucer; *fotch* for fetch; *ye* for you; *hit* for it; *poke* for bag; *antic* for a comical person; *donna* for a sweetheart; the word *spend* as in "I'd rather not spend my opinion," and the word *use* for inhabit as in the bear hunter's explanation, "Day afore to hunt we usually go up to find where the bears are a-using." But essentially this is an American mountain language, born of frontier isolation, matured with lyric softness and utility of words; of yon long and yan way, dusky dark, dogs bold and severe, the preacher-parson, fotched-on furriner, granny-woman, neighbor-people, toothdentist, playpurties; of words like *heer'd* and *afeard*, *mought* for might, *gwine* or a' goin' for going, *hyur* for here, to say nothing of *right smart, right pert, purty*, and *purtiest*. It is not easy for an outsider to comprehend the old-timers, or some of the "young 'uns" either, but these dialects are so localized that I suspect a moonshiner from Cosby, on the Tennessee side, would have some little difficulty communicating with his counterpart across the mountains at Balsam Grove in North Carolina. Kephart himself was the expert on the Deep Creek, Hazel Creek, and Bryson City vernacular.

"In every settlement," he wrote, "there is somebody who makes a pleasure of gathering and spreading news. Such a one we had—a happy-go-lucky fellow from whom, they said, 'you can hear the news jinglin' afore he comes within gunshot.' It amused me to record the many ways he had of announcing his mission by indirection. Here is the list:

> 'I'm jes' broguin' about.'
> 'Yes, I'm jest cooterin' around.'
> 'I'm santerin' about.'
> 'Oh, I'm jes' prodjectin' around.'
> 'Jist traffickin' about.'
> 'No, I ain't workin' none—jest spuddin' around.'
> 'Me? I'm jes' shacklin' around.'
> 'Yea, la! I'm jist loaferin' about.'

"And yet one hears that our mountaineers have a limited vocabulary."

Kephart had no urge to poke fun at his neighbors, nor to exploit them. Money was meaningless to him—so his friends told me, and in his little autobiography he wrote, "I have said nothing about how much money I have made, and lost. But can you not guess how much I care for money, beyond what is needed for books and guns and fishing tackle?"

After three years on Sugar Fork he had moved to Bryson City, living at the main hotel, the Cooper House, which Uncle Bil'y Cooper had remodeled in 1890 from a wooden-pegged lodging house visited by wagons and oxcarts. Bryson City, formerly known as Charleston and before that as Bears Town, was an isolated little place, over two hours on a horse from Cherokee. Once it had been part of the Love family land empire, though it owed its name to Colonel Thad Bryson, who laid out the town lots. D. K. (Kimsey) Collins, son of Robert Collins, the old guide of Professor Arnold Guyot, was a major merchant, owning a store in Bryson City and another in Cherokee; he was also president of the new Bryson City Bank, organized in June 1904. Since 1871 the town was the county seat of the newly formed Swain County. Thus, the Cooper House was the rendezvous of all manner of men, timber cruisers, traveling salesmen, United States marshals, and during court week it was not uncommon to see a murderer handcuffed at the dinner table. As a celebrity, Kephart became one of the attractions; the Cooper House was called Kephart Tavern, and tourists came to see the author in the flesh. But fame was no more his style than fortune. He was unostentatious and reticent; though a well-mannered and well-dressed man-about-town, often when a stranger came in the front door of the Cooper House he would head out the rear door. And in summer, the time for tourists and autograph seekers, he would disappear altogether into the hills.

He fished alone and usually camped alone. A favorite spot was the Bryson Place, eight miles up Deep Creek from the campground, an old cabin site of the Bryson family deep in the woods between Thomas Divide and Noland Divide. He experimented with guns, though more interested in accuracy and bullet design than in killing anything much larger than a squirrel. In the old days mountain men made their own molds out of soapstone, then cast bullets from lead and tin, the lead taken from railroad scrap; and they'd recover their bullets in target practice and cast them over again. So Kephart, the crack rifleman, author of *Sporting Firearms* and countless magazine articles on the subject, carved his own mold and designed a high-powered rifle bullet for use in what was then the new smokeless powder. It was manufactured by the Union Metallic Cartridge Company (later absorbed by Remington) and was popular for years, though apparently he was content to receive nothing more than free molds and ammunition from the manufacturer.

I visited his old camp at the Bryson Place with ranger Bill Rolen. On the way up Indian Creek Trail a timber rattler slithered out of the brush and Bill killed it, but the rattles kept vibrating after it was dead. The Bryson Place was overgrown with blackberry bushes, holly, dogwood, fern, sassafras, grapevine, and sumac—an owl flew out of the jungle growth heading across tangled dog hobble blossoming with corn-like tassels and through a grove of white pine and hemlock. Set in an old grist mill stone we found a marker:

On this spot
Horace Kephart, Dean of American Campers
and one of the principal founders of the
Great Smoky Mountains National Park
pitched his last permanent camp.
Erected May 30, 1931
by Horace Kephart Troop, Boy Scouts of America
Bryson City, North Carolina

It took a little effort to hike up to the Bryson Place, and then the memorial to Kephart was overgrown. But maybe that's the way he would prefer it, for as he wrote in *Camping and Woodcraft:*

"Your thoroughbred camper likes not the attentions of a landlord, nor will he suffer himself to be rooted to the soil by cares of ownership or lease. It is not possession of the land, but of the landscape, that he enjoys; and as for that, all the wild parts of the earth are his, by a title that carries with it no obligation but that he shall not desecrate nor lay them waste.

"Houses, to such a one, in summer are little better than cages; fences and walls are his abomination; plowed fields are only so many patches of torn and tormented earth. The sleek comeliness of pastures is too prim and artificial, domestic cattle have a meek and ignoble bearing, fields of grain are monotonous to his eyes, which turn for relief to some abandoned old-field, overgrown with thicket, that still harbors some of the shy children of the wild. It is not the clearing but the unfenced wilderness that is the camper's real home. He is brother to that good old friend of mine who in gentle satire of our formal gardens and close-cropped lawns, was wont to say, 'I love the unimproved works of God.' "

Kephart's true love in the Smokies was the wilderness itself. It was an unselfish love. He would say, "I got my health back in these mountains and intend to stay here as long as I live,"—then adding, "and I want them preserved that others may profit as I have."

But he saw the loggers arrive and take over the mountains. The timber was difficult of access, but too good to pass by. On Hazel Creek the land and timber buyers arrived in the 1890s. The earliest cutting by large outside firms was for choice poplar, cucumber tree, and ash. Two splash dams were built, one on Hazel Creek, below the mouth of Walker Creek, the other on Bone Valley Creek, furnishing enough water to float the lighter woods to a log boom on the Little Tennessee at Chilhowee, from where they were towed all the way to a sawmill at Chattanooga. But the real exploitation of the drainage began with the arrival of the W. M. Ritter Lumber Company, which acquired land from 1903 to 1910. Mr. Ritter, president of the firm and a leading lumberman of the South, announced that he had found the largest poplar trees and best oak in his entire experience. He proceeded to construct a new community at the mouth of Hazel Creek, where it flowed into the Little Tennessee, and to name it for himself—a practice not uncommon among lumbermen. Ritter built his own railroad, the Smoky Mountain Railroad, a spur from the Southern carrying freight, lumber, and passengers along Hazel Creek. Four miles above Ritter it led to Proctor, where a double-band sawmill, with capacity of 70,000 board feet a day, began operations in 1909. The traces of the old lumberyard, millpond, cement pump house, and brick dry kiln are still visible, overgrown with vines and kudzu, creeping up the banks and spreading through the branches of trees. And from Proctor, the railroad led to Bone Valley and Sugar Fork, where the principal cutting took place in the 1920s, for sound wormy chestnut, red oak, and high-quality maple. By the time the Ritter Company kissed Hazel Creek good-by in 1926 it had cut 166 million board feet of timber, most of it from virgin hardwoods.

Granville Calhoun moved from Sugar Fork to Proctor and lived there until obliged to move by the park. He built a large house, installed lights and running water (the house continued to stand into the 1960s on its stone and mortar foundations, serving as a national park bunkhouse). As the squire of Hazel Creek, Granville took in boarders, built six miles of railroad for Ritter, did supervisory work for the Hazel Creek Mining Company and for the Stikeleather Lumber Company, which later logged the upper reaches above Bone Valley. In 1918, when he took the official census—and who else would take it but Granville Calhoun?—there were 2000 persons along Hazel Creek, workers in the mill, on the railroad, strangers. It was a new world, though not a better one. It was the day of destructive logging, when large companies, desperate for short-term profit, desecrated the land.

"It's spoiling the country," Kephart said one day to Granville, while they were tramping together to a herder's cabin on Siler Meadows. Cattle grazed along the crest of Smoky. It was near sunset, the quiet, magic hour. The pastoral stillness was broken by a logging railroad whistle whining upward from the Little River. They could see the lights flicker in the logging camp at Townsend and even in distant Knoxville. Kephart climbed on a rocky crag—a "view rock"—and watched the purplish twilight settling over the ridges into the misty valleys. To the east it was the still wilderness he had come to absorb; had he followed the trail of Parkman across the Continental Divide he could never have found anything more primeval or sublime.

"The Government should take it over," he said, "and keep it as a national park."

It was the first time Granville heard those two words, "national park." He did not understand them at all. It was his heartland Kephart was suggesting be administered by some remote authority. Granville had his doubts, and asked questions.

"What is a national park?" he asked.

"Would they let us stay?"

"Would they really protect the land?"

"What about fishing?"

"The park would be wonderful for you," Kephart replied. "It would keep the mountains the way you know them. The Government would build trails so you can really travel and see the country across the ridge tops. Fishing? All you want! That's how it is in the national parks out West. But unless we have a national park the lumber companies will destroy the Smoky Mountains."

I am afraid that Kephart did not quite convince Granville Calhoun. The old mountain men would be caught in the middle between the lumbermen and the park movement, although it was Kephart's hope that his old friends would be allowed to stay on Hazel Creek. This no doubt figures in his enthusiasm for the park proposal, and, as on all subjects, he wrote about it from the heart.

"A national park in the mountains of western North Carolina and eastern Tennessee would not duplicate anything in the western parks," he wrote in the *Asheville Times*, July 19, 1925, in an article defining values involved. "The scenery is altogether different from any of them. It is typical of Appalachia at its best. Here stand today, in the Great Smoky Mountains, the last hundred square miles of uncut primeval forest, the most varied and thrifty forest in the world, just as it stood, save for added growth, when Columbus discovered America. It will all be destroyed in ten or fifteen years if the Government does not take it over and preserve it intact so that future generations may see what a genuine forest wilderness is like. . . .

"Certain commercial interests are opposed to the park. One or two large lumber companies own practically all the virgin forest that I have been featuring as one of the chief attractions of this majestic region. They aim to destroy it: to cut down those gigantic trees and cut them into so many board feet of lumber, leaving a desert of stumps and briers in their place. Everyone who has seen the havoc and desolation the lumberman leaves in his wake knows how inexpressibly sad he is when he turns and flees from the sight of it.

"When I first came into the Smokies, the whole region was one of superb forest primeval. I lived for several years in the heart of it. My sylvan studio spread over mountain after mountain, seemingly without end, and it was always clean and fragrant, always vital, growing new shapes of beauty from day to day. The vast trees met overhead like cathedral roofs. I am not a very religious man; but often when standing alone before my Maker in this house not made with hands I bowed my head with reverence and thanked God for His gift of the great forest to one who loved it.

"Not long ago I went to that same place again. It was wrecked, ruined, desecrated, turned into a thousand rubbish heaps, utterly vile and mean.

"Did anyone ever thank God for a lumberman's slashing?"

One can hardly overlook observing the clarity and courage of his expressions. Or, as the *Asheville Times* editorialized the day after his article appeared (and rather boldly, too, on its part, defying the logging giants), "Mr. Kephart knows his mountains. There is no man in this highland region who can write with a larger measure of authority and affection about them. . . . His eloquent appeal should be the textbook of those who are interested in securing a national park for this mountain empire."

Moreover, his concern was not for his own old way of life, but to safeguard a treasure for the nation. "This will probably ruin the old country for me," he wrote his son George after the park was established, "but it will be wonderful for the local people and all who come to see it."

As a man who worked alone and usually camped alone, he made few close friends. One was I. K. Stearns, whose family ran a sawmill in Bryson City. Another was Kelly Bennett, the druggist and Great Smokies enthusiast; Will Wiggins, the timber cruiser, was a card-playing companion at the Cooper House. And then there was George Masa, the short, wiry Japanese photographer of Asheville. Masa had arrived during World War I and became a valet at the Grove Park Inn. Later he opened a photographic studio but became so involved in the Smokies that he neglected his commercial work, sometimes waiting for two days for the right photo effect in the mountains. He tramped the woods with Kephart and with national park officials on their inspection trips and provided photographs to stir public interest in the park.

But there were times when Kephart steered clear of everyone, the periods when he was drunk and lonely—which usually went together. While spending one Christmas at the Cooper House, virtually deserted of cash customers, he and Uncle Billy Cooper were working over a bottle together. "Here we sit," said the infirm Mrs. Cooper to her daughter who had sprained a foot, "two cripples and two fools." When he was well potted, Kephart staggered to his room and stayed for days;

this was his habit, to disappear when drunk, and take no nourishment, almost exactly as when he first met Granville Calhoun. The Coopers' little granddaughter, Helen Angel, carried him buttermilk or tomato juice and crackers, leaving a tray at his door. But he wouldn't come out, or maybe couldn't, until the foggy stupor, loneliness, and remorse wore off.

In 1931 the strange adventure ended. Kephart was killed in an automobile accident while he and a visiting writer were returning to Bryson City in a taxicab from an expedition to his bootlegger. His wife and three of their children came to Bryson City for the funeral.

Kephart has been generally forgotten as an author. And perhaps he should be as far as enduring literary qualities are concerned, though I have tried to indicate his importance as a writer on the outdoors and personally admire his treatment of the southern highlanders. But he figures boldly in any study of the Smokies and his place will last forever. As Secretary of the Interior Ray Lyman Wilbur declared on November 2, 1931, the autumn after Kephart's death, when representatives of North Carolina and Tennessee came to Washington to present the deed for 138,843 acres to be included in the park, "I wish that I could name every one of the men and women who have worked devotedly to see this new national park come into being, but I am sure you will join me in appreciation of the persistent and idealistic interest of Mr. Kephart, who not only knew these mountains and loved the people, but saw in them a great national resource."

One day I went to the cemetery where Kephart is buried, on the hilltop overlooking Bryson City. The caretaker kindly took time out from his work to show me the rock boulder marking Kephart's grave.

The custodian and I fell to talking. For all their reputation of being furtive, secretive, and suspicious, I have found these mountain people surprisingly outgoing and ready conversationalists. This fellow evidently had never been away from the valley of the Little Tennessee, but was a good talker. We got around to politics and international affairs, on which he was well versed.

I was only sorry that he, like most others, knew very little about Horace Kephart.

XIII

The Loggers' Day

Although Horace Kephart and the large logging companies arrived in the Great Smoky Mountains in the same period, their motives and *modus operandi* were somewhat dissimilar. Kephart came to lose himself in the wilderness and in so doing discovered his soul and his place; his only enemy was himself. The lumber companies who came to strip the wilderness and almost succeeded were brash and ruthless strangers. It seems incredible today that 85 per cent of the land within the national park once was exploited by such outside enterprises, but this was indeed the case. They brought lumberjacks, who spoke in the flat accents of the Maine woods and the Great Lakes. They built logging railroads and sawmill towns, scattered in the valleys within and around the limits of what is now the park. And the theme of the loggers' day and the loggers' way was to denude these mountains without mercy. "If your tonnage is too great for a narrow-gauge railroad," so the saying went, "you need a standard gauge. But if it's not large enough for a narrow gauge, you need a mule team. If it isn't large enough for a mule team, get an ox team; if there is not enough for an ox team, then pack it out on your back!"

We are furnished with excellent descriptions of forest conditions and the effect of lumbering in the year 1901, when the large loggers were just beginning to invade the Smokies. In a study of Appalachia, conducted by the Department of Agriculture and transmitted to Congress by President Theodore Roosevelt, two eminent early forestry scholars, H. B. Ayres and W. W. Ashe, investigated the forest cover of 5,400,000 mountain acres from Virginia to Alabama. Only 7.4 per cent, or 303,000 acres, was still in primeval condition—that is, had never been cut or even culled for the choicest timbers. Near railway lines some sections had been robbed of nearly everything of commercial value. The remote areas had been gone over lightly, for walnut and cherry, the rare woods. In between these two extremes, the clearing and culling of a century had made considerable inroads into the Appalachian forests. The woodland connected with farms had been culled and was partially covered with second-growth trees. In many places, where transportation facilities were available, mills were moving into the heart of the mountain region, where much choice timber was being sawed and hauled on wagons to the railroad.

Of all Appalachia, the big forest of the Smokies still stood in its silent grandeur. So far there had been only a nibbling at its edges or a little hole here and there cleared for pasture or a deadening in which to grow corn for the family at the head of a creek. It was an immensely rich timber world containing some of the finest hardwoods that ever stood, plus varied conifers. Ayres and Ashe wrote that the Smokies plus the connecting portion of the Balsams west of Soco Gap contained the largest area of continuous forest with the smallest number of clearings within the total scope of their investigation.

"The broad agricultural valleys of East Tennessee lie against these mountains on the northwest," they wrote, "but elsewhere they are surrounded by a rough country of lower mountains with narrow, intervening agricultural valleys. Less than 10 per cent of this area is cleared. The clearings are few and small, and lie chiefly some miles distant from the crest of the ridge.

"The forests are chiefly of hardwoods, with a large amount of coniferous growth around the higher summits and in the deep, cool hollows. On the drier slopes, and especially on the south sides, oak and chestnut form the greater part of the timber, with some black and yellow pine on the ridges. The timber in the hollows is more varied and the stand is heavier, poplar, birch, linn, and buckeye being associated with the oak and chestnut. The finest and largest bodies of spruce in the southern Appalachians occur here, along the crest of the ridge and the north slope of both the Cataloochee and Smoky mountains. There are about 20,000 acres of spruce and nearly as much hemlock. There is no spruce on the Smoky Mountains southwest of Silers Meadow.

"The forests of the north slope of the Smoky Mountains have been much culled and injured by burning and pasturage. There is yet a great deal of fine timber, however. Fires have done much injury on the south slope, especially to hardwoods, and the growth is often very open on account of the suppression of young trees by burning for a great number of years. The valleys of Cataloochee and Big Creek are heavily timbered, though they have been culled to some extent, and the ridges have often been burned."

The brutal devastation the lumber industry bestowed upon all Appalachia was then in the making. In the same study of 1901, Overton W. Price covered the facts and future prospects of logging, probably as well as any man of his time could have done. Two years earlier he had graduated from the Biltmore Forestry School, the first school of its kind in America, located on the estate of George Washington Vanderbilt near Asheville, where forestry was actually being practiced—the only such place in the southern mountains. His professor there had been Carl Alwin Schenck, the German forestry master; and from Biltmore Price had gone to Washington, where he became the right-hand man of Gifford Pinchot in establishing the new United States Forest Service.

Lumbering, reported Price, already was one of the principal industries of Appalachia and certainly could remain so. Farming necessarily had to be limited because of the rugged terrain and low percentage of arable land. Grazing was hampered by lack of winter forage and temporary life of grass in the lower slopes. But the hardwoods could provide the main resources for future permanent development of western North Carolina and eastern Tennessee. Under systematic, conservative management, the forests would yield a profit and produce a second harvest later to yield another profit. "Not only is there no unfavorable condition in the southern Appalachians which is sufficient to render practical forestry inadvisable as a business measure," wrote Price, "but the opportunity offered for good returns from careful and conservative forest management is a peculiarly favorable one. The forest contains valuable timber trees, which not only command a high price at present, but are rapidly increasing in value for the lack of satisfactory substitutes, notably in the case of Black Walnut, Cherry, Hickory, Yellow Poplar, and White Oak. The transport of timber presents some difficulties as in all mountain countries. These are, however, seldom sufficient to impair seriously the profits from lumbering. Effective protection from fire is practicable without prohibitive expense, while in its rate of growth, readiness of reproduction, and responsiveness to good treatment the forest offers silvicultural opportunities which are seldom excelled in this country."

But, alas, these opportunities were seldom used. The existing supply of timber was being rapidly reduced, wrote Price, while repeated fires and unregulated grazing in many localities hampered the prospect of successful reproduction. He cited the folly of the settler who had built his fence of rails split from prime black walnut for the simple reason the walnut happened to be handier than either oak or pine. As a farmer he girdled many standing trees, so that neither shade nor growing roots would injure his crops. After his trees fell in a few years, he rolled them into heaps and burned them. As a herdsman he turned his cattle and pigs loose in the forest, burning the woodland for the sake of pasturage, known as "greening the grass." In so doing he destroyed the soil fertility, while his browsing stock cut back young trees on their own. When that settler became a lumberman, cutting whatever he could to sell for fuel, fencing, or saw-logs to add to his poor living as a farmer, he was even more destructive. He would cut logs wastefully high on the stump and seldom endeavor to fell trees where they would do the least harm to themselves and to others; the farmer-logger of the hills lacked both capital and knowledge, yet made a fair profit by delivering cherry, black walnut, hickory, and tulip poplar to the nearby markets. His destructiveness, however, was a mere and minor prelude to the havoc wrought by the large lumber company.

Instead of heeding the warnings from Overton Price, Pinchot, the American Forestry Association, and others, the lumberman attacked the Appalachian forest with all dispatch. For the working logger, it was a rough, rugged life. In the early 1900s he received sixty-five to ninety cents a day, in later years a dollar a day, plus lodgings and meals. His bunkhouse was a frame shack, moved about the hills from one site to the next. He packed his own bedroll and blankets, was not permitted to talk at meals in the cookhouse. He worked as long as it was light enough to work, continually facing the threat of accident and loss of life or limb. Despite all the legend and lore, the man with the crosscut saw, the "misery whip," or with pike-pole and peavey on the flumes, was cheap and expendable. Indeed, the only commodity cheaper than human life was land-life. The logging corporation, or syndicate, with roots elsewhere, could hardly care less; for after stripping one woodland and leaving fire in its wake during the glorious "cut-and-get-out" era, it would proceed on its appointed rounds to strip another.

So Overton Price concluded that only remoteness and scattered distribution of merchantable timber saved portions of southern Appalachia from entire destruction. But even as he wrote those words, one railroad was being built up Big Pigeon River in order to exploit the timber in Cataloochee and Big Creek valleys, another railroad was under construction along the Oconaluftee to remove timber from the east prong, and a third would soon be built along the Little River in Tennessee.

The lumber industry today hates to look its own past squarely in the eye. It has learned from many of its mistakes and generally manages timberland with respect for the earth and its future. Yet the sins were needless, especially in the light of experience in Europe, where forests have been cultivated with care and patience for centuries. Here in America, however, the man who did most to exploit the land for his own profit became the most successful and admired; for by our standards he was contributing to national growth and progress. And in this pattern lumbering grew.

In colonial North Carolina the first products of commercial importance came from the coastal piny woods. These were "naval stores," pitch and tar produced from pine sap and given this name because they were used to calk the seams of wooden ships. Then there was the beautiful white pine forest of New England, furnishing masts for the British Navy. The Maine woods were foredoomed by their accessibility, just as destruction of the Appalachian woods was deferred by their inaccessibility. Big-time logging was born in Maine, along the rivers, the Machias, Penobscot, Kennebec, and Androscoggin. It was done best during the long cold winters when logs of pine and spruce could be skidded over ice and snow to the watercourses, then followed by downriver drives to shipping centers on the seaboard.

Still, lumber manufacture was limited. It was the steam-powered circular saw of the 1820s and '30s that really marked a forward stride at a time when the country was growing and pushing westward. And the loggers moved westward, dooming one fine forest after another—but they could always say the prairie schooners and canalboats were made of wood, and railroads were laid on wooden ties.

By the 1880s the "band saw" arrived, a high-powered screaming toothed ribbon of steel, contemporary with the logging railroad and cable skidding. Big lumber outfits were born, often with financial roots in the East and in Europe. It was the same glorious age of expansion that saw promoters and speculators move into the western cattle market and devastate the open range. In the wonderful winter of 1886–87, while thousands of head of cattle were allowed to perish on the northern plains, men by the thousands carved the white pine forests of Michigan, after which the lumber industry spilled its benediction over Wisconsin and Minnesota.

Then, the timber scouts went South. From 1900 to 1920 the South led in production. At the outbreak of World War I North Carolina had the most mills, over 1200, though many were small "peckerwoods" or "coffeepot mills." For the most part Appalachia at first was bypassed for the flatlands of Mississippi and Louisiana. By the 1920s, however, the land was cut barren and the big mills departed, leaving in their wake fierce fires fed by resinous slash scattered on the ground. The magnificent pine forest was replaced by a jungle of scrub oak, rattan, and cat briers.

The loggers moved into the mountains, too. They hunted the hard-woods, the most sought-after lumber in the nation, and had already picked over the forests of Ohio, Pennsylvania, Indiana, and Illinois. Until the turn of the century it was a slowly developing movement. A sawmill was built by Caleb Trentham on the Little Pigeon River, up-stream from Gatlinburg, in 1868 and operated by water power. In the late 1880s outside firms came with capital and skilled loggers, but the tempo was slow. They were after the most precious cabinet woods, walnut, cherry, and cucumber tree, and later birch, ash, and hickory, plus the best construction timber, tulip poplar, white pine, and bass-wood. It was actually a form of selective logging, for mills would not bother with logs less than twenty inches thick at the small end. They logged without the accompaniment of fires or with a few small fires, so that natural reproduction was not halted. Between 1896 and 1900 lum-berjacks cut logs and floated them down the Little River to the Ten-nessee and a sawmill at Lenoir City. On Hazel Creek, logs were floated to Chilhowee, then towed to a mill at Chattanooga. In 1898 Andy Huff set up a mill in Greenbrier Cove, then two years later moved his opera-tion to Gatlinburg; there he would run a boardinghouse for timber cruisers that later became a well-known hotel.

Soon after the turn of the century the larger operators arrived. Colonel W. B. Townsend moved down from Pennsylvania to purchase 86,000 acres in the Little River section, from Tuckaleechee Cove to the foot of Clingman's Dome. In February 1901, his Little River Company was chartered. A band mill was erected where cornfields had lately stood and the town of Townsend was born. The Little River Railroad was built to run on standard-gauge tracks from Walland to the mill and up through Little River Gorge to Elkmont and beyond in the moun-tains. In 1916 Colonel Townsend would report to the Third Appala-chian Logging Congress in Knoxville that after fifteen or sixteen years he was still cutting a phenomenal average of 40,000 board feet per acre. Such were the marvelous forests of the Smokies, where a single tulip poplar, standing 110 feet tall, would yield 18,000 board feet of timber.

Scouts carried the news of these towering virgin forests to other large operators. The trend was downward from West Virginia and Kentucky. The Ritter Lumber Company began acquiring land on Hazel Creek in 1903 and by 1909 installed its double-band sawmill at Proctor with a capacity of 70,000 board feet a day. The Scottish Carolina Timber and Land Company, a Glasgow firm, built a large mill at Newport and operated on Big Creek. Parsons Pulp and Lumber Company built a band mill at Ravensford on the Oconaluftee River and a railroad from Maggie through Cherokee.

Then came Champion, which acquired 92,000 acres in the heart of the Smokies, almost one fifth of the present national park. It purchased four principal tracts. These were located in Greenbrier Cove, on the Tennessee side; along the crest of Smoky, including Clingman's Dome and Mount Kephart; in the watershed of the Oconaluftee; and along Deep Creek. Of all the companies that came into western North Carolina, Champion is the largest and oldest that remains; like Bemis Hardwood, which came into the Nantahalas later, in the 1920s, and is still logging there, Champion had the rare outlook of permanence.

Peter G. Thomson had established the Champion Coated Paper Company in Hamilton, Ohio, in 1903. Ten years later he decided he wanted a steady source of materials—spruce and Fraser fir—to manufacture wood pulp himself. His first move was to acquire 10,000 acres at the town of Canton on the Pigeon River in 1905, at a time when the town had neither electricity nor central water supply. Yet he proposed the most gigantic enterprise western North Carolina had ever seen, a large wood-pulp factory at Canton, to be supplied by an entire village in the forest at the head of the Pigeon River via a huge fifteen-mile-long flume.

In 1908 the factory was completed. So was the company village of Sunburst, with church and school. Thomson engaged the consulting services of the German *Forstmeister* Carl Alwin Schenck, who was then striving to save the loggers from themselves by selling them on the wisdom of forestry from his headquarters at George Vanderbilt's estate outside of Asheville. It was a tough struggle, but that year Schenck ran a highly successful three-day Forest Festival, attended by lumbermen, foresters, state officials, botanists, and newsmen, to whom he demonstrated varied techniques of cutting, thinning, and planting—always explaining profitability against cost. This fair was held to commemorate the tenth anniversary of his pioneering forestry school, of which Overton W. Price already was a distinguished graduate. And another was Verne Rhoades, who later was in charge of land buying for the Great Smoky Mountains National Park on the North Carolina side—an extremely modest man, who never had a mountain named for him, but was devoted to the cause in the same selfless way as Horace Kephart.

As for Peter Thomson, Schenck found that he was not interested in forestry, nor in cultivating a second growth of spruce. But Schenck warned that the volume of standing spruce would be adequate for no more than ten years' supply. Shortly Thomson determined that even the huge flume he planned could not carry the three hundred cords daily required for the plant. He would have to try mixing spruce with North Carolina pine, and he engaged Schenck to survey the pine throughout the western section of the state.

In due course Champion acquired timber rights and logged the mountains from Grandfather and Roan southwest to Robbinsville. Thomson's son-in-law and successor, Reuben B. Robertson, moved to North Carolina and supported sound forestry—though the national park was a bitter pill for him to swallow; for Champion considered the Smokies its own domain. At Smokemont, where campers sleep now, it installed a band mill, cutting high-grade spruce into logs, the tops and scraps into pulp, and continually advancing its railroad lines upward to the crest.

By World War I, the ownership of the Smokies had passed into the hands of the large logging corporations. Logging settlements and mill towns ringed the mountains—Fontana on the Little Tennessee; Proctor on Hazel Creek; Bryson City on the Tuckasegee; Ravensford and Smokemont on the Oconaluftee; Hartford on Big Creek; Greenbrier and Gatlinburg on the Little Pigeon; Elkmont and Townsend on the Little River. Logging railroads had penetrated many of the watersheds and were climbing the slopes.

"Handsome timber in increasing amounts fell to the ax, but there always seemed to be more. Sawmill towns sprang up in their temporary ugliness, thrived, and vanished as the cutting moved on," wrote M. A. Mattoon, a distinguished Government forester who served in both the North Carolina and Tennessee mountains. "When Europe burst into the horror of warfare in 1914, demands on the forest mounted, and postwar reconstruction saw no letup. So the large sawmills, accompanied by many little sawmills, marched across the face of the remaining Appalachian wilderness."

The more distant the logger ran his operations from the main line of transportation, the more costly they grew. The mill itself was a relatively small investment. Getting timber out of remote areas was more expensive—therefore the margin of profit depended upon following the shortest, cheapest way. At first, ox teams were used to drag logs to creeks and streams, and on the skid road to the yarding point or deck. They were replaced by horses, which proved faster and easier to handle; besides, a good woods-wise horse often went about his skidding job without reins or words of command. Erosion was caused by clearing lanes for skidders, though nobody cared. And the best way to get lumber down was just to roll it whenever possible. From the high, steep slopes logs were "ball-hooted"—merely started downgrade with peavey, or cant hook. A sixteen-foot log, three feet or more in diameter, would gain sufficient momentum to smash even fair-sized trees in its path, and when it passed through a dense young growth it left a track like a miniature tornado.

Then there were splash dams and flumes. In setting up a splash dam, the bed of a creek was freed of protruding rocks and fallen timbers, and cleared of all sharp bends. Hemlock logs, snaked to the stream by cattle, were used to build the dam. As the reservoir grew, animals hauled logs to it over the skid trail. When the rains came, raising the creek level, the water would be released by means of a huge trap door creating a force to splash the logs downstream. Sometimes log jams formed a mile long, which the lumberjacks followed to break loose. Where it developed that a splash dam didn't hold sufficient water clear down to the valley, a second dam was constructed on a fork, with the waves of both timed to merge at the confluence. The trouble with splash dams was that no logs heavier than water could be moved by splashing and driving, which eliminated oak, ash, and chestnut. The creek shores and bed were torn, wrecked, and ruined, but in the helter-skelter of the day this counted not at all.

Where streams were too shallow and strewn with boulders, a flume might be built, a narrow wooden trough in which a stream of water carried logs to millpond or log deck. Building costs were high and sometimes the boards had to be "trestled up" to maintain the proper grade. Still, it was calculated to cost $2.00 or less to move 1000 board feet of timber in this fashion as compared with $10 or $13 by wagon. Crews of "lumber herders," wearing calked shoes and armed with pickaroons and peaveys, broke log jams and sometimes rode downhill balancing themselves with a long pole while ducking low branches.

Equipment grew larger, more sophisticated, and more expensive. The geared Shay locomotive, the "Model-T of the woods," was ideal for hauling heavy loads over the steepest mountain grades and sharpest curves of Appalachia. There was the steam-powered Clyde skidder, dragging in huge logs by overhead cables extending nearly a mile in the woods, and the sensational McGiffert log loader, to feed logs of all kinds and sizes into a small circular sawmill. And yet, as I have been told by one who was among them, for every one of the logging companies that made money, a hundred went broke. They were promoters, speculators, syndicates that had to keep skinning the land and selling their lumber regardless of market price, in order to stay afloat.

In their wake, fires were started by sparks from wood-burning trains and skidders. During the dry season the tops and branches scattered over the ground went up in smoke and the sparks would fly from one mountainside to another, with no way to control the problem. In the 1920s, fires burned the slopes of Clingman's Dome, Silers Bald, and Mount Guyot. Another fire leaped from the North Carolina side to attack Champion property at the point now known as Charlie's Bunion, much to the chagrin of Champion officials. They had a good record of fire protection; they were conscious of the need to cut selectively, leaving some trees both as a green protection against fire and to assure regeneration of spruce rather than a new cycle starting with fire cherry. But throughout Appalachia the lumberman left his legacy in the changed land.

His fire had scorched the trees and their roots, destroyed seedlings and forage plants; it had consumed forest litter and humus. The forest no longer could reproduce itself. The chemical elements of plant food were dissipated by fire into the atmosphere, while the residue contained in the ashes was leached away. The pine, thanks to its winged seed, claimed much land once occupied by the hardwoods. The black walnut virtually disappeared.

For all that, the Smoky Mountains still remained the last frontier. The conquering lumberman never quite made it all the way.

Land ownership patterns facing park advocates.

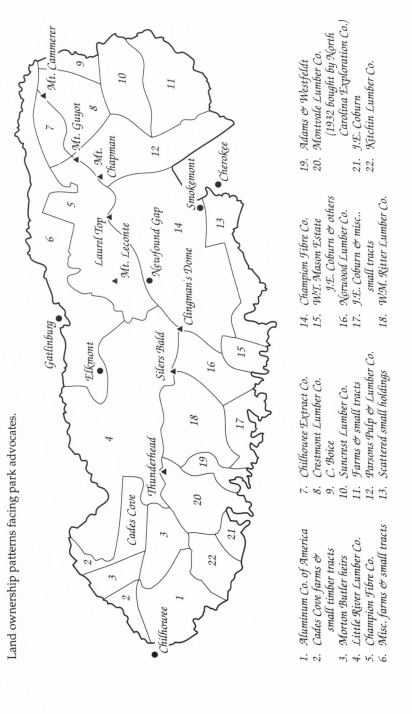

1. Aluminum Co. of America
2. Cades Cove farms & small timber tracts
3. Morton Butler heirs
4. Little River Lumber Co.
5. Champion Fibre Co.
6. Misc. farms & small tracts
7. Chilhowee Extract Co.
8. Crestmont Lumber Co.
9. C. Boice
10. Suncrest Lumber Co.
11. Farms & small tracts
12. Parsons Pulp & Lumber Co.
13. Scattered small holdings
14. Champion Fibre Co.
15. W.I. Mason Estate
16. J.E. Coburn & others
    Norwood Lumber Co.
17. J.E. Coburn & misc. small tracts
18. W.M. Ritter Lumber Co.
19. Adams & Westfeldt
20. Montvale Lumber Co. (1932 bought by North Carolina Exploration Co.)
21. J.E. Coburn
22. Kitchin Lumber Co.

XIV

Coming of the Park

The national park was a long time in coming to the Great Smoky Mountains. More than forty years passed from the time of the first serious proposal to establish the park until it was dedicated in 1940 by President Franklin Delano Roosevelt. They were rough years, but the ultimate outcome was a victory for all the people, from little school children who gave their pennies to one of the richest men in the world who gave his millions to save the beauty of the Smokies.

Establishing a national park in the southern Appalachians, or anywhere in the East, presented a new set of problems and the need of a pattern extremely different from that followed in the several national parks of the West. Essentially, those in the West were carved out of land already owned by the Federal Government as part of the vast public domain. But in the Smokies, park advocates faced an area completely controlled by private owners, in no less than 6600 separate tracts.

Approximately one third of the 508,000 acres finally agreed upon was primeval. It was a larger proportion when the first park proposals were made, but 85 per cent of the total acreage was owned by eighteen timber and pulpwood companies, who were cutting upward, climbing into the high reaches for the last rich timber stands in the East.

The remaining 15 per cent was divided among 1200 farms of various sizes in the valleys, most of them hugging the hillsides, plus 5000 summer homesites and lots. Among these were about 1000 tiny parcels, near Wonderland in the Elkmont section, totaling all of fifty-two acres. Mrs. Kittie Carter had sold these in 1931 at a Knoxville movie-house promotion contest, hoping that each winner would purchase at least two additional lots for a summer cottage.

The first suggestion of record for a national park in the southern mountains appears to have been made by the Reverend C. D. Smith, of Franklin, North Carolina, in the early 1880s. In 1885, Dr. Henry O. Marcy, of Boston, while delivering a paper before a medical meeting in New York City on the subject of climatic treatment of disease, advocated establishment of a health resort in western North Carolina, but as a reservation under state control in order to insure perpetuation of the region's health-giving properties. The paper was published in the *Journal of the American Medical Association* and read by an Ohio physician, Dr. Chase P. Ambler, who was so impressed by the prospects that he moved his practice to Asheville and there became a prime force in the earliest serious Appalachian national park movement.

As early as 1893 the North Carolina General Assembly passed a resolution urging the state's delegation in Congress to seek legislation for a national park. Soon after, the North Carolina Press Association adopted a memorial to Congress for such a park, which Representative John S. Henderson presented to the House of Representatives in Washington on March 27, 1894. Little came of it.

Meanwhile, another force arose that would in time deeply influence and change the direction of the Ambler movement. It centered on two men who sat around a fire one evening in the early 1890s in George Washington Vanderbilt's mansion outside Asheville. One was the state geologist of North Carolina, Dr. Joseph A. Holmes. The other was a young man, recently returned from studies in Europe, who had been hired to develop a forestry plan, something virtually unknown in this country at that time, for the Biltmore estate. He was Gifford Pinchot, who would become Chief Forester of the United States, adviser to Theodore Roosevelt, and possibly the greatest figure in the history of American conservation to this day. While they sat in Mr. Vanderbilt's Brick House and discussed things in general and forestry in particular, Holmes advanced a notion that the Federal Government ought to buy a big tract of timberland in the southern Appalachians and practice forestry on it. Half a century later, Pinchot credited Holmes with the "brilliant suggestion" that led to acquisition of millions of acres of land for national forests in the East.

Advocacy of forest reserves contributed in the long run to the cause of the national park. At times the issue became confused, as between harvesting trees and preserving trees, but the broad effort in forestry's behalf served also to focus attention on the unique values of the Smoky Mountain range.

In 1899, Dr. Ambler organized the Appalachian National Park Association. Forces were joined with the Appalachian Mountain Club, of Boston, an organization of hikers and conservationists, in submitting memorials to Congress in January 1900 on the increasingly desperate need of forest protection in the mountains. It would be eleven years before Congress took positive action, and while democracy moved slowly the hills were well worked over for all the profits they would yield.

For the six years of its existence the Appalachian National Park Association waged an energetic campaign. Senator Jeter C. Pritchard, of North Carolina, and Representative W. P. Brownlow, of Tennessee, were among its best spokesmen in Washington. Senator Pritchard presented the memorial to the Senate, which mustered all possible arguments to the cause of the region. There was the health factor: "Malaria is unknown. It rivals Arizona as a sanitarium for those suffering from pulmonary troubles. No better place could be found for the establishment of a sanitarium for the soldiers and sailors of our country." There was the factor of beauty: "In western North Carolina and eastern Tennessee (or, more definitely, in the heart of the Great Smoky Mountains, the Balsam Mountains, and the Black and Craggy mountains) is found not only the culmination of the Appalachian system, but the most beautiful as well as the highest mountains east of the lofty western ranges. . . . If the national parks already established have been chosen for their unusual natural beauty, here is a national park conspicuously fine, awaiting official recognition as an addition to the number." Then, too, there were all the advantages of the new science of forestry: "No better place in the United States can be found for the institution on a governmental scale of forestry operations, and because of the fine climate, summer and winter alike, it would be the only reserve of the country where such operations could be carried on uninterruptedly throughout the year. The forests and the climate, both incomparable, ordain this as the place for the commencement of forestry operations, and, perhaps, as the location eventually of a national school of forestry." No point stopping with small dreams!

Senator Pritchard introduced two specific pieces of legislation. Through one of them he succeeded in obtaining a $5000 appropriation for the Department of Agriculture "to investigate the forest conditions in the southern Appalachian Mountain region of western North Carolina and adjacent states" during the fiscal year ending June 30, 1901. In the other, he proposed an expenditure of $5,000,000 to acquire two million acres of mountain land in Virginia, the Carolinas, Georgia, Alabama, and Tennessee in order to establish a southern Appalachian forest reserve.

The cause became extremely popular. The legislature of Tennessee voted on April 16, 1901, to cede the lands lying within twenty miles of the North Carolina line in order to "perpetuate these forests and forever preserve the headwaters of many important streams, and which will thus prove of great and permanent benefit to the people of this state." South Carolina, North Carolina, Virginia, Alabama, and Georgia legislatures took similar action. The bill, having been favorably reported by the Senate Committee on Forest Reservations and Game, was passed by the Senate.

But it could not pass the House. One magazine observed that only the great pressure of other business prevented favorable action. However, there was also the strong hand of Joseph Gurney Cannon, the conservative Republican from Illinois, who was on his way to becoming the Speaker of the House and its iron ruler. To Cannon, forests were trees and vistas, on which Congress should not waste good money; his position of "not one cent for scenery" delayed establishment of the eastern national forests until 1911.

Meanwhile, the $5000 study was rushed from one stage to another. It showed all the signs of zestful Gifford Pinchot (who had joined the Department of Agriculture in 1898) at work. On January 3, 1901, Agriculture Secretary James Wilson reported to President McKinley that his Bureau of Forestry and the co-operating United States Geological Survey had mapped the forests of 8000 square miles from Virginia to Alabama, and had studied their streams, soils, the size and nature of present holdings, and the suitability of a national park.

"The movement for the purchase and control of a large area of forest land in the East by the Government has chiefly contemplated a national park," wrote Secretary Wilson in practical words characteristic of Chief Forester Pinchot. "The idea of a national park is conservation, not use; that of a forest reserve, conservation by use. I have therefore to recommend a forest reserve instead of a park. It is fully shown by the investigation that such a reserve would be self-supporting from the sale of timber under wisely directed conservative forestry."

In December 1901, the new President, Theodore Roosevelt, transmitted the full report in a 210-page printed volume, an important historical document of the Appalachian region. Roosevelt gave it his strong support. He sparked the trend that led to reversal of wastefulness in the southern mountains as well as in the West.

"These great mountains are old in the history of the continent which has grown up around them," declared the President, almost as though setting forth the unique qualifications for establishment of a national park. "The hardwood forests were born on their slopes and have spread thence over the eastern half of the continent. More than once in the remote geologic past they have disappeared before the sea on the east, south, and west, and before the ice on the north; but here in the southern Appalachian region they have lived on to the present day.

"In this region occur that marvelous variety and richness of plant growth which have led our ablest businessmen and scientists to ask for its preservation by the Government for the advancement of science and for the instruction and pleasure of the people of our own and of future generations. And it is the concentration here of so many valuable species with such favorable conditions of growth which has led forest experts and lumbermen alike to assert that of all the continent this region is best suited to the purposes and plans of a national forest reserve in the hardwood region."

In those days the need was desperate for a reason other than preserving big trees and providing pleasuring grounds for tourists.

"The rivers which originate in the southern Appalachians flow into or along the edges of every state from Ohio to the Gulf and from the Atlantic to the Mississippi," continued the President's message. "Along their courses are agricultural, water power, and navigation interests whose preservation is absolutely essential to the well-being of the nation. . . . For economic reasons the preservation of these forests is imperative. Their existence in good condition is essential to the prosperity of the lowlands through which their waters run. Maintained in productive condition they will supply indispensable materials, which must fail without them."

But Congress failed to act. Apart from the obstinacy of Speaker Cannon, the lumber industry fought the good fight for dear old free enterprise. One year, as Gifford Pinchot wrote, a forest reserves bill would pass the Senate, but die in the House. Then another bill would go through the House but die in the Senate. And all the while the Appalachians were logged over, then went up in smoke or washed downstream.

Dr. Ambler's group recognized the futility of seeking funds for a national park and changed its name to the Appalachian National Forest Reserve Association; then it transferred its functions to the American Forestry Association in order to place emphasis on a national, rather than sectional, movement. "Nearly twenty years after Holmes's suggestion, which is about the time it usually takes to get a new idea through Congress," wrote Pinchot, "in 1911 the Weeks Law was passed." Alas, the bill that made possible national forests in the East was not named for a southern Appalachian man, rather for Representative John Wingate Weeks, of New Hampshire; but it was, at last, the law.

The effect on the Smokies was felt almost immediately after passage of the Weeks Law. The Forest Service established the Smoky Mountain Purchase Unit as one of thirteen areas chosen for development in the East. Between 1911 and 1916, a total of 61,350 acres belonging to the Little River Lumber Company was optioned for purchase. Over $90,000 was spent by the Forest Service for preliminary fire control and to get the new area organized. Rangers, fire fighters, and trail builders were employed. A fire tower was erected at Rich Mountain, and trails were laid out at Cades Cove and Elkmont.

But a Smoky Mountains National Forest was not to be. Old Tennessee land titles dating to the Cherokee days were too shaky and questionable to be accepted by the Government. When World War I broke out and the price of lumber rose, Little River canceled the option and returned to slashing the forest for profits.

The Forest Service withdrew from this arena. As a devoted and loyal friend of the agency, I am glad that it did so, for here was a parcel of land created to fill a particular role—but not in forestry. If the national park concept ever was sound, it was sound and right in this mountain country.

The idea of a national park in the mountains was not altogether forgotten. Horace Kephart's *Our Southern Highlanders* and Margaret Morley's *The Carolina Mountains* both appeared in 1913 and kindled interest in the natural beauty of the Smokies. At the same time, the movement for national parks was rising all across America. The several parks then existing in the West were administered loosely by the old General Land Office, with protection provided on the ground not by rangers but by the Army. Strong efforts were being exerted, however, to establish a distinctive parks bureau.

In 1915, Stephen T. Mather, a wealthy Californian transplanted to Chicago, was appointed Assistant to the Secretary of Interior (Franklin K. Lane) in charge of national parks. He found on the scene another Californian, a young lawyer named Horace M. Albright, assigned to deal with legal matters concerning the parks. Between them they shaped the framework of the National Park Service after it was created in the Organic Act of August 24, 1916, and became the first Director and Assistant Director, respectively. Both these men were cut from the same cloth as Gifford Pinchot; they were fearless, aggressive leaders, who could walk in the company of Presidents without being overawed, who were willing to work with political figures but unwilling to permit political exploitation of their agencies.

Presently they discussed Niagara Falls, one of nature's marvels, as a potential national park, but commercialization there had gone too far. Mammoth Cave, Kentucky, was mentioned, too. Then George B. Dorr, of Bar Harbor, Maine, presented himself with a portfolio of photographs of Mount Desert Island, hoping to obtain some sort of national status for this parcel of rocky coast and wooded mountain crest. Dorr had interested a number of summer residents of wealth and prominence, including John D. Rockefeller, Jr., and Charles William Eliot, president of Harvard University, in his conservation idea and by 1916 had assembled a number of fine tracts.

"After roaming around Washington offices, he fell into my hands," Horace Albright told me during one of our long and fruitful interviews. "His earnestness and devotion to his cause impressed me very much; finally I came up with the idea that prossibly this area could be made a national monument under the Antiquities Act of 1906, which provided that land could be donated to, and accepted by, the Federal Government for such purposes." Thus, Sieur de Mont National Monument was established in Maine in 1916. Three years later Congress voted to change its name and status to Lafayette (presently Acadia) National Park. It was the first national park east of the Mississippi.

Curiously, in 1917 the Park Service was greeted with an unexpected piece of legislation which would have authorized the Secretary of Interior "to accept for park purposes any lands and rights of way, including the Grandfather Mountain, near or adjacent to the Government forest reserve in western North Carolina." Where had this proposal originated? Grandfather is a superb peak, the highest, most rugged in the Blue Ridge; though not as high as Mount Mitchell in the Black Mountains, it presents a more prominent and massive picture. Albright and his associates looked into the Grandfather possibility closely. The bill had been introduced at the instance of Hugh McRae, whose headquarters was in Wilmington, North Carolina, but who summered and owned land at Linville. But only the top of the mountain, barren of trees, was to be conveyed to the Government and the project was finally rejected. Years later the Service strove to obtain Grandfather for inclusion in the Blue Ridge Parkway, but the McRae heirs had already developed it as a commercial tourist attraction; the heirs, moreover, became bitter opponents in the 1950s and '60s of the National Park Service in the Carolina mountains.

Throughout its early years the National Park Service continued to study various eastern locations. As early as 1918 the Indiana dunes bordering the southern shore of Lake Michigan were discussed—at a time when the dunes yet covered a vast, unspoiled area. So was Mammoth Cave, considered of special value both because of the old underground caverns and the large Mississippi River Basin-type forests aboveground. The need of eastern parks was stressed repeatedly.

"As areas in public ownership in the East are at present limited," declared Director Mather in his seventh annual report, of 1923, "to a number of forest reserves acquired under the provisions of the Weeks Law authorizing the purchase of lands for the protection of forests and the headwaters of streams, it appears the only practicable way national park areas can be acquired would be by donations of land from funds privately donated, as in the case of the Lafayette National Park." Specifically in this report the Director mentioned there should be a typical section of the Appalachian Range in the national park system, with native flora and fauna preserved and made accessible for public enjoyment.

Several bills were introduced in Congress during 1922 and 1923 to establish a national park in one quarter or another of the Appalachians. The Park Service of those years, however, was not seeking to administer land for land's sake alone or for recreational playgrounds. Mather envisioned national parks as providing catalytic action for the states to fulfill their proper roles. In 1921 he inspired the founding of the National Council on State Parks. "A state park every hundred miles" was his slogan. He foresaw the motorist who set forth to visit national parks breaking his journey in state parks, distributed so as to form an interstate park chain across the country.

The states, in fact, were urged to assume responsibility for such areas as Cumberland Gap, in the Appalachians, and Carlsbad Caverns, New Mexico, which, they were told, could be financial assets to them. What the National Park Service stressed for its own system was selectivity. "Due to the great economic value locally of national parks, the Service is under tremendous pressure each year to investigate and report favorably on proposed projects throughout the country," said Horace Albright in 1930 when he came, as Director of the Park Service, the successor to Mather, to visit the mountains of Tennessee and North Carolina. The Great Smokies, he said, were destined to join the select company of Yellowstone, Glacier, and the Grand Canyon. "I think in my office we have over one hundred projects that have to be investigated, in some of these cases Congress having directed an investigation. We turn down dozens of appeals for national parks each year, simply because the areas do not measure up to the great scenic standards. But as has been forcefully said by someone, 'National parks are not created by an act of Congress; only God can create a national park.' "

The groundwork for choosing a national park site in the Appalachians had to be laid carefully. Secretary of the Interior Hubert Work advised the states early in 1924 of his desire to establish a park east of the Mississippi and appointed a special committee to study the entire mountain region. The members were Representative Henry W. Temple of Pennsylvania, chairman; Major W. A. Welch, general manager of the Palisades Interstate Park Commission of New York; Colonel Glenn S. Smith, of the United States Geological Survey, assigned to represent the Secretary; Harlan P. Kelsey, of Salem, Massachusetts; and William C. Gregg, of the National Arts Club, New York. (Kelsey and Gregg were chosen by the Council on National Parks, Forests, and Wild Life, in response to a request from the Secretary for representation by two of its members.)

The five members met in Washington in March 1924, and were duly constituted as the Southern Appalachian National Park Committee. Despite the title, there was no money to work with, so Mr. Gregg donated $500; later John D. Rockefeller, Jr., gave $500 and Stephen T. Mather $250. Harlan P. Kelsey, in particular, played a key role. A landscape architect and horticulturist, he was a former president of the Appalachian Mountain Club and a close adviser to Mather and Albright. Though born in Kansas, he was reared in Highlands, North Carolina, and knew the mountain country. Later in the year, when the focus of the committee was directed toward the Shenandoah country of Virginia, Kelsey would insist forcefully on the values of the Smokies. "He must be given a very great deal of the credit," according to Albright, "for the decision to designate the Great Smoky Mountains as the site of one of our eastern parks."

These developments in Washington fired the spirit of Appalachia. One community after another advised the committee that at its back door was *the* region perfectly suited to become a national park and invited the members to come see for themselves. A summer inspection trip was charted. The committee began in late July at Gainesville, Georgia, and proceeded to work its way north through a round of entertainments by chambers of commerce and mountain politicians. Secretary Work, who started with the party, was overcome by the hospitality by the time he reached Highlands, North Carolina, and begged off going farther, returning instead to Washington.

North Carolina was well primed. The Asheville people were so eager they dispatched one delegation to meet the committee at Highlands, then another delegation, headed by the mayor himself and several county commissioners, to Brevard, where the Washington men were taken directly in hand—almost before they had finished the fine hotel lunch served by the citizens of the town.

Enthusiasm ran high in North Carolina. That summer the legislature established a special commission "for the purpose of presenting the claims of North Carolina for a national park" and generously appropriated $2500 for its expenses. Among its members was E. C. Brooks, president of North Carolina State College. Years later it was recalled that he was chosen because, as a former State Superintendent of Public Instruction, he was well known to the Rockefeller-financed General Education Board and would prove valuable in securing a donation from the Rockefeller family. Many such ingenious and perceptive strokes, an absolute plethora, were recalled in both North Carolina and Tennessee. With all credit to Dr. Brooks, however, there is nothing to indicate that his appointment had the vaguest effect on Mr. Rockefeller's participation in the Great Smoky Mountains project.

The committee planned, according to its records, to take in the mountain regions in the vicinity of Highlands, Asheville, and Linville Gorge, Grandfather Mountain and Roan Mountain in North Carolina, and the Great Smoky Mountains in Tennessee. The Smokies were not the most favored park area among Carolinians. The Linville-Grandfather section was endorsed by the *Asheville Citizen-Times*, as well as the communities of Linville, Blowing Rock, and Boone, and the owners of timber in the Great Smokies.

But on the evening the Washington men arrived at Asheville, hardly before they could sample the hospitality of the Grove Park Inn, or the luxury of solitude, a delegation arrived from Knoxville. It must have been a long, fierce journey around the mountains in 1924, bent, as it was, to invade hostile Carolina country. The delegation of businessmen was headed by Willis P. Davis and Colonel David C. Chapman, while Representative J. Will Taylor added the strength of his office to the cause.

Mr. Davis had been out West with his wife the summer before. Though properly impressed with the scenic grandeur, Mrs. Davis, it is said, asked, "Why can't we have a national park in the Great Smokies?" In some references she is called "mother of the Great Smoky Mountains National Park." Colonel Chapman, who played a leading role in the hard fight, is called "father of the park." Possibly this leaves Mr. Davis in the awkward role of holy ghost. Such terminology, however, applies only on the Tennessee side. You can hear of one "father of the park" or another on the Carolina side. Pride of parenthood is well distributed after a beautiful baby is born.

When the Davises returned from their western trip, they urged a campaign to establish a national park in the Smokies. Their pleas were heeded by the Chamber of Commerce and Knoxville Automobile Club, and from the interest of those two groups the Great Smoky Mountains Conservation Association was organized. Thus, in the strange ways of democracy, the cause of wilderness preservation was led, in that day at least, not by botanists and bird lovers but by energetic civic boosters and businessmen.

The Tennessee delegation presented a handsome portfolio of pictures taken by the Knoxville photographer, James E. Thompson and wanted the committee to proceed to the Smokies (though most of its own group had seen no more of them than Little River Gorge and

Members of Smoky Mountains Hiking Club at LeConte Lodge in 1929, when the climb over primitive trails was strictly for the hardy. Paul Adams established a tent camp on LeConte in 1925 for the Great Smoky Mountains Conservation Association, which members of the park commission visited that year and in 1926. Then he became a mountain guide for guests at the Mountain View Hotel, and Jack Huff built the lodge, which he operated until 1960. Jim Thompson.

Laura Thornborough models early 1930s outdoors apparel. A Knoxville native with a cottage in Gatlinburg, Thornborough hiked and photographed extensively throughout the park. Her book, *The Great Smoky Mountains*, was published in 1937. National Park Service.

Immense tulip poplar dominating the hardwood coves made the Smokies a prime target for timbermen but also gave added reason to establish a national park. The yellow poplar, or "tulip tree," amazed visitors with its size and lovely tulip-shaped flower in spring. Jim Thompson.

Tall trees with straight trunks rise above rhododendron thriving along the banks of beautiful Smoky Mountain streams, while boulders show the power of water to move mountains. Jim Thompson.

Abrams Falls, 2.5 miles from the western end of the Cades Cove loop road, has long been a popular hiking destination. The falls, twenty feet high, are formed by Abrams Creek flowing over beds of Cades sandstone. The plunge pool is over one hundred feet wide. Jim Thompson.

Early hikers making it to the Chimney Tops, a steep two-mile climb to the prominent jutting rock exposure above the head of Sugarlands Valley. In places hikers use their arms to pull up, then find a "scratch-breeches trail" coming down. Jim Thompson.

A Cherokee woman, pictured in the late 1920s or early 1930s, holds her basket as symbol of tradition and history. Members of the Eastern Band of Cherokee dwell in the shadow of their ancestors, the land of high mountains and swift-running streams. Jim Thompson.

David C. Chapman, one of the principal park promoters, takes a break for note-writing. A wholesale druggist in Knoxville, Colonel Chapman became chairman of the Tennessee Great Smoky Mountains Park Commission. In recognition of his driving power and leadership, the fourth highest peak in the park, Mt. Chapman (6,430 feet), is named for him. Jim Thompson.

Clingmans Observation Tower, built in the late 1930s atop the highest peak in the park (elevation 6,642 feet), opened vistas to visitors but required construction of the parking lot and seven miles of road from Newfound Gap. The picturesque wooden tower later was replaced by the concrete structure now standing. Jim Thompson.

The new tunnel on US 441, with the Chimneys behind it, shown about 1940, illustrates sophisticated engineering of the Newfound Gap, or Over-the-Smokies, Highway. Beside the rock formation, meant to suggest a natural opening at the tunnel, other features included wide banked curves, gentle grade, and guard rails of native stone. Jim Thompson.

President Franklin D. Roosevelt himself said he would like to dedicate Great Smoky Mountains National Park on Labor Day, September 2, 1940. A great throng of twenty-five thousand came to hear the president at the crescent-shaped masonry wall at Newfound Gap, straddling the boundary line between North Carolina and Tennessee. Jim Thompson.

Principal personalities at the park dedication, September 2, 1940, included, from left: Harlan B. Kelsey, key member of the Southern Appalachian National Park Committee; Governor Prentice Cooper of Tennessee; Governor (later Senator) Clyde R. Hoey of North Carolina; Newton B. Drury, then newly appointed director of the National Park Service; Arno B. Cammerer, Drury's predecessor, prime mover in the national park campaign, and Charles A. Webb, publisher of the *Asheville Citizen* and *Times*. Robert P. White, National Park Service.

Arthur Stupka snowshoeing to Ramsey Cascade in January, 1940, five years after coming to the Smokies as the park's first naturalist. In his early years he collated the work of scientific observers and assembled basic information. During his long career Stupka personally guided thousands of visitors on hikes and walks, and in evening lectures. National Park Service.

Mark Hannah, at Walnut Bottoms, July 1942, in his early days as one of the local men appointed as park wardens, or rangers. His great grandfather came to the Smokies as a wandering hunter but stayed as a pioneer settler of Cataloochee. National Park Service.

Park officials and local notables at memorial services, June 12, 1960, in tribute to John D. Rockefeller, Jr., whose benefaction was vital to land acquisition for the national park. In the foreground, Fred J. Overly, park superintendent, and Carlos C. Campbell, of the Great Smoky Mountains Conservation Association. Back left, Reverend Charles Maples, First Baptist Church, of Gatlinburg (which Rockefeller attended on his visits to the park), Kelley E. Bennett of Bryson City. Henry W. Lix, National Park Service.

Eliza Walker, last of the Walker sisters, at their cabin in the Little Greenbrier section, in 1962, shortly before her death. When the park was established the sisters received the right of life tenancy. They welcomed visitors and explained the old ways. The cabin still stands, as a point of historical interest and education. Mack Prichard.

Elkmont). But the next days were already booked, with luncheons atop Mount Mitchell and at the Marion Country Club, plus other entertainments, courthouse addresses, and inspections on the Carolina side, so the Knoxvillians were obliged to head home empty-handed. As the expedition advanced, Representative Temple and Major Welch held up as well as their colleagues, until they faced the prospect of being taken by a corps of local men to the top of Roan Mountain on horseback. Both departed in the nick of time for pressing business at home. One or two days later, at Johnson City, Colonel Smith discovered he was urgently needed by the Geological Survey, leaving the field to Kelsey and Gregg.

Now the Knoxvillians urgently requested them once again to see the Smokies and at last they did. From Knoxville they and their hosts went to Gatlinburg, a considerable journey in itself for that day, then proceeding for five or six days on horseback, well escorted around Mount Le Conte and environs by no less than twenty-five Tennesseans. This was a decisive experience in the ultimate decision to establish the park.

It was hardly the end of the Appalachian study. Appeals from governors and civic leaders led committee members to inspect other regions during the fall. The tireless Gregg at his own expense covered the mountains of South Carolina and Georgia, returning to North Carolina for a closer look at Grandfather Mountain, Linville Falls, and Linville Gorge. Part of the committee visited Luray, Virginia, where they were met by a band and hundreds of hospitable Virginians; George Freeman Pollock, the owner of Skyland, a resort on the crest of the Blue Ridge, showed them beautiful country rich in history, near the nation's capital, with the possibility of a scenic skyline drive overlooking the Shenandoah Valley and Piedmont Plateau. This country had many strong selling points.

The Southern Appalachian National Park Committee met December 12, 1924, in Washington in order to determine its choice of a new national park. There were then nineteen national parks, all but one (little Lafayette, or Acadia) west of the Mississippi, although two thirds of the population lived in the East.

"We inspected the northern part of Georgia, whose fine mountains blend with the Highland region of southern North Carolina," wrote Chairman Temple in the committee's report. "We ascended Mount Mitchell and viewed the splendid Black Mountain Range north of Asheville. We went over carefully the Grandfather Mountain region, which for our study included the beautiful country from Blowing Rock to the remarkable Linville Gorge. We responded to the call of the poet —to see Roan Mountain if we would really see the southern Appalachians. We went to Knoxville and from there to the tops of the 'Big

Smokies,' which carry on their crest the boundary line between North Carolina and Tennessee. We went into Virginia to inspect that portion of the Blue Ridge on the east side of the Shenandoah Valley which extends from Front Royal to Waynesboro. Some members of the committee also visited Cumberland Gap, southern West Virginia, northern Alabama, and eastern Kentucky. Several areas were found that contained topographic features of great scenic value, where waterfalls, cascades, cliffs, and mountain peaks, with beautiful valleys lying in their midst, gave ample assurance that any or all of these areas were possible for development into a national park which would compare favorably with any of the existing national parks in the West."

The committee had found many areas which could well be chosen, but it was "charged with the responsibility of selecting the best, all things considered." It listed the requirements it had laid down for guidance, all of noble purpose—though more than slightly contradictory in practice with the passing of years:

1. Mountain scenery with inspiring perspective and delightful details.
2. Areas sufficiently extensive and adaptable so that annually millions of visitors might enjoy the benefits of outdoor life with nature without the confusion of overcrowding.
3. A substantial part to contain forests, shrubs, and flowers, and mountain streams, with picturesque cascades and waterfalls overhung with foliage, all untouched by the hand of man.
4. Abundant springs and streams available for camps and fishing.
5. Opportunities for protecting and developing the wildlife of the area, and the whole to be a natural museum, preserving outstanding features of the southern Appalachians as they appeared in the early pioneer days.
6. Accessibility by rail and road.

Which area, or areas, best met these standards?

"The Great Smoky Mountains easily stand first," reported the committee, "because of the height of the mountains, depth of valleys, ruggedness of the area, and the unexampled variety of trees, shrubs and plants. The region includes Mount Guyot, Mount Le Conte, Clingman's Dome, and Gregory Bald, and may be extended in several directions to include other splendid mountain regions adjacent thereto.

"The Great Smokies have some handicaps which will make the development of them into a national park a matter of delay; their very ruggedness and height make road and other park development a serious undertaking as to time and expense. The excessive rainfall also (not yet accurately determined) is an element for future study and investigation in relation both to the development work, subsequent administration, and recreational use as a national park.

"The Blue Ridge of Virginia, one of the sections which had your committee's careful study, while secondary to the Great Smokies in altitude and some other features, constitutes in our judgment the outstanding and logical place for the creation of the first national park in the southern Appalachians. We hope it will be made into a national park and that its success will encourage the Congress to create a second park in the Great Smoky Mountains, which lie some 300 miles distant southwest."

Colonel Chapman reacted in statesmanlike fashion by accusing the committee of yielding to political pressure when it granted priority to a clearly inferior area. But most of his friends accepted the report as a signal victory and vowed to shorten the interval, if indeed there must be one, between the first and second national parks in the Appalachians. The political strategists suggested that both parks would stand a better chance if their proponents worked together, which the Virginians agreed to do. Thus, on January 27, 1925, Representative Temple introduced a bill in the House, while Senator Claude Swanson, of Virginia, introduced a companion bill in the Senate, to secure lands for not two, but three national parks—the Shenandoah, Smoky Mountains, and Mammoth Cave. Speedily enacted and approved by the President on February 21, the Act did not establish the parks. It authorized the Secretary of Interior to determine the boundaries and areas of the proposed parks; to receive offers of land and money donations for these projects; and to report his findings to Congress. The Government would still not appropriate money for "scenery." For that matter, although the members of the committee were elevated, by terms of the Act, to a duly constituted Southern Appalachian National Park Commission, it was clearly stated they would serve "without compensation."

From this point the complications, conflicts, and struggles began in earnest. Park supporters in Tennessee and North Carolina were wary of each other, to say the least (and still are). The Smoky Mountain supporters were wary of the Shenandoah supporters in Virginia. All of them were wary of the National Park Commission. (The problems relating to Mammoth Cave we shall permit to remain underground in Kentucky.)

The worst headaches of all were within the states themselves. Money had to be raised, a great deal of it, laws had to be passed by the legislatures, and land purchased from logging companies before they logged deeper.

Chairman of the North Carolina Park Commission was State Senator Mark Squires, of Lenoir, who has been described by friends of his as a legal genius, a nervous, hot-tempered debater, and a hard drinking man, a patriot of his state though not a conservationist by instinct. His opposite number, Colonel Chapman, was a wholesale druggist, a civic booster who liked the limelight, and a vigorous leader. Both were men of courage and integrity, who endured political attacks and personal abuse. It is fair to say that without Squires and Chapman there would be no Great Smoky Mountains National Park.

In 1925 it appeared very likely that the state of Tennessee was about to complete an early purchase of the first land for the park, 76,507 acres of the Little River Lumber Company for $273,557—essentially the same land involved in the incipient, ill-fated national forest. When opposition to the expenditure arose in the legislature, the Knoxville Chamber of Commerce chartered a special train to bring the entire legislature out from Nashville to see the Smokies for themselves. And when the bill failed anyway (due to intensive opposition led by James B. Wright, a landowner in Elkmont and attorney for the Louisville and Nashville Railroad, who campaigned for a national forest in the Smokies), Chapman and Mayor Ben A. Morton of Knoxville placed their city on record as being willing to pay one third of the purchase price. The legislature reconsidered and passed the bill.

This was a heroic demonstration, considering that the mayor and his council were subjected to accusations of municipal extravagance. It was a Chamber of Commerce victory, too. The role of the Chamber cannot be denied. One may wish it could be said that the national park was established for sheer purity of purpose, for the preservation of wilderness for its own immortal sake. But in 1925, Robert Sterling Yard, secretary of the National Parks Association, came to see the Smokies. Yard was a brilliant writer, who could rhapsodize poetically, and yet scientifically, about the glories of a national park. Wrote Yard of the Smokies cause: "There is no doubt that it will bear an investment of the first order from an economic point of view. It is impossible to consider this question sentimentally only."

Across the mountains, meanwhile, fellow Carolinians almost destroyed the efforts of Squires, Horace Kephart, and their allies for the national park. For one thing, pressure was still strong to divert the park movement to the Grandfather-Linville area. In addition, the emotional Senator Squires himself created a problem by charging that his state commission was "being played for a bunch of suckers" by the Southern Appalachian National Park Commission. Dr. E. C. Brooks, the educator, who was secretary of the state body, was obliged then and often thereafter, to mollify Squires' outbursts and play the peacemaker's part.

It was touch-and-go when Mark Squires presided at a meeting at the

Battery Park Hotel in Asheville on July 7, 1925, attended by members of his commission, the Asheville Chamber of Commerce, representatives of nearby mountain towns, and all of the members of the national commission, with the exception of Harlan Kelsey. Now it was evident that strong opposition existed to the Smokies project; and the lumbermen would never be stopped except through legal injunction or condemnation of their land by North Carolina. In the next few days, members of the national commission endeavored to convince logging officials that further cutting of virgin timber would damage chances of the Smokies being selected as a national park, but Champion and all the rest were pleased with *that* prospect. After meeting on July 18, the National Park Commission issued a sober warning that it might have to modify its proposal—"owing to the opposition of certain business interests in North Carolina to the original plan for a national park in the Great Smoky Mountains"—and consider the advisability of a national park entirely in the state of Tennessee.

"About one half of the North Carolina project originally designated seems available but the holdings of two or three of the largest timber corporations are difficult to acquire as virgin areas," the commission declared. "If they are not secured until after the timber is cut off, they will not be fit for a national park for recreational use. The companies are at the present time engaged in active operations on some of the higher elevations and are removing the spruce and balsam forests in their entirety."

On the next day, July 19, an article appeared in the *Asheville Times* by Horace Kephart. It told, in sober words, what was going on:

"Our Government has, as yet, no definite policy about the acquisition of lands for park purposes in the East, where there is no public land that might be set aside for the purpose. Such a policy is now in the making, and nobody knows what Congress may do about it. I have heard individual expressions of opinion by congressmen to the effect that if the states of Virginia, North Carolina, and Tennessee should each take enough interest in the park project to donate a part of the fund needed to buy the lands, Congress would probably do the rest. But it is necessary, in order to engage the active support of the Federal Government, that the states chiefly affected should themselves do something worth while."

Kephart took special note of the efforts being made by Champion to save the land for its purposes by advocating a national forest, as a substitute for a national park. The company had gone back to the argument of 1900–01 of conservation through use. It was claiming that a park would cut its jugular vein and destroy it.

"I have the best of good will for the Forest Service and all that it stands for," wrote Kephart. "The waste lands left by former lumbering must be reforested, of course, and the Federal Government is the proper agency to effect it. But if the Smoky Mountain region were turned into a national forest instead of a national park, the 50,000 to 60,000 acres of original forests that are all we have left would be robbed of their big trees. They would be the first to go.

"Why should this last stand of splendid, irreplaceable trees be sacrificed to the greedy maw of the sawmill? Why should future generations be robbed of all chance to see with their own eyes what a real forest, a real wildwood, a real unimproved work of God, is like.

"It is all nonsense to say that the country needs that timber. If every stick of it were cut, the output would be a mere drop in the bucket compared with the annual production of lumber in America. Let these few old trees stand! Let the nation save them inviolate by treating them as national monuments in a national park.

"The Forest Service does not need this small acreage of woodland giants. There are hundreds of millions of acres of cut-over lands, or lands springing up in second-growth, in eastern America, that are perfectly adapted to reforestation.

"In fact, the Forest Service does not want it. A number of years ago the National Forest Reservation Commission established a purchase unit in the southern Appalachians which included the Smoky Mountain area as a desirable one for the Government to purchase as a national forest. But, just recently, the Chief Forester recommended that negotiations for its purchase as a national forest be stopped in order to clear the way for its acquisition as a national park.

"There is no use, then, in talking about conserving the Smoky forest by turning it into a national forest after the lumbermen get through with it.

"The question, the only question, is: Shall the Smoky Mountains be made a national park or a desert?"

The Carolinians and Tennesseans were engaged in a race to acquire land for the park before prices became prohibitive; but they had also to keep abreast of the Shenandoah supporters who, it seemed to them, cared only about establishment of their own park in the Blue Ridge, despite agreement to work for the common cause of both.

Dr. Brooks, secretary of the North Carolina Park Commission, warned Secretary Work in August 1925 of the Virginians' "independent course" that might defeat the whole park program for the Appalachians. Serious efforts were made to bring the groups together. Representatives of the three states conferred in Washington with the national commission, then again in Richmond on September 9. They agreed to a joint campaign to convince the nation of the advantages in establishing the twin national parks at the same time. From this meeting the Appalachian National Park Association was formed in order to raise funds on a broad scale. It was a good idea on paper, but it did not work. Not until John D. Rockefeller, Jr., entered the scene in 1928 did the park boosters obtain the philanthropic interest they had hoped for.

On both sides of the Smokies the park groups tried hard to carry their weight. Horace Kephart pitched in with the publicity work, preparing articles on the wonders of the mountains. Essay contests were sponsored in the public schools on "Why I Would Like a National Park in the Great Smoky Mountains." Across the mountains in Knoxville, Colonel Chapman led the way with a personal contribution of $5000. An enthusiastic force of 250 rang doorbells and organized campaign rallies.

The money came slowly at first. School children in Knoxville and neighboring counties gave pennies, nickels, dimes, quarters, and dollars to the tune of $1,391.72. By January only $500,000 was raised, and almost all of that from the areas immediately surrounding the park-to-be —the desired state-wide support had not materialized on either side. Senator Squires complained that opposition of pulp and lumber companies had seriously embarrassed the campaign in Asheville. The fund finally went over the top, with the Asheville Chamber of Commerce pitching in the last $35,000 to meet the North Carolina goal.

With this vigorous demonstration of local interest as a strong point, Representative Temple, the commission chairman, and Senator Swanson of Virginia introduced identical bills on April 14, 1926, "to provide for the establishment of the Shenandoah National Park in the state of Virginia and the Great Smoky Mountains National Park in the states of North Carolina and Tennessee."

The bill made it clear that the parks were to be acquired by gift, without cost to the United States Government, and presently the bill passed both houses and was signed by President Coolidge on May 22.

It was more of a tantalizing morsel than a full-course meal. The bill provided for creation of a national park at some future date, rather than immediately.

The boundaries would cover a total of 704,000 acres, as recommended by the Secretary of the Interior, but the National Park Service would assume the responsibility of administration and protection only after a minimum of 150,000 acres was conveyed to the Government, while general development would not be undertaken until a major portion of the remaining land was likewise conveyed.

The formidable tasks of raising money and buying land lay ahead on a long, long road. It is true that $1,066,693 had already been subscribed by the state of Tennessee, Great Smoky Mountains Conservation Association, and Great Smoky Mountains, Incorporated; but not one acre of land was firmly in hand, despite the option to buy the Little River Lumber Company tract.

There entered now Arno B. Cammerer, in behalf of the National Park Service, to offer a guiding hand as to the quality of land that should be purchased first, and the standards of land that would be acceptable to the Government. He became the Federal official most intimately associated with shaping the park. For him, Mount Cammerer is named, 5025 feet high, at the eastern end of the national park, east of Mount Kephart, Mount Chapman, and Mount Guyot along the Appalachian Trail.

A native of Nebraska, Arno Cammerer had come to the nation's capital to work in the Government and study law. A man of culture who moved in the circles of artists and landscape architects, including the celebrated Frederick Law Olmsted, Jr., he had joined the National Park Service in its early years under Stephen T. Mather. He was Assistant Director under Mather and Albright, whom he in turn later succeeded as Director.

Cammerer was so committed personally to national park projects in the East that he covered on the ground almost all of the lands now included in the Shenandoah, Great Smoky Mountains, Mammoth Cave, and Isle Royale national parks, and worked hard to push the cause of the Everglades National Park in Florida. He assisted in laying out the boundaries of these parks; he advised the associations, commissions, and state governments on the best methods of securing lands, or funds for securing lands. He was instrumental in obtaining vast donations from private sources; in the case of the Smoky Mountains, Cammerer was the man John D. Rockefeller, Jr., and his associates dealt with most—and he had their trust and respect.

Cammerer's mission to the Smokies was a veritable adventure in diplomacy. In the course of many trips from Washington he became an intimate of all the main park supporters, and many of its foes. Chapman was closest of all to Cammerer, according to Verne Rhoades, "but he was fair to us in North Carolina."

The first 150,000 acres marked as the target for acquisition were along the main ridge, as well as spur ridges and canyons extending from Mount Guyot to Gregory Bald—the very heart of the present park. Cammerer urged the state officials to move expeditiously in purchasing tracts of virgin timber in order to stop logging before it was too late, and before speculation would drive the prices up. Yes, he said, cut-over tracts might also be acceptable; given protection from fire they would be covered with a good growth of vegetation within fifteen or twenty years.

It was a tremendous undertaking, of a nature unknown and unforeseen anywhere in the United States before that time. In the case of national forest purchases under the Weeks Law, villages and settlements were left undisturbed; the emphasis was on the restoration of land no longer wanted, whose value had been destroyed. In the Smokies, Cammerer and his allies in the two states reckoned with clusters of settlements, churches, schools, cemeteries, sawmills, and virgin timber stands. And some of the poorest, least wanted lands became cherished treasures. The same general situation existed in the Shenandoah country, and after a meeting of state officials and the Southern Appalachian National Park Commission in Washington on June 30, 1926, a statement was issued declaring: "It is not the intention of the associations representing the three states to pay high prices for lands which have recently been purchased for the purpose of speculation or which are being held at speculative prices. It is the intention, however, to acquire ultimately all the land prescribed by the act, and it is hoped that these lands may be acquired by private negotiations if possible without recourse to the power of condemnation."

The outlines of the park boundary were changed from time to time. The original "taking-line" of 704,000 acres embraced most of the Chilhowees, Tuckaleechee and Wears coves, Gatlinburg, and the valley into Pigeon Forge; on the North Carolina side, it extended to Waterrock Knob in the Balsams and to the edge of the town of Sylva. Then there was the boundary based on Cammerer's survey, known as the "Red-line" or Cammerer Map, which he prepared with the help of General Frank Maloney of Knoxville and others. Later Verne Rhoades suggested including all the watershed of Cataloochee Creek in place of the original eastern boundary along the creek; after Cammerer and Kelsey made a field trip with him, they agreed and the adjustment was resolved.

Despite co-operation in Gatlinburg, led by Andy Huff, James B. Wright, the L & N railroad attorney, was still determined to fight the park movement with his national forest counterproposal. Carlos Campbell in his book, *Birth of a National Park*, details Wright's provocations and mischief among the Elkmont landowners. Then there was Colonel Townsend, who was on and off again about selling his Little River land. "Let us continue to harvest trees," he said to Knoxville as late as 1929, "for our payrolls will be spent in your stores." But Edward J. Meeman, editor of the *Knoxville News-Sentinel*, countered that while payrolls would last but a few years, the national park would last forever and grow in value to the same merchants. In Knoxville, Meeman was an instrumental figure in the Smoky Mountain park movement. His views and efforts were shared by Charles A. Webb, publisher of the *Asheville Citizen and Times*, and by Josephus Daniels, of the *Raleigh News and Observer*, who had been Secretary of the Navy under Woodrow Wilson and viewed the Smokies with a national perspective.

At last, in November 1926, the first large tract of land was purchased. It was the Little River Lumber parcel, an appreciable package of 76,507 acres. Colonel Townsend generously sold out at the original option price ($273,557.97) but, hardly able to bid his land good-by, stuck a proviso in the agreement that allowed him to keep cutting virgin timber for fifteen years.

It was headway and hardship on one side, then on the other. The boundary line tentatively established by Cammerer gave Tennessee 228,500 and North Carolina 225,000 acres, with a leeway of approximately 10,000 acres on each side, to be acquired for the necessary total of 427,000 acres before the park could become official.

Alas, the North Carolina fund campaign had produced a plethora of promises, but little hard cash. It became apparent that help would be needed from the state in the imminent battle with the lumber companies. After no small struggles, the legislature voted in February 1927 to issue bonds in the amount of $2,000,000 to acquire land for the park and established a new commission to direct the project. Squires and Brooks were re-elected to their respective positions as chairman and secretary; Plato D. Ebbs, of Asheville, a key figure in the park crusade, became treasurer. The North Carolina legislature generously stipulated, however, that its counterpart in Tennessee must take similar action for the $2,000,000 appropriation to be valid. In April, this indeed was done, with an appropriation of $1,500,000 (financed by a gasoline tax). This money came only with a struggle, too. Before the legislators voted, they were all invited by the Knoxville boosters on a sojourn to Gatlinburg and environs. While traveling by car to Elkmont, stronghold of James Wright, the park foe, they were greeted by road signs reading, "Inside Park Area: Will Our Homes Be Condemned?" But the appropriation was made and Colonel Chapman became chairman of the Tennessee Great Smoky Mountains Park Commission to direct land buying and get things going.

To succeeding generations, there is something breath-taking about this whole affair of democracy asserting itself in the mountains. The depression had not yet settled over the country, but North Carolina and Tennessee were poor states even without it. True, the boosters kept assuring themselves that a national park would bring untold prosperity. They foresaw millions of visitors, spending millions of dollars. "All over both states they will go, seeing the immense resources of both states and hearing of opportunities for investment," proclaimed a brochure published by the Great Smoky Mountains Conservation Association. There would be increased land values, increased tax-bearing power, so that whatever these two fortune-struck states would want, "from good roads to improved high schools or from new libraries to better salaries"—all of these could be more readily provided once the magic plateau of the national park was achieved.

But there was more to it, there had to be. A man in New York, quiet, but with a keen mind and eye for such things had been well aware of the Smoky Mountain campaign since 1924. John D. Rockefeller, Jr., was certain there was more to the motives of the Carolinians and Tennesseans than increased tax-bearing power, so certain that before long he would enter into partnership with the people.

The states needed and looked for an angel. Between them, North Carolina and Tennessee had $5,000,000 in the kitty, which, it now developed, was about half as much as they would need.

In 1926 a Knoxville delegation energetically mobilized a flotilla of Lincoln automobiles and sailed due north for Cumberland Gap, intercepting Henry Ford, the auto magnate and antiquarian, while he was visiting Lincoln Memorial University. Would Mr. Ford like to visit the Smokies, the very stronghold of yesteryear?

He would and did. He was interested in the mountain people and their ways, but bought nothing besides homespun. Ford was then building his Greenfield Village back at Dearborn, collecting houses, trains, covered bridges, county courthouses and shipping them home. These mountains were too tough to crate. But surely Ford was glad the Knoxville fellows were thoughtful enough to come see him in Lincolns.

On February 28, 1928, following an urgent appeal from Cammerer, John D. Rockefeller, Jr., noted for his philanthropic largess and interest in conservation, agreed to contribute up to $5,000,000 through the Laura Spelman Rockefeller Memorial, named for his mother. Cammerer was not the first person to direct Rockefeller's attention to the Smokies (as we shall observe later), but he did find the wealthy New Yorker eager to save the wonderful primeval forests. Thus Rockefeller agreed to match dollar for dollar funds made available by the citizens of the states and the states themselves. The money was to be used "only in defraying the cost of acquisition of lands and property rights in the area approved by the United States Government for the establishment of the Great Smoky Mountains National Park," and would be expended through the duly established trustees of the Great Smoky

Mountains Memorial Fund, composed of Cammerer, as chairman, Colonel Chapman, and Senator Squires.

As soon as the money was in hand, both states took immediate steps to halt all lumber cutting within the park area. This was no easy job. The companies were defiant. They did not want to sell and would yield only to condemnation. They wanted to cut timber and would have decimated the virgin stands if they had not been stopped by law.

The first major showdown came with the Suncrest Lumber Company, an outfit headquartered in New York, which owned 26,000 acres in the eastern end of the park. This tract was the remainder of 94,000 acres which Suncrest had purchased, together with a railroad and sawmill, for $1,000,000 in 1916. The company had a sawmill at Waynesville, from which it operated a standard-gauge railroad to its woodlands within and around the park boundary. It made clear that it would fight for the highest dollar, demanding a total of $2,000,000 for the 26,000 acres.

Litigation in Superior Court in Buncombe County set the value at $600,000. The North Carolina Park Commission brought suit and obtained an order to stop the company from logging and destroying park values. But this hardly ended the issue. In the Circuit Court of Appeals, where the case proceeded, the three-man court issued its decision on January 14, 1929, denying the Suncrest appeal for a restraining order. "To do so," ruled the court, "would be to hold up the acquisition of lands for the Great Smoky Mountains National Park, a great public enterprise which should be of inestimable value to that section of the country as a help toward flood control and as providing a beautiful recreation park for the benefit of the people. The restraining order would enable the complainant to continue its cutting of timber, and instead of preserving the *status quo* would result in depreciating the value of the property for which it is desired by the public."

Nevertheless, the Suncrest case ultimately went to the Supreme Court and was not completely resolved until 1932. The fate of the Ravensford Lumber tract of 32,700 acres also was fought upward to the Supreme Court. It would not be until 1937 that the state completed its purchases, although a thousand-acre mining company holding remained unacquired almost thirty years later.

"We actually had fewer problems in North Carolina than they had across the mountain," Harry Sanders recalled years later. "The holdings we had to contend with were large ones, relatively few compared with the vast number of small farms and lots in Tennessee." Sanders came on the scene as a young man employed as clerk in the office of the North Carolina Park Commission. This office was established at Asheville in 1928 with Verne Rhoades as executive secretary. He employed foresters and surveyors, operating from field offices in Bryson City and Waynesville, whose jobs were to cruise and appraise timber, and to examine titles as the basis for condemnation proceedings. When I talked with Harry Sanders in late 1964, he was Assistant Chief of Lands of the National Park Service in Washington.

On the North Carolina side there were 401 separate tracts. On the Tennessee side, the Park Commission faced the forbidding job of surveying, mapping, appraising, and negotiating the purchase of more than 6200 separate tracts, including 5000 lots in summer colonies and proposed developments, plus over 1000 small farms in the valleys and coves, and several large timber holdings.

The reaction of the settlers to the park situation varied. In the late twenties a new set of "furriners" invaded their mountains—land buyers, scientists, botanists, foresters, surveyors. To some of the natives the idea of the national park provided the chance to move and buy better land near roads and towns for their children. They were willing to sell and felt they were treated fairly, particularly those who dared set a price of $500 for their land and then were astounded when the buyer offered twice or three times that much. To others, the park was uninvited, unwelcome, and "plumb foolish"; the whole purpose was to provide a playground for rich people. Though more summer residents filed suits for damages, a few mountaineers held out and "lawed" the Government, too. They could fight for the highest dollar as well as anybody, contending they could hardly stand to be torn away from the cherished homesteads.

Despite many a story about the typical mountain man's devotion to the soil, perhaps equally typical is the yarn told of the "furriner" who came upon a mountaineer tilling a perpendicular farm. "Why don't you sell this miserable patch of ground and get out?" asked the stranger. "I ain't so pore as you think," retorted the mountaineer. "I don't own this patch of ground."

Or, as another stranger said, "You'd get along better with this property in the long run if you'd care for it." To which the native replied hotly, "Don't tell me! This is the fourth patch I've had and I've worked out every one of 'em."

Yet those places rich in memories emptied one by one: Greenbrier Cove, Copeland Divide, Tater Ridge, Cow Path Branch, Horse Shoe Mountain, Big Laurel, Bear Pen Gap, Injun Creek, Scratch Ankle, Upper Dudley, Snag Mountain, Rooster Town. Some left behind harness and plow, mule and hound dog, shoe box of letters, Bible, songbook with shaped notes, when they moved to the towns and were confronted with the strange ways of town living.

John W. Oliver, owner of 375 acres in Cades Cove, descendant of the settler often accepted as first of record in the Cove, refused to be pushed. Through his influence, Colonel Chapman was not especially welcome in Cades Cove. Condemnation was not the happiest procedure, but it was filed against Oliver in July 1929. He won the first suit. He lost the second suit and filed an appeal. The John W. Oliver case went before the Supreme Court of Tennessee three times before he accepted the inevitable. Some mountain men could hold their own against the Government almost as well as the corporation lawyers.

In 1932 Congress passed a law granting lifetime leases to the Smoky Mountain settlers. They could stay on and a few did, like the celebrated Walker sisters of Little Greenbrier Valley, but most departed the isolation for town and "flat country" living.

The large holdings were another matter. Next to the Cades Cove farms, the Aluminum Company of America owned the land almost from Chilhowee to Gregory Bald on the Tennessee side; Kitchin Lumber Company was its neighbor on the North Carolina slopes. Montvale Lumber Company held a very large tract from the Little Tennessee River to Thunderhead, which it sold in 1932 to the North Carolina Exploration Company, a mining subsidiary of the Tennessee Copper Company. The Ritter holdings extended up through Hazel Creek drainage to Silers Bald; Morton Butler Lumber owned up to Ekaneetlee Gap in the heart of the park between Cades Cove and Gregory Bald; Norwood Lumber Company owned the Forney Creek drainage up to the state line, from Clingman's Dome to Silers Bald. The Ravensford Company owned lands adjoining the Cherokee reservation; Parsons Pulp and Lumber holdings on the North Carolina side reached the slopes of Mount Chapman and Mount Guyot. Crestmont Lumber Company shared the North Carolina side of Mount Chapman, and the Suncrest Company surrounded Cataloochee. Little River Lumber Company had been the big owner on the Tennessee side (and kept logging until 1938).

Then there was the Champion Fibre Company, the giant of them all.

Champion owned 92,800 acres, almost one fifth of the national park. It owned the core of the virgin timber. It owned the slopes of Newfound Gap and part of Clingman's Dome, all of Mount Le Conte, the Chimney Tops, the Three Forks and Greenbrier wilderness, part of Mount Guyot. Besides the main mill at Canton, it owned another at Smokemont.

Champion was set against selling. Reuben Robertson, president of the company, and his associates said the spruce in the high Smokies was the reserve necessary to insure continued operation of the plant in Canton. It was the spruce that was a required ingredient for the sulfite process of paper making, although the high tops of the Smokies would be tough to get to, and costly to harvest.

In 1930 the Tennessee Park Commission filed a condemnation suit against Champion in Sevierville in order to acquire at a fair price the 39,549 acres lying in Tennessee. Champion had stopped cutting timber on its property (possibly because of the high costs, as Colonel Chapman claimed), but it demanded top money for its land, at least $4,000,-000 for the Tennessee portion in question. After a seventeen-day trial, the court handed down a verdict of $2,325,000, plus $225,000 for its investment in the mill and railroad. (The price of the land, before improvements, had been $643,500 when Champion acquired it in 1917–19.)

Colonel Chapman protested that the price was exorbitant and would destroy the park movement. Threatening to appeal to circuit court, he offered Robertson $1,500,000 for all the Champion land within the park boundaries. This placed the burden on "Mr. Reuben," the squire of the hills, who preferred more respectful treatment from his neighbors than Chapman gave him.

Robertson did not want to be the villain of the piece. But in March 1931, he began preparing for the possibility of the case going before the Supreme Court by hiring a high-class attorney, John W. Davis, Solicitor General of the United States under Woodrow Wilson, and the Democratic presidential candidate in 1924. First, however, Robertson and Davis made an effort at peaceful settlement by asking the leaders of the National Park Service to arrange and referee a bargaining session with the two park commissions. After three days of negotiations in the Interior Department at Washington, with Albright and Cammerer as mediators, the case was closed. Champion accepted an offer of $3,000,000 for all of its land inside the park. (North Carolina paid $2,000,000 for the 53,265 acres on its side; Tennessee paid $1,000,000 for the other 39,549 acres.)

J. Herschel Keener, a long-time official of Champion through the years involved, told me that after losing the Smokies, Champion bought spruce in the early 1930s in Nova Scotia, Newfoundland, and New Brunswick; even with the ocean freight to Charleston, the company found it was just as cheap to import wood as it would have been to build a railroad along the crest and spurs of Smoky.

Following the hard fight, Robertson picked up the pieces of his company's image. He did not like Colonel Chapman (with good reason—about $2,000,000 worth), but got on well with Squires, Brooks, and the North Carolina commission. In 1932 he wrote Squires: "You and your commission have engaged in a task which holds much hope for the advancement of western North Carolina. It so happened that the project threatened to disturb the favorable position of our particular industry. Whatever the ultimate effect upon us may be we shall nevertheless rejoice as citizens of western North Carolina."

It is possible to conjecture that if Robertson had pursued the case through the courts, there might never have been a national park—although some ancient land titles might not have looked too impressive in court. It has also been said in Champion's defense that by holding the high Smokies for its future reserve, the company was able to deliver the wonderful forest nucleus of "national park caliber." This could well be true. Robertson and Champion could not defeat the public interest, but they both survived in the mountain country with a good reputation.

It was much tougher, in fact, for the two heroes of the park movement, Squires and Chapman, to protect their reputations.

The opposition to the park movement focused on them. It came from politicians in both states who were trying to get their hands on the Rockefeller money; from other politicians who honestly felt the park was a waste of money; from timber interests, land speculators, summer home owners, settlers who did not want to sell or move, the Nashville press. The wonder is that Squires and Chapman survived as well and as long as they did.

By early 1930 the two commissions had purchased more than the minimum 150,000 acres required under the Act of 1926. On February 6 large delegations, headed by the governors of both states, arrived in Washington to present Ray Lyman Wilbur, Secretary of the Interior, with deeds to 158,799.21 acres of land.

"The Great Smoky Mountains National Park, when established," declared Governor O. Max Gardner, of North Carolina, "will create in the heart of the Appalachians a permanent sanctuary for animal and bird life and a botanical garden and arboretum which scientists say will be unequaled in the world.

"This great undertaking, when accomplished, will preserve the last remnant of the American wilderness of any considerable size east of the Mississippi River, and a great tract of virgin timber which will be allowed to stand in its natural grandeur, safe forever from the usual forces of devastation."

What further could Governor Henry H. Horton add, asked the Tennessee chief executive in his presentation, about "one of the greatest projects ever undertaken by any state for the benefit of mankind, and for conservation of beautiful scenic areas for the enjoyment of this and future generations."

Quite aptly, he expressed appreciation of the people of Tennessee to the Southern Appalachian National Park Commission, to the Secretary of the Interior, to John D. Rockefeller, Jr., and to Arno B. Cammerer, "unfailing in his co-operation, official and personal, in the enterprise and in his assistance in solving many unforeseen problems that constantly arise in a new project of this magnitude with few precedents to turn to for guidance."

As for Colonel David C. Chapman, a grateful state, said the Governor, could not heap too much praise upon this original park advocate "who unstintingly, without thought of self or his private affairs, has for years given his time, both personally and as chairman of the Tennessee Great Smoky Mountains Park Commission, toward the furtherance of this project." Colonel Chapman shortly would be in a position to use the support of all grateful friends.

In response to the governors, Secretary Wilbur accepted the deeds in the largest real estate operation he had ever handled. He expressed the proper and profound thanks of the American people, who would always remember the noble work of North Carolina and Tennessee, "for in the long run we are the sons and daughters of nature, and nature is at her choicest in the Great Smoky Mountains National Park."

Thus was the area granted something called "limited park status," and the United States assumed responsibility for its protection and administration. J. Ross Eakin, formerly superintendent of Glacier National Park, Montana, arrived in 1931 to become the first superintendent of the new park (who paid the price, alas, of also being its most vilified).

In 1929 members of the legislature went after Chapman. Instigated by James B. Wright, the old enemy of the park, an investigation was conducted into the affairs of Chapman and his commission. Who was this bullheaded wholesale druggist from East Tennessee, they demanded, to hold the money of Rockefeller and the state in the palm of his hand? The *Nashville Banner* and *Tennessean* were delighted to cover the hearings charging misuse of funds and to add a few gossipy comments of their own. According to Horace Albright's recollection, one of the lowest accusations against Chapman was for "indecent exposure," based on an observation of the fellow relieving himself from the porch of a lodge above Cades Cove in the middle of a night.

A majority report of the investigating committee cleared Chapman and praised his work, but the park issue was back before the legislature again and again. In 1932, in the heat of an argument over a bill authorizing condemnation (in the Elkmont and Cherokee Orchard sections) a flurry of fist fighting broke out on the floor of the House—almost a brawl by the time the aisles were cleared.

In August of that year, the *Knoxville News-Sentinel* warned of efforts to replace Chapman and the other members of the commission. "It seems inconceivable," the paper editorialized, "that the commission should again be subjected to the attacks of selfish interests who have lands to sell in the park area, friends to be favored, or personal malice to satisfy." But a new commission was appointed, only Chapman and one other member surviving. The Smoky Mountains Hiking Club was so furious at one of the new commissioners that it expelled him from its ranks and returned his annual dues, even though he hadn't paid any lately. Colonel Chapman was pretty furious, too. He and his successor, George R. Dempster, disputed each other's words during a commission meeting, and one called the other a "damned liar." Chapman struck first, but Dempster struck hardest and oftenest, inflicting body bruises, two broken ribs, a black eye, cut lip, and knocking out one tooth.

However, Chapman did not lose his tooth and pride in vain. Before the new commission was seven months old, his friends pushed through a bill to abolish it and turn its duties over to the Tennessee Park and Forestry Commission, though Chapman himself received no appointment.

Progress came hard, painfully hard, every foot of the way. The raucous behavior and disharmony in Tennessee endangered the payment of the remaining Rockefeller funds. Then there was the question of whether to build the road across the mountain, and what effect it would have. It was completed in 1930 as the first link between Gatlinburg and Cherokee (the Park Service had later to reconstruct almost the entire length on both sides) and increased land values.

Squires was fated to suffer from the same harsh treatment and abuse as Chapman. His commission was attacked with charges of squandering money and confiscating land. In 1931 the legislators considered abolishing the commission altogether, even while the touchy negotiations with Champion were under way, but softened the blow by merely demonstrating their lack of faith: all members of the commission, voted the legislature, would be retired in January 1933—to be on the safe side the state auditor would check all their account books as soon as possible.

When the legislature convened in 1933, it screamed loudly and bitterly in opposition to the park commission, charging gross extravagance, pork-barreling, failure to account, demanding investigation of the commission, abolition of the commission, and generally endeavoring to match the low political level in Tennessee. Robert R. Reynolds, a petty politician of Asheville known as "Buncombe Bob," newly elected to the United States Senate, urged the Governor to withhold the reappointment of Squires.

"It would be impossible for me to say how embarrassing to me this continued talk in the General Assembly has been," wrote John G. Dawson, a member of the commission and a prominent citizen of his state. "I have taken more pride in my efforts in connection with the establishment of the Great Smoky Mountains National Park than I have ever taken in anything in all my life."

"Appointed as we were, to please a thought deemed fanaticism and folly, we have brought the movement to a position where our successors will have nothing to do," said Mark Squires when he, like Chapman, was on the outside looking in at a new park commission, a totally political commission. "The hard work has been accomplished, and those now our detractors have done nothing to speed us on our way."

The investigation was never held, although large quantities of testimony were presented to the Governor in late 1933. Arno Cammerer wrote from Washington: "There has been no dissipation of funds; it has been a really magnificent project carried through very well." Of course it was a magnificent project, conducted by men of courage and integrity, who gained the respect of John D. Rockefeller, Jr., the admiration, though possibly grudging, of Reuben Robertson, the affection of Albright, Cammerer, and Kelsey. For their pains, they were bloodied and bruised by the politicians who tried to control their respective states.

Funds were running out. After the initial presentation of 158,000 acres, the Governors and appropriate delegations returned to Washington November 2, 1931, with deeds for 138,000 additional acres, including the Champion tract, bringing the total to almost 298,000 acres. Timber cutting continued, affecting park values, and yet the states could not match the last $506,500 of Rockefeller funds.

Representative Zebulon Weaver, of North Carolina, tried to get an appropriation from Congress in 1933, but failed. President Franklin D. Roosevelt, however, felt the national importance of the Smokies. On December 28, 1933, he issued an executive order allocating $1,550,000 out of funds authorized for the Civilian Conservation Corps "and other purposes." The Rockefeller Memorial then made an additional contribution to the project, most of which went to acquire the Ravensford land in North Carolina. In this period the Government began optioning and buying land directly with its own money.

By March 1934, the North Carolina Commission had completed its land purchase program, except for one tract of sixty acres, and presented all its deeds to the Government. The following month the Tennessee Park and Forestry Commission filed a condemnation suit to acquire the Morton Butler tract of 24,929 acres. The action was initiated only one day before the commission's authority to file condemnation suits under state law would expire—and all it had left in its accounts was $11,800. Cammerer boldly came through with a pledge that the National Park Service would pay the judgment. It took more than a year of litigation before the final judgment of $483,500 (the owners had demanded $1,400,000) was decreed.

At long last, in October 1935, nine years after passage of the bill providing for the establishment of the park, a total acreage exceeding the 400,000 set by Congress as a requirement for full national park status had been acquired. The Smokies were now ready to be taken over, operated, protected, and developed by the Federal Government.

Much land still remained to be purchased. An appropriation of $743,265.29 was made by Congress in 1938 to insure early completion of the Tennessee portion—this was maneuvered by Senator Kenneth D. McKellar, of Tennessee, by tacking an amendment to an appropriation for a western national park. It was in the days before McKellar undertook his campaign to undermine the park superintendent and harass the National Park Service.

Who really bought the park? Without denying the states their full credits, the figures show that North Carolina and Tennessee purchased only a part of it. Both states paid a combined total of $4,095,696 from appropriations and private subscriptions. The United States Government gave $3,503,766 for land purchase, plus the cost of developing and maintaining the park. The Rockefeller Memorial gifts totaled $5,065,000.

As I stated earlier, Tennesseans were wary of North Carolinians, and both were wary of the Government people in Washington. Has this changed since the great day of dedication in 1940?

"Over the years approximately twice as much money has been spent on the Tennessee side as compared with expenditures on the North Carolina side," complained the North Carolina Park, Parkway, and Forest Commission in its report of 1952. "During the years following the date the former North Carolina Park Commission became inactive and the date the present commission was created, unfortunately, relations between the state of North Carolina and the state of Tennessee, with respect to the Great Smoky Mountains National Park, became deteriorated to a point of indifference and acrimonious competition."

But that's democracy for you. It's not always right, but it's often right, in the long run. John Oliver shook his fist at the big government in Washington, and the big government shook its fist at Reuben Robertson. Granville Calhoun was "lawed" for killing a park bear that broke into his chicken house at Proctor. But Judge Webb in Bryson City told Granville he had a right to protect what he had. And after all the rights and wrongs were tallied up, and the pennies of school children and the millions of Mr. Rockefeller, there was the Great Smoky Mountains National Park, one of democracy's wonders to behold.

XV

Why the Rockefeller $5,000,000?

Franklin D. Roosevelt, the President whose physical infirmity prevented it, would have loved to hike, climb, and romp in the Smoky Mountains. Although a subtle and sophisticated man, he treasured the simplicities of nature and the out-of-doors, as even the casual visitor can tell by learning of his way of life at Hyde Park, New York, and especially at Warm Springs, Georgia. He took a considerable interest in the Smokies and had an idea about establishing a herd of roe deer from Europe, which he continued to suggest almost until the outbreak of World War II.

The President agreed to participate in ceremonies officially dedicating the new national park. Over a period of many months tentative dates were scheduled, then canceled because of depressing international developments. In June 1940, word was received that the event might have to be carried out on a few hours' notice, but in early August the President himself suggested that he would like to dedicate the park on Labor Day.

The Roosevelt entourage arrived by car from Chattanooga, where the President had dedicated Chickamauga Dam. It was a hot drive through the valley that had once been the Overhill Cherokee country, and then it was cool in the mountains, almost too cool for summer clothes. The presidential party was three quarters of an hour late arriving at Newfound Gap, which Harold L. Ickes, the temperamental Secretary of the Interior, blamed on the sad miscalculation of whoever had made up the itinerary.

Ickes was there and so was Arno Cammerer, whom he disliked intensely. Senator McKellar was there and so was Superintendent J. Ross

Eakin, whom *he* detested. Governor Prentice Cooper, of Tennessee, and Governor Clyde Hoey, of North Carolina, were there. Newton B. Drury, scholarly San Franciscan long the champion of the redwood forests, who had already succeeded Cammerer as Director of the National Park Service, was there. So were Colonel David Chapman and Mrs. Willis Davis. (Her husband and Mark Squires were dead.) Ten thousand cars rode up the mountain bumper to bumper, carrying a tremendous throng of 25,000 to hear the President and see the park officially opened.

The ceremonies were held at the crescent-shaped masonry wall and platform, straddling the boundary line between Tennessee and North Carolina, where the bronze plaque bears this inscription:

> For the permanent enjoyment of the people—
> This Park was given One-half By the Peoples and States
> of North Carolina and Tennessee and by the United States
> of America and One-half In Memory of Laura Spelman
> Rockefeller by The Laura Spelman Rockefeller Memorial
> Founded by Her Husband John D. Rockefeller.

The minister who delivered the invocation irritated Ickes. The Secretary became nervous and impatient. The Reverend continued to warm up to his subject before the illustrious audience and the vast crowd. "One of those pests who thinks that the whole nation wants to hear him harangue God ad lib," was how Ickes described him later. Finally Ickes could contain himself no longer. He touched the minister on the arm and brought him to a halt. Worst of all, he had to cut his own remarks to four minutes. The two Governors spoke, and the President delivered his speech on the international situation and its threat to American liberties. Then the official party descended the mountain into Knoxville and pulled out by train. It took the 10,000 cars until dark to disperse, despite all efforts to control and channel the flow of traffic.

Only John D. Rockefeller, Jr., was not there. He was the missing witness.

Although invited to attend, he had declined politely, writing to Secretary Ickes as follows (on July 11, 1939, when plans for the dedication were first being formed):

Dear Mr. Secretary:

Since I am just leaving for an extended absence, I greatly regret that it will not be possible for me to be present at the dedication of the Great Smoky Mountains National Park in which important ceremony you kindly invited me to participate. That the President of the United States is planning to honor the occasion with his presence is indicative of the high value which he places upon this newest park. That the governors of Tennessee and North Carolina are also to take part in the program is peculiarly fitting in view of what they and the commonwealths have done so generously and so untiringly, to make possible this noble result.

As president of The Laura Spelman Rockefeller Memorial when it pledged five million dollars to the Great Smoky Mountains National Park and as the son of my mother in whose memory the gift was made, I rejoice profoundly in the opening of this great area of outstanding natural beauty for the permanent enjoyment of the people of these United States. May the beautiful spirit of my mother, who was a loyal and devoted wife, a wise and loving parent, and an earnest Christian woman, descend upon those who visit these mountain fastnesses, who find refreshment in the shaded valleys and new courage by the side of the sparkling streams! May the peace of the Father of mankind, the Creator of all this beauty, to Whose service my mother's life was dedicated, dwell in their hearts and make beautiful their lives.

Very sincerely,

John D. Rockefeller, Jr.

"You see, this was the extent to which he felt that he should participate. He did not want the spotlight," said Kenneth Chorley when he showed me this letter from the files at the Rockefeller headquarters in New York. Chorley was Rockefeller's close associate for forty years, and served as president of Colonial Williamsburg, as emissary to the two states of the Smokies, and as a confidant. "He didn't feel entitled to it. He was the most modest human being I've ever known."

I never met John D. Rockefeller, Jr., and therefore have been unable to ask him what he was thinking when he decided to go ahead and contribute $5,000,000 to the cause. Once, at Williamsburg, I overheard a visitor comment to his wife, "Rocka-fella could afford to do all this, with his millions. He had to spend that money somewhere and didn't care where." Well, that was one theory expounded by a curbstone expert.

Writing about Rockefeller, or any man of immense wealth, is difficult, because you find yourself currying favor with his establishment or currying antifavor with the disestablishment (from the servilely subsidized to the carpingly critical, as James Warner Bellah once characterized the range of writing about the Du Ponts). But I want to treat John D., Jr., in terms of the Great Smokies and areas related to them, without concern for where he got his money, whether he had too much of it, or where he spent the rest of it.

This is not easy either, for he has often been dealt with and portrayed as an institution rather than as a human being. His own phraseology doesn't make it easier. The purpose of his benefactions to Acadia was to make accessible "one of the greatest views of the world." When he made a gift of Forest Hill, outside Cleveland, it was so the people of the community could enjoy, "as I did during the happy days of my childhood and youth, the beautiful area comprised within the park." When he came away from the Redwoods, he was "speechless with admiration at anything so beautiful as the forests we came through today." He gave funds to preserve Linville Falls in North Carolina because it was "that beautiful area." He gave the $5,000,000 for the Smokies in memory of "the beautiful spirit of my mother."

He was a man who indeed felt a natural love for beauty, in architecture, painting, nature, and the landscape, a love that he wanted to share. I have seen this demonstrated time and again in the course of my travels over the years—in the Smoky Mountains and Acadia, the Grand Tetons, the Redwoods in California, Williamsburg, the Cloisters in Manhattan, Tarrytown on the Hudson, the old Baptist Church in Providence, and at Versailles (he contributed millions after World War I to preserve and restore the palace and gardens).

Many places where he expressed his interest in restoration and conservation reflect his personal taste and touch. A Rockefeller road is always built with native material; the borders are landscaped naturally and never look ugly—they're not allowed to. He wanted and had things done right, well ordered, never left raw nor displayed too loudly, but always neatly. He was meticulous to a fault and wanted the national parks to which he contributed kept as clean as his own development at Williamsburg. Once, after fire swept over Bar Harbor and Acadia in 1948, Park Service naturalists wanted to leave the burned and downed timber to serve as a breeding place for insects, which in turn provide food for bird life, but Rockefeller shuddered at the unsightliness and paid to have nature's messiness tidied up. It is also true that he personally selected the site of Jackson Lake Lodge, in the Tetons, though it otherwise would have been located at a less conspicuous setting.

If these incidents indicate flaws in his viewpoint, they were minor flaws, negligible when weighed in the balance. Rockefeller came on the scene with great wealth and clear vision at a time when relatively few Americans were concerned with conservation. He plunged into projects concerning endangered areas, as Chorley recalled, or projects that might never have been undertaken. Sometimes these were daring in size and concept, and stirred fierce opposition. At the same time he was involved with the Smokies, Colonial Williamsburg was just getting started; there he was not interested in restoring a single building in inappropriate surroundings, but in reviving an entire segment of the past. And concurrent with the Smokies and Williamsburg, he was active in Jackson Hole, Wyoming, where he bought up 30,000 acres between 1926 and 1950, despite the wrath of local ranchers, and assured preservation of one of the most beautiful mountain valleys in the world.

As for the Smokies, he didn't write a check for $5,000,000 as a contribution to a worthy charity. He knew exactly what he was buying—it was virgin primeval wilderness to be safeguarded for generations hence —and he insisted through Cammerer that the states block timber cutting before it went too far.

He respected North Carolina and Tennessee. Maybe they wouldn't have been able to raise their matching funds, or sell their bonds, without the stimulus of his $5,000,000 gift, but it was overwhelming to him that the people of the two states should have the foresight and courage, in the midst of a depression, to spend their money for the national park and for their children's children.

In short, above all others involved in the Smokies, John D. Rockefeller, Jr., who could not, because of his immense wealth, have experienced much intimate contact with the common man, demonstrated his faith in the people and faith in the future. He believed in them both. In his own way, these ideas must have been in his thinking when he decided to contribute to the cause.

"No fuss and feathers about young John D.," wrote O. O. McIntyre, in his newspaper column of October 8, 1930. "He walks up the avenue window-shopping every evening he is in town to his home around the corner in West Fifty-fourth Street. Many in his neighborhood do not recognize him. His home is not particularly pretentious. Around his doorway or loitering nearby are always two guardsmen in plain clothes. Mr. Rockefeller often stops to talk to a street sweeper in his block. He is seldom seen leaving his home after dinner.

"Those who know say John D., Jr., is the most dutiful of sons. He phones his father wherever he may be daily. He visits the family home at Tarrytown twice a week and father and son take long walks together about the Pocantico Hills estate."

He had a fixation about his parents. He was trustee, not owner, of the Rockefeller fortune—that was his father's money. Everything he did was in the name of his father, or of his mother, as in the case of the Smokies.

He developed his lifelong interest in landscaping as a boy on the family summer estate outside Cleveland (which he later presented as a city park). When he was sixteen, Rockefeller became involved in clearing underbrush, resurfacing roads, and planting scores of trees. If he

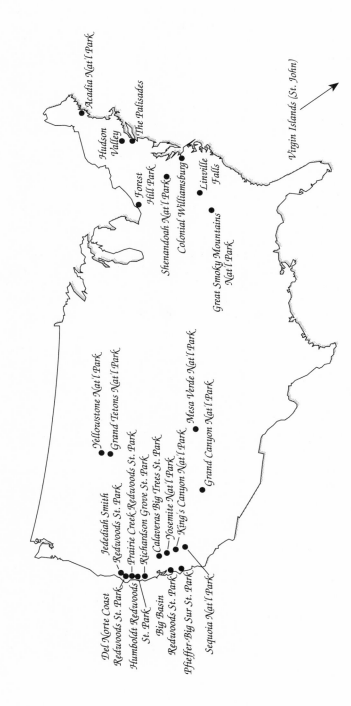

Acadia Nat'l Park

Hudson Valley

The Palisades

Virgin Islands (St. John)

Forest Hill Park

Shenandoah Nat'l Park

Colonial Williamsburg

Linville Falls

Great Smoky Mountains Nat'l Park

Yellowstone Nat'l Park

Grand Tetons Nat'l Park

Mesa Verde Nat'l Park

Grand Canyon Nat'l Park

Jedediah Smith Redwoods St. Park

Prairie Creek Redwoods St. Park

Richardson Grove St. Park

Calaveras Big Trees St. Park

Yosemite Nat'l Park

King's Canyon Nat'l Park

Del Norte Coast Redwoods St. Park

Humboldt Redwoods St. Park

Big Basin Redwoods St. Park

Pfeiffer-Big Sur St. Park

Sequoia Nat'l Park

State and national parks to which Dr. John D. Rockefeller, Jr., contributed aid.

had had to work for a living, he might have become a landscape architect (much later he was awarded honorary membership in the American Society of Landscape Architects) or a nurseryman. He surprised the park naturalist in the Smokies, Arthur Stupka, with his knowledge of trees and shrubs and his close examination of the veins of leaves. Not so the people who worked for him at Williamsburg. They became accustomed to his recognizing trees not only by species, but as individuals; whenever he visited Williamsburg he could tell where a tree had been cut and wanted to know the reason.

Rockefeller's first association with national parks was at Acadia. He was among the elite Bar Harbor summer residents who responded to George B. Dorr's appeal to preserve Mount Desert Island, leading to the establishment of Sieur de Mont National Monument in 1916. He not only donated 2700 acres of land, but offered to build and maintain a road system. Acadia was a bit of prelude to the Smokies, for it had been well scarred with resort developments, logging mills, and a cog railroad to the summit of Mount Cadillac, all of which are gone today.

However, it was his meeting with Horace Albright in the summer of 1924 that marked his full entry into philanthropy for conservation.

He had contacted Stephen Mather, though he didn't know him personally, asking for aid in planning a tour of the western parks with his three oldest sons, John, Laurance, and Nelson. Mather instructed the superintendents to make themselves available, but to restrain themselves from talking about their financial problems unless the gentleman of means asked specific questions. This, apparently, was precisely what John D. had in mind. At Mesa Verde, the shrine of the cliff dwellers, he asked Superintendent Jesse Nusbaum a few questions and before he knew it, he was giving money to help establish a park museum because Congress had given nothing to house and display the treasures of the ancient culture.

Then he proceeded on to Yellowstone. In those early years Horace Albright was there each summer as park superintendent, then he would return to Washington to pick up legal and administrative problems of the whole park system as Assistant Director under Mather. At the moment of their meeting before the railroad depot at Gardiner, Montana, John III, eighteen, was recording in a notebook the amounts paid in tips to Pullman porters, while Nelson, the future governor of New York, then sixteen, was engaged in helping porters transfer baggage from the train to Yellowstone Park buses for a group of tourists. As the superintendent guided the Rockefellers over the park during the next few days, John D., Jr., was disturbed to observe timber that had been slashed years before, in the 1870s and '80s to open the way for park roads, stacked and rotting along their route. He later corresponded with Albright about whether it could be cleaned up, and how much it would cost, and in the next three years contributed $50,000 toward a tidier Yellowstone.

In 1926 he returned to the West to have another look around, but perhaps to see Albright more than the sights. They began their long period of association based on mutual respect and trust. "I felt close to Mr. Rockefeller from that year until he died in 1960," Horace Albright told me. "He regarded me as his adviser on conservation problems and affairs and I often had visits with him in his office and at lunch." (Albright left the Government in 1933 to become general manager, then president, of the U. S. Potash Company, with headquarters one building removed from Rockefeller's office in Rockefeller Center.) Rockefeller was reticent, cautious, alone. For all his wealth and generosity he could be cautious with his money, too. When his wife wanted to restore the interior of their house at Williamsburg, he resisted at first. "They can use the money elsewhere," he said. Finally, he gave in but quipped in his wry manner, "Just so you don't take in tourists." Albright had the gift of penetrating with sound advice in questions of principle, policy, and ideals, of suggesting where money must be spent in the right places. In the course of thirty-five years his advice and judgment influenced the expenditure of millions of dollars to acquire historic and natural treasures for the public.

Rockefeller placed his trust in people like Albright. And Chorley, who joined the inner organization as an assistant to Colonel Arthur Woods, educator, industrialist, and first president of Colonial Williamsburg, whom he succeeded when Woods became Herbert Hoover's director of unemployment emergency relief in 1930.

It was in 1924, as the records studied by Chorley show, that Rockefeller became aware of the campaign to establish a national park in the Great Smokies. And it was Willis P. Davis who made a pilgrimage from Knoxville to New York in order to talk with one of Rockefeller's associates, in the hope of enlisting financial support. Davis went away empty-handed, but later that year Director Mather sent Rockefeller a request to join him in making a contribution toward the expenses of the Appalachian National Park Committee. He contributed $500, as I have written earlier.

"In 1926," according to Chorley, "the treasurer of the Great Smoky Mountains National Park Purchase Fund Campaign wrote Mr. Rockefeller requesting a subscription to express his interest, but the request was declined. Actually, the National Park Service and others interested had told the local people that, if they would meet certain conditions, help would be given them in getting citizens throughout the country to support the effort, and Mr. Rockefeller's declination was doubtless based on the fact that he would be called on in the later effort and therefore was not inclined to contribute at that time."

In August 1927, after the legislatures of North Carolina and Tennessee had taken action to furnish funds, Cammerer wrote to Rockefeller with an eloquent plea. It would require some $9,316,000 to establish the park, he advised, of which $4,950,000 had been raised or pledged. The two states had done all they could—now public-spirited men all over the nation must be counted on for the remaining $4,400,000.

It is possible that Cammerer came to New York for a conference later that year, at Rockefeller's invitation. "Mr. Rockefeller respected Cammerer's judgment highly and liked him personally," recalls Horace Albright. "When it comes to discussing who convinced Mr. Rockefeller of the importance of the project, and who furnished him with the information necessary to make a decision, I feel we must give credit to Cammerer. It was he who did the big job of making financing certain."

Rockefeller at first pledged $1,000,000. He interested Edsel Ford in pledging $50,000. By early 1928 the campaign for public subscriptions had made no other headway; only the Rockefeller and Ford pledges had been received. Then he decided to contribute the whole amount. He would do so through the Laura Spelman Rockefeller Memorial Foundation, a relatively small foundation established by his father. Surely, as Rockefeller said, preserving the beautiful Smokies would have appealed strongly to his mother. At a meeting of his staff in February 1928, he discussed his plans. "Gentlemen, this is something that interests me. I hope it interests you."

The first week of March, Chorley went south to review the precise terms of agreement with the Governors and other officials of both states. The announcement of the gift was made simultaneously in North Carolina and Tennessee on March 6. It was greeted in Knoxville with the sound of whistles and bells throughout the city at 4 P.M. Across the mountains, two days later, the *Raleigh News and Observer* (whose editor, Josephus Daniels, and Rockefeller were in correspondence about the national park) commented thoughtfully: "It must give large satisfaction to the two Rockefellers to make the $5,000,000 donation in the name of wife and mother and thus associate her with the loftiest of God's creations, which for all time will be the resort of those who seek sweet communion with nature."

However, on March 27, still finer words were written by an unforeseen correspondent, the president of the Bank of Lenoir, a North Carolina mountain community.

Dear Mr. Rockefeller:

I note from the papers that the Governor of North Carolina and probably other officials in some way connected with the Great Smoky Mountains National Park have written you in acknowledgment of your recent magnificent contribution to that great project. This you of course expected, but I am wondering if it would not be even more gratifying to you to know of the very deep and sincere appreciation on the part of a warmhearted southern people—the rank and file of a great deal of just plain "everyday folks." It has occurred to the writer that, while this sentiment of gratitude for so munificent a gift exists and is freely expressed among the thousands, it may occur to all too few of them to tell you so, therefore I am, without authority, taking the liberty of acting as spokesman for this individually unknown and un-numbered multitude in conveying to you this expression of unbounded admiration for your generous act.

Very sincerely,

J. H. Beall

The reply was dated March 31:

Dear Mr. Beall:

Your gracious letter of March 27 is received. Nothing in connection with the gift to the Great Smoky Mountain Park in memory of my mother has touched me so deeply as the warmhearted and sympathetic appreciation of the people of the South of the memorial aspect of this gift. Your letter only emphasizes that appreciation, and in so doing adds to the satisfaction which my father and I feel in the making of this gift.

Please accept my thanks for the friendly spirit which has prompted you to write me so delightful a letter.

Very sincerely,

John D. Rockefeller, Jr.

Having committed himself to the Smokies, Rockefeller decided that summer to go and see the region for himself.

He and his wife stayed at the Mountain View in Gatlinburg, attended the First Baptist Church, and visited Cades Cove. It was the first of several visits. After his wife died and he remarried, he took the second Mrs. Rockefeller on a honeymoon trip in 1954, traveling down the Blue Ridge Parkway by motorcar to the Smokies. Always he tried to plan these trips quietly (on his 1924 tour of the western parks he traveled with his sons under his middle name of Davison), with arrangements through Horace Albright and the park superintendents.

Long after he had assured the future of the Smokies, he paid a friendly call in 1950 with his youngest son, David, that cost him $100,000 to acquire a parcel of Blue Ridge scenery he would never see personally.

Grandfather Mountain by then was a lost cause for the Park Service. The Service had hoped to manage it as a unit of the Blue Ridge Parkway, together with Linville Falls, ten miles southeast, where the Linville River pitches over a towering outcrop of rock, then tumbles between the dark walls of Linville Gorge. In the early 1940s, the McRae family, the owners of the mountain, had granted the Government an option to purchase its 5500 acres for $165,000. Another 14,000 acres was to be transferred from the surrounding Pisgah National Forest. Under this plan, the 6700 acres in Linville Gorge were to remain under the Forest Service to be administered as a wilderness area, the first in the East, devoted to a completely primitive environment, with a simple trail system down into the gorge and into side canyons.

True to its ancient policy, Congress would appropriate nothing toward the purchase of Grandfather. True to his tradition, Rockefeller had offered to pay half the required amount, if the other half could be raised through other sources. When the option expired, the McRae family granted a renewal, raising the price to $180,000. Harlan P. Kelsey, the conservation leader who had played a key role in the Appalachian Park study of the 1920s, arrived on the scene and barnstormed North Carolina on a fund-raising drive. Not one cent was pledged in the entire state. "What's wrong with Grandfather the way it is?" Kelsey was asked. "What makes you think they'll spoil it?" Although Asheville people in the twenties had urged Grandfather-Linville as a national park, in the forties they turned their backs on the same cause. Finally, in 1948, the option was canceled, Grandfather no longer was for sale. The finest mountain of the Blue Ridge chain was lost to public ownership, where one day it must properly find its place.

This was not, however, the end for Linville Falls. From New York, Albright telephoned Superintendent Sam P. Weems, of the Blue Ridge Parkway, that Rockefeller wanted to tour the southern mountains on a quiet father-son vacation with David. It was the hope of both Albright and Weems, a man known and admired throughout the mountains, to interest Rockefeller in the appealing beauty of Linville Falls, whose primeval environs had never been logged.

The reservations were made in Weems's name. The first night the Rockefellers and their chauffeur stopped at a hotel in Shenandoah Valley, adjacent to the Parkway in Virginia. The second day they continued south through Roanoke. David was now driving, with his father in the front seat and the chauffeur in the rear—so the park rangers reported by radio to their superintendent. Weems and his chief ranger, E. M. Dale (later superintendent of Chesapeake and Ohio National Monument), departed from Roanoke in cautious pursuit of the three-year-old Cadillac with New York plates.

At Floyd Plateau, near the Virginia-Carolina border, the Rockefeller car pulled off and parked on the shoulder of the road. David clambered down a steep hillside in the direction of a cabin far below. He was carrying a large bundle. A green-painted official ranger vehicle came along and stopped behind the Cadillac. The two men in uniform got out and approached the big car.

"Oh, are we in violation of some regulation?" asked John D. Rockefeller, Jr., looking just like any other citizen (and perhaps secretly hoping to be apprehended).

"No, Mr. Rockefeller," replied Superintendent Weems, with a laugh. He introduced himself. "I just happened to be driving down today. The chief ranger and I thought we'd see how you're getting along."

"Well, you had that hotel pack such a large picnic lunch for us that we decided we'd share it with some needy family. That's why we've pulled off here. David has just gone down to that cabin with the basket."

In a few minutes David returned with a proud announcement that they had found just the right place, the home of a poor widow with several children and a "fantastic story"—of how her husband died in the middle of one night and she didn't know he was dead until she happened to touch his feet under the covers and they were cold.

The two cars traveled down the Parkway. Rockefeller was deeply impressed with its management. "I want to compliment you on doing a fine job," he told Weems at one stop. "This is the most picked-up park I've seen."

The entire party stopped for the night at the lodge at Doughton Park, one of the loveliest settings in all Appalachia (located in Wilkes County, celebrated for mountain music and moonshine). Rockefeller, as always, showed his interest in landscaping and road construction. "How can you afford such fine stone curbing?" he asked. "Why, it looks like the entrance to a private estate." When Weems explained that, with native materials and local labor, the Government paid ten cents a foot, delivered, Rockefeller replied, "Do you know how much this would cost at Tarrytown? At least ten times as much."

Next morning Weems proposed that Rockefeller and David ride in the Government car, with the chauffeur following. They carried a basket of food, complete with linen, for a picnic lunch. Superintendent

Weems was determined to make his play for Linville Falls, where a lumber company was then cutting virgin timber on the ridge top and endeavoring to obtain the rights to the property directly surrounding the Falls.

After a generally pleasant morning (during which the chauffeur became lost on a side road in the hills and had to be rescued by a ranger), Rockefeller asked where they would stop for lunch. Weems checked his watch, calculated thoughtfully, and announced that the logical place would be Linville Falls—where else?

They stopped under a big old hemlock and unloaded the basket.

"Before lunch, Mr. Rockefeller," suggested the superintendent, "wouldn't you like to walk up and see the falls?"

"I'd better not. It looks like a steep climb. My doctor cautioned me against overexertion. David, you go with Mr. Weems."

They climbed the hillside. David asked about a little heath plant, the Allegheny sand myrtle, questioning whether it might grow at Tarrytown. He stood briefly at the brink of the watery chasm in the wilderness and took but one photograph with his camera.

While they lunched, Weems told the Rockefellers about the logging encroachment and the possibility of saving the beauty spot. His hope rose when Rockefeller asked, "How much could it be bought for?"

"The asking price is much higher, but I think one hundred thousand dollars would do it."

"That's very interesting."

The superintendent reached in his brief case for a folio of photographs, maps, and descriptive material on the Falls. Rockefeller accepted it without comment, or even looking at it, but passed it to the chauffeur to be filed in the luggage. The superintendent's hopes fell.

That evening in Asheville, after dinner at the Battery Park Hotel, Rockefeller said that he wanted David to have a suit made of the famous Biltmore Industries homespun cloth. The Industries shop itself was then closed, Weems advised, but the hotel gift shop carried a rack of bolts of Biltmore homespun.

They went to the gift shop across the lobby, where David bought dolls for his children and his father selected four or five hundred dollars' worth of cloth, while the young girl clerk stared at the slight, average-looking man picking out all that merchandise.

"May I write a check for the amount?" he asked her.

"Well, I'm not sure," she hesitated. "You've spent an awful lot of money. I don't know whether I can take a check for that much. Do you live in Asheville?"

Superintendent Weems came forward and volunteered his good confidence, as a Government official in uniform, in the gentleman's honesty and the integrity of his check. When she accepted the check rather reluctantly, the girl looked as though she was going to ask Weems to endorse it with his signature. But when she read the name, she turned purple, looked faint, and gasped inaudibly.

The next morning, at their parting, Weems thought he was bidding farewell to his dream of acquiring Linville Falls. It appeared so hopeless that he did not even mention the area.

Six months later, Albright wired: "If you can buy Linville Falls for $100,000, Mr. Rockefeller agrees to contribute full amount."

And so he spent his money. Though probably he had more of it than any one person should have, he spread it where it was needed in behalf of all people, filling a deep void during a period of Congressional indifference, and asking little personal recognition. Mr. Rockefeller foresaw his responsibility. He was, by all odds, a man worthy of his role in the Great Smokies.

As for his purchase on the Blue Ridge Parkway, when he returned in 1954 on his honeymoon trip with the second Mrs. Rockefeller, Sam Weems served as his guide once more.

"Would you like to go to Linville Falls, Mr. Rockefeller?" the Parkway superintendent inquired.

"Oh, that's right. I did buy something down here for you."

"Yes, Mr. Rockefeller, you sure did."

XVI

Crucifixion of Ross Eakin

On June 30, 1939, the Honorable Arthur H. Vandenberg, Republican from Michigan, rose before the United States Senate to question the need of a proposed investigation into the administration of J. Ross Eakin as superintendent of the Great Smoky Mountains National Park.

"I want to be sure," declared Senator Vandenberg, "that the basis of the investigation is something different from the basis of his crucifixion on the floor of the Senate a few months ago."

His colleague and sponsor of the investigation, the Honorable Kenneth D. McKellar, a powerful and vitriolic Democrat from Tennessee, was a difficult man to resist. "The Senator knows that the Secretary of the Interior wrote an eighteen-page letter," persisted Senator Vandenberg nonetheless, "which, evidently, a terrific effort was made to suppress before the Senate was called upon to vote on the matter involving Mr. Eakin. The Senator listened to the Secretary's letter, and it seemed to the Senator that the Secretary of the Interior gave Mr. Eakin a thoroughly clean bill of health."

J. Ross Eakin was placed in this manner on trial before the United States Senate. It was not only a national park superintendent standing judgment, however; for as the *Knoxville News-Sentinel* editorialized, "The Eakin fight is more than the fight to 'get' or 'save' one man. It is a symbol. Somewhere, sometime, the people are going to have to make a last-ditch stand against the political patronage monster."

Patronage was not the only question. "He has depended upon a man by the name of Cammerer, who happens to be at present the head of the National Park Service," said Senator McKellar, in the course of the earlier Senate dialogue, on April 17, 1939. "Mr. Cammerer has been woefully negligent in his duty."

Secretary of the Interior Harold L. Ickes, a man of many moods, defended Ross Eakin, but persecuted Arno B. Cammerer. Perhaps it was more than one national parks director that he was determined to tame, but the spirit that characterized the age of Mather and Albright. Ickes felt the Park Service was too independent and loyal to its cause, and decided to teach the agency and its career men a lesson in obedience and responsiveness.

Kenneth D. McKellar was a rough, tough, crusty machine politician, who built his strength in Tennessee by "bringing home the bacon" from Washington and by demanding every bit of his share in control of patronage (which earned him the title of "grand-pappy of all political pie-hunters"). He built his strength in Washington through the system known as seniority, which recognizes and rewards the talents of those who can survive one election after another. McKellar entered the Senate at the age of forty-seven in 1916, halfway point in World War I, and was returned again and again, for a total of thirty-six years, through World War II and the dawn of the atomic age, until Tennessee voters turned him out as an old man in the election of 1952. Meantime, however, he became a power of the Senate Appropriations Committee, a man who could by his yea or nay grant or deny funds for the pet projects of his colleagues. His outlook was partisan, and heaven help the man who crossed him—for McKellar spit nails and spewed venom. David Lilienthal, chairman of the Tennessee Valley Authority, a highly honorable and able public official, was another, besides Ross Eakin, whom McKellar tried to destroy.

As for the Great Smoky Mountains, it is undeniable that McKellar gave valuable aid to the national park much of the time. "The establishment of the park," he had said during the trying formative years, "would not only help Knoxville and East Tennessee but the whole state. And anything that helps Tennesseans should have the support of all good Tennesseans." Then again, it was McKellar who obtained the appropriation of $743,000 in 1938 for land buying when the money was sorely needed.

"He was a friend when he thought it would help him politically," said Horace Albright, "an enemy when he thought there was political profit in being an enemy. Park Service people had to be extremely cautious with McKellar because we didn't know which way he would go."

Albright, who was Director of the Park Service from 1929 to 1933, told me a typical and revealing story. One day he was out with Herbert

Hoover at the President's fishing camp on the Rapidan River in Virginia. Hoover was impressed with the possibilities of the emerging Shenandoah National Park. He directed Albright to survey the crest for the road that would open panoramic views of the Piedmont Plateau on one side and the Shenandoah Valley on the other. In due course McKellar learned about the scenic road project and demanded the Park Service provide one just like it for the Great Smokies.

The national parks Director went to see him and endeavored to explain that because of the rugged topography there could never be a road along the eastern crest of Smoky, and moreover that there never should be—that a large portion of the Great Smokies should be preserved as roadless wilderness. The two national parks were designed to complement each other, Albright emphasized; it would be ridiculous to develop them exactly alike.

McKellar exploded. He couldn't bother with such details as the meaning of a national park and the methods of its management. He blasted Albright and for good measure blasted Albright's parentage. That a damn career bureaucrat would dare to stand in the way of the welfare of Tennessee! McKellar would have liked to punch the rascal (who had to be a Republican anyway, since he was serving under Hoover) squarely in the nose, and he said so.

Albright withdrew. He was a tough man in his own right, but knew when to advance and when to retreat. In a few days he returned to Capitol Hill. McKellar refused to see him, but Albright had brought along an intermediary, a mutual friend, who insisted that he listen to the parks Director and held him strongly by the arm while he did. "I will explain to you the difference between the two parks, of Virginia and North Carolina-Tennessee," began Albright. After so doing, he concluded, "I will not, under any circumstance, go ahead with the road you demand. Furthermore, Senator McKellar, I resent your personal insults."

Despite McKellar's power and influence, that road was not built. The politicians were obliged to accept the National Park Service as a bureau that ran its affairs on non-partisan integrity. They may not have liked it, but they respected the Service all the more because it lay beyond the spoils system. The tradition had begun with Mather. Like Gifford Pinchot, in the Forest Service, Mather didn't have to come to Washington to work for a living. And like Pinchot, he established a high level of pride in his agency. ("From the day I entered the Division of Forestry under President McKinley until I was dismissed by President Taft, not one single person in the office or the field was appointed, promoted, demoted, or removed to please any politician, or for any political motive whatsoever," wrote Pinchot in his autobiography, *Breaking New*

Ground.) Mather was tough. When, after he had ordered a lumber company to dismantle its mill and depart the bounds of Glacier National Park, the company disregarded him, Mather headed a brigade that exploded the mill with thirteen charges of TNT. Perhaps Mather reflected the philosophy of President Woodrow Wilson, under whose administration the Park Service was established—Wilson, who fought the issues before the people on principle, rather than among the politicians on expediency. Thus, when it was suggested to Mather that park superintendents be appointed under the same terms as postmasters, with the consent of the President (and the gentle advice of congressmen), Mather replied that he was going to pick his own people according to capability alone. And so he did, building a career force of trained parks people with loyalty to the Government and with a wonderful *esprit de corps.*

Mather was gone when it came time to choose the first superintendent of the Great Smoky Mountains National Park, but his successor, Albright, was cut from the same cloth. He had to pick a top man. Taking charge of half a million acres is no small responsibility (and neither is managing *any* area in the national park system). The Smokies would present special problems. "No hunting is permitted in any national park," explained Director Albright during an inspection trip in October 1930, but adding quickly, "which protection in time results in an overflow of the game to outside the boundaries, thereby furnishing excellent hunting in the areas next to the park." There would be other regulations to enforce: prohibiting distilling of liquors; occupancy of houses inside the boundaries without permits; digging of flowers or shrubs; cutting of timber, setting of fires—none of which the local backwoods mountain men looked upon with favor. In preparing to transform the wilderness into a park, the Government would have to establish ranger stations, campgrounds, field museums, and lay out roads, trails, telephone lines.

"We chose J. Ross Eakin with deliberation," recalled Albright. "He had had experience in the Geological Survey as an explorer and topographic engineer. He was strong and stocky and gave the impression of a man who could not be intimidated or frightened. He had the qualifications of a superintendent who would deal fairly with the public on both sides of the mountains, who would steer clear of political intrigue and reach his decisions without partisan influence. He had a solid background in running a big park at Glacier and served very well when he was moved to the Grand Canyon in early 1924, at a time when mining claims around the rim threatened to destroy the whole park. Moreover, though most of his experience was in the West, Eakin was a native of West Virginia, who understood the eastern mountains."

But he didn't understand McKellar, and for McKellar his being a native West Virginian was not good enough to put him on a Federal payroll in Tennessee.

The eminent Senator began a personal vendetta against Eakin, but the principle at issue was the right of a United States senator to have his say in the appointment of a national park superintendent and how that superintendent should run his park.

McKellar was determined to use the payroll of the Civilian Conservation Corps in the national park as an outlet for Democratic patronage. His idea was to give every Democrat in Sevier County, regardless of qualifications, a job in the emergency conservation program.

"Be damned if I will!" protested Eakin. He was brusque and businesslike, a stocky five-foot-five or -six, an ex-major of the Coast Artillery, who had commanded a battery of heavy guns in France during World War I. He was devoted to national park principles, though sometimes he bypassed bureaucratic procedures, and had the backing of Colonel Chapman and the conservation leaders in Knoxville. His staff admired him. "Hell, yes" or "Hell, no," he would bellow in response to a question, but still he knew how to delegate authority. "I want this done by such and such a time," he would order. If one of his staff asked *how* he wanted it done, Eakin would reply, "That's your problem." In 1940, while he was on vacation, Miss Mary Ruth Chiles was hired to work in the office. On finding a woman among those present when he returned, his comment was, "I'm damned glad of it. Maybe it will cut out some of the rough talk around here."

McKellar disliked Major Eakin so intensely for his refusal to play politics that he arranged secretly to receive reports from agents on the park staff.

In 1939 McKellar dragged his noble crusade before the nation. "Eakin is from West Virginia and he's got a setup of men from out of the state, except two or three lower-paid men," he declared as the year opened. "All but one or two of them are Republicans. I think the superintendent should come from Tennessee."

Furthermore, Eakin had refused to authorize the purchase of land from a handful of McKellar's patriotic constituents at prices considered exorbitant by the land appraisers. "He's got no business," protested McKellar, "passing on the value of lands acquired for the park."

The New Deal may have been shot full of politics, but Secretary Ickes protected the National Park Service from being manhandled (except by himself). "I wouldn't remove a man except for cause," he replied to McKellar's demand for Eakin's removal, "and his political affiliation is not a cause. Eakin has done a good job."

McKellar did not think Eakin had performed well at all. For one thing, he didn't like the way the superintendent had voted in the election of 1936—or the way he thought he had voted in 1936. And how did the Senator know? Very simply, by having the election clerks mark the ballots of Eakin and park employees with ink smears, then transmitting the ballots to McKellar. A simple case of the democratic process as practiced in Tennessee country politics.

But McKellar, shrouded in the cloak of probity, also unearthed accounting irregularities concerning CCC funds in the books of the Great Smoky Mountains National Park, which he magnified into proportions of graft and corruption on Eakin's part. These were probed by the Department of the Interior in 1937 and 1938. Eakin was cleared of mismanagement and fraud; because the CCC camps had been flung up overnight, with inadequate provision for record-keeping, funds had been recorded in the wrong columns of the ledger books.

With malice aforethought, the distinguished Senator from Tennessee made the ledger books of the Great Smoky Mountains National Park the main issue of the day at the Capitol of the United States on April 17, 1939. It was just a few weeks after the Park Service had decided to knuckle under to the political pressure and announced that Eakin would be shifted to Shenandoah, Virginia. But he had too many boosters and the *Knoxville News-Sentinel* could scream as loudly as McKellar. The transfer was rescinded. McKellar, in righteous wrath, urged the Senate to adopt an amendment to the Interior Department appropriations bill eliminating the salary of the "present superintendent of the Great Smoky Mountains National Park."

The junior senator of Ohio, Robert A. Taft, asked why the man should be punished. So did Senator Vandenberg of Michigan. Both, of course, were Republicans, although Taft in particular was noted for following his convictions of rectitude wherever they might lead.

"My friend from Ohio is exceedingly suspicious; he is the most suspicious man in the world," declared the gentleman from Tennessee. "I do not know whether it is ambition or what it is, but something makes the Senator from Ohio very suspicious."

What made Taft suspicious, as the discussion evolved, was that the Appropriations Committee had conducted hearings into Eakin's conduct. The only member present at the hearings was the diligent Tennessean himself. The principal witness of the star-chamber proceeding was one Herman E. Myers, Regional Fiscal Officer, or examiner, of the National Park Service—a good man and true, McKellar called him— who produced the evidence damning Eakin.

But apparently there was another piece of evidence, too, a letter from Secretary Ickes to the Honorable Carl Hayden, of Arizona, chairman of the subcommittee on Interior Department appropriations, in defense of Eakin.

What about that letter? asked Taft.

Hayden had forgotten all about it, didn't think it was important, hadn't really read it—and all the while Eakin was being smeared and derided on the Senate floor.

McKellar was having so much fun that at one point, when he referred to the Secretary of Interior's proposal to shift Eakin to Shenandoah, the Honorable Carter Glass felt constrained to join in.

MR. GLASS: "Mr. President, what business had he to transfer a crook to Virginia?" (Laughter)

It was strictly a Democratic joke. The Honorable Alben Barkley wondered aloud whether, since Senator Taft was so solicitous about Eakin's welfare, the subject of debate could be transferred to Ohio.

But Senator McKellar rose tall and statesmanlike, declaring:

"Mr. President, is it possible that our Government has sunk so low that we are going to keep a man like that in the Government employ? I am glad the Senator from Virginia is present. I decline to let a man like that go into his state, and notwithstanding the fact that he is being defended by the distinguished candidate for the Presidency, the Senator from Ohio (Mr. Taft), on this floor, I would decline, even under those circumstances, to let him go to Ohio, if I had anything to do with it."

The Honorable Tom Connally, of Texas, wondered whether the language of the amendment preventing any of the appropriation going to the superintendent was really strong enough. He wasn't really interested in the affair, he said, but suggested tougher wording to prevent the Secretary of Interior from transferring Eakin to another division and paying him out of other funds. Just before the final vote to seal Eakin's fate, the junior Senator from Ohio claimed the floor.

MR. TAFT: "Mr. President, in the first place I wish to say that I never heard of Mr. Eakin before last week. I do not know him. I do not know what his party affiliations may be. I have read the testimony which the Senator has submitted; and it seems to me to show a large number of minor irregularities. I do not see, however, that the gentleman has ever been charged with any moral turpitude.

"By the amendment, particularly as amended, we are throwing out, without any trial or any hearing, a man who has spent his entire life in the Park Service, who has grown up in the Service until he has reached the position of superintendent of one of the great parks in the United States. The Senator conducted some kind of star-chamber session in which he examined Mr. Myers, the accountant. Mr. Myers did not come before the committee. The committee did not have the opportunity to cross-examine him. The chairman of the subcommittee has just admitted that Mr. Eakin, or his representative, requested an opportunity to appear before the committee if the question came up. He had no hearing before the committee. If Mr. Eakin has committed any offense he can be tried, and if he is convicted he can be removed. This is not the place to do it. It seems to me that the proposed procedure is simply trial by lynch law because of the personal feeling of one member of the Senate against a particular man.

"I have not been able to obtain the letter from the Secretary of the Interior, but certainly the Senate will not act unfavorably to this man without at least hearing from his superior officer. We have a right to that hearing."

At long last, the Ickes letter was somehow discovered and read. The proceeding grew confusing, even to the Democratic wheelhorses, including Scott Lucas, of Illinois.

MR. LUCAS: "Whom is the Senate to follow? It seems to me we are in somewhat of a dilemma. The examiner says that this man is a crook. On the other hand, the Secretary of the Interior, by written testimony, says that the general reputation for uprightness and good character of this man is excellent, and he wants him retained."

But the gentleman from Tennessee staked his case on the accountant, Myers, whom he had seen but once. "He impressed me as being a very honest man and a very able accountant."

Senator Vandenberg joined Taft in pleading for Eakin. Of the amendment to cut off his salary, Vandenberg said, "That is his death warrant."

In this manner was a national park superintendent put to trial before the Senate of the United States, known as the greatest law-making body in the world, but never as a court of law. I doubt that such an episode could ever be repeated. Senators do not dictate the appointment of park superintendents; on the other hand, as an official of the Park Service once confided to me, "Now we would be careful to transfer a superintendent from a state *before* a senator or congressman objected to him."

The Senate rejected the McKellar rider by three votes (31 nays to 28 yeas and 36 not voting), but the persistent Tennessean continued to hound Eakin. In May he introduced a resolution calling for a Senatorial investigation of the superintendent. It was in consideration of the resolution, when it reached the Senate floor, that Senator Vandenberg decried the raw crucifixion of Ross Eakin.

"But did the Senator read that which is in the *Record*," demanded McKellar, "which shows that the Secretary of the Interior sent an auditor down to examine the accounts and affairs of the park under Mr. Eakin, and that the auditor after a careful examination reported innumerable derelictions of duty? Did the Senator read that, or did he pass it over?"

The mysterious Myers, that efficient and honest accountant, was still the key to the case.

The resolution was adopted, $5000 was appropriated to indulge McKellar's passion, and the committee proceeded to investigate. The members were Senators Carl A. Hatch, of New Mexico, the chairman, and Henry F. Ashurst, of Arizona, both Democrats, and Gerald P. Nye, of North Dakota, the Republican. Unfortunately, I have not been able to locate any documentation of the hearings or the printed report. However, I have had the benefit of an interview with Jackson Price, then a young attorney in the Department of the Interior, later Assistant Director of the National Park Service. Price was assigned by the Department to represent Eakin as his attorney at the hearings.

Before the hearings began, Price was called in by Ebert K. Burlew, Assistant Secretary of Interior for administration. Burlew was a Republican holdover, whom Ickes had insisted on retaining as an able and essential officer of the Department; because he was not of the party in power, Burlew himself had been subjected to a bitter investigation and a scurrilous attack.

"You won't gain anything by arguing," advised Burlew. "The more you try to defend your man, the more they will carry on the attack. Let them wear themselves out. Report to me every day after the hearing."

McKellar brought a criminal lawyer from Knoxville to be sure that justice was served. The committee, however, endeavored to be fair to both McKellar and Eakin. Senator Hatch, in particular, demonstrated repeatedly that, while deferential to his colleague, he was determined to reckon squarely with the park superintendent.

At first, nothing detrimental to Eakin transpired. When McKellar accused Eakin, supposedly a Republican, of claiming to have voted for Roosevelt in the 1936 election in order to curry favor with the Interior Department, the committee saw the absurdity of the charge. McKellar showed his embarrassment. But not for long.

"I want the accountant brought in," he said. "I demand the subpoena of Mr. Myers."

Attorney Price advised that a subpoena was unnecessary, that if the committee wanted to question Myers, the National Park Service would have him available the next morning.

Herman E. Myers appeared at the Capitol of the United States to impart vital information to a subcommittee of the Senate. He was slight of build, mild of speech, self-effacing, and he wore a hearing aid. Senator McKellar endeavored to set him at ease by introducing him to the committee as a fine, courageous, and able man.

"Now, Mr. Myers," continued McKellar gently, asking a series of questions regarding expenditures and account books of the national park in the Smokies.

Strangely, however, Myers seemed to be answering contrary to the record McKellar had revealed to the Senate.

The Senator's face reddened. His questions grew sharper.

"Mr. Myers," he said, no longer gently. "You remember when you came to my office and gave answers?"

Myers stiffened, rose from his chair, looked squarely and stubbornly at McKellar, and replied, "When I came to your office you didn't tell me a reporter was present. I couldn't understand your questions. I couldn't hear, being without my hearing aid, but you insisted on answers. The answers to many questions were taken down incorrectly by the reporter."

Senator Hatch entered tactfully to rescue the deflated McKellar. As chairman, he gave a statement of generalities concerning the hearing and announced the committee planned to look closer at the accounting system of the park. (The committee's report, in January 1941, cleared Eakin of any wrongdoing, but recommended changes in procedures of accounting.)

In the winter, after the hearing and furor subsided, Eakin invited attorney Price to visit the Smokies. Price found him a quiet, mild-mannered, and likable person. He was bewildered by McKellar's unrelenting bedevilment, but not too upset or concerned, feeling that he, as a national park superintendent, could hold his own, with the support of his agency and of understanding national park boosters. Eakin showed Price over the park, but while they were driving down from Clingman's Dome their car skidded on a patch of ice or snow. The car spun and fell twenty-five feet over an embankment. Price threw himself from the car and broke two ribs. Eakin, however, struck his head and suffered a concussion. He also received an injury to his back from which he never fully recovered. In late 1944 he suffered a paralytic stroke and lapsed into unconsciousness. For eighteen months he lived in a coma, until his death at the veterans' hospital at Johnson City.

McKellar, always a hard man to cross, grew doubly bitter after the Eakin hearings in Washington. He fought Ickes and the Park Service. The Secretary and the Service refused to knuckle under. McKellar made it difficult by cutting appropriations for the Great Smokies. The park suffered until after World War II, while other national parks moved ahead with their developments. In 1945 McKellar got part of what he wanted. Eakin's successor was a Tennessean, a veteran of the Corps of

Engineers; he may not have been too experienced in parks work, but he was the brother-in-law of a congressman.

Meanwhile, Harold L. Ickes couldn't stand Arno B. Cammerer and couldn't wait to get rid of him. When Ickes had come on the scene in 1933 he found Horace Albright serving as Director of the National Park Service. Albright was the kind who stood up to him in a discussion and refused to be talked down or berated; the Secretary of the Interior respected him, and others, for such behavior. But Albright departed in August for the mining business (he might also have decided it was time to avoid the Secretarial slings and arrows) and left Cammerer as the logical and inevitable choice to succeed him.

Ickes was a strong member of Franklin Roosevelt's cabinet. He felt that he could resist, or even insult, members of the Senate like McKellar because he had the President's backing. He worked hard at conservation and left noteworthy accomplishments (although he was thwarted in his highly questionable crusade to transfer the administration of the national forests from Agriculture to his own Department). However, he suffered from shortcomings in his own personality—which he recognized. He was temperamental, unpredictable, stubborn, given to tantrums, a many-sided man, difficult to understand, who could look out his office window and shudder with sentiment at the sight of a tree being removed from Rawlins Park, then turn around and blaspheme some well-intentioned and perfectly competent subordinate.

Once Kenneth Chorley came to see him to discuss Rockefeller's plans for Jackson Hole in the Tetons. Ickes proceeded to denounce Cammerer roundly, which was one of his favorite activities, both in front of the parks Director and behind his back. "I asked Chorley whether he would come in to run the parks," Ickes wrote in his diary. "He did not know whether I was serious or not and neither did I."

Another time William G. Shirley, highway commissioner of Virginia, came to attend a meeting in Ickes's office about a national park matter in his state. Shirley, a courtly southern gentleman, was highly regarded in Virginia and in Washington. He made the mistake of asking a question of Ickes. "I told you to have the answer before you came to see me!" Ickes exploded. "Shirley, get out of my office!" Two subordinates of Ickes's led the Virginian away and endeavored to soothe his jangled nerves.

He was especially rough on national parks people, whom he considered to be ingrained bureaucrats in need of spanking. Charles Goff Thomson, superintendent of Yosemite, a sensitive man who appreciated the finest qualities in nature and conservation, suffered a heart attack after being browbeaten by Ickes. At another time, a superintendent was summoned to his office. The man stood before his desk. The Secretary did not look up but continued working through his papers. "Rogers," said Ickes after a time, without ever greeting the man or even looking at him, "you're fired." The man's jaw dropped; he was wordless. Ickes continued with his desk work. The superintendent withdrew from the Secretary's office to national park headquarters, where he reported the grisly episode to Arthur E. Demaray, the Associate Director, whose special facility was handling Ickes. "Don't worry," Demaray directed. "Go back to your park. We'll take care of it." Not another word was heard from Ickes.

He respected those, like Albright, who would not be pushed around. Colonel John R. White, superintendent of Sequoia National Park, had occasion to help a Hollywood motion picture company find a suitable mountain location for a film. The producer wanted to reward him with money for his effort, but White advised that he couldn't accept such a gift. The moviemaker persisted and, instead of cash, presented him with a fine new riding horse. When Ickes learned about it, he was furious and ordered the park superintendent to return the horse. But White bounced back with a message that he had done nothing wrong, and saw nothing wrong in accepting the horse, which he had no intention of returning. The episode ended there.

Cammerer lacked the disposition to stand up to Ickes. He felt a compulsion to respect and defer to his superior in the Government. It was the wrong way to handle Ickes. Cammerer, the man of refinement, was inclined to like everybody he met. But Ickes couldn't understand that outlook and took advantage of Cammerer's good nature.

Ickes delighted in putting Park Service people, Cammerer in particular, on the carpet. He had a group in one day about a land transaction. "The lawyer over whose desk the papers passed seemed so dumb that I asked him whether his conception of his duties was that of a legal robot," wrote Ickes later in his diary. "I gave him hell and ordered an investigation with the full intention of suspending him under charges if I find that he really knew what was going on and failed either to protest to his immediate superiors or to bring the matter to me." The worst treatment he saved for the Director:

"I was particularly rough on Cammerer. As usual, he sat by my desk vigorously chewing gum in an openmouthed manner. I asked him who was responsible for his bureau and when he acknowledged that he was, I told him the facts seemed to prove what I had charged him with some time ago, namely, that he is in total ignorance of what goes on in the Park Service."

Cammerer had to go, one way or the other. For a time the Secretary considered appointing Robert Moses, of New York, to take his place.

Then he thought of Michael W. Straus, Director of Information in the Department, and later Commissioner of Reclamation. When he discussed it with Roosevelt, the President thought well of giving Straus the job, but asked Ickes what he would do with Cammerer in the Park Service. "I told him that I would offer Cammerer a job as a Regional Director. No doubt remains in my mind that the Park Service needs new blood and a strong man."

Ickes was spared the trouble. In April 1939, Cammerer suffered a heart attack, which led him to submit his resignation as Director. When he recovered, he continued as Regional Director at Richmond, Virginia. He visited the Smokies, which came under his region, from time to time until his death in 1941.

However, more than Cammerer was involved. The Mather-Albright era was shaken. Maybe not all at once, but the pieces that shaped the great tradition were loosened around the edges. The tale is told that Stephen T. Mather, not liking certain conditions he encountered in a national park, so wrote his old friend of college days, Secretary Franklin K. Lane. The Secretary, the story goes, wrote back: "Dear Steve, if you don't like the way the national parks are being run, come on down to Washington and run them yourself." Those days were over. The career people would have less and less to do in determining the destiny of the national parks. The Ickeses and the McKellars and the party in power would take over; they might not know as much about parks, but they would know more about politics and patronage.

Ickes was suspicious of the Park Service. Besides being "stereotyped" with "too many incompetent people," it needed "new blood" to purify the "bureaucracy." He couldn't understand the *esprit de corps* or the devotion to purpose, complaining about the bureaucracy being "so well established that no one down the line dares to go over the heads of his immediate superiors and bring to me important information." (But he resented anybody in the Department "short-cutting" him by going to the White House.) When he received a report about a questionable method of land appraising, he quickly concluded that Park Service people "had been in a conspiracy to defraud the Government, not for personal profit, but to build up the park system." He was convinced that it was a "criminal conspiracy" traceable to the Hoover Administration, since the appraising method was started under Albright. It turned out that there was no conspiracy at all; the report from the General Accounting Office was in complete error, but Ickes, with his deep suspicion of the Park Service, had leaped to a conclusion and given it credence.

As the new Director, Ickes brought in Newton B. Drury, a distinguished Californian (and, much to Ickes's credit, a Republican). Drury was a genuine conservationist, who kept the standards of the National Park Service at a high level. I believe that he and every other Director of the National Park Service have tried their best to serve the interests of the nation, for today and for the long tomorrow; and so, too, have the superintendents of the Great Smoky Mountains National Park.

XVII

Social Workers in High Places

A social worker who had ventured from the Pi Beta Phi Settlement School in the early 1920s to engage in extension work in the region called Sugarlands reported to her headquarters on what life was like. She was not only at the remotest possible outpost of education, but in "a land of poorer homes" as compared with Gatlinburg—which itself had been chosen by the women's fraternity, after careful study, as the community most in need of help anywhere in the southern Appalachians. She wrote that one family with which the teachers ate Sunday dinner provided the food on lard pail lids. Three broken dishes held the other food to be served. Four grownups were privileged to sit on the only chairs but the boys stood. Chickens picked up crumbs underfoot while the meal progressed. Although the walls were blackened with smoke, large bright blue paper bows had been fastened upon them by the little girls to brighten this cheerless atmosphere.

There she was, our social worker, feeling like a pioneer in a primitive world, a part of the movement of Pi Beta Phi that carried books into the hills and hollows up Baskins and Spruce flats, and Mill Creek, Little Dudley, into the Sugarlands and Little River. She was part of the broader movement, too, of welfare people working their way into the crannies of Appalachia, bringing with them instruction not only in reading and writing, but in sanitation, personal hygiene, homemaking, and how to earn a living. Some of these fit together, for the teachers encouraged the mountain people to revive the vanishing old crafts, like weaving, and to perfect their work in basket making, which they hoped would prove profitable.

It was the age of the settlement houses in the teeming cities, the Henry Street Settlement in New York and Hull House in Chicago, and of the humanitarian social workers, the Lillian Walds and Jane Addamses. They provided nurseries, adult education, libraries, all sorts of training that brought hope and help to poor immigrants crowded in the tenements of a strange new land. And in Appalachia, the spacious, rich, and beautiful country, these were no less needed by the so-called pure Americans; where lives were cribbed, cabined, and confined, and typhoid fever and tuberculosis were widespread—strange diseases for mountain people who spent most of their time in the clean country air.

Berea College in Kentucky was an early vital influence (and still remains so), affording students from eight Appalachian states the chance to "barter for larnin'." In North Carolina, Miss Frances Goodrich, a social worker, early in the century started Allanstand Cottage as a crafts center in Asheville in order to bring "healthful excitement" to mountaineer ladies. It became evident to these people, who had hand-hewn and hand-made almost everything they owned, that they could use, swap, and even sell their products. Mrs. George Washington Vanderbilt was another of note; despite her wealth, she was deeply social-conscious (and after her husband's death arranged transfer of most of the Biltmore Estate to become the nucleus of Pisgah National Forest). Observing that many homes still had looms, she inspired the establishment of Biltmore Industries in order to widen the opportunities open to the mountain people. Their weaving proved successful not only as a craft but as a business venture which is still thriving. Then there was Mrs. Olive Dame Campbell, who organized the John C. Campbell Folk School at Brasstown, near Murphy, in memory of her husband, director of the Southern Highland Division of the Russell Sage Foundation.

One of the heroines of this movement in Carolina, Miss Lucy Morgan—widely known, admired, and loved as "Miss Lucy"—was born in the mountains at Franklin. When I met her she was settled in her retirement villa, a complete house of crafts on a hilltop at Webster, facing the Smokies; despite age, she was youthful of spirit, radiant, and beautiful, clearly one of God's chosen and blessed, an exemplar of teaching and social work, who asked little during her lifetime but to associate with humble mountain people, to believe in them and reveal to them their own creativity.

Miss Lucy had been out in the world, teaching in a Chicago suburb and working in the Children's Bureau in Chicago, before she returned to the mountains. In the early twenties she came to Penland, tucked away between Mount Mitchell and Linville in the Blue Ridge, where her brother, Rufus, an Episcopal minister, had lately founded an institution of rural learning known as the Appalachian School. Her experiences of the next forty years became the basis of her book, *Gift from the Hills*, written with LeGette Blythe.

Her inspiration derived from the people themselves. One day, early in the Penland years, she went to see Aunt Susan Phillips, in the hope of learning to do a little weaving. Aunt Susan was in her nineties and yet was the only person in Mitchell County who still knew how to weave. The old lady showed Miss Lucy all of her hand-woven coverlets, some in blue and white, some in rose madder, blue, and white, mostly woven in the traditional pattern called Cat's Track and Snail's Trail. She and her two daughters were wearing linsey-woolsey skirts and basques; they showed yardage in reserve which Aunt Susan had woven years before. Most of the materials were colored brown, having been dyed with walnut hulls or walnut or roots (also known as "warnut"). At the bottom of the skirts there were strips in various vegetable-dye colors—indigo blue, the yellow of hickory bark, tan from onion skins, green produced by dyeing yarn first in the ooze of hickory bark and then, after it had dried, in an indigo bath.

"There was nothing harsh in Aunt Susan's colors; all were soft and mellow and rich," wrote Miss Lucy. "For me her coverlets were the greatest attraction; I fairly ogled them, I felt their softness and perfection of texture, I marveled at their color. I yearned to know how to create such materials and such patterns. All the way home I thought of those beautiful specimens, each worthy of immortality in some museum, and of what a tragedy it would be were the art of creating such things lost to succeeding generations."

In time, on a song and a prayer, but no cash to speak of, Miss Lucy began the Penland School of Crafts in order to perpetuate native skills and to provide the people of the Toe River Valley a means of livelihood. After she herself had mastered the art of weaving, Miss Lucy had to walk the hills to the homes of her weavers, and teach them how to warp, beam, "thread up," and follow designs.

One cold winter's afternoon she stopped at the home of a mountain woman who had been weaving scarves requiring only two harnesses; but Miss Lucy wanted her to try a four-harness operation.

"Law," the mountain woman sighed, looking hopelessly at the draft. "I never could learn to do that."

"Yes, you can. You're a smarter woman than I and I learned to do it."

"Why, Miss Lucy," she insisted. "I hain't had no education."

"Education doesn't put brains in your head."

"Well, I reckon it don't. But it helps you use what you got. Don't it?"

"Sometimes, I suppose. You can do it, though, and I know it."

With this encouragement, the woman did learn to thread the new draft on her own and from then on solved many intricate loom problems. To be told once was all she required.

The weavers of Penland produced goods for sale. They created things with which to beautify and make their own homes more comfortable. They wove curtains, towels, table linens, dresses. One bravely wove her husband a suit—and he bravely wore it. They revived a cultural heritage.

Such incidents were in the genesis of Penland. Miss Lucy had also to build markets and sales outlets; though never operating on more than a shoestring and a prayer, she displayed the work of her craftsmen in the sophisticated North and in Europe, and attracted enthusiasts and teachers who came to Penland for study and work. The United States State Department on many occasions has sent official visitors and students to observe this little center in the hills.

In the winter of 1928 Penland was the scene of the organization meeting of the Southern Highland Handicrafts Guild, which brought together the workers of Berea, Pi Beta Phi, Brasstown, plus similar schools and shops throughout Appalachia. Allanstand offered the Guild its facilities in Asheville as a sales outlet for jewelry, wood carving, pottery, wrought iron, and weaving. The Guild has grown so well that every July members converge on Asheville to set up their looms, benches, and wheels for the five-day Summer Craftsman's Fair; they do it again in October at Gatlinburg for the Fall Craftsman's Fair. These crafts have been more than preserved, they have been revived from the brink of extinction.

When the Guild was still young, Miss Lucy and other members thought of interesting National Park Service officials in helping to assure that only quality craft products would be sold in the Great Smoky Mountains National Park and along the Blue Ridge Parkway. These two areas were just being developed, but Miss Lucy conceived the idea of going to Washington to see the head of the Park Service, whoever he might be. Off she went, armed with a letter from the Governor of North Carolina.

Who was it she saw but Arno Cammerer himself, then Assistant Director.

"Not at all what I expected a Washington bureaucrat to be like," Miss Lucy reminisced. "He was just as natural and real as someone down under Bailey's Mountain at Penland. I gave him my letters and hoped he wouldn't read them until I was gone, but he did.

"He asked why I was so interested in the people and the crafts of the mountain region, and I told him I was a mountain girl myself. 'I'm from the sod houses of Nebraska,' he said, and right then he won my heart. Mr. Cammerer remained a friend as long as he lived, and he came to Penland often."

From the Cammerer day, Penland and the Park Service have had a love affair (rather unique considering that nowhere else but in these Appalachians does the Service encourage native crafts, or emphasize the sale of craft souvenirs as an important educational function within national parks). When you visit the Oconaluftee Pioneer Museum, composed of log buildings assembled inside the park near Cherokee to depict a typical mountain farmstead, the display you will see in the Pioneer Handicrafts Room was planned and arranged by Penland. For a time, the Penland crafters demonstrated carding, spinning, and weaving; perhaps they will again one day. The greatest achievement of the weavers, however, came in connection with the extensive restoration of Independence Hall, the birthplace of liberty in Philadelphia. As part of that patient, minute search for authenticity, historians examined four million manuscripts in this country and in the British Museum. The Park Service commissioned the manufacture of blinds and curtains in England. But where could it find weavers of eighteenth-century baize for desks and tables to match the little sample located abroad? The place, of course, proved to be Penland.

Across the mountains, the sisters of Pi Beta Phi arrived at Gatlinburg under severe handicap. Miss Lucy Morgan had the advantage of being a mountain girl when she went to Penland. Her brother already had a school going and was accepted, even though he was the first Episcopalian to live in the neighborhood. But the Pi Beta Phi workers entered into the hardest of hard-shell, foot-washing Baptist country, appearing to the natives like some kind of missionaries promoting a foreign religion.

Pi Beta Phi, the first national college fraternal organization for women, carefully selected Gatlinburg for its special project, designed as a memorial to its founders. College settlements early in the century were not unusual; many important universities maintained at least one and sometimes more in the tenement districts of large cities, where they endeavored to serve foreigners in the great melting pot. But magazines and newspapers had stirred the world with accounts of the primitive life of mountain whites in North Carolina, Kentucky, and Tennessee, and stirred no less the fraternity. In 1910 it decided to establish the Pi Beta Phi Settlement School somewhere in the southern mountains. Where was it needed most? The Commissioner of Education in Washington unhesitatingly pointed his finger at Tennessee. The state Board of Education narrowed the field to Sevier County, which had the fewest schools. The county Superintendent of Schools said the folks around the hamlet of Gatlinburg, also known as Little Pigeon, were certainly in need of educational training, with special emphasis on industrial and agricultural subjects so they could make a satisfactory living in their own homeland.

When the first term of school opened in 1912, the children did not know how to play even simple games like "Button-Button" or "Farmer-in-the-Dell." The little ones had "such sad faces," reported the teachers. "They are the most stolid little things I ever saw, with the least affection that is visible," wrote one teacher, "but I hope to bring some to the surface before spring." Here they learned the stories of Christmas, many of them for the first time. Miss Dell Gillette, of Illinois, was surprised at how little their parents knew about Christmas either—there were no family dinners or even Christmas trees at home. Not one of her pupils knew who Mary was, when she related the story of Mary and Joseph. "It is surprising," she wrote, "as these people are supposed to be religious, and it seems as if the Bible stories might have been handed down by word of mouth, if nothing else." Their first dolls, given to them by the school (from a box sent by the Philadelphia alumnae), were hung on the walls to be looked at, but not touched.

In the beginning, thirteen children attended irregularly. School was conducted under the direction of Miss Mary Hill, of Nashville, a trained mountain worker, in the old schoolhouse at the junction of Baskins Creek and the Little Pigeon River. The little house was leased for $1.50 a month. The local people were slow in giving the co-operation they had promised. They were proud and dubious; skeptical about the religious motivation of the "Pi Phis"; suspicious of outsiders seeming to interfere with their affairs, and yet plainly hopeful of educational opportunities for their children. It was as much a trying time for them as for those who sought to help.

These were people who dwelled in the world of magic sunsets, mist-covered mountain peaks, and deep solitudes, for the Gatlinburg community, at the opening of the Pi Phi School, was shut in by the rugged mountain ranges and by almost impassable roads. It comprised about six houses, three general stores, a blacksmith shop, and a Baptist Church beside the little tumble-down schoolhouse. The two hundred families lived in log cabins, or shacks, along the creeks that spilled down from the mountainside, and in the tiny fertile coves that turn up unexpectedly at the bend of a mountain stream. They raised a little grain, corn, a few potatoes and other vegetables, orchards here and there, enough hay for their few cows and horses, and hogs and chickens for their own use. Gatlinburg was the hub for visiting and trading, when any trading was done. Few had much ready cash. They bartered eggs at the store for sugar, coffee, salt, and tobacco, maybe sold a bushel of potatoes or chickens for cash. Some grazed cattle during summer on the hills above Cades Cove. Sevierville lay seventeen miles distant, but a long, long trek from Gatlinburg by wagon or buggy, requiring the fording of the river and creeks (and sometimes floating). As for Knoxville, it could have been New York—it was so far away, and just about the biggest place on earth. Church services were held once a month by a lay preacher, whose main recommendation was his earnestness.

Their primitive schoolhouse had long benches, no desks, a very low ceiling supported by half a dozen poles. Many times the teacher (before Pi Beta Phi) had little more than a fifth-grade education. He or she received about thirty dollars a month—one of the best paying jobs around. The number of boys and girls in attendance varied from ten to forty, their ages from four and five to twenty-four and -five. The oldest ones came for a short time, sometimes a week or so in winter, and the very young ones came with the older children because there was no one with whom to leave them at home. At best, school lasted three months.

In those plain and simple days there were no undertakers in the mountains. The body of the dead was simply placed in a wooden box lined with calico, with the lid nailed down and the whole covered with black calico. It was not uncommon to place a photograph of the departed one in a glass container atop his grave. Or, bits of bright-colored glass, paper flowers, toys, or trinkets he had known and liked.

One funeral the Pi Phi teachers remembered well took place in the Sugarlands. Late one afternoon a teacher saw a group of people from her window in the little churchyard. Presently a pair of small children were dispatched to fetch her to read the funeral service, there being no preacher available. She went over with her Bible, read a few verses, and said a prayer over the grave of an infant. The grief-stricken young mother and her family stood nearby. The father of the baby was at his wife's side, but presently he departed, for he was handcuffed to a revenue officer waiting to take him "down the river" for moonshining.

They were people with many serious problems, but no solutions could be forced upon them by "furriners." Yet Pi Phi wanted to get on with acquiring land and establishing a permanent school.

"It is customary in most places for businessmen to support movements such as ours," they told the natives. "The people must do their part in buying land and show they want our school. Otherwise, we will have to close it and leave."

Andy Huff carried his small daughter to school each day in order to encourage attendance. But this was not enough. The ladies wanted the money to buy the Ogle property so they could build a real schoolhouse for Gatlinburg. Pi Beta Phi was ready to contribute $600—why wouldn't the people invest money for their children's future?

They weren't even certain that Eph Ogle would sell. A final hour was set, at which time the school would be moved elsewhere, where it might be considered more welcome.

The day of decision arrived. Mrs. Andy Huff, one of the pioneer boosters of the school, sent for her husband at his logging camp in the woods and pleaded with him not to let the school get away. Andy and Steve Whaley thereupon chipped in $250 each. With the $600 of Pi Beta Phi, they now had a total of $1100, but were still $700 shy of the purchase price of the seventy-acre Ogle property. A hack had already been ordered to come and take the ladies and the school equipment away. Others chipped in, too, but there was serious doubt enough money would be raised in time.

Kate B. Miller, of Iowa, one of the Pi Beta Phi committee, who waited on the porch of the teachers' cottage while groups of people gathered around Ogle's store at the foot of the hill, reported later on the scene and events:

"Just before noon Mr. E. E. Ogle came up to say that he had decided to sell the tract if the money could be raised, that he would give as much as anyone toward the purchase price. He would give $250. He said he would rather have the school than his land—provided he could get a fair price for the land. His neighbors said that if Eph had wanted to sell to anyone else he could have gotten $2000.

"The last stage of the transaction was at hand. The hack from Sevierville now arrived and raised the excitement to fever heat. Soon after its arrival, word was sent to us that we were wanted at the store. Men were crowding around the outside of the building, on the steps, in the doors, and were standing inside and sitting on the counters.

"We found Mr. Ogle busy writing a title bond to be held by us till the deed could be made and sworn to. Almost all the money had been subscribed and Mr. Huff and Isaac Maples had agreed to make up any final deficit. When the terms were finally and satisfactorily embodied in this preliminary instrument, it was signed and given to Mrs. Elizabeth Helmick, the chairman of our settlement school committee.

"The wave of relief that passed through that assemblage was almost audible."

To commemorate the event a boy named Charley Ogle, who later ran the biggest store and shopping center for tourists in town, fired off a round of firecrackers.

Thus did schooling come to stay along the Little Pigeon. Much more than book learning was involved, however. Often it is said that the national park made Gatlinburg. Probably so, although it should have been a pretty good mountain resort anyway, with the coming of roads. Pi Beta Phi had much to do with making Gatlinburg, and these mountain people made the Pi Beta Phi Settlement a classic of social work in the hills.

I have interviewed some of the old graduates and the social workers. Andy Huff's family, for instance. It is true that Andy was almost a "furriner" himself, having transplanted from Greene County, Tennessee. In 1916, Andy built the frame Mountain View Hotel for loggers and hunters, on the site of the spot where Will Thomas and his Cherokee warriors had camped during the Civil War. Andy's children not only attended the Pi Phi School, but Jack married Pauline, a Pi Phi worker, and between them they built the lodge for hikers and climbers on Mount Le Conte. The story is told of how Jack's mother, when she became seriously ill, told him she wanted to see the Smokies once more from the top of the mountain. Having toted heavy supplies up and down the slopes, his mother appeared to be an easy parcel. He carried her all the way to Le Conte, in a chair contraption strapped to his back, crossing roaring streams on stepping stones, and pulling himself up perpendicular slopes by grasping tree roots.

Dick Whaley, who was born at Bull Head, halfway up to Le Conte, told a different kind of story. His father, Steve, built a house and farmed along the creek back of the present Riverside Inn. After World War I, he ran a boardinghouse that did fairly well. Both the Mountain View and Riverside were full during the summer, when school was out, though they were not as popular as the bigger resorts in Elkmont, Kinsel Springs, and Walland—for it took a dry day to motor from Pigeon Forge to Gatlinburg. The Riverside had a very simple price scale: 50 cents per person, regardless of the number in a room; 50 cents per meal; or, $2.00 a day, $10 a week, $35 a month. Steve had no such gadget as a cash register, but kept his money in his pocket, and if any of it was left after paying expenses during the season, that was his profit. In the early 1930s, having learned his lessons at the Pi Phi School, Dick set up an office at the Riverside. One day a pair of internal revenue agents came to call.

"Let's see your books," the Government agents asked.

"Books? We have no books," Dick and his father replied. "We make barely enough in summer to keep going in winter."

"But you've got to keep books and file returns."

"Maybe so, but we don't know bookkeeping. We can't afford to hire a bookkeeper," protested the Whaleys. "It would break this business to hire somebody just for that. We couldn't afford to operate."

The revenue men laughed and looked around. They concluded there couldn't possibly be any tax payment due and departed. But the Whaleys were among those who decided the national park was going to do something for the town. They held on to and developed their property. It took a few years before business rose, but Dick Whaley became a big hotel operator with a big house on the hillside. He hired a bookkeeper or two, plus a tax accountant.

Despite such advancement and affluence, many of these people kindle the pictures of their past and of their parents' past as though they are only hours or days old. Orley Trentham remembered the first time he saw an automobile in the Sugarlands. It was 1922 and it took the vehicle all day to come from Cleveland, Tennessee, a little over a hundred miles away, on trails hardly fit for a wagon. He remembered how the farmers never hired hands for wheat threshing, but would help each other; how the boys and girls shucked corn together and had a time telling tales and singing, as they did at spelling bees and " 'lasses boilings." He remembered the story of how his grandfather came across the mountain from Car'liny, toting a "budget" of clothes on his hog rifle. On the way, he shot a bear cub, then its mother and, frightened by the prospect of meeting other bears, started running down Indian Gap— smack into a big black "painter." The animal and man both fled, in opposite directions.

Orley remembered the Pi Phi days, when Miss Mary Pollard flung up her hands and shouted, "How do you handle these doggone mountain boys?" One of them piped up, "Get a hickory switch!"

There was very little sanitation; no outhouses at the old schools, but one section of the woods reserved for the girls and another section for the boys. Doctors brought in by Pi Phi found most of the boys had hookworm from tramping barefoot in the woods. The kids loved to go around shoeless and their feet got tough enough to crack chestnut burrs without getting any stickers in them. One lad claimed that when a snake bit him on the heel, the snake died but he was unhurt.

There were no doctors, no nurses, only the home remedies and superstitions. In 1920, the first trained nurse arrived in Sevier County to set up shop and develop a hospital at the Settlement School. She was a Canadian member of Pi Beta Phi, Miss Helen Phyllis Higinbotham (who later became State Supervisor of Public Health Nurses for Tennessee). In her six years, nurse Higinbotham examined school children for eye, nose, and throat troubles, the first physical examinations they had ever had. She taught their parents personal hygiene and the cleaning up of premises, including the swatting of flies, and trained a corps of midwives, "granny women," to help with obstetrical cases. She answered calls on foot and on horseback over terrible roads, fording swollen streams, plowing through mud, crossing rickety foot-logs and swinging bridges. She enlisted four doctors in Sevierville and Knoxville to keep office hours in Gatlinburg once a month. Before she left, the State Medical University cited the Pi Beta Phi hospital as a model for rural health centers in the state; and Federal, state, and county funds were added to the program at Gatlinburg.

Nurse Higinbotham and her successors (including Mrs. Marjorie Chalmers, who arrived in 1935 and was still the school nurse almost thirty years later) were called upon to minister not only to humans. "Gave vaccinations today," as one nurse recorded, "to 229 people and 37 dogs at a three-room school."

Pi Beta Phi has been synonymous with creative mountain handicrafts. One may deplore the transformation of Gatlinburg since World War II from a charming mountain town into an over commercialized, neon-lit resort, but the splendid craft shops inspired by Pi Beta Phi are in the finest tradition of the Great Smokies. From the beginning, the Settlement School urged the mountain people to sing their old folk-songs, to perfect their work in basket making, and to revive the almost lost art of weaving. This was not always easy.

"In the yesteryear this country was a community of weavers," wrote Miss Caroline McKnight Hughes, of Minnesota, who introduced the arts and crafts program in 1915 as part of the effort to foster home industries, "but after the Civil War 'store cloth' was so cheap that one woman after another put the old loom aside. Today, many of our neighbors know how to spin and weave, though it has been a 'tol'able long spell' since any have done such a thing. One woman not far from the school has her old loom up and is willing to make 'kivers' and these are dear to the hearts of old-timers. Many women still use the big hand wheel to twist stocking yarn but the little wheel for flax has disappeared. All the looms about here are either the one 'grandpap brunged from Car'liny when he coomed in,' or are copies of these old ones. All are crude homemade affairs, clumsy and big. All the weavers are old women. 'Up yander in the mo'tains' there are many looms in use, and the women have little or no use for 'store cloth' but down in our Burg all are fond of it."

The Settlement School workers benefited from the talents of Aunt Lydia Whaley and Aunt Lizzie Reagan, true mountain women of the old tradition. Aunt Lydia, or Liddy, after her husband's death in the Civil War (he was a Yankee shot down while trying to rescue a neighbor captured by the Rebels) tended her own crops, took her own corn to mill, made shoes for her children out of the old ones she ripped up, and often, for the sum of $1.00 each, made coats by hand in order to pay the taxes on her land. She knew how to make "ooze" out of barks, roots, and weeds and could explain every step in the making of "county pins," (counterpanes, in the outside world), from the raising of sheep, through shearing, washing, spinning, twisting, and dyeing of wool to the making of such old patterns as the "Rattlesnake" and "Gentleman's

Fancy." She was best known, however, for her Aunt Liddy baskets, which the Settlement School found could actually be sold through its alumnae clubs, thus opening the market for Gatlinburg's fireside industries. Copies of the Aunt Liddy baskets are still made and sold.

When the school bought the big old-fashioned loom that belonged to Aunt Liddy, the only one who could set it up was Aunt Lizzie Reagan, even though she had been away from a loom for thirty-five years. From her childhood training she knew many a little turn that proved to be revelations to the weaving teacher. She helped train other women, some of whom needed only a refresher course. Old looms were hauled out of the attics and reconditioned. Forgotten "drafts"—the patterns handed down from mother to daughter for a century or more—turned up on yellowed and wrinkled paper. Aunt Lizzie, besides doing some of the finest weaving in the mountains, worked for nine years at the school, where she milked the cow, made the butter, picked and canned wild berries, helped tend the garden, and kept the house in order. Women were eager to learn. When Winogene Redding became the first full-time weaving teacher in 1925, she had to walk the hills to provide instruction. But presently the mountain ladies came to her. On a cold winter morning one such lady appeared at the Settlement School, having walked five miles with her little daughter. It was more than the chance to earn money that brought her out to learn weaving. "I've worked hard all my life, I started to hoe corn and 'taters when I was a little 'un and I been hoein' ever since," she told the teacher. "I've had nine chillun, seven are livin' and two air dead. I've lived in the same holler twenty year—sometimes I think I'd like a sight to change. When I heerd of this weavin' I thought I'd quit workin' in the field and let the young 'uns do hit. I'm forty-four year old and I'm tired, so I aim to work inside now."

The men were willing, too, and had much to learn. In 1922, O. J. Mattil came from Chattanooga as a vocational agriculture teacher. He went around giving lessons in animal husbandry, horticulture, and poultry raising; he taught the simple lessons of crop rotation, weed eradication, spraying, and pruning. But he also conducted classes in shop work, in how to remodel furniture and make new pieces, how to use tools more sophisticated than the saw, plane, and hammer. This was to be his calling. In time, Mattil set up his own shop, the Woodcrafters and Carvers, where dozens of talented mountain cabinetmakers have studied and worked, learning how to produce quality furniture and how to price it for sale.

The national park and the mountain crafts have grown up together, not solely in Gatlinburg, and in Cherokee, but in the entire Appalachian environs. The roads brought visitors who were exposed for the first time to the craftsman's wares at Pi Beta Phi's Arrowcraft Shop (and at Pigeon Forge; the Qualla Crafts across the mountain; the gift shop at Fontana Village; Penland, Brasstown, and the way stops along the Blue Ridge Parkway). Mountain people by the hundreds have found markets for handwork they love to do, despite the surrounding mechanized world; along with the old traditional work, they have created new forms in pottery, basketry, metal, textile design, and jewelry.

By the 1960s more than one thousand looms were busy in the Gatlinburg area, producing about one million dollars' worth of coverlets, towels, table linens, handbags, and petticoats. In 1923 the Pi Phi ladies had been overjoyed when the sales had reached $1000 a year.

The social workers have taught many things to mountain people. They have shown children how to eat foods unknown to them, like hot chocolate; shown their mothers homemaking skills, like cooking, sewing, canning, and shown their fathers how to read and write and earn a living. To gather from those I have observed, the smart social worker recognizes there is plenty to learn as well as to teach in these parts. For instance, a friend of mine in Gatlinburg joked, "Today, us natives go around dressed, while the tourists are half nekked." Years ago, he continued, when the boys at the Settlement School first learned to play basketball, they were given uniforms to wear. "We had never seen a real game before and refused to wear those funny little suits," he said. "We were told that we must. Finally, we agreed. Would you believe it, but every single boy came down wearin' his overalls *underneath* that scarce uniform."

XVIII

Mountain Missionary

When Dr. Robert F. Thomas, the Methodist medical missionary, arrived as a stranger at Pittman Center in 1926, he was struck by the ancient ways of the hills. The town of Gatlinburg, barely fifteen miles distant, could have been fifteen hundred. Pittman's people were dressed as their grandparents must have dressed. The women, in their Mother Hubbard dresses, still sheared sheep and wove wool into cloth. The men with mattock and hoe tilled the steep hillsides, mostly for corn. They were religious, in their way, turning to church for a social rendez-vous, where they favored the old-time "harp singing," and turning to God, who they expected would unlock the gates to the beautiful place in the sky called Heaven. The young doctor found many mountain people in poor health. Almost as soon as he arrived he was busy caring for typhoid victims—not of an epidemic, but of an endemic disease. Some were not only sick physically, but were mentally and emotionally disturbed. "You're going to work with isolated Americans. Don't tell them you're a missionary," he had been directed before coming. "They'll resent it. Just be useful."

To Dr. Thomas, going to the Great Smokies was almost like traveling halfway around the world to the jungle mountains of Malaya, where he had already served as a missionary. There he had gone in 1916, a twenty-five-year-old Pennsylvania-born minister, teaching English to boys of high school age and preaching in the English-speaking church. His island station, Penang, between Singapore and Bangkok, was a mixture of tropical splendor and tropical squalor, where wealthy European and Chinese merchants lived in palaces resting on alabaster foundations while their plantation field hands lived like coolies, or slaves, in crowded huts perched precariously on rotting stilts. The missionary had traveled out through the villages and jungles and seen the school children suffering with beriberi or amoebic dysentery, their parents languishing with leprosy, dengue fever, or malaria. In the Straits Settlement of Malaya there were over one hundred Methodist missionaries, and only one of them a doctor. The Reverend Thomas had seen the sick people in need of help that only medical training could provide, and felt inadequate.

He returned to the United States at the age of twenty-eight in order to study a new profession. He had little money (and would not have much more in the Smokies), but with the aid of his wife, Eva, worked his way through six years of training at Syracuse University and internship at Binghamton, New York. Then, he prepared for his chance to return to Malaya by practicing medicine in the Adirondack Mountains and preaching on the side. The chance for Malaya, however, never came. Instead, he found himself interviewed and accepted for a position in the rough halfway-to-heaven country of southern Appalachia, where there were plenty of preachers "a-hollering at the Lord" with hosannas, hellfires, and hysteria, but where doctors were as scarce as in the jungles of Penang.

Only the backdrop was different. He traded a setting of palm tree for pine tree, the jungle pass for the mountain trail, the Malay vernacular for the backwoods English vernacular, the elephant for the saddle horse, the suffering from beriberi and dengue for typhoid, pellagra, and malnutrition.

Furthermore, he discovered that not a single cabin in his new environs had an indoor toilet or lavatory equipment as known in the outside world. Screens for windows didn't exist. There were no bridges, barely anything resembling a road, and certainly no telephones for miles around. Grown men couldn't read or write, as the local draft board had discovered in World War I when 30 per cent of those called marked their names with an X or touched the pen while a "writing man" signed for them.

Families with ten or twelve children were crowded into one room, sleeping in four beds. Meager, patched clothes hung from nails on the walls; the children ran shoeless winter and summer. Often there were not enough 'taters and beans to go around.

On the best lowlands of the Tennessee Valley farming produced fifty bushels of corn per acre. But in these hills, where the land had been divided from one generation to the next, the average farmer reckoned he was harvesting about sixteen bushels per acre.

"The country's mighty purty," as one said, "and the land's mighty poor. Hit's so pore hit wouldn't hardly raise a fight."

The ranger staff in front of park headquarters, December 1960 (all men in those days). Front row: Rodney Royce, Superintendent Fred Overly, Fred A. Wingeier, Clifford Senne, Robert I. Kerr, William J. Watson, Carlock Johnson, Frank Oliver, William Rolen, Management Assistant John Morrell. Rear row: Assistant Superintendent David DeL. Condon, Norman H. Roy, Mark Hannah, Thomas Lewis, Dunbar Susong, Harvey Wickware, Robert Peters, Max Hancock, Larry Freeman, Joe Lynch, Buford Messer, Luther Winsor. David DeL. Condon, National Park Service.

Taking a break along the Save the Smokies Hike on October 23, 1966. Stan Murray, of Kingsport, a leader in the Appalachian Trail Conference (standing right), makes a point to Liane Russell, of Oak Ridge, of Tennessee Citizens for Wilderness Planning; daughter Evelyn Russell (then age 14), and the author, William L. Russell.

Harvey Broome, of Knoxville, president of the Wilderness Society, long active in the Smoky Mountains Hiking Club, speaking to a rally of park defenders at the 1966 Save the Smokies Hike. Ernie Dickerman, Smoky Mountains stalwart, is at left. Leroy Fox.

Hikers take a break under the massive overhang at Alum Cave Bluff on the foot path once known as "the trail with the continuity of thrills." The trail starts at the Grassy Patch parking area and climbs beyond Alum Cave to Mt. LeConte. Mack Prichard.

The author hiking to LeConte on the Alum Bluff Trail, 1983, uphill into a late wintry blast while anticipating early spring. Mack Prichard.

A winter view of the mountains, ridge after ridge extending to the horizon, framed by frosted tree limbs on the Alum Cave Trail. Mack Prichard.

Signs in the Smokies generally are unobtrusive and helpful. This one, looking northeast from Fighting Creek Gap near park headquarters, identifies key points north of the main Smokies range. Triple-peaked Mt. LeConte, at far right, is the highest (6,593 feet) one here. Dean Stone.

This sign, on the Foothills Parkway, facing LeConte straight ahead, tells a story of problems that come with park popularity and heavy use. Mack Prichard.

Bernard Elias, of Asheville, active campaigner of the Carolina Mountain Club, has led hikes and taught hikers for more than fifty years.

Alan Householder, the first Ridge Runner (left), shows the author how he patrols the Appalachian Trail, while they hike from Fontana Dam to Shuckstack Tower in June 1992. Mack Prichard.

Reliving history. Barbara Ambler Thorne shown in 1992 sharing her scrap-
book with the author. Her father sparked the Appalachian conservation cause
early in the century, while during the 1930s she herself was a pioneer Smokies
hiker. Mack Prichard.

The beautiful Oconaluftee River enriches the biology and scenery on the North Carolina side of the Smokies. Summer thunderstorms turn such peaceful streams into torrents of rushing water. Mack Prichard.

Guided wildflower walks like this one along the Appalachian Trail from Newfound Gap draw visitors from all over the world, especially during the annual Wildflower Pilgrimage the last weekend in April. Tennessee Department of Conservation.

The snail darter of the Little Tennessee River, though measuring only three inches long, stirred a cause célèbre in efforts to protect a free-flowing river and historic Indian sites. Jim Robertson, Tennessee Department of Conservation.

Before Tellico. Reconstructed Fort Loudoun, near Vonore on the south bank of the Little Tennessee River, recounts the story of England's strategic frontier outpost during the French and Indian War. Dean Stone.

After Tellico. The fort, in one respect, was spared, since the site was raised seventeen feet before the closing of the dam. Its context, however, was lost and the nearby Indian villages were buried under the waters of the reservoir. Dean Stone.

Higher altitudes were favorable to fruit, grass, and vegetables. Orchards were planted with apples, peaches, grapes, and plums but weren't cared for properly and produced little for market. The streams from cleared land were muddy and fluctuated. Some cattle grazed on Pinnacle, above Greenbrier Cove. Hogs roamed the woods, getting fat on chestnuts and white oak acorns.

People believed in witches and wild superstitions. One lad explained that if a certain old lady had bewitched a man or boy, he should draw a picture of that person with a representation of a heart upon it, then take the picture into the woods and fasten it to a tree by driving a knife through the heart. This action, coupled by refusing to lend anything to the "witch," would cause her to grow sick and lose her power.

In this climate the Pittman Community Center was established in 1921 by Eli Pittman and the Methodists of Buffalo, New York, who perhaps were attracted by the stories of Bishop Francis Asbury's arduous expeditions through the region a century before. Pittman established a grade school that first September, a considerable improvement over the one-room log cabin where school had hitherto been conducted for all of three months each year. Now a small army came a-walking to class, some from as far off as six miles and on bare feet. They were given shoes and carried by wagon, those who lived in the far hills and hollows.

Just as Reverend Thomas had decided that prayer wasn't enough help in Penang, the Methodists concluded that schooling wasn't enough in the Smokies. In the two hundred square miles of rough, isolated country where Pittman Center was striving to serve some five thousand mountain people, there had never been a single M.D. in residence. Along with the elementary school and the church work, it needed a health clinic, run by a doctor willing to sacrifice himself and family.

To fill this void, the Reverend Dr. Thomas led his wife and two children into the Tennessee mountains barely one year after the celebrated "monkey trial" of John Thomas Scopes, who had dared to teach evolution in his biology class at Dayton, a small community less than one hundred miles from the Smokies. The philosophic level of the state was laid bare before the world. It was a level of rigid fundamentalism, of anti-evolution and anti-science, in a state where country politicians denounced the Sunday opening of gasoline stations in Nashville as a sure and certain step toward hell. H. L. Mencken, writing from the trial scene, gave Tennessee a dose of cynicism for its "anthropoid religion." Worst of all, he observed in *The Nation*, the hills above Dayton were "full of reliable moonshiners, all save one Christian men." Having spoken, Mencken withdrew, along with his colleagues, to the comforts of the northern cities. There was no such hit-and-run therapy for Thomas.

In 1926 the nearest hospital from Pittman Center was at Knoxville, forty-two miles distant, over rough roads. From Pittman to Sevierville, the beginning of the journey, it was seventeen miles of mean and narrow track. Thomas was isolated, on his own, as diagnostician, obstetrician, surgeon, anesthetist, and also as marrying parson and baptizer of babies he had brought into the world.

Probably his greatest obstacle was the backwardness of the people. Their doctoring was done by the "granny women," who administered herbs and potions with righteousness and ritualism. For typhoid, the granny woman's treatment might be a pan of cold water under the bed to stop the fever. For another ailment it might be a potion concocted of anvil dust, diluted in sugar. For childbirth, it was believed that if a father sent an ax into the puncheon floor under the labor bed, the pains his wife must endure would be eased. Ginseng was prescribed for colic and stomach trouble. Sheep dung, or "bullets," boiled down and sweetened, was sometimes used to "break out" measles. Spider webs were placed on raw wounds (where they were apt to cause infection). For constipation, or "locked-up bowels," a granny woman might decide to use the boiled-down root of the May apple, rolled up with flour and eaten with sugar. And ground ivy tea was prescribed for colic in an infant. The mountain families "confidenced" their granny women and home remedies. They "suspicioned of a furriner" toting a little black bag, filled with the evils of black magic. When faced with the choice of disease or vaccination, a man might prefer to run the risk of disease, even smallpox.

"Don't you never put Velva to sleep with no hydraulic needle. That's one thing I hain't wantin', Doc," said a young man grimly on one occasion while Thomas prepared to help his wife give birth. It was a terribly poor and poorly kept home. Openings had been hewn crudely in the walls to let in air and light and let the swarming flies out. The floor was earthen. The wood stove was piled with rubbish, the table littered with food and dirty dishes. The bed had no sheet, the blankets were matted and soiled. There lay the young wife, a sixteen-year-old who had had no prenatal attention. The doctor pushed the man aside and examined her. She was in pain, nearly at term, and the position of the child was not good. But the husband leaned forward and whispered hoarsely, "No cuttin', hear!"

Infants were dying of diarrhea, of parasitic worms in the intestines. Even with the best home remedies and rituals of the granny women, the family graveyards had too many little rocky, red earth mounds, on which the slate headstones bore the crudely carved inscriptions: "Our baby" . . . "agd 1 month" . . . "1 yeer" . . . "10 days" . . . "belovd son 11 yeers."

The medical missionary was there to stay, having been greeted by the dread plague of the mountains, typhoid, caused by unsanitary living conditions. Two years later, smallpox struck. It was first observed on a newborn baby in Bear Pen Gap. Two granny women had diagnosed it simply as the seven-year itch. By the time Dr. Thomas was called, the infant's body was confluent with pox. The father, it developed, had been visiting in Knoxville a while before, in a home afflicted with small-pox; he fled the quarantine (associating quarantine with jail) for the hills. And from Bear Pen Gap the smallpox epidemic swept the mountain end of Sevier County, overworking and exhausting Thomas and five other physicians. He went around giving inoculations by the hundreds—and thereafter by the thousands, for typhoid, paratyphoid, diphtheria.

"I'll be at Jones Cove School Thursday at ten o'clock," was how Thomas would spread the word through preachers and teachers. They would be waiting for him, down from the hollows, and he would immunize them one after another down the line. Some looked fearfully and suspiciously at "that thar needle," but the needle became a popular symbol in due course, and he who had been shot with serum was a man with something to talk about. "Typhoid shots help the rheumatis'," it was also said.

The people suffered poor nutrition from a lack of variety in the diet. They absorbed excess carbohydrates and starches, from the steady helping of corn at three meals a day, plus potatoes, beans, soda biscuits, and sorghum. They did not get enough protein, or enough fruits and vegetables. The women did plenty of canning, but with little variety. It was quite the usual thing to feed green beans, fried eggs, and cheese to babies of five or six months. Children were apt to have an insufficient supply of milk, due partly to the lack of proper feed for cows—and the lack was filled with coffee. Blue denim was sometimes used for diapers and water on a baby was "sure death unless used in small doses."

He saw patients—sometimes whole families—suffering from pellagra, depressed and melancholic. They were so downcast they had lost their appetite, and were ready to die.

He saw patients suffering from tuberculosis, a disease born of crowded and poor living conditions, which found a breeding place in the inadequately heated and poorly vented little cabins.

He saw patients suffering from trachoma, the contagious eye disease of unknown cause associated with poverty and crowded conditions. As many as twenty and thirty a day would come to his clinic and sit quietly, with their thick, reddened eyelids testifying to the inner irritation of the eyes, and of the path to blindness.

A man would have to be strong, I venture, even for a physician, and buoyed by a strong God, even for a missionary, to pursue his course through years that grew into decades in the luxurious hills of under-nourished people. Thomas went among them, on horseback, his saddle-bags loaded with medicine and doctor tools, to relieve suffering and to share it, sometimes to feel the heartbreak of being called too late—for some families struggled to overcome fear and suspicion before asking his help, even in cases of fractured skulls, diphtheria in babies, and advanced tuberculosis of the bone.

Once he went to a cabin where a woman lay very ill. There he found the large family living on a steep, high hillside, flanked with hemlock, poplar, and "spangly-limbed pines." His examination showed her heart was severely strained. He instructed the husband to prevent Oda from overexertion: she was not to haul any more water from the spring, or even the young ones up the steps. Three months later, however, she died and the doctor returned to fill out a death certificate. He was astounded when John gave her age as twenty-nine, for he had judged her to be in her forties. Then he looked again. The young face was lined deeply beyond its years, the hands were gnarled with the hard work of years, the body was worn and aged with childbearing.

The family prepared a fresh coffin of poplar, lined it with black calico, the "mourning cloth," and sent for Reverend Thomas to officiate at the "funeralizing." At the burial ground on the hill, graves were spiked with faded, weather-stained paper flowers, each wired and left from the last Decoration Day. It was the custom, like a tribal rite, that on a certain day, weeks before Decoration Day, the women of each family would make paper flowers and the men would clean the graveyard; the rules were that not a blade of grass must be allowed to grow on any mound, and the mounds must be kept heaped and rounded. Rarely have people been more mindful of their graveyards than in the Smok-ies. It proved to be a hard funeral of raw emotion. Oda's mother and sister fainted. John, the strapping husband, was kept up on his feet by the arms of his brothers. It could have been a harrowing experience for the preacher, but he was sustained by his instructions to be useful. "Oh God of infinite compassion," he prayed, "look down upon thy servants. We entreat for them thy sustaining grace. Be Thou their stay, their strength, and their shield, that trusting in Thee they may know Thy presence near, and in the assurance of their love be delivered out of their distress."

When I called on Dr. Thomas in his hilltop clinic, I inquired where his role of physician ended and that of religious missionary began.

"It isn't that simple," he replied. "The medical missionary's attitude is that the sick need to be helped, regardless of any message. You do your level best. Sometimes prayer, or a word fitly spoken, becomes even more useful than medical attention."

He recalled being summoned on a murky, rainy night to a log house where a young man lay sick. The examination proceeded by a flickering light while the large family stood nervously by. Based on symptoms such as dizziness and poor co-ordination, the doctor concluded the young man had a brain tumor and would have to be carried to Knoxville for surgery. He thought, "This is a tremendous problem. I must tell them the diagnosis. But *how* can I tell them?" The father was a moonshiner, the mother a Christian, and both were frightened and upset. "We ought to realize what kind of situation the boy is in," he said. "We ought to pray." It appeared to help. The parents grew quieter, they faced their problem with poise.

Often, Dr. Thomas continued, patients came to him who were not sick physically but were mentally upset. They would confront him with their family problems, their dreams, their psychiatric disturbances. One troubled woman pleaded for help. "Evil thoughts have passed through my mind," she said. "I must be terrible bad. I pray to God, but it don't help. Night after night the thoughts come to me in bed. I get up at night in my bed clothes and sit on the bridge over the creek and hope the evil thoughts will go 'way. Why won't they go?"

They were very keyed up people about their physical and psychological problems. As nurse Helen Phyllis Higinbotham, of the Pi Beta Phi Settlement School at Gatlinburg during the early twenties, wrote, "I have had to get used to getting most of a woman's symptoms from her husband, and not having heart failure when a messenger comes with the news that so-and-so is 'bad off'—'about to die' or 'got the fever.'"

Along the Pigeon River section of the Pittman Center district a man fell from a barn loft, dislocated his shoulder, and began screaming, "Oh Lord, have mercy!" When Dr. Thomas arrived the man could be heard over a half mile away. But when he was given a dose of ether and put to sleep, the shoulder was set very easily, without any of the fear or fighting he would have shown while awake.

The special genius of Dr. Robert F. Thomas was that he entered into the fundamentalist world of the Great Smoky Mountains and respected it but insisted upon ministering to its true needs. An evangelist performing histrionically to the emotions would have been great on a Sunday and forgotten on a Monday. Thomas was the man who was there on Tuesday, with vitamin pills and antiseptics, and soft prayers where they were fitting in place of the frenzied exhortation of the old circuit riders.

The old religion could be harsh and demanding. A true practitioner would never countenance liquor in his home and would consider playing cards sinful, and the same for round dancing. The worst fate that could befall a man was to be "unchurched"; he might accept it philosophically, as a license to live his own life, but to his neighbors, for one to be 'churched, it meant that he could not possibly be saved.

On the other hand, there was the beauty of the song in the little mountain churches of Greenbrier Cove, Jones Cove, Emerts Cove and all the other hollows of the Smokies and Appalachia. A local singer would teach the gospel hymns using books with an unusual system of notation. The sound of the note was recognized by its shape, rather than by its position on the music staff. The simple and sensible system of "shaped notes" has enabled thousands of people who cannot read or write their own names to read music. In the Four Shape system, the first and fourth degrees of the scale, called *fa*, are represented by a right triangle; the second and fifth, *so*, by a circle. For the third and sixth, *la* is used and symbolized by a square head, leaving a diamond for the seventh, *mi*. The Seven Shape system has a different form of notation. Both are said to spring from the *sol-fa* method of sight reading, used in ancient England and handed down from the age before the musical staff came into being.

Harp singing—all-day conventions for religious singing—were major social occasions. Churches in different communities would take turns as host. Choirs of the best harp singers would come from miles around and the sound of singing went on in relays from morning till sunset. The leader of each group used a tuning fork, tuning pipe, or a guitar to set the proper tones. Anyone who grew tired was free to help himself to a dipper of water from the rostrum or to stroll outside for his picnic lunch, of fried chicken, naturally, and country visiting. The all-day sings have gradually faded, but harp singing and the shaped-note music books continue as part of the culture of the hills.

This was part of the personality and dignity of the Smoky mountaineer that Thomas learned to admire, as well as to respect. He told me of how his wife, Eva, once was obliged to take a young girl to Knoxville to visit a medical specialist. It was in the days when it took four hours from Pittman Center to the nearest pike road, and four hours more to Knoxville. Martha had never seen Sevierville, never seen a paved road or a sidewalk, never been in an elevator, a streetcar, or a railroad train. At her first sight of Knoxville she murmured, "Well, well . . ." "From that moment," said Dr. Thomas, "Martha never let on that anything was strange. She acted completely poised."

Another time he lost his way on a bright moonlit night in fall (as he must have more than once, in the roadless Smokies). The path was so rocky and steep that he walked his horse. The region, wild and beautiful, was unknown to him. Not for an hour did he near the first cabin, nestled in a hollow. Not a lamp or candle was lit.

"Who's thar?" he heard the strong, suspicious voice of the mountaineer demand.

It was followed in a moment by the time-honored greeting extended to strangers. "Come in and stay the night."

The cabin was spotless, the coffeepot gleamed in the firelight, the floor was white with scrubbing, the sheets were hand-woven linen. The man warmed the coffee and corn bread. "Eat all you want," he said. "Don't be backward none." Next morning from the cabin he saw the Greenbrier Pinnacle, wreathed with smoke in the distance, and left, with a word from his host hoping he'd come by another time purposely.

A visitor never was turned away, but might find himself in the same bed with two or three children. Certain procedures were followed in the one-room cabins whereby everybody's modesty was properly regarded. The visitor was put to bed first. Or all the men turned in first; then, after the lamp was out, the women took their turn. One night Thomas was in one of those typically overcrowded cabins, shared by a husband, wife, five young boys and four girls. It consisted of one room with four double beds, plus a shed for a kitchen, and a loft.

"I reckon yore tired, Doc," said his host about 7:45 P.M., "and would like to go to bed. Hit's a-gettin' late. You can have that bed over thar."

While the doctor crawled into bed (and left his trousers on), the family faced away and sat around the fireplace.

About 4:30 A.M. he was stirred. He smelled the salt pork frying and the coffee boiling. "Doc, hit's time to get up," he was told. "Hit's soon in the morning."

When I visited Dr. Thomas he was in his seventies, a tall and slender, gray-haired, thoughtful man. His clinic at Pittman Center was old and worn, clearly a place getting by without being touched by American prosperity.

"Oh, this is not a good place for a physician to become rich," the doctor said. "Not here, nor anywhere in the county. We have six physicians in Sevier County for twenty-five thousand people. On the busiest day last year I saw one hundred ten sick people.

"We charge a modest fee for medical services at Pittman Center, but spend as much for drugs and supplies as we take in. You must not forget that conditions of the twenties and thirties have by no means disappeared. Hungry children must be fed. Sick children must be cared for. Late one night word came for the doctor to go to see a sick baby. I found that what that baby needed was food, and for a considerable time we furnished the special milk formula. Fortunately, vitamins and iron tablets in large quantities have been furnished by the Council of the Southern Mountains and many medical supplies have been contributed by friends. But I really need another doctor, a social worker, office secretary and bookkeeper, another nurse to help do the work that needs to be done so badly."

A great man of the Great Smokies, though unknown outside his own county, he is perhaps one of a vanishing breed. His rewards have been very scanty by our standards. Maybe he finds his reward in the passion for medical practice, and in remembering how he taught mountain women to assist in emergency operations in the dirtiest threadbare cabins; they had to be shown how to wash their hands with hot water and green soap, then how to let ether fall drop by drop over the mask on the patient's face, how to stand on one side to hold the patient firmly while the doctor cut and blood flowed. Maybe he finds his reward in the raising of his two sons, who have become teachers. Or perhaps in having their mother, Eva, share his work at Pittman Center and its Pinnacle Handicrafts Shop, going into the homes as nurse when he needed her.

An old woman sitting next to me while I waited to see him at the clinic said to me, "Nobody but those who live here appreciate what he's done. There might be other doctors just as good, but I wouldn't go to no other. He's *my* doctor." Perhaps that is his reward.

God, or whatever we presume to be God, can be awfully close in the natural sanctuary of the Smokies. Maybe when he saw a rainbow by moonlight, or a bluish-green sky at dawning, or when he heard the thunderheads over Pinnacle, or the roar of the Little Pigeon, or the drumming of the ruffed grouse on a fallen log—maybe that was his reward.

Whatever it was, he appeared to be envious of no man. The work that engaged his time and energy was important, part of the work of the Kingdom of God. It was the real missionary work that he had set out to do over fifty years ago, halfway across the world.

Despite the problems and difficulties, there was no "perhaps" in his knowing that "he that goeth forth and weepeth, bearing precious seed, shall doubtless come again with rejoicing, bringing his sheaves with him."

XIX

Last Day of a Bear

The Bear

At dawn it was raining lightly, as it had been through the night, and the clouds settled low in the hollows. He felt the falling leaves of late November against his full-coated fur but ignored them. He paid not the slightest attention to the rain. He had only one object in mind, being driven by a powerful natural force. It told him, through the instinct given to creatures, that soon a change would come in the seasons and with it a scarcity of food. He must be prepared for it by feeding an insatiable hunger now and thus accumulate enough fat to carry him through the deep sleep of winter.

He halted in his prowling before an old hemlock and sniffed. Then he raised up on his hind legs and clawed deep into the bark high on the tree. This was his signpost. It told him and other bears who might come this way where he had been and where he would return. Within his five or six square miles (possibly more, depending on season), he would follow a meandering course, avoiding open spaces, marking his trees by clawing or biting. He might have been saying that he would keep to his own territory, as long as there was ample food, providing others would keep out. Strangely, however, though the black bear is the most familiar mammal (to human visitors) in and around the Great Smoky Mountains, the reasons for its behavior are virtually unknown. Biologists know pretty well *what* bears do, but a good deal of research is still required to answer the question of *why*.

The bear ambled on, impelled by ravenous craving. He turned rocks over and dug for insects. He ripped open decaying logs, hunting for wood roaches, salamanders, ants, and larvae. He wanted anything and everything edible, though mostly he was counting on acorns and nuts for his autumn diet.

This bear was three years old, not yet in his full maturity. His domain was outside the national park, in the rough country under Devil's Courthouse, in Pisgah National Forest. The year before, his mother had left him to his own devices and during the mating season of the recent summer he had tasted the excitement of love for the female for the first time, an early age for such affairs. He was jet black of color and weighed about 190 pounds.

A remarkable fellow, this young he-bear, as are all his kind, with their fantastic humanlike qualities. Black bears are considered not exactly the brightest of creatures, but they are not the dumbest either. They always appear well fed—no one has yet observed a starving bear; nor is there record of a bear ever dying of exposure. The bear has no effective natural enemy, except for man and dogs, and his own kind. Much to their credit, bears have survived in America long after saber-toothed cats have disappeared.

Survival in the Smokies and surroundings has been no small feat. Bears have been hunted, and hunted hard, from the days of the first white settlers and the Indians before them. Although bears were given a revered place in the ancient mythology, modern Cherokee consider the bear their special prey. "When a bear comes off the park, he's a goner," said an Indian friend of mine. Bears seem to be smart enough to know they're protected in the national park, but piratical Indians and whites hunt them down within the sanctuary in the dead of night. They either slay them on the spot or capture them for a life of torture. You will see them in communities surrounding the park, displayed in sordid cages before souvenir stands, to the delight of unthinking people, who stop and hold up their children and laugh, "Look at the bear!"

Such is the introduction for throngs of visitors to the Smoky Mountain bears. It is followed, along the transmountain road inside the park, by the spectacle of other bears uprooting garbage cans for food or begging for it, like demoralized buffoons.

In its native element, the black bear is shy. Even the backpacker on the trail scarcely gets a more inspiring perspective. When he catches a glimpse of a bear it is usually the hindside of a shy animal heading for cover. Both the hiker and bear are content to have the other go his separate way.

The hunter knows the bear more intimately than the hiker or casual motor tourist. He respects and admires him, for a bear can defy and elude the best of men and dogs; despite the odds against him, he can deal them death fighting on his own grounds and terms. The bear demonstrates the power, courage, and swiftness of his kind, and the proud urge for life.

The three-year-old was born in the still of a winter. The she-bear, his mother, had mated the summer before, following the sexual cycle of being receptive to intercourse, "in heat," every other year. The egg was fertilized but grew very slowly or not at all until late fall; then the embryo developed rapidly in the last two or three months. Alone, the she-bear chose her place close to the earth to give birth. She dug out a depression in the ground, then lined her bed with leaves and twigs; or it might have been under fallen trees or an overhanging ledge or upturned roots. But it had to be secluded and undisturbed. If a human had accidentally come upon and frightened the she-bear near birth, she likely would have fled and aborted her young.

The bear was one of a litter of three born in January or early February. At birth he was no larger than a red squirrel or chipmunk, weighing less than one pound, with a thin coat of fine black hair. His eyes remained closed and his vision poor for several weeks. He was wholly dependent upon his mother. While they lay holed up in the deep snow, he and his brothers (or sisters) suckled of her milk, while she ate nothing and gave them life. The milk was highly nutritive and the bears continued at her breasts for months. The cub discovered early that he had a voice. In the warmth next to his mother, he hummed as a human baby might; when he was pushed at the breast by his brothers, he moaned or cried and pushed his way back.

When the first spring came, he was over five pounds in weight. The she-bear nudged her cubs into the sunlight and bloom of late March and April. They blinked many times, for a bear's eyesight, even in maturity, is poor. Our little black bear found himself blessed with keen smell and hearing, and a natural curiosity. He needed little training from mother in how to feed himself, to pick fruits, berries, and nuts, to dig for insects and larvae, to plunge in the streams after fish, to trap rodents —mostly a vegetarian diet, though meat that lay handy was not to be overlooked.

The concern of a mother bear for her young is legendary. No stranger is allowed in the family group. Once our black's mother was swimming with her cubs, she out front and they trailing ten feet behind, when suddenly she sensed trouble. She turned and swam back; the cubs hooked their paws in her rump and she towed them safely ashore.

They roamed together, mother and young, throughout the entire year. The black kept growing and learning, and sometimes climbed trees in a spiral fashion, chewing at the bark and into the cambium layer. He grew fond of walking on fallen logs—possibly because he associated logs with food—and crossed with marvelous balance. He learned to run in a straight line over the roughest ground and his wind was twice as good as a deer's. He did some foolish things, too, or things that would look foolish to the human eye, like getting himself muddy with earth digging up woodchucks, or sitting on his rump in a blueberry patch, gathering up branches with his front legs and chomping and blowing at masses of leaves mixed with berries.

As the autumn leaves fell, the she-bear and the young ones began to eat more. When it came time for their first winter sleep they were still dependent on the mother for protection and all denned together, even though each cub weighed at least fifty pounds.

In the spring it was different. The mother protected them still, but became increasingly restless as the onset of oestrus, the period of sexual heat, grew closer. One day they passed a male bear sitting and crying like a baby. It was caught in a steel trap, set by man and concealed on a worn bear trail. He was a chicken-hearted bear—as some are apt to be—for only two of his toes were imprisoned. Another animal would have left the toes and fled with his life, but there he sat moping and sobbing like a baby. The she-bear sniffed at the scent of man associated with the trap and led her cubs away. Alas, many an unwary bear has met its end walking into a camouflaged log pen or steel trap. The trouble with traps in years gone by was that they also caught dogs. Once, an old man living in Tennessee set out to find work at the Everett Mine on the Sugar Fork of Hazel Creek; he stepped in a bear trap, broke his leg, and starved to death. Bear traps are illegal, but so are other activities that go on in the hills.

The she-bear turned her back on the cubs in late June. The mating urge now moved her more strongly than the protective urge. The sexual drive was irresistible. The family divided ranks. She proceeded to pair with a male bear for a few days. The deserted cubs stayed together at first, then parted to become wanderers for the rest of their lives, and to start families of their own.

The black bear became accustomed to a career of solitary prowling. Whenever he encountered another bear at a feeding place, he became quarrelsome. Through most of his waking moments he had one object: the search for food. His habits and schedule and almost all his movements revolved around hunting for something to eat. Food supplies influence his location—as a result of an acorn failure in the autumn of 1946, about half the bear population left the Great Smoky Mountains National Park and never returned. No item of food was too small for him to pass up, none too tedious to dig out. He spent hours clawing for woodchucks, mice, and chipmunks and in uprooting an acre of stumps for ants. He worked for days at a bee tree to get the honey to satisfy his sweet tooth. His hide was too tough to bother with a sting; whenever he was stung on the tip of his nose, he brushed it and kept digging.

He was a good fisherman, better than most men with rod and reel. Perhaps he should have been a good hunter as well. He was powerful enough to kill deer and most other animals, but bears generally are inclined to forego fresh meat as a matter of economics, considering that vegetation is more abundant and requires less energy to secure. He would not pass up a stray fawn, a dead animal, a ground squirrel, beetles, or anything handy, but essentially he was a vegetarian feeding on the crops of the earth. In spring he ate roots and grasses, or nibbled at the base of moist tree trunks. June was the hardest time, before the growing season. In summer he became a browser and grazer, feeding on grass and green plants, chewing wild white clover close to the ground. In autumn he would fill himself with berries and nuts, climbing old beech trees abundant with the nuts that many animals find delectable.

This little black bear gave the human race a wide berth. He was a primitive of strong character who tended his own affairs in the dense woods under the Pisgah Ledge and Tennessee Ridge and bounded away at the approach of man, whether moonshiner, revenuer, hunter, or logger.

Other bears have behaved differently, particularly after frequent contact with man. Their love of man's food masks their fear and they become bold, sometimes foolish. A bear is apt to raid a cabin for flour, pork, bacon, or anything that smells good, even though he knows there is someone to chase him off. He might invade a farm, ripping down fences in order to foray into the beehives, or to eat a pig, or carry off a sheep. Or sit in a stupor in the middle of an orchard while munching apples and getting drunk, feeling the same effect as with apple cider. When bears lose fear, they reach the point where they are not duly alarmed by sticks and stones, or even being shot at. Dogs will chase them off, but otherwise the bears retreat far enough to get out of the way, then circle around for new adventures.

In the Great Smoky Mountains National Park, bears constitute one of the principal attractions—and problems. Once they were hunted unmercifully. They became few in number and were rarely seen. After protection was given to them, they reproduced but mostly stayed in the inaccessible mountains and ridges. In time they found campgrounds and garbage cans an easy source of food, easier than foraging in the forest.

Tourists have contributed further to the tragic transformation. By feeding incessantly along the roadside, the bears have been robbed of their dignity and induced to abandon the natural way of life. A number have become degenerate beggars and marauders. Rarely do they molest human beings unless attacked, unfairly disturbed, or in defense of their cubs, but they are apt to poke into tents and trail shelters in search of food. One bear practically demolished an automobile in the Chimneys campground while its owners slept in a nearby tent. It climbed atop the car and battered it, then broke the glass in a window and tore up a cushion, hunting for something to eat.

But our black bear was not of this kind. He was not very large and never would have been, even if he had lived his full life expectancy of twelve to fifteen years. Few bears in the southern Appalachians ever do weigh over six hundred pounds. According to the celebrated hunter of years gone by, "Black" Bill Walker, the biggest bear he ever killed weighed four hundred pounds net—"which, allowin' for hide, blood, and entrails, would run full five hundred live weight." As stories have been handed down, the famous bears slain by the hunters have grown into immense proportions in the telling. Honest John, the scourge of bear dogs, for example, has been credited with a weight of between seven hundred and one thousand pounds. He earned his name by raiding farms only when the berries were scant and then killing but one animal at a time to sustain his needs for food.

The black bear had neither the weight nor the legend of an Honest John. He went about his own business, as a child of the wilderness growing into manhood. Going into the second winter of his life, he was fat and full, ready to build his bed for the long sleep. His fur, the deep, black pelage which began to renew itself in August, was glossy and rich; though he might be exposed to snow, this full coat would warm him. He would never know the cold.

He lay down early in the winter, in a hidden spot, having prepared himself by dining for days on end on "mast," the crop of nuts and acorns of the forest. His layers of fat, the "blanket," were heavy. Though the seasonal temperature is a critical factor, the accumulation of sufficient fat determines when a bear retires. Some other bears, less energetic or fortunate, might have to continue their activity, possibly on and off through the winter, but by December a healthy bear contains sufficient fat within him to yield ten to fifteen gallons of oil.

The bear became dormant, but did not hibernate. In the cases of ground squirrels, woodchucks, and jumping mice, hibernators all, the breathing and heartbeat are barely perceptible; the animal is cold to the touch. The bear, like the raccoon and skunk, goes into a deep sleep, but the heartbeat, body temperature, and breathing remain much more regular than in the hibernators. It would be physically impossible for a hibernating mammal to bring forth young, cut the umbilical cord, lick life into a newborn offspring, and guide it to the breasts. Yet the old she-bear had done all of these in late January and February.

However, with dormancy the black's physiology and digestive organs changed. His stomach and intestines shriveled. A plug or obstruction of dry leaves, pine needles, bear hair, and mucus, called a tappen, formed in his throat. It blocked the food passage and the bear lay still, subsisting placidly on his fat and letting winter go its own way.

When the bear awoke in the spring he had lost little weight and was still fat. It was not until after the early springtime activity that he became lean. By June, while shedding his winter fur, he was scrawny. He moved into the larger cycle of life with his first encounter with a female, then leaving the mother-to-be to her own devices in order to rest himself by lying down in damp, dark places. For a few days he was suspended in semi-dormancy, wisely skipping the hottest part of the year.

Soon it was fall again. In forests all across America, members of the species known as black bear, or *Euarctos americanus,* felt the instinctive weather forecast of winter. They must all stir in order to feed themselves, accumulate fat, and perpetuate their lives.

The Dogs

At dawn the dogs were restless. They were tied to trees and cars, as they had been all night, and clamored to be free and on the move. Earlier they had howled, whined, and snuffed mournfully, disturbing the hunters in their sleep. "Shut up, dammit!" one man had shouted intermittently through the night, wakening the camp as much as the dogs did. Another hunter had tried feeding a bone to his dog, but the dog bayed anew as soon as it was done chewing. A third got up from his bed and kicked his dog hard in the ribs. That dog winced in pain and was quiet.

They were not the kind of dogs that one would ever find in a show ring, going through routines with precision and good manners. The members of this pack were lean, on the scrawny side. One was minus an eye, which he had lost to a bear in a fight long ago. They were hardly distinguished by their color or conformation—that is, unless you were looking at them as bear dogs. As such, they were bred in the same patterns as the champions of the show ring, and then as finely trained for their own demanding performances.

They were whipped, kicked, treated fiercely. In the relationship between hunter and dog, however, the harsh disciplines do not reflect the full feeling of the man. He also protects the dog from abuse by another person. He places a high valuation upon his bear dog, maybe $250 or even $500, or wouldn't sell him at any price. Once a hunter parted with his dog because he needed money badly; before the day was out he had bought the dog back—he'd sooner have parted with his wife. Nothing to him could be more valuable or cherished than a dog of "good bear stock" or with "bear blood in him."

As Vaughan Plott, of the famous bear-hunting and dog-breeding Plott family, told me at Waynesville, "The dog is as good as the hunter. It must be a good hunter to have a good dog." Certainly in the drama of the bear hunt, the quarry itself has not been bred for certain, pre-ordained death, as in the case of a fighting bull, but for life. It is the dog who must gamble his stamina and perseverance against the power of death, and who far more than the hunter must show the courage of his breeding.

The dogs were ten in number, mostly blue ticks and black and tans, plus one big reddish-brown Plott hound, a sad-eyed fellow. The ancestors of that Plott were crossed and bred into a fighting bear hound, known wherever bears are hunted, with the Great Smokies and the Balsams as their proving ground.

The original dog of the breed may have come from Germany with Johannes Plott. His descendants, George and Vaughan Plott, who raise and sell Plott hounds, have told me that Johannes migrated from Heidelberg to Philadelphia, then to Goldsboro, North Carolina. Several of his grandchildren took up land on Jonathan Creek and it was for this generation in particular that the Plott Balsams were named. John Plott, grandfather of George and Vaughan, owned the farm outside Waynesville now shared by their families. His brothers, Amos, Enos, and David, were celebrated hunters and many stories are told of their exploits. On one hunt Amos advanced on a wounded bear hiding under a creek bank. He began his thrust but lost his balance and fell into the jaws and claws of the desperate beast. The bear chewed his arm and mauled him badly. But Amos was left-handed and had fallen with his right side to the bear, enabling the use of his knife hand to the best advantage. He drove it into the short ribs and the bear was finished.

George Plott told me the Plott hound originally was a bigger dog. It was crossed with a hound for a keener nose. The bears of the Smokies and Balsams gave its offspring trial by combat. Unworthy dogs that weren't slain by the bear were culled from the pack. George said his grandfather used the hounds to track slaves, as well as wolves and bears.

The family started to sell Plott hounds in World War I at $50 a puppy. They now sell twenty-five or thirty a year to hunters all over the country, and in South America (where they fight the small peccary). One dog has sold for as much as $700. Vaughan Plott, who first hunted in the rugged Plott Balsams when he was six years of age—old enough to hold a hunting dog on a leash—told me that his grandfather and father were very guarded about their ways of training the hounds. Once, when Vaughan was sixteen, a New York man came down to hunt and buy dogs. The old hounds were fought out. Six or eight had been killed by Old Reelfoot, a ferocious and much feared bear, who bit many dogs to death.

" 'Take the six young,' said my father," George recalled. "They never fought before. I couldn't believe it. 'Take them,' he said. 'Set them on a bear track.' We went into the Snowbirds. I was nervous of fear to humiliate those young dogs.

"I gave the old dogs a chance afore turning the young loose. Jack Dillard cut two loose, then I cut two more, and then the other two.

"There were a big fight. The bear got in a hole. The dogs charged in, one after another. They got bit up pretty bad but they stayed at it and charged till they got 'im.

"I never had any question about my daddy after that.

"If the dog wouldn't stay all day, my daddy killed 'im. He had to stay and fight, he had to stay with the bear at the tree.

"This breed of dog won't quit. He may get clawed and chewed, but he'll be back next week. It is one with plenty of gut. The man who isn't game isn't fit to have him."

Sam Hunnicut, a famous Smoky Mountain hunter, has written, "When I go out to hunt, I want a dog that I can depend upon." Hunnicut is credited with killing thirty-three bears, including the famous Old Roundfoot, on Noland Creek, and being in on the kill of 104 more— plus claiming to have killed a thousand coons. "If anything would cause me to kill a dog," he continued, "it would be when I told it to go after game across the ridge out of my sight and hearing, and then I should climb to the top of the ridge and, instead of hearing him after the game, meet him coming toward me. This would cause me to shoot him on the spot. That is the kind of dog you will have unless you get a thoroughbred hound; a hound one or two times crossed does very well but I would not advise anything except a thoroughbred hound."

Each of the master hunters has his own idea about what makes a great dog, or hound. "Some people," according to Hunnicut, "think a dog with long keen ears and a long tail is a hound, but they are mistaken. A real hound has fur instead of hair. The best dog I ever owned was a redbone a beagle crossed, not the little family of beagles, but the large family. A cherry red, redbone, which is known as a Florida tan, or black and tan, is a good hound or a cross from either of these species. Some think if they have a dog cross with hound it will hunt anything or any kind of game, but this is a great mistake. If, for instance, you have a bloodhound and you have any other kind of blood in this hound, he will not perform his duties. Cross up a collie and he is no good; the same with a bird dog, he is not a good bird dog if he has any other species besides the bird dog blood in him. It is the same with a hunting dog; if you want a good hunt get a thoroughbred hound, as it is nature for them to be thirsty for game."

Well, that was Sam Hunnicut's notion. But when Horace Kephart was out on the crest of Smoky with a hunting party that included Granville Calhoun, Little John Cable, Bill Cope, and Matt Hyde, he set to asking questions. Kephart wondered whether the dogs had the Plott strain, observing, "They were dangerous to man as well as to the brutes they were trained to fight; but John was their master and he soon booted them into surly subjection."

"I've been told," ventured Kephart, "that the Plott hounds are the best bear dogs in the country."

" 'Taint so," snorted John. "The Plott curs are the best: that is half hound, half cur—though what we-uns calls the cur, in this case, raelly comes from a big furrin dog that I don't rightly know the breed of. Fellers, you can talk as you please about a streak o' the cur spilin' a dog; but I know hit ain't so—not for bear fightin' in these mountains, whar you cain't follow on hossback, but hafter do your own runnin'."

"What is the reason, John?" asked Kephart.

"Waal, hit's like this: a plumb cur, of course, cain't foller a cold track —he just runs by sight; and he won't hang—he quits. But, t'other way, no hound'll raelly fight a bear—hit takes a big severe dog to do that. Hounds has the best noses, and they'll run a bear all day and night, and the next day, too; but they won't never tree—they're afeard to close in. Now, look at them dogs o' mine. A cur ain't got no dew-claws—them dogs has. My dogs can foller ary trail, same's a hound; but they'll run right in on the varmint; snappin' and chawin' and worryin' him till he gits so mad you can hear his tushes pop half a mile. He cain't run away—he haster stop every bit, and fight. Finally he gits so tired and het up that he trees to rest hisself. Then we-uns ketches up and finishes him."

In other words, the back-country hunter will breed his dogs and cross them until he produces the choice offspring that can run like a rabbit dog, trail like a foxhound, stay with a treed bear with the tenacity of a coon dog, and fight like the dickens until the bear or dog lies dead. "The redbone and blue tick mixed makes a good dog, bold and severe," said Shoof, a rough and ready mountain man, as the hunting party below Devil's Courthouse ate a breakfast of eggs and coffee. "The blue tick has a little colder nose—he can pick up a cold trail a fur distance— but your redbone is a little better fighter. That Plott has meanness and is a good dog for a short race. A Plott is a good fighter, but not a good tracker. The full-blooded Plott hankers to fight other dogs. When they have whupped the bear, Plotts'll set upon other dogs in the pack, and when they have whupped them, will start fighting among themselves. Mix a Plott with blue tick or black and tan or redbone, I say. Breed him down to about a quarter. Then you got good bear stock—a one hunnert per cent dog to live up to!"

The Hunters

Eight or ten of the hunters had gathered at the camp the evening before. It was late November, when much of the red foliage had faded into a dull russet, but here and there splashes of color still covered the hills. The camp was along a stream, part of the mountain headwaters of the French Broad, overhung with rhododendron and hemlock and carpeted with fallen hardwood leaves. The hunters were roughhewn, the old vanishing breed of mountain men, gathered from Canton, Hazelwood, and Balsam Grove, the kind who could never be content or at home in grown towns and cities. They wore simple sturdy clothing and heavy boots, the same sort of boots worn by the hiker, the moonshiner, the revenuer, to protect themselves in the forested jungle that draws them all.

There was Shoof, a woods worker, the boss of the hunt, big and heavy as a bear, yet agile on his feet. He was a fellow overjoyed in his environment; he loved to talk, to do any or all of the work around the camp. There was Abraham, lean as the usual concept of a mountaineer, whose two brothers were currently in prison for arson (rising out of a moonshining dispute); he was quiet but friendly. Among others were Frank, Bump, Lindsey, and Monty; most were in their thirties, but one or two younger and the same number older. Most of them were on speaking terms, if not practicing terms, with the old dark arts of moonshining and game poaching. The only "furriner," outside of myself, was an Asheville physician, a splendid man who had been with them before and earned their respect: he was "stout." But several of the fellows were very reticent around me. As Shoof confided later, they took me in only on his word (he had taken me on someone else's word), but insisted on their suspicions.

They set up a tent and cooked a thin stew. After supper around the fire, I offered a bottle to warm the evening.

"This is beary country, I tell you, turribly rough," said Shoof in a rich baritone. "I have hunted this place since I was a chunk of a boy big enough to tote a rifle gun, and every year since they opened it for bear on the management hunts. The Pisgy now has more game—better bear, coon, deer, or nigh anything than any district in the state of North Carolina."

He was one native hunter willing to recognize that the old free and easy days had their faults. Hunting was so intensive and destructive that when George Washington Vanderbilt bought his lands outside Asheville, western North Carolina was virtually devoid of deer and he was obliged to import stock in order to build the herds anew. The wild turkey and bear were hunted relentlessly, too. The management hunt on the Sherwood Area of the Pisgah National Forest was started in the early 1950s with some benefits for the hunter as well as for wildlife. The Forest Service plants food and cover for game and keeps the boundaries posted, while state game wardens patrol it from poaching and stray dogs. A party of hunters gets its date for use of the area by drawing for it.

Granville Calhoun, great old bear hunter of the Smokies, once recounted a revealing experience of a single day. Granville was the kind of mountain gentleman who, when he said he killed a bear weighing over six hundred pounds, I would not doubt or think a braggart. "Oh, that was one stout hunter!" said George Plott of him. "Now with roads everywhere, they ride to the sound, but Granville done it the hard way."

On the day long ago, Granville and his father-in-law, Crate Hall, tramped with their dogs to the cabin on Hall Field. It was a little hut twelve feet square used by the herdsmen when they were grazing cattle on the high grassy balds or rounding up razorbacks. The bearded hunchback, Bill Cope, was staying in the cabin. Presently they were joined by their friends, the four Cables, and six Tennesseans, who were looking to stay overnight. They set their rations inside the cabin and were preparing to build a fire and camp outdoors, when somebody said, "Let's bring in some fresh meat."

"Sure," piped up another, "let's everybody kill something."

There were plenty of signs of turkey and bear around.

"We might even get up a bear race!"

They agreed to return by four o'clock; in case anybody was missing they would still have time to look for him before dark.

The hunters spread out. In the first mile and a half toward Thunderhead, Granville and companions killed two squirrels and a pheasant. His dog ran into a drove of twenty-five or thirty turkeys. While old man Hall held the dog out of sight, Granville commenced turkey-calling and killed five, shooting from one spot.

"Hold this dog," his father-in-law shouted, "and let me have a shot!" He killed one. "Let's hang them on a tree and look some more!"

When they returned to the cabin, some of the others had already arrived. One pair of hunters reported they had treed a woodchuck when a frightened bear ran downhill past them. Their dogs chased and trapped it and a Tennessean killed the bear with a buckshot hog rifle.

At four o'clock all hands were present. The game count was eleven turkeys, twelve squirrels, one bear, one deer, one ground hog, two pheasants, three boomers, or red squirrels. It was the biggest hunt Granville had ever had in a single day.

"Well," he said, "we wanted some fresh meat in camp!"

They cooked a stew with a little of every kind of meat and feasted around the campfire from 11 P.M. until 2 A.M. Next day they decided to hunt again, but nobody killed a thing, except for a single boomer. As Granville well knew, he might hunt six or eight solid days for bear, or he might kill three in a single evening.

His generation, and those before him, hunted for the sheer sport, the thrill of the bear race, for the bear meat, skin, and oil. They hunted, too, to keep the bears out of their pastures. The hunters in whose company I sat were of the same old stock.

"I've had the bear fever all my life," said one, "and will hunt till I get so old I cain't hear them dogs and my legs get so shaky they won't carry me through the brush."

"They's more real sport in coon hunting," allowed another. "Hit takes but one man and one dog. When you tree a coon you got 'im."

"Hear now!" sang Shoof. "That bear is out thar—he's a-feedin' himself for tomorrow. If there's no mast there's no bear; he'll move on. But he's hongry, and this is good country.

"You 'uns'll see. For the first hour he'll outrun those dogs, but he's got too much fat to last all day. They'll catch him.

"I raise bear dogs and when you raise the stock once you turn 'em loose and get right up to them, you've got nothing but a continuous roar!"

The hotter the fire the more animated the conversation grew; and the more colloquial. Draining the bottle of "Government liquor" helped it along. Back-country courtesy dictated the last drop should be mine. But I insisted that it was Shoof's to down, and he was "right obleeged." A first-class promoter in his way, and bear hunting was his product and pride.

"We was a-bear hunting on the Champion property," he said, adding quickly, "when it was still allowed, I mean. We had a stander down in the gap 'twixt the Champion property and Sherwood property. He shot at the b'ar and crippled him. I lay down my gun and went under the cliff. Signs of blood were in his trail. The bear, he was hid seven hunderd or eight hunderd yards away under logs, and hurt bad. I crawled close and heaved rocks right at him. Finally he came a-chargin' out. When he went past, I lay my knife to his throat, then stove it into his stomach. He went off, but couldn't go far, for I had caught him in the neck. He was two hunderd eighty pounds and dead as four o'clock."

Then it grew late and the hunters crawled into the tent, or slept in the station wagon or on the ground, while the dogs bayed and yelped nervously, and when it rained those outside scrambled for cover.

The Hunt

It was raining lightly in the predawn and a mist shrouded the hunters' camp. Sparks flew up from the fire under the limbs of an old hardwood tree, glinting the red galluses, red shirts, red vests, and red hats, while the men stood around trading insults in the traditional manner.

"Why, this Monty'd swipe a chaw of tobacco out of your mouth if you'd open to yawn," Bump warned me.

"And that old coot would steal the hat right off your head, and you a-looking at him," retorted Monty. He was a tall, handsome young fellow, built like a football player who should have gotten an athletic scholarship and gone to college; he had a feeling for the woods and might have become a forester or wildlife biologist.

"Twenty hunters and twenty-five cars show up," someone said, referring to the new arrivals, and to new ways of comfort crowding the old.

The state game warden checked the licenses. He was a serious fellow, who faced serious problems. In a way, the procedure was a bit of a charade, and the same for the "management hunt," for most bears killed are killed illegally without regard for rules and regulations. Backwoods men hunt for bear summer, winter, in any season. There aren't enough game wardens and rangers to apprehend them—perhaps one out of twenty-five poachers is caught. Inside the national park, the wildlife sanctuary where hunting is forbidden, poachers use traps and dogs, striking by night or by boat on Fontana Lake. It is known that some poachers are not above baiting a mother bear with sardine, honey, or beef bones and then, after they kill her, capturing the cub for display in the cages before tawdry souvenir stands.

The moisture in the air was favorable and the hunters were anxious to get started.

"In this weather a dog'll smell a bear fart a half mile away," said Monty.

"I am chief cook around here and there'll be bear on the slab tonight!" proclaimed Shoof. "We'll hunt till she's dusky dark."

He deployed his hunters like a general. The "standers" were posted in the gaps along the main divide, or near it, that is, in front of the bear, while the "drivers" would be holding the dogs on leash. For the latter it was to be a day of rapid-fire action, charging through the brush with dogs raring. But for the standers, a lonely, cold vigil.

"It is hard on a fellow's nerves to sit there, praying with all his soul that the bear may not run some other way, and yet half doubtful of his own ability to head it off if it does come his way," wrote Horace Kephart in behalf of all standers.

"Chances are that it will by no means run over him, but that it will come crashing through the brush at some point on one side, toward which he will have to run with all his might and main before firing. Now if he does let that bear go through, after all the hard work of dogs and drivers, his shirt-tail will be amputated that night by his comrades and hung from a high pole in the midst of the camp—a flag of distress indeed!

"Can you hit him? That is the question. The honor of the camp is on your shoulders. Ah, me! it is easy to follow the pack on horseback— to chase after something that is running away. But to sit here clenching your teeth while at any moment a hard-pressed and angry bear may burst out of the thicket and find you in his way—nothing but you between him and nearby freedom—gentlemen, it tests nerve!"

However, something new was in the offing to make life simpler for the standers and render the whole affair of hunting more direct and to the point. I hadn't realized it, but our Asheville physician was not only the camp doctor but its communications expert, who was going to modernize the whole procedure of hunting. He had brought along and distributed four or five handy little walkie-talkie radios. The drivers would communicate their whereabouts, and presumably the bear's, when they found it, to him at his command post operating from the battery of his car at the camp, and he would relay the signal to prepare for action to the stander in line with the bear. Perhaps he figured, as a good doctor, that the charge of an angry bear tested a man's nerve too much and all trauma should be reserved for the bear.

Shoof himself elected to operate from what he called (and may have invented) a "roving stand." He took Abraham and me along with him in one direction, while the drivers headed in another looking for the scent of the bear. We made our way through the haze along an old logging road, bordered with dogwood, scarlet oak, and laurel. Now and then we passed bear trees with old claw marks and tracks with dried droppings. A woods hen scurried into the brush.

The pale misty morning brightened. Shoof tested his walkie-talkie with command headquarters at the doctor's car. After we had passed a deserted moonshining location, he tested again—with one of the other mobile units. Imagine the potential of the walkie-talkie when placed in service between lookout and still!

The day dragged. We joined with the drivers, who followed the dogs on a slow track over a cold trail through the brush. They'd cut one loose and he'd meander through the brush snuffing with his nose to the ground. Then they'd try one or two more, but each followed a different course. The men chewed tobacco, grew discouraged, and cursed the dogs for taking after a deer trail.

It began to look futile, but Shoof refused to quit. "Look at the mark on that hemlock. The bear's been here today," he insisted.

Later on the trail, "See there! He rolled over the rocks to get at the grubs. He tore them rotten logs to ribbons, a-huntin' for ants."

The dogs pulled at their leashes like chained dynamite.

"Cut that strike dog loose!"

"Go get him, Little Joe!"

The men turned another dog loose. He followed hard. They turned another, and then another. They started baying like coon hounds, strung out, their noses straight ahead following the fresh scent of a hot trail.

The bear sensed they were coming. He left all his acorns and thoughts of acorns and fled for his life, traveling a straight line over the roughest ground available. He zigzagged, then doubled back like a fox. He would rather have climbed a cliff and made his escape, but calculated he might be safe, for the present, high in a tree that had given him nuts, and let his pursuers roar by. As soon as they were beneath him he realized his mistake.

The bear leaped forty feet to the ground and bounded off, rolling downhill. The dogs were fast, but he was faster in the downgrade. On the upgrade he climbed with hind legs moving like pistons. The race was on! Some dogs were deep-throated, others shrieked. They charged through the tangle of rocks and stumps, through laurel and rhododendron, howling and screaming as though these were the moments they'd been born for, and death held no fear.

The bear crashed through the brush, loping, heading for the jungles in the reaches of the high hills, or a den in a rock cliff. The dogs nipped at his flanks, trying to pull him down, but avoided his paws. He slapped at them and shook them off, but they kept coming back, like true bear dogs. Then he reared in rage on his hind legs, snorted in ferocious warning, and struck with powerful front paws. The engagement grew bloody but the race went on.

It grew bloody for the drivers who came up behind, too. Their pants were torn, they were cut and scratched. As for the wonderful walkie-talkie, it was forgotten.

The bear made his stand to fight, leaping to a big rock, there sitting on his haunches, his big head up and swaying, sniffing the breeze for the scent of man. He was tired, and the dogs were tired except for the big Plott who charged without letup. Monty circled on hands and

knees. "Keep to the lee," shouted Shoof, "so he don't get wind of you!"
The fight rose again. The bear was atop a tangle of logs, popping his
teeth, snorting and blowing. He let out a full-throated roar, a startling,
humanlike cry that shook the woods. One of the young dogs scrambled
up the logs and leaped. The bear reached down and crushed it and the
snarling dog crawled away limply. Monty raised up, took aim, and fired
his rifle. It struck the bear in the eye. The animal reared up to its full
height and then fell backward, flat, like a man.

The signal was given: one shot, then two more.

The standers had missed their chance at the bear, but were glad to
come in. It was dusk and their day was done.

The bear is now dead. The hunters regroup, treat the dogs' wounds,
and start to yarning. "You got to cook a bear through and thorough,"
says Monty, who killed it, "for even though it suits my taste hit carries
trichinosis, like a hog."

"Heck no," retorts another. "The way to cook that wild pork is: drap
several hot rocks in a pot o' bilin' water with the meat for several hours.
Then, throw the meat away and eat the rocks."

It is quite a task to skin a bear, and a grisly business. Shoof must
begin from the feet. He must slit it up inside each leg to the belly.
He must leave the head attached. He must slit along the belly between
chin and tail. The beast is covered with fat, the source of sustenance
for the winter sleep that will never come; it sticks to the hide and must
be scraped free. It is rendered into bear's oil, better and wholesomer
than lard, by cooking in a pot high over a slow fire. The smell is acrid,
but the hunters know that bear's oil will serve its purpose in shortening
biscuits and frying good food at home. They can mix it with sugar,
spread it on bread, and use it as a substitute for butter and syrup.

I wish that I had saved the last drop of my whiskey. My friend, ol'
Shoof, perspiring before the fire of late November, disappears for an
instant and returns from his car with a bottle of soothing-syrup too new
to have paid tax. I despise the taste of white moonshine but cannot
refuse.

The bone is hacked with an ax. The dark, fleshy bear meat is fried
slowly on the coals, turned and turned again until, as Monty said, it is
cooked thoroughly.

So, the bear's last day is done.

XX

The Boar on the Loose

The strangest dwellers in the Great Smoky Mountains are frightfully unpopular and unwelcome. Park rangers trap at least fifty of them a year and wish they could catch more. Biologists refer to them impolitely as "exotics," which means they are alien to the environment. They are roundly denounced for their nasty habits of uprooting grassy balds and heath balds covered with azaleas, of depriving the black bear population of acorns in fall, of killing snakes and smaller animals, and of generally making troublesome nuisances of themselves. Besides, they're a fierce-looking lot, and dangerous.

They may be unwanted and despised, these intruders, but they like it in the Smokies, being true creatures of wilderness. They have adapted themselves, alas too well, and have multiplied to a level beyond hope of stamping them out. In Germany, where their grandfathers may have originated, their breed is called *wildschwein*, wild pig, or wild boar. Around the mountains between Robbinsville, North Carolina, and Tellico Plains, Tennessee, where they first arrived early in the twentieth century, they are known as "Rooshians," on the theory they came from Russia, if not Prussia.

Whatever the source, the European wild boar appears fixed in the fabric of the southern Appalachians and deserves recognition of his place, if not acceptance and a kind word.

And who is to say that the boar is any more the stranger than the old-fashioned razorback or the pure-bred swine? For after all, the modern swine is understood to be descended from a domesticated version of this European boar crossed with a smaller Asiatic species, then introduced into America by the Spanish and English settlers. In the same sense that only the Indians were un-strange among the human dwellers, so the peccary, or musk hog, of the Southwest and Mexico, was the only type of native pig in North America.

Our European wild boar, Sus scrofa, furthermore, is endowed with a savage untamed spirit, fighting speed, and stamina; and, while his facial features may be frightening to all but his own kind, those razor-sharp tusks, or "tushes," have a beautiful and versatile utility about them that help him to survive, as many a hunting dog has learned the painful way. In short, this creature, standing three feet high at the shoulders, weighing over two hundred pounds and sometimes four hundred, is worthy of his environment; and if the mountains are to be respected, so too should he.

It was in 1908 when the notion of importing boar to North Carolina was conceived. In that year, the Great Smoky Mountain Land and Timber Company sold a vast tract of land, containing huge stands of hemlock, yellow poplar, ash, and maple in the Nantahala and Snowbird ranges, to the Whiting Manufacturing Company, one of a number of English and Scottish investment concerns that exploited the southern hardwood forests. As part of the transaction, Whiting's agent, George Gordon Moore, of St. Clair, Michigan, and New York, was given 1600 acres on which to establish a shooting preserve, of the European type. According to one report I have read, he planned it for the entertainment of wealthy friends and clients. According to another, bonds were sold to them and the proceeds used in construction of a clubhouse and other buildings. Take your choice. For his location, Moore chose a high, remote, and roadless corner of the densely forested Snowbirds. It lay twenty-five miles from Robbinsville, surrounding Hooper Bald, 5429 feet high, a stone's throw from other high places on the main ridge bordering Tennessee, like Haw Knob, Laurel Top and Stratton Meadow; his nearest neighbors included some of the "Snowbird Cherokee" scattered about the isolated coves and hollows below.

Three years of preparation were required before the first animals arrived. The road had to be constructed to the summit of the Bald. Twenty-five tons of barbed wire had to be hauled by wagon to fence game lots. The distance around a single enclosure, designed for buffalo, measured almost a mile. The boar enclosure covered 600 acres. A ten-bedroom clubhouse and four-room caretaker's cottage were erected, a horse trail laid out, and telephone lines strung from the village of Marble across the top of the Snowbirds.

In 1912 the chosen game animals arrived in wooden crates by railroad. They were constituents of a sportsman's ark—bear, buffalo, boar, deer and elk. Some were hauled by wagons, drawn by oxen or horses, from Murphy over Hanging Dog Mountain. Others were sent on to the Andrews depot for transfer to a lumber rail line (the Snowbird-Unicoi) extending into the Snowbirds. This was a large-scale operation, which began in springtime and continued all summer. It was facilitated by the participation of State Guard cavalrymen, under Captain Frank W. Swan, of Andrews, who probably found more excitement than in ages of drilling. The boar were young, weighing sixty to seventy-five pounds, thus not as fierce or hard to handle as mature animals. Moving the buffalo was another matter, for it took a wagon and four horses, or oxen, to haul but one of them.

At last they were present and accounted for, and almost all had survived: eight buffalo; thirteen or fifteen boar; fourteen elk; six Colorado mule deer; thirty-four bears, including nine huge Russian brown bears; two hundred wild turkeys, plus ten thousand eggs of the English ring-necked pheasant. Moore then purchased locally one hundred and fifty sheep and one hundred and fifty turkeys, most of which were placed within the lot as victuals for the bears, and another one hundred and eighty turkeys which he ordered scattered about the woods in an effort to get them started.

Of all these introduced species, the wild boar alone would become well established in the new environment. It was the only one of he strangers that would adapt itself to the hills and endure the difficulties of nature and the harassments of the native predators—hunting men and their dogs.

As to where the boar came from originally, was it Russia, Prussia, or where? George Gordon Moore in a letter to Garland "Cotton" McGuire, his foreman to whom he later presented the Hooper Bald preserve for whatever it might be worth, wrote:

"I got my knowledge of wild boar through Walter Winants, the famous sportsman, who had his own wild boar hunting lodge in Belgium. He told me that the largest and fiercest wild boar were found in the Ural Mountains in Russia. I purchased the boar through an agent in Berlin who represented that they came from Russia. You will remember the number. I think there were 10 or 11 sows and 3 boar originally."

The boar could have come from other sections of Europe, as well as the Urals, for they are found in wilder forests and marshy woodlands of Austria, Germany, Spain, and Turkey; numbers of them are preserved on large hunting estates to be hunted by the nobility either by boar hounds—setters or terriers—scrappy little dogs which I have seen (though not in action) at the Kaiser's old estate near Hanover, in northern Germany. Another species, Sus cristatus, slightly taller than the European, is found in India. An old custom there was to stage pit fights between tiger and wild boar; often the odds were on the boar.

Moore's European boar, the "Rooshians," were not exactly the first of their kind imported to the United States, nor the last. As early as 1885, a railroad magnate named Austin Corbin developed a preserve near Newport and Grantham, New Hampshire, which he stocked with red deer, wild sheep, boar, and boar dogs, little setters, from Austria, as well as bison and elk. Theodore Roosevelt bagged one of the Corbin boar on a hunting trip in 1902. The land, which became known as Corbin's Park, is now owned by the Blue Mountain Forest Association, a private hunting club whose members still shoot elk and boar.

I have also seen the telltale destructive signs of boar—the uprooted soil and damaged shrubs—at the Aransas National Wildlife Refuge in Texas (the famed sanctuary of the whooping crane). "Razorback?" I asked the refuge manager.

"No, European wild boar," he replied, "stocked before the refuge was established. They have mixed with local hogs, but their strain dominates. We shoot them on sight."

Moore himself, when he became disenchanted with the rigors of the Appalachians, moved to California in the early twenties, built an estate in the Monterey vicinity, and transplanted a dozen of his Carolina boar. These have grown into a sizable herd and are hunted in season in the Santa Lucia Mountains, a part of the Los Padres National Forest.

The mountains of Carolina and Tennessee proved ideal for boar. They discovered early that they could root their way out of the split-rail enclosure any time they wanted, though most chose to remain; for eight years they were fed and permitted to reproduce unmolested. By 1920 they had proliferated to about one hundred in number. Local mountaineers observed the tuskers with keen interest. They knew the razorback and acorn-splitter hogs, but these Rooshians were something to behold, and to make a man wonder how he and his dogs would fare in hunting them through the woods.

For all the time, effort, and investment, Moore's hunting preserve was ill-fated. Moore might have come a few times himself and occasionally sent some guests, but the location was much too remote and rugged for English gentlemen, or any other kind. Besides, the big bears learned to climb out of their stockade and head for the nearest food, which happened to be at the lodge; they had to be roped and tied by Cotton McGuire and other hands, and dragged back to their own quarters. As for hunting, local poachers got to the turkeys first and quickly exterminated them. The buffalo, though protected from shooting, survived poorly at best and were later driven to Andrews and disposed of. The elk did well, and even multiplied, but they eluded Moore's hunters and ultimately were sold, too.

Although much of the Hooper Bald story is based on twice-told tales, it appears that about 1920 Moore and his guests set dogs on the boar within the enclosure for the first time, whereupon the boar decided the time had come to leave, and one hundred of them ran through low places in the chestnut fence, heading for the open woods. Or, they may have crashed out two or three years later when Cotton McGuire invited some of his local friends to bring their dogs up to the Bald for a grand hog hunt. The boar, however, had other ideas. According to this version, only two of them were killed as compared with a dozen dogs killed or maimed, and the boar tore their way through the fence while the hunters shinnied up trees.

In this period, the early 1920s, Moore lost interest and prepared to liquidate his mountain estate for more civilized parts. The easiest way proved to give McGuire title to the land, animals, the two houses, and $1000 for good measure to keep up the menagerie. For a while thereafter sportsmen paid McGuire $75 for the right to come up and shoot elk, but he sold off the herd here and there, including twenty-five to North Carolina for stocking around Mount Mitchell. The bear fell prey to native hunters, who paid nothing for their shooting privileges.

Only McGuire remained.

And the boar.

In 1926, Champion Fibre Company acquired the Bald, along with 39,000 acres of the Whiting tract, but McGuire, a quiet, well-respected man of the mountains, continued as fire warden. Word of the fighting boar spread through hunting circles and attracted sportsmen from distant places. They sought McGuire, who knew the animal's ways better than any man in the woods, as their guide until his death in 1957 at the age of sixty-two.

Following their escape, many of the boar crossed the state line into the rugged uplands above Tellico Plains, within the boundaries of Cherokee National Forest, ranging back and forth between Tennessee and North Carolina, and finding both to their liking. They thrived, multiplied, and claimed their place as kings of the wilderness. They extended their range—the boar probably has a larger cruising radius than any other species in the southern mountains—and cross-bred with razorbacks. The tougher characteristics of the European prevailed in the mixture, while full-blood stock grew rare.

The bold body structure of the boar resembles the buffalo's, high and heavy in the shoulders. "He's a big 'un up front," as the native says. Over each shoulder the animal is armed with extremely thick cartilage, which the teeth of a hound cannot rip and which will stop any small-caliber rifle bullet. From his shoulders, extending to the neck, the boar has a shield of skin, which may become two inches thick, that defies the knife.

The prevailing color of the adult, a grizzled dark gray, is produced by the cover of coarse hair which develops into a pronounced mane of long, heavy bristles from atop the head to the back of the hips. The bristles differ from those on an ordinary hog for each bristle splits at the end into silvery prongs. There you have one of nature's camouflage marvels, for on a dark night the wild boar appears black while on a moonlit night the silvery tips blend with the shine of the moon.

The head and face are the unforgettable features of old *Sus scrofa*, being as grotesque as a gargoyle, though designed as an integrated unit for usefulness and survival. His head is wedge-shaped with a pointed snout, which enables him to root up the ground, or to push through thick underbrush when under pursuit. The small, hairy ears are streamlined to a point. The top canine tusks curve upward, like bony handlebar mustaches two to eight inches long. The straight, angular lower canines grind against them and are thus kept sharpened to a razor's edge. With these tushes, the boar is admirably equipped to dig roots, mushrooms, and plant matter of all kinds. These are his swords in dueling another boar, aiming for the belly or flank. The tushes are so finely honed and lethal that when the boar slashes out and upward at a hunting dog he is apt to split the dog open from head to tail with a single thrust.

The boar is loaded with power in his hoofs as well as the tushes. The hoofs are narrower than a domestic pig's, and more sharply edged; the legs are longer, stronger, and more supple. Thus, the boar can stomp on a rattlesnake and cut him to ribbons for his dinner. He can run or jump up steep banks, cross streams over narrow logs, while the domestic hog must wade through the stream. He can leap over obstacles like rocks or downed logs.

This animal has been shaped to survive a harsh environment. From 1920 until 1936 the wild hog was hunted relentlessly in all seasons, without regulation or control, by fierce mountain men and fierce dogs. In addition, it found itself competing for food with other wild creatures. Wildcats, bears, and possibly foxes preyed upon its young, an age of high mortality. As a result of these pressures, *Sus scrofa* of the southern Appalachians has developed as a nervous, alert, graceful beast; in all its movements and behavior it demonstrates the wild animal's protective vigilance. It is rarely seen near inhabited sections. Never does it stand still more than a second or two, remaining remote and difficult to observe. The sense of smell and hearing are acute, more important than sight. Mostly the boar is a nocturnal creature, feeding under the cover of darkness. Unlike the bear, who moves alone, boar band together for mutual protection, with herds traveling up to twelve miles during one feeding period. The old boar, who have lost their fight, usually spend the day in safety and solitude on the high ridges, then feed with the band at night. The large young males range over extensive areas looking for sows to perpetuate their species, demanding survival of the fittest and the wildest. They kill tame boar, or cut them and scar their hides, then breed freely with domestic sows. The ablest, strongest boar sire the most pigs. This is why the qualities of the stranger have dominated: the big chest, the armored cape of skin around neck and shoulders, the bison-shaped hips, the defiant fighting spirit. The young are born in some secluded spot, the sow denning in a cliff recess, rocky ledge, or dense thicket, to insure safety from enemies. After giving birth to a litter of four or five, and sometimes more, the sow keeps constant vigil, but the little pigs learn rapidly to care for themselves. At the age of one year, the permanent tusks begin to grow, and soon after the boar are mature and on their own.

In other circumstances, the wild boar is not as wild. Kenneth Flewelling, of Sherwood Forest, Lebanon, New Hampshire, wrote me in 1962 about a visit to his neighbors at the Blue Mountain Forest Association. "At the headquarters today, four boar were grazing in the field in company with about a dozen deer," wrote Mr. Flewelling, a trained forester. "No shooting is done in this area and all the animals become rather tame. In fact, the wife of the superintendent had a young boar as a house pet a few years ago, until its size forced its banishment to the yard. He allowed me to scratch his head and would trot behind one to the point of being a nuisance." Likewise, in the same year in Germany, when I visited the Saupark at Springe, the Kaiser's old hunting ground, the *forstmeister* told me that some boar, such as those in the *Tiergartens* of German cities, have been so tamed by kind treatment they will stand still to be stroked like a baby. The meat of tamed animals, he said, contains more fat than that of the wild ones.

"The purely nocturnal and wandering life is not in the least characteristic of the hog," it has been written by another German. "They very soon give up those habits if one gives them peace, or if they are well fed." At the Saupark, I saw how food was set out for a herd of boar along a roadside, and down they came from the woods in early evening to have their dinner of corn in full view of hikers and tourists. When these boar are hunted in late October by the president of Lower Saxony and party, there are grand festivities, said the *forstmeister*, with much dining and wining. The scrappy little hunting dogs, led by the "beaters" or drivers, track down and chase the boar within shooting range of the president and his guests. The year before my visit, I was told, some thirty or forty hunters bagged twenty-two boar, including ten males, plus a few stray foxes and rabbits. And after the shooting, the festivities proceeded.

In the mountains of southern Appalachia, however, the fighting wild boar has seldom been seen feeding in public view—and hunting them down is one of the roughest pursuits of man and dog. In the early 1930s there was discussion of exterminating the boar officially from the national forests (although the local poachers were doing a good job without sanction), but it was decided instead to give them protection in order to perpetuate the species and to permit reasonable hunting seasons. The first open season was conducted in the Cherokee National Forest in 1936, followed a year later by the first season in the Nantahala National Forest.

Boar are hunted in much the same way as bears, with the same kind of fearless, tireless dogs, including Plott hounds, many of whom show the years of combat on their cut, scarred bodies. Old-time hunters at Tellico Plains, including Jess Brooks, Perry Swainson, and Joe Floyd, have told me they can never quite anticipate the movements of a boar, who can be as fleet as a deer, as cunning as a bear, as elusive as a fox. A boar may run in circles or in a zigzag trail, with the stamina to run hard all day. He may double back and charge, at dog or hunter, and often has been known to keep unarmed men treed for hours. Experienced dogs, once they bring the boar to bay after the chase through the woods, give him lots of room, nipping legs and flanks but dodging the tusks—while young, headstrong dogs may be cut to pieces. The boar shows that he's ready to take on any and all dogs by croaking deep guttural coughs, champing his jaws furiously until he froths at the mouth; and then he rushes. The hunter will get a shot at the boar, unless the animal charges him first. If the shot misses, chances are the hunter will turn and run, leaving the dogs to cover his rear.

Yet, the boar invites his own downfall, becoming more and more belligerent with each victory, counting on using the same escape trick that worked before. The old mountain guides, built with the same constitutional cunning and leanness as the boar, plan their moves accordingly.

Hunting is not the sole factor controlling the population of the Appalachian wild boar. Man has left little area wild enough to suit his needs. The sleek predatory animal of the wilderness, the bobcat, takes a toll of young pigs (though it would hardly be capable of killing a full-grown boar). The black bear can prey upon the hog, killing both large and small animals, but the two species are believed not to occupy the same areas at the same time. They depend upon much of the same foods, but their feeding habits differ, the bear depending upon claws and teeth while the hog uses its nose or snout as a plow; and while the hog's activities continue during winter, the bear is dormant, easing food competition at the time of year when it is least plentiful. The abundance or absence of food supply—particularly of fall "mast," crops of acorns and nuts—is one of the principal factors governing the number of boar, their whereabouts and movements. For instance, during the winter and early spring of 1946–47, when mast was in acutely short supply, most boar shoats in North Carolina apparently starved to death before reaching maturity. (The boar season was closed to insure survival of breeding stock for the following year.) The adult boar were forced to range greater distances, crossing ridges into new valleys, in the hunt for food.

In this way, a band of Rooshians may have found its way across the Little Tennessee River and taken up residence inside the Great Smoky Mountains National Park (bringing along the ticks and hog lice that make their dwelling place in the hides of almost all hogs). This could have taken place in the 1950s, or possibly earlier. An estimate of wild boar population in 1956 was given as 800 in the Cherokee National Forest, 300 in the Nantahala National Forest, with no report at all from the national park. However, the boar must have found plentiful mast, for their number doubled, redoubled, and redoubled again until, by the 1960s, they were into the hundreds in the western portion of the park.

The wild boar keeps active throughout the year, feeding on both plant and animal matter of all kinds, shifting wherever food is to be found, devouring insects, June bugs, hardshell beetles, crayfish, frogs, salamanders, mice, lizards, destroying birds' nests for young and eggs, relishing the rattler and literally eating him alive, and for a vegetable supplement succulent herbs, tuberous roots, grains and acorns. During spring and early summer, he may locate at the head of a high, heavily shaded moist cove, then drifting into thickets lower in the coves for berries. In fall, he roots out hoarded nuts hidden by squirrels, and in winter feeds along the mast-producing ridges vacated by the bears.

The boar leaves a trail of devastation. He tramples bare the ground around trees. A ranger has shown me where eight or ten hogs tore up an acre of ground, leaving it barren of vegetation. The boar roots in a straight line, takes a few steps, then repeats the operation, over several miles in a single night. He roots the heads of streams, damaging vegetation *and* the watershed. He wallows in almost each stream he crosses, then picks a small pine for a rubbing tree or as a sharpener for his tusks. He digs a bed in dense thickets of rhododendron or laurel, first loosening the dirt because he prefers to lie on bare soft soil.

All of this is not necessarily evil. In one German forest, where the number of boar was kept under careful control, the *wildschwein* were considered an economic asset, for, while they continually dug up the forest soil to eat the chrysalises of insects, they were mixing leaf and twig litter to enrich the soil and increase its growing capacity. In our

Appalachians, by exposing insects and small root tubers, the boar benefit keen-eyed birds. Ground squirrels probably suffer the most from hogs, since their winter stores are destroyed and the animals themselves occasionally eaten; but on the other hand the red and gray foxes, which proved useful in controlling squirrels in the Smokies, themselves suffered years ago as a result of disease and have been reduced in number. Perhaps the boar have filled their role. Though their food habits differ, both also have a propensity for preying on eggs and small young of ground-nesting birds.

The Rooshians may be destructive and damaging, but have made their way in the wilderness. Should they be exterminated? Trapped more intensively in order to keep the number under control? Permitted to roam free and work out their own ultimate destiny in the forest community? Whatever the decision, I would only hope the wild boar is never reduced to the pitiful beggarhood of his neighbor the bear.

At Hooper Bald, meanwhile, Champion sold its land in 1946 to two other lumber companies, Genett and Bemis, and in due course it came under Government ownership, as part of Nantahala National Forest. Old logging roads circle the Bald, but the summit itself, with the crumbling remains of George Gordon Moore's hunting camp, can be reached only by jeep or horseback. That is, by you and me. The Rooshians have their own way of getting around.

XXI

Revenuer

When he leaves home for the office and his work in the field, Paul Byron hardly resembles a law enforcement officer. He favors worn denim clothes and scuffed boots. These serve a practical purpose in carrying him through the woods afoot and also give him the appearance of an average, balding mountain man in his late thirties, to those unaware of his true calling.

He drives an old car, a black Ford, that formerly belonged to a taxicab driver in Murphy who made the mistake of selling a case of moonshine to an undercover internal revenue agent, or, more properly, an alcohol tax investigator. Most men in Byron's line drive such vehicles, seized from runners of illegal whiskey, and find them well suited, for usually they're deceptively ancient cars equipped with modern high-powered engines.

Byron's office is located in an obscure corner of the basement of the old Federal Building in Asheville. He and his two partners, Sievers and Hart, receive few callers in person. They have no secretaries and type their own reports. They answer the phones themselves and speak in hushed tones, for they may be receiving tidings that will never be offered again. One caller, a jealous woman, in a fit of spite may disclose the location of her own husband's illegal whiskey operation. Another may be a defeated ex-sheriff hoping to punish his political foes. Or a religious zealot stirred to passion against a neighbor who has fostered the whiskey sin. Or a moonshiner double-crossing a competitor in order to improve his own selling position. The three agents know that many calls are a waste of time: people want them to hunt here and there in the hills, often on wild goose chases, but informers are vital, so they listen. Their best informers are men in the moonshine business, who provide them pipelines into the mountain underworld and thus are cultivated with care.

"The facets of human nature are never in greater play." These are Byron's words (though Byron is not his real name), which explain the fascination of his work to him and the common bond between the moonshiner, or blockader, and the revenuer. At their best, they respect each other as honorable men constantly testing each other over the years to determine whose skills are the sharper honed.

Once, for example, Byron was chasing a moonshiner's car through the mountains. He thought he was gaining ground when suddenly he missed a curve and spun into a ditch. The moonshiner could have made a clean getaway, but instead his car backed up as fast as he'd been moving forward.

"You hurt, captain?" asked the mountain man. He insisted on calling Byron captain, even though he'd only been a sergeant in the Marine Corps.

Then, however, he saw that Byron was unhurt and could back the car out of the ditch. "How fur ahead of you was I?"

"Down to the turn, I think," replied the revenue agent.

"Reckon it was a quarter mile more, captain."

Byron knew that man was being truthful, according to the codes. If he or any other agent were to testify in court that a moonshiner on a chase was driving 120 miles per hour when he actually was doing only 90, that would not be playing "far and squar." An agent who lies is an unworthy competitor.

They resumed their positions and the pursuit went on. Byron failed to catch the man. The next time he came into Balsam Grove, he was asked with a smile, "How's your driving, captain?"

And he was obliged to reply, "Improving."

One of Byron's partners, Sievers, had been a special agent for a railroad before joining the Alcoholic Tax and Tobacco Division (called "A and TT" or "ATU") of the Internal Revenue Service. The other, Hart, was a graduate optometrist, of all things, who discovered he didn't like being cooped up indoors. Byron himself had rather an ideal background for his work. Besides being mountain bred, he was a graduate in both agricultural economics and law, who had taught on-the-farm subjects to veterans after World War II. He knew the ways, needs, and psychology of mountaineers.

The life of an alcohol tax investigator leaves much to be desired. The pay is low, hours are long, work is hazardous, the future uncertain, and the concept certainly not as popular or glamorous as that of an FBI agent or a T-man tracking down narcotics smugglers. The letter of the law itself is not necessarily the most important consideration in dealing with some of the terribly backward, underprivileged, and undernourished people—morally as well as physically—who are bred to moonshining. As an example, two young brothers of Balsam Grove, an impoverished community once rich in timber treasures, were hailed before Judge Wilson Warwick in Asheville, but the stiffest sentence he would impose was that they be out of bed at 7 A.M. every morning and keep wood cut for their mother at all times. When Byron came by two months later, he found them at noon lying in beds that probably hadn't been made all year, with dogs and cats roving about at will. "Have you still got the wood cut?" was all he could ask.

Most moonshine operations in the western mountain districts bordering the Smokies are small operations, averaging fifty to sixty gallons capacity. They differ considerably from syndicate productions in Wilkes County, North Carolina. In that Blue Ridge country, the big-timers have been known to use coke-burning boilers with capacity of up to 25,000 gallons and to pay farmers $100 a week to go through their yards in order to service stills hidden in the woods. Their flotillas of delivery cars are powered to make 150 or 160 miles per hour in the straightaway —with or without lights on. These cars are equipped with all manner of devices, including oversize racing wheels, truck power brakes, air-lift springs, and extra shock absorbers to keep from rolling on mountain curves in the midst of a chase. When agents narrow the gap, the skilled moonshine racing drivers can pepper the road surface with tacks released by a dashboard lever. The stakes are high, of course, for the average "road" car hauls 20 cases, or 120 gallons, of 100-proof moonshine for transfer at secret rendezvous to the "town" car for delivery; and while the cost of the merchandise at the still varies from $18 to $22, it will rise to $32 at the wholesaler, $60 at the "drink house," and $5 for a half-gallon jar to the customer. Coping with these operators and distributors has demanded new techniques by the Federals: transistor walkie-talkies; movie cameras to observe activity on roads and in cities in order to learn the "set-in," or delivery points, and infrared scopes called "snooper scoops" to penetrate total darkness. Investigators have learned to skim over mountain roads in captured cars at 140 miles per hour, and have installed huge steel bumper guards to ram or wreck the moonshiners when they get close enough, rather than be dusted off themselves.

Such activities reflect more than a way of life but impersonal big business, illicit trafficking on a grand scale. Since prohibition and postrepeal periods, whiskey supplies from Wilkes County and from Cocke County, Tennessee, flush against the Smokies, have been delivered to big cities of the Middle West, including Cincinnati, Indianapolis, Detroit, and Cleveland—and not just "to the neighbors."

Byron has very few, if any, of the big fellows in the counties surrounding Asheville. The little moonshiners are more appealing to him, people who have lived out of the mainstream of history for generations, to whom morals and religion are not quite the same. Back in Ireland, from whence some of their ancestors came as runaway indentured servants, one might say of another, "Surely, he's an honest man. I was in jail with him."

"The little moonshiner is a more interesting character (than the big fellow)," wrote Horace Kephart, "if for no other reason than that he fights fair, according to his code, and singlehanded against tremendous odds. He is innocent of graft. There is nothing between him and the whole power of the Federal Government except his own wits and a well-worn Winchester or muzzle loader. He is very poor; he is very ignorant; his apparatus is crude in the extreme, and his output is miserably small. This man is usually a good enough citizen in other ways, of decent standing in his own community, and a right good fellow toward all the world, save revenue officers. Although a criminal in the eyes of the law, he is soundly convinced that the law is unjust, and that he is only exercising his natural rights."

Such men have been the core of the ancient illicit whiskey trade that somehow cannot be eradicated. Nobody knows the exact figures, but an estimate has fixed the number of stills operating in North Carolina at about one thousand. Probably it's about the same, or a little less, in Tennessee. The Internal Revenue Service has reported that 95 per cent of all liquor law violators apprehended are in the eleven southern states. (These included, in a typical year of the early 1960s, 10,000 persons arrested, 3000 cars seized, 7000 stills smashed, plus 4,000,000 gallons of good mash spilled into the creeks.) The A and TT terms the South the "pre-prohibition moonshine belt," where illegal distilling has been inherent in the population and the technique handed down from generation to generation—particularly in the mountain districts. "It is in these states, where over 40 per cent of the population is located in so-called 'dry' or local option counties and liquor is not readily available," according to an A and TT report, "that we have encountered extreme difficulty in combating the moonshine traffic, despite extensive seizures, arrests, and prosecutions."

This statement impresses one as a tribute to various forces at work. The internal revenue agents clearly have been on the job cracking down as hard as they can. So have the hardshell Baptist ministers, shouting to the rafters about the evils of drink and denouncing any editor or politician who dares suggest that perhaps drinking in public is less of an evil than getting plastered in private. The bootleggers cheer the ministers onward, and keep their politician friends well oiled in the cause of righteousness. In the state of Mississippi, sinfulness is not exactly sanctified but simply recognized *sub rosa:* bootleggers can sell anything to anybody as long as they pay a ridiculous levy called the "black market tax." All these enlightened folks—ministers, bootleggers, and politicians—make our mountain distillers look like scholars and gentlemen.

The market for their merchandise has never disappeared, despite all efforts at suppression. Some customers prefer the taste of moonshine to legal liquor. Some buy it because they must go too far, into Asheville or Knoxville, in order to purchase the legal; and others, because the price is right. Consider that Federal taxes come to $10.50 a gallon. A moonshiner can produce and bottle a gallon of 100-proof whiskey for $1.25 and can sell it profitably at $5 per half gallon—less than half the Federal tax. Thus, the moonshiner has genuine incentive, despite the risk, and so has the consumer.

The popular version of the origin of the term "moonshiner" is that the early practitioners confined their working hours to nighttime, by the light of the moon, for security reasons. The term "bootlegger" supposedly originated from the manner in which peddlers of liquid contraband concealed bottled wares in their boot tops. Whatever the source of these words, the contest between moonshiners and revenuers has been underway in the hills for a long, long time. In a sense, it began in the seventeenth century in Ireland, where the natives distilled spirits out of their own barley in small pot-stills. They preferred their own brand to "Parliament" or "King's" whiskey and resisted the revenuers of their day, known as "gaugers." Around the big cities, like London, Edinburgh, and Dublin, the common practice was to bribe the gauger, who received a "duty" upon every still in his jurisdiction; but in the impoverished Irish back country people couldn't afford to share profits with the gaugers. They also disdained to do so, for they were governed more by clan law than by law of the central government, and hid their little pot-stills in wild mountains and glens, defying intrusion with force of arms.

The Scotch-Irish, who absorbed many of these ways from contacts with the Black Irish, brought with them a certain fondness for whiskey when they migrated to America; but presently they ran into the excise tax of 1791, of nine to eleven cents per proof gallon. In western Pennsylvania and the mountains southward, where they had settled, the Scotch-Irish farmers found it profitable to turn much of their corn and rye into whiskey, for in such concentrated form it was much easier to ship their crops to market over woefully poor roads of the day. Along came a band of Government agents, excise men, authorized to enter homes and collect money from the small producers. These intruders were given short shrift, occasionally a coat of tar and feathers, by the "Whiskey Boys," who dealt just as harshly with any local citizen friendly or favorable to the collectors. All of which led to the celebrated Whiskey Rebellion of 1794, with pitched battles raging on the Pennsylvania frontier between farmers and United States marshals until President Washington sent the troops. Such habits and precedents journeyed south with the settlers and were combined with the harsh actualities of life—the barter economy, the difficulties of transportation, the isolation from government—to stimulate the worst forms of guerilla warfare between revenuers and moonshiners.

Ironically, it was after the Civil War, during which many mountain men were loyal to the Union and fought in the Union Army, that the Federal Government struck hardest against the Appalachian dweller who turned his apples and peaches into brandy and his corn into whiskey.

"The extent of these frauds," wrote the Commissioner of Internal Revenue in his report for 1876–77, "would startle belief." There were, according to his calculation, no less than 3000 illicit stills scattered in the southern mountains, each producing ten to fifty gallons a day. "They are usually located at inaccessible points in the mountains, away from the ordinary lines of travel, and are generally owned by unlettered men of desperate character, armed and ready to resist the officers of the law. Where occasion requires, they come together in companies of from ten to fifty persons, gun in hand, to drive the officers out of the country.

"These frauds had become so open and notorious that I became satisfied extraordinary measures would be required to break them up. Collectors were each authorized to employ from five to ten additional deputies. Experienced revenue agents of perseverance and courage were assigned to duty to co-operate with the collectors. United States marshals were called upon to co-operate with the collectors and to arrest all persons known to have violated the laws, and district attorneys were enjoined to prosecute all offenders."

Despite these official pressures, complained the Commissioner, moonshining flourished. The Government was being deprived of its revenues. Even worse, officers and witnesses were often dragged from their homes at night and cruelly beaten, or waylaid and assassinated. What he needed, what he pleaded for, was a tougher law, granting the right of arrest without warrant, and stronger support for revenue officers. He was determined in 1877 to smash moonshining in the hills, once and for all, and forever.

One trouble was that few revenue agents were much better, if better at all, than the moonshiners. A handful were tough, fearless and fair, devoted to the law in the same sense as Paul Byron. But the work was so rough and unpopular that, in the main, it attracted rough, unpopular characters, old moonshiners themselves. In the early days, to make things worse, tax collectors—even those high up the ladder—were paid by commission and fees; out in the mountains the income of agents depended upon the number of stills they cut and upon the arrests made. For long years it would take a fine-tooth comb to find anyone with a kind word for "the revenue."

I have talked with Charley Branton, a splendid, well-liked gentleman of years, at the attractive guest house he operates in Bryson City. Forty years before, in 1921, Branton was appointed a revenue agent. His headquarters then was in Bryson City and his territory the Great Smoky Mountains and surroundings.

"I knew nothing about the work and learned as I went along," he said. "There were ten times as many stills then as now, for there were logging camps and big band mills, where liquor sold for twenty dollars a gallon. It was all blockade, of course."

"Blockade" is one of those strictly Smoky Mountain expressions, which I've heard here but nowhere else. Perhaps it derives from the Irish practice of running the English blockade. The distiller, among the old-timers especially, is called a blockader, and his merchandise is either blockade or blockade liquor. The ancient craft and the ancient expression are honorable badges almost everyone respects.

"Most information came from informers," continued Branton. "Church people were some of the best. They would write us letters and mark out the setting of a still on a map. It was all on horseback. The officers would go to the still when it was ready to run, and wait for the operators. We would tie our horses and walk a half mile. Then came cars. We got them about 1925 and walked three or four miles instead. Still, cars and roads were hard on the blockaders, took away their privacy.

"The Smoky Mountains were just right for them. They could set a still miles from any wagon road along a little side branch choked with laurel and rhododendron, almost unapproachable except by such worming and crawling as to make a warning noise. But we'd manage somehow.

"I recollect many times breaking into a still setting and saying to somebody I knew, 'You oughtn't to be a-doing that.'

"All he'd say was, 'I have to be a-doing something.'

"There was good money in the blockade, but they throwed it away."

A few Smoky Mountain fellows, said Branton, made good liquor. Jim and Wick E., for instance, made it from pure corn, with just a little sugar. They used a copper still and sold to special customers they knew and trusted, not school kids, young folks, or anyone who might prove to be an undercover agent.

But such craftsmen were scarce, even in Branton's day. Few mountain folk felt they could afford a proper aging process. Quill Rose, a famous blockader and champion of drinking bouts, who lived on Eagle Creek (now inside the national park), rode a little jackass with his Winchester on his arm. He was almost eighty before he was hailed before a judge for blockading. On that occasion the judge leaned forward on his bench to inquire whether it was true that moonshine whiskey improved with age.

Rose denied it. "I kept some for a week one time and I could not tell that it was one bit better than when it was new and fresh."

Kephart recounted the same story a little differently: "A slick-faced dude from Knoxville," said Quill, "told me once that all good red-liquor was aged, and that if I'd age my blockade it would bring a fancy price. Well, sir, I tried it; I kept some for three months—and, by godlings, *it ain't so.*"

The small blockader couldn't afford to hold on to his merchandise for several reasons. He was too poor to wait, the product was small, the local demand urgent. There was also considerable hazard in concealment and the safest procedure was to dispose of the product while it was still warm from the still.

A revenue agent, whether in Branton's time or in Byron's, must be well versed in the habits, techniques, and timing of the moonshiner. He knows that sugar fermentation takes three days and can tell by dipping his hand into the mash at a deserted still how near ready it is to run. If it's heavy with sugar, the conversion is not yet complete. But if there's bubbling action, it's near ready and the moonshiners will be back; they can be nabbed in the act.

In the old days, no sugar was used. Mountain dew was made on the same principle as legal whiskey, by letting grain ferment under the barn for a year to mellow. Then somebody learned that adding sugar would speed fermentation, which meant the quality came down, while the output rose.

In making spirits from corn at a little still-house screened from habitation, the first step is to convert the starch of the grain into sugar (which regular distillers do in a few hours by using malt). The corn is placed in a vessel with a small hole in the bottom, and warm water is poured over it repeatedly for two or three days and nights until the corn begins to sprout. Then the sprouted corn is dried and ground into meal, mixed with boiling water into mush, or sweet mash, and let stand another two or three days. At that point a little rye malt might be added and fermentation would begin at once. Or, molasses, sugar, and yeast to speed fermentation. Having no yeast, a small-scale moonshiner must let his mash stand eight or ten days, giving constant attention to assure the right temperature for fermentation. Then it becomes sour mash, or "beer," to be thinned with water and poured into the still. The old-fashioned still, a vessel with closed head connected with a spiral condensation coil, the worm, properly is made of sheet copper—but also of oil drums, wash tubs, or anything handy, and the worms of half-inch galvanized pipe. A fire is built under the still and containers set in place to catch the hot liquid trickling down from the worm. The product of this first distillation, called "singlings," is a weak, impure liquid which must be run through a second time. If the redistillation is not carried far enough, the "doublings" will be weak and rank; if carried too far, it will approach pure alcohol. Regular distillers have their own devices and instruments to determine "proof," but in the mountains testing is done purely by taking a sample and shaking it. Good whiskey will bubble or "bead." The bead is everything. If the bead rises and persists, the proud blockader nods his head and lets it go. If it lacks bead he shakes his head and condemns it. The sloppy moonshiner, however, can add washing lye to increase the yield and give an artificial bead—it may not be healthy but it looks good to the eye. This is just one of many tricks to make a cheaper, faster, if not altogether safer, product. The final process is to run the liquor through a crude charcoal filter in order to rid it of fusel oil, or at least most fusel oil. And there you have it, ready for drinking, uncolored moonshine, which accounts for its name of white liquor, white lightning, or plain white. And also ready for confiscation.

Charley Branton told me about an experience of his in the early 1920s regarding confiscation of fresh merchandise. He had received a report on a still operating in the Cataloochee section and went tracking for it with Deputy United States Marshal Jim Worley. A well-known figure to the blockaders, Worley had the reputation for courage and the nose of a hunting dog. On this excursion the two men could tell they were on the right track when they observed soot on the tips of tree leaves and shrubs. Then they found a cache of six fifty-gallon barrels. Across the Pigeon River Branton saw the glitter of glass in the sunlight.

The Federal agents waded across the river and crawled a half mile up through the dense brush to a rocky ledge. Through a screen of rhododendron they could see two men working at a still. "You stay here," Branton whispered. "I'll go in."

He had overalls on and looked like any other mountaineer in search of a drink of whiskey. The blockaders poured a warm half pint for him right from the worm.

"That's too hot," Branton said. "Ain't you got none cold?" The men, who had been standing some distance apart, moved toward a five-gallon keg. Branton reached into his pockets swiftly, pulled out handcuffs, and grabbed them both and cuffed them.

That wasn't the end. While he and Worley were heading down the mountain with their prisoners, they were stopped by a local woodsman. The man called Branton aside.

"You caught more than blockaders," he said. "Them men killed Scott B—— and Mims W——, —the double murder." The two bodies had been found a day or two before on the slopes of Scottish Mountain, the rough and notorious Bend of the River section.

Worley and his partner took their prisoners to Asheville, where they were booked on $25,000 bond—considerably higher than for a moonshining charge. They were placed in separate cells, in due course confessed the double slaying, and were sentenced to sixty-six-year terms.

On another occasion, Branton was testifying in a perjury case in Bryson City, involving a man who had married into his family. He had arrested the fellow on Noland Creek for blockading. The culprit denied knowing anything about the still and furthermore, he said, if he did know about it, he hadn't been there.

"Mr. Branton," asked the judge, "can you be certain this was the man?"

"No sir, not absolutely. But he is, to the best of my knowledge. I've knowed him for years. He married my first cousin."

A young lad of fifteen, who had been arrested at the scene, sat in the courtroom. The judge waved him to come forward.

"Little boy, I want to ask you something," said the judge. "Will you tell the truth?"

"Yes sir."

"Do you know this man?"

"Yes sir, he owned the still. We 'uns was just helping."

Although operating a still drew a jail sentence of but thirty to sixty days on a first offense, the judge awarded the lying blockader two years for perjury.

Another ex-revenue agent of Bryson City, John D. Norton, recalled for me his experience during the period from 1933 to 1944.

"There is hardly a branch I haven't been on," he said. "I'd work stills of a day, chase liquor cars of a night, co-operating with highway patrolmen or any state officers whose assistance I could associate. It was a rough go, searching and raiding stills, then laying on the Tennessee or

South Carolina road for liquor cars. One week Roy Reese, my buddy, and I went ninety-six hours and never had our boots off.

"In the early days I used to hear about the number and size of stills in these extreme western counties. But when I went to work for the Government I soon found the big stills were not in these mountains. I have helped to cut and dynamite some really big whiskey and beer stills, up to twenty-five thousand gallons, but they were in Wilkes County and the eastern parts of the state.

"My experience was that the bigger the still the sorrier the liquor. In the middle and eastern parts of the state they used sugar and shorts. Their whiskey never saw a dust of corn meal.

"However, in this end of the state, I must say, nearly all stills were of copper, ranging in size from thirty gallons to sixty gallons. There also were stills producing one hundred to five hundred gallons of beer, all contained in sixty-gallon oil barrels—pretty small compared to other sections of Carolina.

"I have cut five stills that I considered were making pure corn whiskey. Every one was right here in these mountain counties. When you get a thirty-gallon still making fifteen to twenty gallons—well, that man is drinking some himself and selling to his friends."

Norton gave me a little episode of the unending cat-and-mouse game between revenuers and moonshiners.

"It was really an accident one day when I heard a beating and banging and saw a little smoke in the woods," he recalled. "I was sure it was a still and nabbed a pair red-handed.

" 'Who set me in?' one of them asked. He was more upset about being informed on than being caught.

" 'The man who set you in is making more liquor than you are,' I told him. Every time I caught a man, I'd make him think somebody set him in. One way to keep getting informers."

Branton told of a logging superintendent on Forney Creek—let's call him Norvel—who operated with six bootleggers in selling blockade whiskey to lumber hands. He was turned in by his wife, because she was tired of having smelly whiskey jars clutter up the house. When Branton arrived and poured the liquor on the ground, Norvel was furious and fighting mad.

"Don't you fellows know better than to do what you done?" the logging bottlegger demanded.

Branton's attitude was never to back down. He was shot at twice in the line of duty, though not hit. Marshal Jim Worley's views were tougher yet. When he went to serve a warrant to a blockader near Sylva and the man leveled a .30-.30 at him over the banister, Worley wanted to open fire and Branton had to restrain him.

In the case of Norvel, Branton kept pouring whiskey and said, "I'm an officer of the law and I did what I'm supposed to do, and if you don't like it, you can lump it."

Norvel, however, was not discouraged. A few months later Branton received a tip that Norvel was coming to Bryson City with whiskey. He obtained a search warrant.

"He reached for his gun but I shoved it in his face," said the old revenuer, "and got ten gallons of liquor out of his grips at the hotel."

Norvel knew the law had him dead to right. He feared going before the dread prohibitionist, Judge E. Y. Webb. "If you help me, I'll help you," he said, offering to lead Branton to some of his own confederates who ran a still on Forney Creek. "Just meet me after dark."

Branton agreed and asked a Bryson City deputy to go along. "No," the deputy declined, "it's a trick. He's a-going to kill you." Then he asked Jim Worley, with a warning that death hung in the balance. Worley liked that fine.

"Now," said Norvel to them that night, "you follow me. I'll buy the whiskey, then step on the porch. When you see me light a cigar, that's the signal."

Worley charged from the front and Branton from the rear when the signal was given. They caught the moonshiners, who never discovered the trick played on them.

As for Norvel himself, he was half drunk at his trial for aiding and abetting the manufacture and sale of liquor, but was sentenced to only one year instead of two or three and might have gotten off with less if the story of his attempted assault on Branton hadn't gotten out.

Paul Byron faces many of the same problems, the same situations as his predecessors.

Technology changes the world, but very slowly in the back hills. He has had the advantage of training as a criminal investigator. "There's an army of revenuers out there," as a modern moonshiner might say. "They have college degrees. They know every trail, gully, and ridge. They have become tireless branch walkers, who climb like a mountain goat and track like an Indian." But it is not the college degree that counts, nor the training in criminal investigation, as much as the branch walking, the patience, the understanding that mountaineers are the hardest people to deceive and that the best way to play the game is "far and squar."

I have seen and been with him and know that Byron is wise enough to realize that his gun is best left in the glove compartment of his car.

When he arrests a man his first efforts are directed to showing him the issue is not personal, but a simple matter of law.

The second efforts are directed to helping him in his defense, although exactly why is another question. Does he want to keep him out of jail out of goodness? Or is it because the odds are fifty-fifty that every man he helps will become an informer? Does he want to send him to jail because the man has violated the letter of the law? Or because he'll eat three meals a day in jail, and for the first time have his teeth cared for—and when he comes home return to the old ways and sooner or later become an informer?

Byron knows he can catch the little man with the least amount of trouble. But he'll pass up the "pinter," (who sells by the pint) to trap a still operator. He'll leave a small still operator in business as long as that man informs on a larger one.

He'll take inside information from a local sheriff who can't touch it himself because of the political power of a bootlegger. Then, he must face the sheriff in court and hear him testify to the bootlegger's good character; or watch the sheriff appeal for a parole for the criminal he helped secretly to convict.

He works outdoors, much more than in the office, climbing the laurel and rhododendron jungles, looking for signs and running down clues —not necessarily near water, because moonshiners have learned to use hoses and to carry stills uphill on their backs, with fantastic strength and endurance.

He feels a sense of pride when he knocks over a big one, like notorious old Hillary, of Poplar Hollow, who had never been caught before.

Byron prospected that area long and hard, looking for signs. Then he came one day to an old frame house with galvanized roof, deserted, but the trail to the outside toilet was still in use. In the woods behind the house he discovered a still. Should he have wrecked it then and there? Out on the road he spied two women. They were Hillary's wenches, serving as lookouts.

He knew then to leave the still alone for a higher stake and returned a week later. The "machine" was mashed in for the three- to six-day ferment cycle. He estimated when it would be ready for running off and was back again with his partner, Hart. Briers and thorns ripped their clothing. A cow bellowed in the distance. A dog barked. Dim lights from a nearby farmhouse appeared spectral.

"Smell the goop?" asked Byron. His partner nodded. It was the unmistakable odor, full, ripe, yeasty, and downright pleasant, similar to home brew, or rising bread dough.

In the thicket, the firebox gave off barely a glow under cover of dense laurel and pine—moonshiners run off their liquor in the thickness of blackness and gullies. And there sat Hillary and two others, with sandwiches, canned food, crackers, and soft drinks. Byron invaded from one side of the stream, Hart from the other. The moonshiners started to run, but the agents had them and Hillary was caught.

The worst part of this work, I think, must be the need to stare the ill effects of moonshine squarely in the face. There is some good whiskey made with pride and craftsmanship, but much of the output is straight poison. I was with Paul Byron one day, scouting the back country in his black Ford, when we turned to a little dirt road and arrived at a dismal shack. Bottles and trash were strewn everywhere. It was the hangout of a small bootlegger or moonshiner; though it appeared deserted, Byron kept looking, convinced that someone was around. Finally, huddled and hunched behind a tree, we found a man, unshaven, poorly clad. His face was swollen red and blotched—"the liquor pellagry." The poor fellow was drunk, incoherent and terrified. Obviously he had run out of whiskey and was trying to beg or borrow anything he could get from a pinter or batwinger (who sells little thin bottles). He lacked the strength to stand or to speak sensibly. He was a man destroyed morally and physically by the rawness of moonshine, a tragic, pitiful sight to behold. I felt that for him the ultimate disaster must be near. Moonshine whiskey often contains poisonous lead salts in large quantities, which, accumulated in body tissues, result in blindness, paralysis, or death. Certainly this poor fellow could not have been drinking anything but the cheapest, poorest-made booze loaded with lead.

Still the chase goes on. Commissioners of Internal Revenue come and go and ask for new rules so they can *really* finish off the moonshine trade. Currently the Major Violators Program makes it easier to prosecute principal offenders, but these are mostly syndicate operators who are inclined to play rough. Then there's the Mandatory Raw Materials Program, known as the sugar control act, which makes it very difficult to obtain sugar—the lifeblood of moonshining—and yeast in large quantities. It has worked to an extent, and also has broadened the base of law violations to include bakerymen and grocers.

Let us say the Paul Byrons have plenty of ground to cover. Moonshiners on both sides of the mountains will move their galvanized iron pots and portable oil burners inside the Great Smoky Mountains National Park every chance they get, or in the surrounding national forests. It was easier in the old days, of course, before the roads, campers, and "dern tourists," yet the ancient contest between the blockader and the revenuer does manage to endure.

XXII

Moonshine Maker

"I've been making it thirty year, since I war twelve. My daddy showed me how and I got the habit. Hit don't take long to learn. Daddy made whiskey all of his life, though I don't know whether he was borned to it by my granddaddy. He started me off a-gathering wood, carrying water, and being lookout.

"Hit's all ever I done. I know it's wrong, but hit's something to do. The Baptist preacher, he's pretty rough. Gets on me every time he sees me, but I don't pay no attention.

"My daddy was lawed by the revenue at least three times. He allus had a feeling when he'd get caught. One time he'd say, 'Something told me not to come down here today.' Or, like he'd say to the revenue, 'I knew you were a-going to catch me today.' Daddy went right back to it, every time. Like he said, the Government should spend more time chasing robbers and other people that really done wrong. He learned me to be careful, *extry* careful.

"There war more show of rifleguns and pistols in the prohibition. Daddy never fired but onct or twice and from a fur distance, just to scare them off. Them investigators sometimes shot upon each other. One gang'd come from one side, another gang from 'cross the branch and open up on each other.

"Today, them fellows are tough. They get special training in shooting. They got all the equipment in the world. They can watch one place, or one man, seven, eight months. They wait till hit's time to run it off and then cut the still.

"I had more stills cut than I made money off of. You can lose money having stills cut. I tell you, it costs me a hunderd twenty dollar, maybe a hunderd thirty-five, each time.

"Most of the ATU is good men. Sure, I respect them. That Byron is truthful. I don't have nothing against him. But he give them hell in Gloucester. He's a-hunting signs around here right now.

"They's different ways of knowing when the revenue comes in. Maybe a lookout'll holler or shout. Or somebody down the highway says, 'Byron is around.' Or you hear an old-fashioned 'mountain shaker'— that's a blast of dynamite.

"One buddy of Byron is an SOB. He's mean; run you all day. He told all kinds of lies against one brother down here. Byron got him off. It warn't him, I knowed it warn't, 'cause I saw him in the bed when he was supposed to be at the still.

"They say, 'I'll turn you loose if you tell and get another man in trouble.' Then you never know who set you in.

"I hate airplanes. They spot from the air. The ATU uses helicopters and cub-planes. Marine helicopters come over every day in summer. How'd I know they don't spot for the revenue? They got about five men in the ATU at Asheville—it used to be eight—with radio equipment.

"No sir, a man don't have time in the woods now. He don't have time to run hit off. The law never messed with me till two, three year ago. I got to know when to lay off. When the ATU is around, well, I just say to the people who buy from me, 'This is the last you're going to get for a while.'

"You would be surprised at some of these customers who drink blockade whiskey. Folks with high, important jobs. Churchgoers. Price is the main thing, but not the only thing. I can sell more'n I make 'cause these people like the blockade better'n Government liquor. I don't mean the rotgut, you know what I mean, but my whiskey will never hurt you. I'll tell you just what is in it.

"Shoot, I hain't drank a whole pint o' Government liquor in my whole life. I cain't see the taste to it. I keep me a drink all the time. I never do take no chaser. You can just bite it off. If I get drunk tonight, there'll be no headache tomorrow, I gu'rantee.

"I never sell to people I don't know. If I don't know the man, he don't get nary a drap. Not even on a recommend.

"They's no money selling to pinters. You don't get your jars back. They's too many chances.

"You *got* to be careful with your customers. You got to be careful how you answer questions. They got to be careful, too. 'Oh,' I'll say to a fellow who inquires about my cousin, 'I don't even know if T.S.

drinks.' And if anybody asks what we do, the answer is, 'We'uns all work.' See what I mean?

"The price is seven dollar a gallon. Some others has it up to ten, twelve. Maybe I'll go up, too. It still costs less than half as much as bottled liquor. If I sell you a gallon, I don't want to tell you a lie. I don't add for beads—I don't want to kill anybody.

"Sometimes I'll have a run o' whiskey that's bad. I wouldn't sell hit to my customers. I can sell a bad batch to a fellow in South Car'liny. He moves it to them coloreds down thar for three dollar a pint. They'll drink anything, for they don't know good whiskey. South Car'liny is a big market for moonshine 'cause the legal is so high priced, but the law is rougher 'n hell.

"The way you tell about your beads is: when you shake that whiskey, if them beads goes two thirds under, that bottle is made with corn. If the bead rides up top like a leetle duck, well, that bottle is made with sugar n' shorts. The longer the bead stays up, the higher the proof.

"Hit takes some doing. One whole day to hunt a place in the hills. I takes one trail in, then another 'un through the woods. Use another path each time, mighty good, too. ATU looks for a man coming out of his favorite spot so I don't stay too long anywhere, but move every month or two. The best place is away from water and use a hose, maybe five hundred feet or more. They'll track less on the mountainside than the branches.

"Winter's bad. I'm skeerd o' tracks in the snow. Besides, mash ferments too slow of a cold night. Summer works too fast, dammit. Them whiskey factories control the temperature but I got to ride with the Lord's thermometer. Also, in hunting season I got to be specially keerful. March, April, May—they're good months. October, too. I can make four hunderd or five hunderd dollar a month, if I don't have bad luck.

"I get eight tubs up thar and use eight bushels o' corn meal and two bushels o' rye. I'll buy the corn meal, sometimes raise hit but not much. Yaller corn don't make good whiskey. Straight corn's not so good—it'll burn you up.

"I'll put out the sack of corn in the creek and take her out tomorrow. In winter, it takes two, three days, I'll throw hot water on her. In summer, throw cold water.

"What you want is a quarter-inch sprout, or two inches long for straight corn. I'll use twenty-five pound of sugar, one bushel of corn meal, plus a half bushel of rye and one peck of corn malt with sprouts.

"I hain't never used yeast to ferment. Horse dung works good sometime, like rye meal. You cain't hardly get no sugar. The grocer charges eleven or twelve dollar for a hunderd pound. He takes more chance than the man who makes the whiskey. I got to buy it from the right man. Else, they'll take your name and car number. Big outfits has the money to work with. They can go anywhere in the country with a big truck and pay big money for sugar.

"I can tell how she's a-running by the taste. If she tastes too strong, I can add water. If she's too weak, I got to pour her out and run another one. I never spill anything in the branch—that's a dead giveaway. The ground'll soak hit up. You'll allus find ground around a still covered with spent mash.

"I keep the outfit covered best as I can, with laurel and cane, tar-paper when hit rains. Rain is hell. It's damn hard to make moonshine in the rain. I cain't keep the fire even, or running right. If rain gets in the tubs, it'll stop the fermentation. And there I am, cold, wet, disgusted, worryin' about that mountain goat Byron—I cain't tell whar he's at or what he's up to, but he's allus after me.

"I don't reckon I'll ever stop. Sometimes I wisht I had a job, any kind. Hit wouldn't be dangerous. But I was raised in the woods to these ways, for better or for worse. The woods and moonshining is in my blood."

XXIII

For Tomorrow, a Ballad

Each one of us who comes in contact with the Great Smokies foresees the fate of the mountains and their people differently, based on his own traditions, individual experience, and special set of circumstances. A man from the city might think, "Here is a beautiful wilderness that should never be touched," while a mountaineer might feel, "I've had enough wilderness for a while; now I want some comforts of the city." On the other hand, if the city fellow was a businessman he might prefer to build a housing development or a motel, or to get hold of a parcel of Indian land if he could. The mountaineer might like to do the same. Or he could be content in his home valley with a few modern conveniences, like electricity, telephone, and plumbing, though it has grown increasingly difficult for him to survive as a farmer following the old ways.

The present of the Great Smokies is complex and the future is uncertain. The fact that a national park embraces half a million acres is encouraging, but then each of us could have a different notion of what a national park should be and how it should be run, including those who pass laws and those who administer laws. It may sound encouraging to listen to the Bureau of Indian Affairs report on all that it is doing to help the Cherokee Indians help themselves. Somehow, however, it has sounded to me too good to be true; I am not sure whether the Government is at long last leading the Indians forward or leading them backward.

The twentieth century has changed the Smokies in a manner that could be compared with the violent geological changes of ages ago. First came logging to destroy land, alter the natural balance, and shatter the isolation of the hill dwellers. Early in the century, too, the Aluminum Company of America began to harness the Little Tennessee, building dams and lakes to provide power for its factory in Alcoa, the company town at the edge of the hills. The creation of the national park, though designed to preserve natural resources, brought forth roads and more roads, people and more people. Then came the Tennessee Valley Authority, constructing the highest and largest dam east of the Rocky Mountains at Fontana, displacing rural settlements, filling fertile valleys and the old stamping grounds of timbermen, miners, and stumphole whiskey distillers with a mammoth lake thirty miles long. Symbolically enough, the first customer to utilize Fontana's hydroelectric power was the engineering works at Oak Ridge, Tennessee, in devising the atomic bomb.

The ancient mountain ways are fading under the pressure of these influences, but have still not quite vanished. People up the hills and hollows live on the brink of tomorrow and the edge of yesterday. Some of the settlers who dwelled within the national park, and some of the sons and daughters of settlers, are strongly devoted to the old places, particularly to the burying grounds and churchyards. Homecomings draw people from distant towns and cities to sit by their former homes, picnic, and drink the "uncitified" water of the high streams.

A few resent the national park; they resent Government regulations that deprived them of unrestricted hunting and fishing. They recall how they would burn the woods in order to "green the grass" and to kill off snakes and ticks. In those days, when *they* managed the land, the woods were full of small game. Chestnuts were plentiful, which they could use at home or haul to market as a cash crop. Then came the park, with its rules and "book learning." What happened since? The mysterious chestnut blight struck. Small game isn't what it used to be. Neither is fishing. All of this, of course, they attribute to the way the Government runs the Smokies.

Still, the game poaching continues, and the moonshine making, the occasional case of arson (either for spite against the Government or for sport), and the illicit ginseng digging. Wisely, soon after the national park was established, local men were hired as rangers (first called wardens) to face the problems of law enforcement. Every one of them was a Smoky Mountain woodsman himself. They formed a unique corps in the national park system, and have tracked down many poachers and discouraged many others. In the old days, for instance, whole families would turn out to collect ginseng for the China trade. It cost them nothing to harvest the fleshy-rooted herb from the shady hardwood coves where they thrived; they would dig in autumn, when "'sang" shrinks the least on drying and thus brings the highest market price.

Digging went on so hard and relentlessly year after year that all natural beds were destroyed, except in the park. The diggers have dwindled in number, only the old-timers persisting. In groups of three or four they tramp far off the beaten track, digging in one drainage of "rich covey land," then following ancient paths into another drainage, camping out, feeding on squirrel, and fitfully trying to stay one step ahead of the mountain-bred rangers.

Varied attempts have been made, in the national park and environs, to snatch one creative facet or another of the dying mountain culture and save it for the future. Sometimes it has taken an outsider to recognize what really is worth saving, among everything taken for granted, and sometimes it takes a native fellow like Bascom Lamar Lunsford, the music man of Buncombe County.

"It's as much a language as anything else, you know," said the old minstrel to me. "People sing songs that remind them of some little romance or tragedy. Few mountain ballads were written down—somehow, the printed page crowds out spontaneity. Some songs were handed down from one generation to another, with words and music changing, and varying from valley to valley. Others were composed as they went along by people who enjoyed doing as they pleased, not being bound down. They get a kind of lick out of music."

While he spoke we were sitting in his little house not far from Asheville (the location, he reminded me several times, was "South Turkey Creek"). He held a fiddle in his old freckled hands. He was seventy-eight, but unstooped, a man renowned for the vibrance of his square dance calling, and the lively cadence to his music on the fiddle and five-string banjo. With him was his wife of less than a year, much younger than he; a musician too, naturally.

The odd thing about folk lyrics and tunes is that mountain people began to lose interest and pride in their true cultural expression once they felt the influence of roads and the outside civilization. The more exposed to exterior sophistications, the lower became their esteem for fiddle and banjo; the music of their ancestors seemed crude, severe, and unmusical, relics to be dated with the oxcart and rifle. It took an Englishman, the celebrated Cecil J. Sharp, ballad collector and president of the British Folk-Lore Society, to stir a new twentieth-century appreciation of mountain songs and dances. When he came into the southern Appalachians, he was greeted by Mrs. John C. Campbell, of Brasstown, who with her husband had studied the folk movement of Denmark. With her guidance, Sharp visited scores of mountain homes and set down the songs which people sang for him, some of which traced back to his own country, but had been lost there. Sharp stayed nearly a year in 1918, then wrote glowingly of his discoveries in Appalachia. Bascom Lunsford subsequently became one of the foremost collectors—certainly the outstanding collector in the Smokies and environs—to continue Sharp's work.

Lunsford may be recorded as a part-time lawyer, politician (who once was reading clerk of the North Carolina House of Representatives), auctioneer, and full-time folklore scholar. Over the years he collected more than three hundred songs for the Library of Congress and Columbia University, a truly phenomenal achievement, writing down and arranging many of them for the first time, and composing new songs in the traditional spirit. "It's a nice way to bring modern expression," as he said, "into an old thing."

He went around the hills, attending bean stringings, corn shuckings, shoe-arounds, and shindigs. "Let me get the young 'uns out of the house," more than one mountain mother would say to him before disclosing ancient songs and musical instruments. "We make a rule never to cuss or sing love ballets while they are in hearing." Such tunes, as well as fiddle and banjo, were pure anathema to their mountain preachers.

In due course, Lunsford awakened the pride of his people in the traditional music, and in creating new pieces worthy of the old. He convinced them that a good time with their own music isn't sinful. In 1927 he began as impresario of the annual Mountain Dance and Folk Festival, held in August, a successful rendezvous of square dancers, fiddlers, banjo pickers, and mouth-harp players, all of them amateurs. In 1939 he brought the Soco Gap dance team to the White House for a command performance before the King and Queen of England. Sam Queen, the famous caller, made the square dance tunes sound as though they came from the jigs and reels and hornpipes of the British Isles. For instance:

> Hold your hands just like I do
> And let King George's men pass through
> Halfway round and halfway back.
> Hold your hands as high as the sky
> And let King George's men pass by.

One of Lunsford's favorite performers was the late Samantha Bumgarner, one of many Bumgarners on the North Carolina side of the Smokies, a spritely lady of years who played a five-string banjo and sang choice mountain ballads. Think of the self-respect of the balladeer and all her kind inherent in the song she has conserved, and Bascom Lunsford recorded for posterity, such as:

There was a ship that sailed upon the sea,
And the name they gave it was the Merrie Golden Tree,
As it sailed upon the lonesome lowlands low,
As it sailed upon the lonesome sea.

Now let us consider the fate and future of Samantha Bumgarner's neighbors, the Cherokee Indians, and the efforts to conserve and advance their cultural heritage.

A new marvel came to Cherokee in 1964. It was an amusement park called Cherokee Frontier Land. It was represented by the state of North Carolina and the Bureau of Indian Affairs as having reference to the past and future of the Cherokee people.

Officials of the state heralded Cherokee Frontier Land as a splendid asset to the reservation and to western North Carolina. It would prove a delight to the throngs of visitors attracted to North Carolina by its mighty cultural and natural heritage. It would be an attraction "without equal in eastern America," predicted the president of the Cherokee Chamber of Commerce in a publication issued by the state.

The Bureau of Indian Affairs, equally enthusiastic, encouraged the tribal council to make available one of the finest parcels of land on the reservation for the new wonder called Cherokee Frontier Land. "The Indian agency officials greeted the announcement and the beginning of work on the project," recorded the state, "as another milestone in the growth and development of the Indian reservation. One official remarked that this 'could well be the greatest thing that ever happened to Cherokee. It promises to increase and stimulate the entire economy of the reservation.' "

How could it prove to be anything but an asset? It would be operated, of course, by the same extraordinary outfit that had bestowed Ghost Town upon Maggie Valley, just beyond Soco Gap.

The state had studied all of these things. It classified Frontier Land and Ghost Town as "Participating Attractions," which provide one of the surest ways to earn tourist income. Not quite as good as "Super Attractions" like the State Fair, but better than "Dynamic Spectator," "Static Spectator," and "Static Display."

The trouble with "Static Spectator," a classification that includes the outdoor drama, *Unto These Hills*, according to the study, is that attendance must be limited by the seating capacity of a theater. As for "Static Displays," like museums, exhibitions, and displays of objects under glass, they have large attendance, but, unfortunately, relatively small revenues and must be publicly subsidized.

Thus, reasoned the state of North Carolina and the Bureau of Indian

Affairs, it made sense to exploit the Cherokee name and the final fragment of Cherokee land.

Despite the state publicity that Frontier Land represents "an authentic re-creation of the old West," however, the only authenticity is that it stands as a classic form of tourist blight—a tawdry amusement park, abusing and misusing history.

It may employ a few Indians, but certainly not as descendants in the line of Junaluska, Sequoyah, and Drowning Bear—while the high profits in serving low fare to the traveling public go out of the hills.

The Cherokee Indians face the future in the Great Smokies from a very special set of circumstances. They dwell in companionship with disease, malnutrition, poverty, illegitimacy, illiteracy. Their own leadership, unfortunately, lacks the vigor of youth and education; it gropes with the problems of its people, but cannot project comprehensive long-range thinking.

As for the guidance the Indians look for in Washington, after almost one hundred years of administration in Cherokee, the Bureau of Indian Affairs has little it can point to with pride.

Consider the broad and basic question of environment. In 1963, at my request, the Public Health Service, of the Department of Health, Education, and Welfare, prepared a memorandum on conditions in Cherokee. The Public Health Service has been charged, since 1955, with responsibility for providing comprehensive health services to the American Indians and Alaska Natives (formerly the responsibility of the Bureau of Indian Affairs, of the Department of the Interior).

"The incidence of disease associated with *poor environment* indicated that large percentages of reservation Indians were in need of safe water supplies, water disposal facilities, improved housing, and health education," advised the Public Health Service memorandum on conditions it had found in 1955 (italics mine).

"In the early years of the environmental health program, a concentrated effort was made to survey these needs. Native Indians, on nearly every reservation, who were respected among their respective people, were selected and hired by the Service as Sanitarian Aides, were trained to demonstrate the proper methods of healthful living to their own people and to identify the needs for sanitation facilities.

"The Cherokee Reservation of North Carolina was found to be typical of the conditions reported throughout the reservation areas of the country. The house-to-house survey of the Cherokee Reservation (606 homes with population of about 3000, located in seven districts) completed in 1957 by the Sanitarian Aide working alone, indicated the following conditions existed:

"(1) Occupants of more than 90 per cent of the homes obtained water from unsanitary and unprotected sources (springs, surface drainage, dug wells).

"(2) More than 80 per cent of the homes had no inside running water.

"(3) More than 70 per cent of the homes utilized privies for excreta disposal, of which only 6 per cent were of an approved type; 15 per cent had no facilities at all.

"(4) About 90 per cent of the homes disposed of garbage and refuse improperly.

"(5) More than 60 per cent of homes had improper cold storage for food even though electricity was available to about 70 per cent of the homes. (Economic status prevented purchasing refrigeration units. Average income $600/year/family).

"(6) More than 95 per cent of the housing was of log or frame construction and for the most part structurally unsound. The average house had three rooms with an occupancy of 1.5 persons/room; about 26 per cent were 1- or 2-room houses.

"(7) Prevalent diseases included impetigo, intestinal worms, septic sore throat, diarrhea, and scabies. (All traceable to poor environment.)"

The early physical efforts of the Public Health Service included: spraying and explaining public health; clean-up, elimination of insect and rodent breeding places, and screening and privy construction.

"The sanitation programs were fully accepted by the Tribal Council and limited monetary support was given by it to correct the most glaring deficiencies until a broader program could be initiated by the Public Health Service. The interest of the Cherokee people in environmental sanitation ran high. . . .

"The Cherokee Indians are very responsive to the health education activities now available and are ready and willing to accept additional services."

Why the Cherokee circumstances should have to be described in this manner in the 1960s, almost one century after the Act of 1868 recognized the Federal responsibility, is difficult to explain, let alone to understand. Perhaps the reason was best summarized by John Collier, who endeavored during his tenure as Commissioner of Indian Affairs from 1933 to 1945 to treat the native peoples with dignity and respect. "It was not individual corruption but collective corruption," he wrote in Indians of the Americas, "corruption which did not know it was corrupt, but which reached deep into the intelligence of a nation."

In short, why face the hard, cruel, human issues of a small minority, the "weaker race," as Theodore Roosevelt called the Indians, when it stands in the pathway of the stronger majority? Yet there have been able, diligent men, like John Collier, working in the Federal Government in the Indian's behalf against heavy odds, pressures, and indifferences from the white majority. I have also been appalled to encounter people working for the Bureau of Indian Affairs, in responsible positions, who are not in sympathy with Indians, who dislike Indians, and have little understanding of them.

"You *know*, of course," I have been told, "that Indians lack initiative, are lazy, and can't be depended upon."

This could be a question of how you look at it. A few years ago a Big Cove Indian fellow, June Wolf, walked over the top of the Smokies in the dead of winter, a tremendous physical feat, a show of initiative and sustained endurance. On the way home he was trapped in a blizzard. Though he stopped to build a little fire, it was not enough and he perished in the mountains. Now if I add that he had gone to Cosby in order to obtain a supply of moonshine whiskey, do you then see him in a different light, as a "typically degenerate Indian"? Or, would you see him in reference to the influences upon him, all the influences, all the history, all the "benefactions" of the Government in Washington?

With every change of administration, the Indians have been presented a new policy, a new program, a new manifesto. "Forget the old with which you have fallen in step," they are told. "The step has changed." Osley Saunook was flogged at the Indian school in Cherokee because he spoke in his native language instead of English. Three years later, however, when he returned from the Haskell Institute in Kansas, he was astounded to find Will West Long, the patriarch, teaching Cherokee at the same school under Government auspices. Later, under the Eisenhower Administration, the Indians were advised to prepare to assume the "rights of full citizenship," a polite way of saying the long history of Indian nations and communal land ownership were doomed. When the New Frontier arrived, the Indians were told to forget the Eisenhower philosophy. They might be reeling with confusion from the endless changes, but they were assured that now everything would be different.

The New Frontier and Great Society boasted of fantastic amounts of money going into their program for the Indians, as though money represents the cure-all in dealing with human beings suffering two centuries of abuse. In three years (1962–64), almost half a billion dollars was appropriated for Indian affairs, an amount exceeding the total spent in the preceding 150 years. Many millions have been poured into underwriting small industries, on the theory that what the Indians really need are factories on their reservations, like Jersey City or Youngstown. Would these plants be owned and operated by Indians? No, not quite. This plan has really amounted to an easy way for businessmen with proper connections to obtain tax-free locations and a cheap labor supply. Some of these businesses have been shaky affairs at best. Some employ few Indians, though occupying Indian land.

In Cherokee, some of the finest land in choice scenic locations that could be used to represent the cultural history of these people has gone over to unattractive factories. The tribal council or the Government is responsible for paying for "training," which assures the outside factory owners a continuing source of cheap labor.

It might have been otherwise. The Cherokee Historical Association wrote a wonderful record and demonstrated the vivid potentialities. The Association began as a creation of business groups in western North Carolina who wanted to provide worthwhile evening entertainment for summer visitors to the Great Smokies. The superintendent of the Cherokee Reservation, Joe Jennings, a devoted conservationist and Indian scholar, welcomed the project and became a key figure in the Historical Association. In 1950, the outdoor drama *Unto These Hills* was performed for the first time. To the credit of North Carolina, the state legislature voted $35,000 to underwrite the drama and assure its success. It made the nation conscious of the Cherokee; it opened a page of history that had lain forgotten and neglected for more than a hundred years; it stirred the Indians to rediscover their heroes. Three years later the Oconaluftee Indian Village was opened in a lovely mountain setting next to the theater. The state legislature gave $25,000 to erect the village—even though it might now be classified as "Static Display" or "Static Spectator." Unlike the later rage, Cherokee Frontier Land, this village was re-created in authentic detail, under the supervision of the Tsali Institute for Cherokee Indian Research, established by the Historical Association with the co-operation of the Universities of North Carolina, Tennessee, and Georgia.

These ventures of the Cherokee Historical Association provided employment to Indians. The activities of the Village helped rekindle their interest in crafts, an outlet for the talents of a creative people, a source of prestige, pride, and revenue.

Much more of this might have been done and expanded in the true interest of the Cherokee. It should have been done, considering the Department of the Interior for many years has proudly proclaimed its devotion toward conservation of water, land, forests, wildlife, and people.

The needs in Cherokee are terribly acute. The number of people has trebled in a century, yet they live within the same bounds. The ownership of land has been confused for years. Some nine hundred parcels are poorly marked and defined, from tree to rock pile. The entire reservation of 56,574 acres theoretically is communal property, yet these parcels, held by individuals under "possessory" or use rights, can be sold, exchanged, or leased among the Indians themselves. Presumably, no land can be sold to whites, yet it can be leased. An unsatisfactory procedure to all parties, accounting for the poor-grade establishment prevalent in Cherokee; and the question has never been resolved as to whether leased land and improvements on the land revert to the Eastern Band at termination.

The white world is confused as to whether the Cherokee are wards of the Government, or citizens of the United States. The Indians are confused about their relationship to the world around them. They do not want to lose their identity; nor should they be expected to.

And the Great Smoky Mountains National Park, that wilderness jewel of eastern America—how does it fare with the passing years? What of its future?

"We used to have eleven hundred cars on a busy Sunday in 1938 or 1940," said my friend John Morrell, the veteran of national park headquarters. "Now we have that many *an hour* on a good hot sunshiny day."

On almost any given weekend from late spring through fall, or any day during the summer season, visitors of the 1960s hoping for a glimpse of mountain majesty find themselves embroiled in bumper-to-bumper traffic on the transmountain highway. Though coming to the Smokies for a respite from the mechanized intensity of our age, they must contend with the same racing motors, exhaust fumes, tension, and traffic jams from which they fled in their home cities. The parking areas are congested, the campgrounds overloaded night after night. The picnic areas are trampled. The scenic overlook at Newfound Gap is so completely swarming with people and littered with trash (despite all efforts at cleanup) that the thrill of the scene is often destroyed.

Such conditions were unforeseen by the best park planners. They can hardly be allowed to endure into the 1970s; but the solution, if there is one, has been difficult to achieve. More roads, of one type or another, could be constructed, but it isn't that simple.

"It must be clear that the demand which now looms over us can never be satisfied," writes Harvey Broome, apostle of the Great Smoky Mountains Hiking Club and president of the Wilderness Society. "Even modest annual changes will ultimately destroy the wilderness. The choice will have to be made between supplying facilities for everyone who asks, or adopting clear measures to preserve what is left.

"Slow attrition follows development. Almost without exception, wherever there is a road, or dug trail or shelter facility in the virgin forest, there is slowly spreading damage. The areas contiguous to developments become littered, eroded, or threadbare from heavy use and abuse.

"No further developments of any character should take place in the virgin heart. No more trails; no more shelters; no more roads; no expansions, extensions, or additions to existing facilities. To protect what is left we must learn to live with facilities we now have. The hardest thing will be the decision itself."

Harvey could be correct, and I believe that he is, but others will disagree. Business people and politicians in Tennessee and North Carolina lament that the only way to enjoy the largest virgin wilderness in eastern America is on foot, that only 150 miles of road are open to the public in a 500,000-acre preserve. After all, how many hikers are there compared with all the rest of us? What's the use of having all this natural beauty if folks can't get to it?

"We're not wanting roads up every valley and across every peak," reasoned Dr. Kelley E. Bennett, the pharmacist of Bryson City, in 1955, when he was chairman of the North Carolina Park, Parkway, and Forest Development Commission. "We just want a few that will make it possible for folks to have access into the wilderness areas where they can enjoy the beauty that is going to waste."

Others, of course, want just a few more roads to insure that additional portions of beauty are not "wasted."

The question becomes, What are the capacity limits beyond which use will destroy natural beauty and the true quality of a national park experience? If an additional 150 miles of concrete are completed, what will happen when they become congested, as they must—another network after that?

The National Park Service has endeavored to satisfy the demand of its public as best it can, with a plan to "improve circulation by automobile" by constructing a loop road and a second transmountain highway, and by designing something called a "motor nature trail" so that more citizens may take to the open trail without ever using their God-given feet.

How much of an answer will these really provide in the long run, or how much of an escape will the park provide from the frenzy of the motoring age should it become laced with such highways?

A national park experience, whether in the Great Smokies, Yellowstone, Big Bend, or where have you, should really be the antithesis of haste. I mention this point especially because local boosters have tried one device or another to slow visitors down, to make sure the Great Smokies are more than "a one-day show." Motoring has its place, principally as the means of arriving, but not of exploring. The surprising truth is that there are many nature trails in the park, some gems of only a half mile in length that almost anyone can walk and find himself immersed in natural beauty and feel a part of it, rather than a spectator as he must from a car window.

"Democracy should accommodate a great variety of tastes," Justice William O. Douglas has written judiciously and aptly. "There should be bits of wilderness, the edges of which people can reach by car. Roadside picnic areas fit some needs. Some want comfortable beds at night though they tramp the heights by day. The demands vary. Yet certain it is that we can have no wilderness where wildlife flourishes, unless 'civilization' is kept out. If 'civilization' is brought no closer than the fringe of these wilderness areas, one who can walk only one hundred yards may enter the sacred precincts and feel and see the wilderness that once possessed America. Then even invalids may experience wonder and beauty beyond expression."

But as far as the Great Smokies are concerned, as the number of visitors each year has risen from one million to two million to three million to four million, with the probability of ten million visitors by the 1970s, the need has made itself plain for creative and imaginative thinking, for a plan that goes beyond construction of still another road or another campground. The same holds true of all national parks, if they are to survive as an endowment of riches and a gallery of American treasure.

In 1930, when Horace Albright and Arno B. Cammerer visited the Smokies, they rode over the logging railroad of the Suncrest Lumber Company from Maggie Valley. "What about the tracks?" they were asked by reporters. "Any chance of using them to carry visitors around?" The answer was unequivocal: "The operation of a scenic railway within a national park is not in keeping with the plan of the Department." The tracks were removed and the roadbeds used as fire trails for patrol rangers. Looking back thirty-five years, this doubtless was the sound decision. But looking ahead thirty-five years, perhaps this system could provide part of the solution to the conflict between rising human use and preservation of land values for the benefit of generations hence.

Who really needs an automobile inside this national park? Leave it at the gateway community. Board public transportation. Ride a train, or tram, if it should be determined as the most feasible type of conveyance, or a small, quiet bus. Enjoy the scenery and vistas as you ride over the loop. The vehicle will stop at campgrounds, picnic areas, scenic overlooks, and the beginning of hiking trails. There will be another along in thirty or forty minutes or an hour on which you may continue the loop.

Can this kind of procedure work? It *does* work at Colonial Williamsburg, where visitors ride on buses instead of in their cars; and where, on the principal street, Duke of Gloucester, they either walk or ride in a horse-drawn carriage and feel the eighteenth century instead of the twentieth. Without suffering or objecting, either.

Some form of public transportation should be the beginning, but not the sum total, of a plan for the Great Smokies. Campers bound for the park could receive their campground assignments and ticket arrangements at the entrances. When all the spaces are gone, others would be directed to campgrounds of the adjoining national forests, the Indian reservation, and commercially developed resorts. In this manner, the entire region, and not just the national park itself, would absorb and serve the rising tide of visitors. Such was the original design of the proposed Appalachian National Park and Forest of sixty years ago. Such was the intent, too, thirty-odd years ago when the national park was created. On the Tennessee side, Pigeon Forge and most of the Chilhowee Mountains were inside the first boundary line of the park. On the North Carolina side, Waynesville was forecast as the eastern gateway.

"Not only is the part of the park area we visited very beautiful, but the entire approach from Asheville, Waynesville, and the intermediate points is entrancing, and interesting," declared Horace Albright in Asheville in 1930. "North Carolina must guard against cluttering up that beautiful drive with billboards and unsightly structures. It should legislate at an early date to prevent the marring of the views that are available to the approach to the park. The state would do well to adopt a zoning law similar to that in California relative to billboards, signs, and various structures."

But North Carolina, Tennessee, and the mountainside communities fell down on their responsibilities. They turned their backs on a genuine partnership in the development of the Great Smokies. They benefited from the throngs of visitors drawn to the national park, but refused to enhance their own settings as attractive foreground gateways. While demanding the Federal Government build additional roads inside the park so that scenic beauty would not be wasted, they destroyed beauty outside the park by lining their roads with the caged bears, jerry-built souvenir shacks, and tourist attractions of a low order.

Maggie Valley, one of the loveliest mountain valleys in Appalachia, was destroyed with the blessing of the state of North Carolina. Through the willful erosion of its God-given beauty this section would prosper—and that was all that mattered.

"Due to the amount of business it has generated," boasted an official publication of the state, "Ghost Town has been considered by many state officials as the equivalent of an industry employing two thousand persons."

What is Ghost Town? On the word of that scholarly journal, the *Asheville Times,* Ghost Town is an "authentic" re-creation of a frontier settlement. The newspaper's authority on such matters explains precisely what this means: "Gun-totin' youngsters and nostalgic adults visiting Ghost Town find themselves transported into their favorite television western. From the team of bearded cowboys who enact the shootout to the waitresses and dancers in the saloons, costumes and architecture reflect the pioneer western atmosphere."

But this is not all. The newspaper continues breathlessly, and tastelessly, to report: "Even the building of Ghost Town was spectacular. In September of 1960 bulldozers climbed the mountain and shaved 45 feet off the top for the town site and moved thousands of yards of dirt to make way for its companion attraction. Anyone who has ridden the incline railway from the valley floor to within 200 feet of the mountaintop can well imagine the daring of the bulldozer operators who drove the huge machines up the mountainside to fashion the 3364-foot-long roadbed."

I think of the inherent splendor and greatness surrounding the national park toward which the boosters of Appalachia could direct their interest and energies, and with at least a shade more pride than to Ghost Town, the animal farms, and the brutally caged bears.

On one side of the mountains the Federal Government has constructed the Blue Ridge Parkway and on the other side the new Foothills Parkway in the Chilhowee Mountains. These are for easy adventure by motoring, with picnic areas at high, cool elevations, and expansive vistas of the Smokies and the southern ranges spilling into Georgia.

On the North Carolina side of the national park, there is the popular and worthwhile outdoor drama *Unto These Hills.* The adjacent Oconaluftee Village and Qualla Crafts Shops are more than manifestations of the Indian culture, but part of the network of crafts centers that rings the Great Smokies. A traveler could spend an entire summer, or a year, going from one to the other. This is mountain culture at its finest—at Penland, the school of textiles, wood, iron, silver, pottery, and furniture; at Brasstown, the Campbell Folk School, for wood carving, American square dancing and country dances, folk songs and dulcimer; across the mountains at Gatlinburg, the Mountain Craft Workshop conducted during the summer by the University of Tennessee and Pi Beta Phi; at Pigeon Forge, the pottery of Douglas Ferguson, a talented innovator who has shown and lectured on his sophisticated work all over the world.

Knoxville opens the way to water sports on the TVA reservoirs, surrounded by forested ridges, providing a type of recreation a national park cannot match. The restored schoolhouse near Maryville where Sam Houston taught and restored Fort Loudoun near Tellico Plains depict chapters of history that many Tennesseans have forgotten. Surely they tell growing school children and tourists a more meaningful story of the state than do the assorted snake pits and other tourist slums.

Across the Little Tennessee from the national park, the Fontana Village resort stands on the site occupied by 4000 men and women involved in the construction of Fontana Dam during World War II. It provides some of the best boating and bass fishing in the country on Fontana Lake, with access by water to Eagle, Hazel, and Forney creeks, choice trout streams inside the national park; as well as craft classes, square dancing, and horseback riding.

Near Fontana, in the direction of Robbinsville, the Joyce Kilmer Memorial Forest constitutes a virgin hardwood forest of 3800 acres as superb as almost anything in the Great Smokies, and very likely as superb as any woodland of its size on earth. Patriarchs five and six centuries old stand 150 feet tall and 20 feet around in almost endless arboreal variety—poplar, hemlock, cherry, birch, walnut, oaks, basswood, sycamore, and beech. The Veterans of Foreign Wars petitioned the Government in 1934 for a fitting memorial to Kilmer, the author of the poem "Trees"; after a long study of areas throughout the country, this tract was chosen. How had it remained untouched, out of millions of acres slashed and burned around it? In 1961 I walked in this cathedral-forest with Earl A. Parsons, district ranger of the Nantahala National Forest, who said that during the lumbering era two syndicates were logging everything within reach and extending a railroad straight toward the Kilmer tract. "When they were within two miles," said Parsons, "those outfits went broke. If it wasn't the hand of God at work, then it was fate."

The three national forests within proximity of the Great Smokies afford exceptional and varied opportunities for recreation. The Nantahala, the Cherokee "land of the noonday sun," embraces the country William Bartram visited and described. Along with facilities for camping, hunting, and fishing, there are beautiful waterfalls like Bridal Veil and Cullasaja, and Lake Santeetlah, glistening among the high mountains; and scenic drives from Robbinsville, Franklin, and Highlands. The Pisgah National Forest was developed around the nucleus of the George Washington Vanderbilt estate, where young Gifford Pinchot, newly returned from studies in Europe, discarded the old destructive logging ways and began selecting and marking trees for cutting. To commemorate the "Cradle of Forestry in America," the Government

Protected areas of the Appalachian Ecosystem.

announced plans in the mid-1960s for a museum and recreational complex in a portion of the old estate called the Pink Beds. The Pisgah covers an area one hundred miles long and forty miles wide, including eighty miles of the eastern hiker's dream boulevard, the Appalachian Trail. Across the mountains in Tennessee, the Cherokee National Forest had begun to develop in the mid-sixties the largest single recreation complex in the national forests of the South. Located at Indian Knob, only a few miles from the southwestern corner of the national park, it was projected to include beaches, hundreds of camping and picnic units, boating, nature trails, and campfire theaters. The Tellico-Robbinsville Scenic Highway, also under development, was designed to open vistas of the Unicoi Range that have scarcely been touched or seen. The national forests also embrace a host of other outstanding wilderness and scenic areas like the Fall Branch and Unaka in the Cherokee, Craggy Mountain, Linville Gorge, and Roan Mountain in the Pisgah.

Federal law has decreed that national forests should furnish a wider range of activities than national parks. Taken together, the two types of reservations provide a harmonious balance to fill the needs of a people. The reservoirs of the Tennessee Valley Authority and the Aluminum Company of America furnish still further alternatives.

Looking toward the future, the national park, the parkways, national forests, and reservoirs are but pieces of a large system of the Appalachian region. This system must include the cultural and craft expressions, the historic sites, the participation of the two states, local communities, resorts, and private interests with vision and pride. Through regional co-operation, additional millions of recreation seekers could enjoy in many ways the scenic land and be shown new opportunities for healthful recreation.

Each component of the system would serve its own purpose. The Great Smoky Mountains National Park would be understood and appreciated anew for the special role that it must fill as an outdoor sanctuary, rather than as a playground.

Benton MacKaye, who thought of the idea of a footpath through the wilderness that became the Appalachian Trail, wrote of the past and future in these words: "The old pioneer opened through a forest a path for the spread of civilization. His work was nobly done and the life of the town and city is in consequence well upon the map throughout our country. Now comes the great task of holding this life in check —for it is just as bad to have too much urbanization as too little."

The future of the Great Smoky Mountains delineates this great task. It challenges one generation to match the wisdom of the preceding generation that created the national park. It gives a people the opportunity to write their own testament of belief to the glory of nature's ways and to the kingdom of nature's God. The old mountain culture may be conserved in a loom or a ballad, but the ballad for the Great Smokies is the enduring majesty of the Smokies themselves.

Amanda Swimmer demonstrating pottery at the Indian Village in Cherokee. The Qualla Arts and Crafts Mutual sustains the cultural heritage of the Eastern Band of Cherokee with quality products from fingerwoven scarves to animals carved in walnut. Cherokee Historical Association.

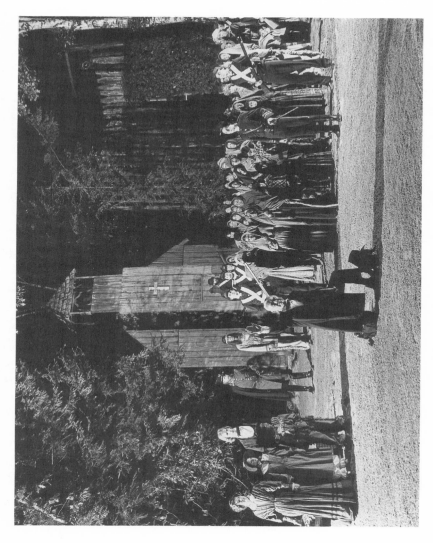

Unto These Hills, the summer outdoor drama at Cherokee, North Carolina, tells of tragedy and heroism in the forced removal of Eastern Cherokee over the infamous "Trail of Tears." Cherokee Historical Association.

Boyd Evison, park superintendent, 1975–78 (left), with the author. Evison conscientiously defended wilderness in the Smokies. He closed roads, converting them into "quiet walkways." Mack Prichard.

"This is beary country, I tell you, turribly rough," said Shoof (obscured but for the cap) while he and friends take a moonshine whiskey break in a rhododendron thicket. (See Chapter XIX.) Photo by the author.

Bear hunters take a stand. The author (second from left) and friends at the Twelve Mile Strip in Pisgah National Forest. They were tough, determined mountain stock, but not tough enough to change the government's mind about road building in bear country.

Tasting the delectable at the Ramp Festival at Cosby, Tennessee, a celebration of spring and the tasty ramp, or leek—"stronger than garlic, sweeter than ary onion." Mack Prichard.

Environmental issues of the 1990s include the fate of the Pigeon River, "the most polluted river bordering the nation's most popular national park." Mack Prichard.

Abundant water and rocks and vegetation as dense as a tropical rain forest characterize the southern highlands of Appalachia, as the author discovers anew in the Gee Creek Wilderness in East Tennessee, the day it was dedicated in 1975. Mack Prichard.

XXIV

A Slight Case for Exercise

It was not the season to encounter a rattlesnake, though I am certain that if we had, Arthur Stupka would have pointed calmly to the special gracefulness of the serpent and the part it plays in the total ecology of nature. As it was still late winter, the Smoky Mountain rattlers, as well as copperheads and the twenty-one kinds of non-poisonous snakes in the national park, presumably were denning peaceably.

I remember the time of year very clearly. For one thing, Arthur had remarked on the extremely early arrival of fringed phacelia, which appeared here and there like patches of snow left in the shadows. A cluster of birdfoot violet added the touch of lilac color. But also, when he reached into the Park Service box that normally contains folders to guide visitors on the nature trail, he touched one of a group of little white-footed woods mice that had taken over the box for their hibernation headquarters. At once he closed the lid; the mice may never have known they were disturbed.

Arthur Stupka wrote the folder about the Big Locust Nature Trail where we walked that day. The manner of the markers on the ground aided by the text of the leaflet exposes visitors to a splendid primeval forest, surprisingly near a heavily traveled road, as a living, vibrant interrelated community. Considering the fact that the trail itself spans but three fourths of a mile, this may not seem much of an achievement on Stupka's part. However, he was also responsible for the same contributions to almost every other nature trail in the park (though the trails were laid out by his associates, Vernon C. Gilbert, Jr., Henry Lix, Neil J. Reid, and A. Randolph Shields), and he personally guided thousands of individuals on conducted hikes and walks, and lectured to thousands more during evening programs. The pattern in which the Park Service interprets the natural scene in the Great Smokies to the American public was his design He was on more intimate and knowing terms with nature in all corners of the park than any other man during his time, which began in 1935 and continued until his retirement thirty years later.

It is impossible to visit the Great Smoky Mountains National Park without feeling the influence of Arthur Stupka, a circumstance which very probably will continue long into the future. The scientific community, in particular, will be mindful of his role, for he accumulated exhaustive records relating to the biology and botany of the park and kept a nature journal throughout his career. During his last five years he worked on the organization of a series of catalogued works, the first of which was his *Notes on the Birds of Great Smoky Mountains National Park.* In this exceptional book he recorded the status of 210 birds, with data relating to their altitudinal range, dates of arrival and departure, and nesting habits. Besides his own observations on hiking trips, he collected reports, facts, figures, and fables from all manner of citizens—visiting professional ornithologists, park rangers, amateur bird watchers, and old-fashioned mountain men, whom he learned to respect for their keen eye and who, in turn, respected him. This he followed with an important botanical study, *Trees, Shrubs, and Woody Vines of Great Smoky Mountains National Park.*

By way of showing there was always something new and surprising to record, he recounted the story of how Roger Tory Peterson walked into his office on April 30, 1953, accompanied by James Fisher, the British naturalist, during the course of their tour of America. "What is the status of the Laughing Gull in the park?" was the first question Peterson asked. The Laughing Gull? As far as Stupka knew, the bird had no "status" in the Smokies and he so informed them. But Peterson retorted that he and Fisher had just observed one of these gulls along the transmountain road, between Smokemont and Kephart Prong, at elevation 2700 feet. Stupka never was able to explain the accidental appearance of that Laughing Gull—and never saw one himself in the Smokies. This was no laughing matter, except for the gull.

When Stupka first came to the Smokies in October 1935, he had no idea that his work would involve amassing a body of information. He was not sure of what he was supposed to do when he reported to J. Ross Eakin, the park superintendent.

"A park naturalist?" asked Eakin in disbelief. "What in the devil would we do with a naturalist?"

Stupka assured him that he had indeed been sent out for duty in the Smokies by the National Park Service and was eager to begin. Four summers earlier he had worked as a naturalist-ranger in Yosemite and then, after graduating with a degree in zoology at Ohio State University in 1932, had been appointed as the first junior park naturalist at Acadia in Maine. Now he had come to establish a program for the new park in the southern mountains. He was the first full-fledged naturalist in any national park in the East.

"But there's nothing in this park that visitors can get to at this stage of the game and damn little to show except along the transmountain road," Superintendent Eakin insisted. "I've got to concentrate on protection, not interpretation. When the boys in our sixteen CCC camps get finished constructing hiking trails, fire control roads, and some facilities for visitors, maybe then you'll have something to do.

"Meantime, Stupka, build your collections. Get around the park. Also, please don't bother me if you can help it."

For the first three years he concentrated on assembling basic information that had never been assembled before and in collating the work of scientific observers who had explored the Smokies. His first love was the world of birds. He found that William Brewster, the eminent ornithologist, had written an account of twelve days spent in western North Carolina (but short of the Smokies) in 1885, followed by Arthur Lemoyne one year later, who, in *Notes on Some Birds of the Great Smoky Mountains*, reported on twenty-one species, one third of them warblers. Among those who followed were Albert F. Ganier, of Nashville, the dean of Tennessee ornithologists; Dr. Alexander F. Wetmore, of Washington, D.C., the Secretary of the Smithsonian Institution, and E. V. Komarek, who had conducted a study of fauna under the auspices of the Chicago Academy of Science and also had prepared an *Incomplete Checklist of the Birds of the Smokies* in 1934, including 147 species and subspecies. Stupka also benefited from the investigations of wildlife technicians attached to the camps of the CCC. Raymond J. Fleetwood, for example, who arrived in the park in 1934, kept a daily journal of his hiking in the field, which led to preparation of a list of 137 species and subspecies.

Although Stupka concentrated at first on birds, mammals, and insects, this plainly was a world of unending natural dimensions. "More than 1300 kinds of flowering plants, almost 350 mosses and liverworts, 230 lichens, and more than 2000 fungi have been found here," he would write years later. Then there were the trees, the precise number of varieties unknown—and still unknown but totaling at least one hundred. About twenty of them, Stupka and other experts have concluded, reach their record size in the Smokies; among these, red spruce, eastern hemlock, mountain magnolia or cucumber tree, Fraser magnolia, yellow buckeye, and mountain silverbell. In addition, he saw plants that normally would be considered shrubs thriving in the proportions of trees—that is, standing erect with a tall, woody stem at least nine or ten feet high. Such, in favorable Smoky Mountain locations, is the case with staghorn sumac, witch hazel, rhododendron, and mountain laurel. "The world's largest mountain laurel" was called to Stupka's attention by a mountaineer friend, "Uncle Jim" Shelton. The laurel measured a fantastic eighty-two inches in diameter, seeming like the aggregate growth of sprouts fused into a single stem. The late Dr. Harry M. Jennison of the University of Tennessee named it officially Shelton's Ivy Stalk, in honor of its discoverer.

All of these, the trees, shrubs, flowers, insects, birds, and mammals, are components of the whole, each having little true meaning without the other. I recall once walking with Stupka and asking repeatedly, "What use is this plant?" or "What good was that flower to the mountaineers?" After answering patiently for a time, Arthur stopped in his tracks and pointed a long finger under my nose.

"I wish you would stop asking what *good* this or that may be," he said. "Do you mean good for you or me? Or in terms of this place where they grow?"

He was right, of course. The most important lesson to learn from the primeval forest is that nature capably writes its own rules. "The outstanding scientific discovery of the twentieth century," as Aldo Leopold, the pioneer scholar on wildlife management and wilderness, wrote in 1947, "is not television or radio, but rather the complexity of the land organism. The last word in ignorance is the man who says of a plant or animal, 'What good is it?' If the land mechanism as a whole is good, then every part is good, whether we understand it or not."

This same philosophy of the land guided Arthur Stupka. In 1939 he began a program of guided hikes and walks, pointing to the explicable and inexplicable miracles of nature. In the evenings, on his own time, he would deliver illustrated talks at the spacious Mountain View Hotel, in his own studious but convincing fashion. The program that he began of interpreting the national park grew into a well-rounded naturalist service of hikes and talks open to all visitors. The conducted hiking trips begin May 1 and continue through October, with a team of park naturalists leading the way to waterfalls, big-tree groves, concentrations of wildflowers, and outstanding views. Talks are given every evening during the summer in the campgrounds and in the Sugarlands Visitor Center, where the displays include many of the bird and animal specimens assembled by Arthur Stupka.

Trails there are of all sizes and shapes, guided and unguided, of thirty minutes, half a day, all day, or all week on the Appalachian Trail. Each trail reveals a distinctive story.

The Big Locust Trail, for example, which begins at the Chimneys Campground, passes through an area where settlers cut the trees and cultivated the land; then it plunges into a fragment of virgin forest, including the rare yellowwood and giant tulip tree or yellow poplar, black locust, and buckeye—a real cross-section of the Smokies. On both sides of the trail at the beginning are piles of rock, vestiges of laborious clearing before the steep slopes were cultivated in corn and potatoes, now overshaded by a young woodland. The waters of the West Prong of the Little Pigeon River, draining Sugarland Mountain and the south slope of Mount Le Conte, rush downward toward Gatlinburg.

Presently the trail bends into the wilderness, passing an eastern, or Canada, hemlock, a species that grows to greater size in the Great Smokies than anywhere else in its entire range from Nova Scotia west to Minnesota. The tree appears to have been a favorite with sapsuckers, which have punctured their drill-marks systematically in straight horizontal rows.

A few steps beyond stands the biggest black locust in the park, a species ordinarily considered a "weed tree" but here fifty-two inches in diameter, with the rough, deeply furrowed bark of age. In April or May, white and fragrant sweet-pealike clusters of flowers appear, drawing droves of bees. Because the wood is so durable when in contact with the ground, the numbered posts along this trail are aptly made of black locust. For me, however, the most interesting tree on the loop is the yellowwood, or gopherwood, a smallish tree, rare even on the limestone slopes of Tennessee, Kentucky, and North Carolina, where it is native; perhaps because a yellowwood was the final survivor of all the specimens collected by John Bartram and planted by him in his garden in Philadelphia. The clustered white flowers which appear in late spring are not unlike those of the locust, to which it is related as members of the bean family, or Leguminosae.

A sloping field along the trail, strewn with jumbled boulders, tells of an ancient age and its colder climate, when these massive rocks were torn loose from a higher ridge by the process of alternate freezing and thawing. The bouldery debris moved slowly down the slope, churned and heaved by frost and the pull of gravity, continuing even now its downward movement toward disintegration, sliding at an imperceptibly slow speed. The variety of plant life along this one little trail is incredible—the gray-barked white ash that was growing here above the rock-strewn stream long before the white man arrived, the large old sugar maples, the young silverbell, basswood, and yellow poplar; the evergreen walking fern, or "sore eye," a strange, ancient plant growing on moist mossy rocks, spawning offspring when the tips of its finely tapered fronds touch the ground, and the wildflowers that usually begin with a burst of spring beauty and hepatica and reach *their* greatest variety in April. Then, as the trail circles back to its starting point, the signs of old human activity reappear. A rocky pile is all that remains of a "sugar camp" where the sap drawn from the maples in early spring was boiled down in big iron kettles. Then, the contrast becomes strikingly clear between the second-growth young forest, at the upper limit of lumbering operations in this little cove, and the mature stand of big trees left behind.

Most trails are leisurely pathways. Five separate routes lead up to Le Conte Lodge, the only overnight facility (with four walls and running water) inside the park, and possibly the highest resort east of the Mississippi River. Despite the elevation of 6593 feet, 4000 feet above the valley in Gatlinburg, the shortest route one way, via Alum Cave Bluffs, is but 5.2 miles. The lodge is the house that Jack Huff built, and which he and his wife, Pauline, ran until 1960. Actually, it consists of several balsam log cabins for sleeping and a large shingle house for the dining room, with a capacity of about fifty persons. When the Huffs gave it up, the lodge *had* to go to members of the Smoky Mountains Hiking Club, the Herrick Browns, who promised to preserve the tradition. The loudest sounds around the lodge are the serenades and chirpings of bird life. At sunset it requires a quarter-mile walk from the lodge to Cliff Top in order to view hundreds of square miles of mountains, lowlands, East Tennessee towns, lights of Knoxville, and the western horizon darkening through the colors of red, orange, bluishwhite, and the intensity of a natural night. And at dawn, a mile from the lodge, Myrtle Point affords another vista, to be shared with juncos, warblers, vireos, and other high fliers.

The trails have their different seasons. The choice time to hike to Gregory Bald from Cades Cove is in late June, for the flower show of wild azaleas in diverse hues, running from pure white through all the pinks, yellows, and flames to deep, saturated reds, ranged around the fringe where grass and forest meet. Could these colors have been done by design? Perhaps the answer is that good landscaping follows some mystic pattern of natural informality.

The same month the forest nears the fullness of green and leaf. Clearly now, plants, flowers, and trees are to the Smokies what granite domes are to Yosemite and geysers to Yellowstone. This is the month of rhododendrons on the trail. It begins with purple rhododendron of the mountain slopes, then the densely flowered Piedmont, or punctatum, waist high, and the towering catawba, or rose-pink, blooming at different altitudes from June into July and the rest of the summer; and the *Rhododendron maximum* forming a gigantic garden of waxywhite to deep pink under the streamside hemlocks.

Americans of all ages take to the trails of the Great Smokies. I have been to Gatlinburg the last weekend in April for the annual Spring Wildflower Pilgrimage, a program begun in 1951 by Arthur Stupka; Bart Leiper, manager of the local chamber of commerce, and the botany and zoology departments of the University of Tennessee. Of several hundred participants, four fifths were older citizens. They had arrived from New York, Chicago, Florida, and more distant places, armed with cameras, binoculars, botanical guides, sketch pads, and notebooks, above all with enthusiasm and tirelessness. Their desire was to learn as well as to enjoy, and learn they did from early morning until late at night.

Almost thirty field trips, conducted by park naturalists and botany instructors of the University and other nearby colleges, comprise the annual program. Each trip is a new adventure, a many-sided display, varying in length and physical effort. Many pilgrims have turned out for the 7:30 A.M. bird walks to see the wild turkey, that noble American favorite of Ben Franklin's; the ruffed grouse, the log drummer; the hummingbird, warbler, catbird, wood thrush, and the olive-sided fly-catcher heard at great distances whistling his tune, "What peeves you?"

The longest walk of the Pilgrimage, about six miles round-trip, leads to Ramsay Cascade, the most beautiful falls in the park at an elevation of 4200 feet. The trail passes through virgin forests of towering hemlock, four-hundred-year-old yellow poplars, black cherry, and white ash, along streams shaded thick with rhododendron. The Ramsay Prong of the Middle Prong of the Little Pigeon River running down from Mount Guyot has a great roar in its throat that drowns out conversation. This may not be the easiest climb; it cannot be made hurriedly. The reward, however, is to sit at the edge of Ramsay Cascade and feel the cool air current and the spray of water splashing and shouting while it tumbles one hundred feet into a shallow-pan pool before proceeding on its way.

On the trail to Ramsay Cascade, I noticed that Arthur Stupka was much less a hiker than a walker. That is, his pace was easy and leisurely. Perhaps this was the result of adjusting his step to match the thousands and thousands of untrained trampers whom he had guided through the woods during his career. Or, perhaps from his absorption in the surroundings rather than in the physical process of locomotion. We all hike, I thought, for different reasons. Some take to the trails to search for solitude, where they can find a large and quiet enough spot for unrestrained thought. Others look for natural beauty, finding their wonder in trees, wildflowers, and wild animals. The scientists hike in order to study and to advance the knowledge of the human race about the planet on which it lives. Others want to match their muscles and stamina against the long trails to the highlands.

It does not make much difference, really, why we hike, or tramp, or walk, as long as the trails and the expansive natural environment are there so we can do these things. The Great Smokies are that kind of country. The heart of the national park is a hiker's park, where the Appalachian Trail follows the crest of the mountains from Davenport Gap to Shuckstack and Fontana Dam, a distance of seventy miles, touching civilization only at Newfound Gap and from there to Clingman's Dome.

The Appalachian Trail is the longest marked path in the world, covering 2021 miles along the crest of Appalachia from northern New England into the Deep South. It is more than a footway, however, it is a concept of recreation brought to reality almost entirely through the voluntary efforts of patriotic people who felt the need to stir the pioneer spirit and to provide new generations of Americans the lure of exploration. "This is to be a connected trail," declared the constitution of the Appalachian Trail Conference, after its organizational meeting in 1925, "running as far as practicable over the summits of the mountains and through the wild lands of the Atlantic seaboard and adjoining states, from Maine to Georgia, to be supplemented by a system of primitive camps at proper intervals, so as to render accessible for tramping, camping, and other forms of primitive travel and living, the said mountains and wild lands, as a means for conserving and developing, within this region, the primeval environment as a natural resource."

The idea of the Appalachian Trail was first proposed in 1921 by Benton MacKaye, a trained forester and regional planner, of Shirley Center, Massachusetts, who later came to Knoxville as a member of the staff of TVA. MacKaye formulated the project for the mountain footpath from his wanderings in the New England forests, although others had already begun localized trails. In an article titled "An Appalachian Trail—A Project in Regional Planning," he envisioned "a 'long trail' over the full length of the Appalachian skyline from the highest peak in the North to the highest peak in the South." Few proposals in regional planning have fired the imagination as did MacKaye's. Almost at once scattered groups and individuals began to work, including some of the leading personalities connected with the Great Smokies. In 1922 the first part of the Trail was constructed by hiking clubs of New York and New Jersey in Palisades Interstate Park; Major W. A. Welch, general manager and chief engineer of the Interstate Park, who later was to serve on the Southern Appalachian National Park Commission, designed the standard "AT" copper marker. Harlan P. Kelsey, another member of the park commission (who played a key role in the selection

of the Great Smokies), suggested Lookout Mountain, near Chattanooga, as the southern terminus of the Trail. This appealed to Paul
Fink, of Jonesboro, Tennessee, who, familiar with the trails and woods
of his state, in 1922 developed a map showing a route down the western
range of Appalachia to Cohutta Mountain, then crossing the Great
Valley to Lookout in the Cumberlands. However, the idea of crossing
a wide, cultivated valley was ruled out and Lookout was dropped from
the Trail. Subsequently, it was determined that existing Forest Service
trails could link the Great Smokies with Mount Oglethorpe, then
known locally as plain old "Grassy Mountain," in Georgia, and so the
southern terminus was chosen.

But connecting the Great Smokies with the Nantahalas presented
a problem. Routing of the Trail through the entire length of the Great
Smokies to the Little Tennessee River involved a circuitous, almost
backtracking, course to the Nantahalas at Wesser Bald. Suggestions of a
more direct approach to Wesser from Silers Bald had been rejected in
favor of the more attractive route through the western Smokies. In
1931, the Smoky Mountains Hiking Club pledged to construct this
extremely difficult thirty-two-mile link, crossing the Little Tennessee
to Tapoco, then bending east toward Wesser Bald. This work was completed under its chairman, Carlos C. Campbell, by 1933.

The Smoky Mountains Hiking Club had been organized in Knoxville
in the summer of 1924. Even before then a few planned trips had been
taken in the Smokies under the auspices of the Knoxville YMCA, driving out in model-T Fords over the uncertain roads of East Tennessee.
The members of this club have also hiked in the Blue Ridge and Cumberlands, but the Smokies are their special domain. Through the years
they have been responsible for 110 miles of the Appalachian Trail, including marking the portion within the national park. The point I
admire most about all the Appalachian Trail clubs is that they set an
example of giving to the land resources as well as taking pleasure from
them; they try to improve the experiences of other park and forest
visitors, as well as those of their own members. One of the first nature
trails in the park was mapped in 1937 by the club, principally by Dr.
Stanley A. Cain in co-operation with the botany department of the
University of Tennessee, under Dr. L. R. Hesler. Tens upon tens of
thousands of travelers have walked on trails cut with ax and mattock
and maintained by this club and others like it without ever knowing of
their existence. In 1947 and 1948, after the construction of Fontana
Dam, the club engineered a major relocation of the Little Tennessee
crossing, eliminating the dogleg via Tapoco, substituting instead the
magnificent view from the Shuckstack fire tower and the 2000-foot

descent from the dramatic crossing of the Little Tennessee Gorge at Fontana Dam.

On the other side of the mountains, organized hiking had begun in 1920 with establishment in Asheville of a southern chapter of the venerable Appalachian Mountain Club. Three years later it withdrew from the parent organization in New England and incorporated as the Carolina Mountain Club, emerging anew in 1931 as the Carolina Appalachian Trail Club. The earliest of these groups had been headed by Dr. Chase P. Ambler, who figured prominently in the conservation campaign leading to passage of the Weeks Law; the second group by Dr. Gaillard S. Tennent, who continued to lead walking trips into the mountains until well into his seventies, and the last group by George Myers Stephens, who was intimately involved with the Great Smokies since 1928 when he served in the woods as a young member of the timber cruising party whose calculations helped to determine valuation of the Champion Fibre Company lands. Later, as a publisher and printer, Stephens produced many maps and booklets for the guidance of hikers and other vacationers in the Smokies and surrounding mountains. Besides the Trail Club, he was associated through the years with the Cherokee Historical Association, the crafts movement, and efforts to develop a planning program for western North Carolina.

One of the founders and active members of Carolina Appalachian Trail Club was George Masa, the Japanese photographer, who is credited with having a remarkable knowledge of the southern Appalachians and with solving many trail location problems. Masa labored on the Trail project in companionship with Horace Kephart until he, Masa, died in June 1933.

The primary project of the Carolina club was to get the Appalachian Trail routed, measured, and maintained from the Virginia border to the Great Smokies, where the Knoxville group took over, then again from the Nantahalas past Standing Indian Mountain to the Georgia border. Its members have had the benefit of a happy hiking land in the Blue Ridge Mountains at Asheville's back door, but its veterans have known the trails in the Smokies intimately.

To hike the full length of the Appalachian Trail from Maine to Georgia is impossible for most people. Within six or eight days, however, a good walker with backpack can cover the seventy-one miles in the Great Smokies from Davenport Gap to Fontana, traversing a host of major peaks, Cammerer, Old Black, Guyot, Chapman, Laurel Top, Kephart, Clingman's Dome, Silers Bald, and Thunderhead, stopping at cool campsites or trailside shelters (closed on three sides with bunks for six persons) above the 5000-foot level. The Trail can also be taken in portions, of a day, or a half day, from either end, from Newfound Gap, Clingman's Dome, or up from Cades Cove.

What makes a mountain trail a supreme adventure is the combination of natural diversity, the touch of intimacy at hand, and the fullness of distant vistas. The high footpath of the Smokies has all of these elements. In the eastern half, the crest is narrow, at times so narrow that the tramper must imagine himself walking with one leg as the guest of North Carolina and the other of Tennessee. The round wooden lookout tower at Cammerer perches high on a rugged treeless ledge overlooking the Great Valley and Pigeon River curving through farmlands, black in color, unfortunately, from the pollution bestowed upon it at the Champion Fibre mill in North Carolina. The rose-pink rhododendron blooms high on Cammerer, its rich color contrasting with the light rock.

This eastern portion is forested with red spruce and aromatic fir of the north country, though yellow birch sometimes keeps them company; and modest plants like mountain sorrel, or wood shamrock, thriving beneath the trees because they demand little sunlight, yet blooming a delicate white threaded with pink. Rain and fog, alternating with streaming sunshine, keep the hiker company. The trail winds past Mount Guyot, dominating the main range to the west, at Tricorner Knob, high above the Three Forks Wilderness, passing patches of low growing wintergreen and blackberry thickets to the steep slopes of the Jumpoff and Charlie's Bunion.

Across Newfound Gap the trees change to hardwoods. Approaching Silers Bald, the spruce forest reaches the limit of its southern range before the hiker's eye. Trees are gnarled and wind-blown. However, in late July wild Turk's-cap lilies standing eight feet tall blossom near Silers with huge orange-red flowers flecked with brown. Each of the balds, thick with wild grass, is a little mystery of its own. Looking at Silers Bald or Spence Field, and being told that these actually covered a larger area when cattle ranged here, one might wonder whether it was a mistake to ban grazing on these old grassy knolls. Or, is it better to allow nature to have its own way, with patches of aromatic wild strawberries invading the abandoned pasture lands? In any event, the thick wild grass makes a welcome mattress after lunch and the berries are good eating for hikers in the fall. Finally, from Shuckstack, at 4020 feet elevation, one of the finest vantage points in the entire park, the Trail leads downward past dead chestnut stumps and honeysuckle, with Fontana Lake dead ahead.

It spells the end of the trail, except for those who plan to rest a while at Fontana, then continue south. But anyone who has walked in the high places once will return to walk again, as long as he is able.

The visitor views Cades Cove, a meadowland about five miles long and two miles wide on the Tennessee side of the national park, as a cameo of living history. This it is. Though other settlements within the park have disappeared and have reverted to woodland, Cades Cove still presents the scene of open fields and farms, growing hay, and grazing cattle, and of water-powered grist mill, homesteads, and frame churches.

More isolation has been fancied into the Cove with the passing years than actually existed, but it is the nearest thing anywhere to the kind of valley community that dotted the back country of Appalachia long ago. It has the charm and beauty of earlier American ages, or perhaps I should say that it evokes nostalgia for ways that are gone.

The development of Cades Cove as it stands today was not altogether simple. The park originally was envisioned as a wilderness; the plan was to let the Cove revert to nature along with the other settlements, when the inhabitants moved out or when their lifetime leases expired.

Still, it was recognized that something would have to be done about saving, or recording, or collecting traces of mountaineer history. "The Great Smoky area is one of our most important depositories of native culture," stressed Dr. Waldo G. Leland, of the American Council of Learned Societies in a letter to Arno B. Cammerer, Director of the Park Service, in 1935. "The Government has a very definite obligation to make as complete and accurate a record as possible of this culture without delay, and before intrusive influences have been exercised in any considerable degree."

Three years later, in June 1938, a "Mountain Culture Program" was submitted by Arthur Stupka, Charles S. Grossman, and Hiram C. Wilburn. As the first essential of the program, a mountaineer museum was proposed for the site of the historic Mingus Mill in North Carolina, with the mill itself to be included in the museum complex. Grossman, a National Park Service employee, inspected over one thousand buildings in the park and collected invaluable materials and records relating to mountain life and home industries, becoming a foremost authority on log hewing, iron making, tanning, sugar making, and much else. Wilburn, a native of Waynesville, North Carolina, worked for the national park as a technician during the CCC days, investigating and writing original reports on many facets of its history, including the early Indians. In this same period, Joseph S. Hall was engaged as historian student technician in the CCC in order to study and record the language of the mountain dwellers.

When Dr. Hans Huth came to study the historic picture in the Smokies in 1941 as a consultant for the Park Service, he found there were still traces of pioneer culture that could not be found in any other part of the country—but they were going fast. About two hundred families lived in the park on lifetime leases. Their houses were being kept in more or less good repair. Others already deserted had tumbled down, or been destroyed by fire or storm. It was practically impossible, he said, to imagine how the settlement of the Sugarlands looked when it was open, so rapidly was nature reclaiming its own.

In his report Dr. Huth endorsed the proposals to designate "an area of living mountain culture," providing that it was done in the right place and in the right way. Such an area could not be established in one of the narrow, steep valleys, afflicted with soil leaching and erosion, where conditions were unfavorable to farming, and where visitors would hardly have sufficient room to move about without destroying the scene. But Cades Cove was a broad and prosperous valley, where selected settlers could live and work. "The aim," he suggested, "would be to make these settlers, as far as possible, economically independent and self-sustaining. Such a program would be educational with respect to both visitor and settler. Though such an evolutionary program would be started in one way, there is no possibility of telling how and where it might end."

Cades Cove achieves such reality that visitors never stop to think of it as a synthetic creation designed to force back the wilderness for a show of history and folk culture. The eleven-mile loop road leads past the half dozen farms, smokehouses, and "bee gums" buzzing on the front lawns. The farm dwellers are granted leases and educational assistance to make them economically independent and self-sustaining. In return, they must fertilize, maintain the rail fences, and keep up their properties. From April to November the John P. Cable grist mill, built in 1868, the only mill left in the park using an overshot wheel, grinds corn the old-fashioned way. In October, sorghum cane is ground by a mule turning the mill slowly and laboriously, followed by the "boiling off" into sorghum, or "long sweetnin'," the old sugar of the hills. Campers can purchase these freshly made products and have hot cakes and sorghum for supper on a crisp fall evening.

Ringed with mountains, Cades Cove affords a variety of walking trails—the easy climb along Abrams Creek, the largest stream entirely within the park, to the rocky ledge where Abrams Falls plunges into the dark pool below on its journey to the Little Tennessee; the hike up the mountain to Gregory Bald, following the trail of the old herdsmen; or the short hike up to Rich Mountain lookout, giving a view of Townsend, Tuckaleechee, the Chilhowees, and the broad Cumberland

Plateau. Returning from these walks one may spot wild turkey and deer, animals that once were nearly decimated, in the open fields of Cades Cove, and grouse in the shadows. It's the ancient scene, more or less, not perfectly re-created, but it wasn't perfect to begin with, either.

A fellow named Randolph Shields worked as a summer naturalist in Cades Cove during the 1950s and early '60s, answering visitors' questions and giving evening lectures. He sounded like a modest, well-educated young man but one who knew all the lore of Cades Cove. It was his birthplace and that of generations of his family before him. His family had moved out when the park was established, and he had gone off to become a college instructor, preparing for his doctorate in biology when I met him, but he had returned during the summers to work as a naturalist.

Dr. Shields showed me a great deal of Cades Cove. Arthur Stupka, John Morrell, and others told me about a few other items that reveal there is more to the story than meets the eye.

The first marvel of Cades Cove is its geology. History here can be traced back to 400 million years ago, when limestone containing fossils of primitive sea animals of the ancient seas was buried here. During the Appalachian Revolution, pressures from the southeast thrust older rocks, sandstone, and shale over the limestone toward the northwest—the end of the upthrust was at the foot of the Chilhowees. Then constant stream erosion which ensued cut through the ancient rocks, exposing the younger limestone beneath. Running water has been ceaselessly wearing away the mountains, removing several thousand feet of rock and producing a level-floored valley—a "limestone window" —surrounded by steep-sided cliffs formed of rocks said by the geologists to be 200 million years older. Cades Cove is one of the two places in the park with evidence of fossil deposits, White Oak Sink being the other.

When the first permanent white settler arrived in this part of the Cherokee domain ruled by Abram of Chilhowee is a matter of conjecture. John Oliver is credited with establishing residence here in 1818, although the region was not legally open for entry until the Indian treaty of 1819, and William Tipton is credited with arriving two years later in 1821. Regardless of whether these dates and the order of settlement are precisely correct, it is well known that the Olivers and Tiptons came early. Robert Shields arrived in 1828, his family having followed the usual pattern of moving in stages from Pennsylvania down through Virginia into East Tennessee. Also in the usual pattern, most of his several children headed West for new land and a new opportunity. The two older ones stayed behind, becoming permanently settled here with families. These were Henry and Fed, or Frederick, who had married Oliver sisters. The families of Shields, Gregory, and Oliver were variously related and there were plenty to go around—Fed, for instance, had seventeen children and most families averaged about six or eight offspring. But one of the Shields married a McCauley, "Black Irish," not a Scotch-Irish, who was born near Maryville. The songs sung in Cades Cove were as much Irish as they were English.

These people were not totally isolated, as often pictured, but through the years were linked with Maryville, Sevierville, and other parts of the outside world. For instance, Dan Lawson came into the Cove in the 1840s, married Peter Cable's daughter, inherited her father's property (his fine old cabin, smokehouse, and corn crib are still intact), and at one time owned a swath of land one half mile wide from Cades Cove Mountain to Big Smoky. As justice of peace and owner of a general store, he had a telephone line run during the 1880s across Cades Cove Mountain to Tuckaleechee, and thus Cades Cove had phone service in operation until about the turn of the century. Old Dan deserves further remembrance for starting his own church, in the Methodist denomination, on an acre of hillside property and deeding it to "God-almighty." This complicated procedures for the United States Government in acquiring land for the national park, for how does a government condemn land from God-almighty?

During the Civil War most of these people stayed home and tended their own business. Those who did fight joined the Union because they opposed slavery on religious grounds. It is often written that Appalachian whites knew nothing of their black brethren; yet at the time of the Civil War several free Negro families dwelled in Maryville, including one in which the head of the household operated a livery stable. In the period of the early 1900s to 1920s Negro herdsmen came into the Smokies driving cattle and were welcomed to stay in Cades Cove homes, sleeping in the same beds with three or four children.

One of the showpieces of mountain cabin construction on the Cades Cove loop is the little place on the old David Shields property built for his sister, Matilda. She was known in later years as Aunt Tildy. As a young girl in the 1870s, she married a Gregory and departed the Cove with him. But when their child, Joe, was born, the father deserted and she returned to brothers Dave and Jonathan, who built for her the low, squat house with roughhewn logs, saddle-notched corners, and a large stone chimney. Later she married a "widderman," Henry White-head. The whole family pitched in to build the larger house in 1895–96, his two daughters helping to saw the pine logs, plane the joists, and mold the bricks by hand. One of these girls, Nancy Ann, later became the wife of John Oliver, the great-grandson of the original John Oliver;

the later Oliver, who made his mark by fighting the national park on general principles, was represented as a backward mountain man, whereas he had actually studied at Maryville and at a business college in Louisville, Kentucky.

Joe Gregory, the son of Aunt Tildy Shields Gregory Whitehead, meanwhile grew into manhood as a splendid churchgoer and manufacturer of some of the best corn whiskey in the East Tennessee mountains. Before prohibition Cades Cove was distinguished for its high quality of legal liquor. Julius Gregg made corn whiskey and brandy in a substantial two-story distillery, kegging the raw products and hauling them out in barrels to age elsewhere. George Powell was another brandy maker who provided a market where farmers could sell the apples of their orchards at a good price. Though it was a terrible calamity for the legal trade in apples and corn when the Volstead Act took effect, Joe Gregory was undaunted. He refused to merchandise "popskull" or rotgut, continuing to age his whiskey in wood for at least a year.

Two rivals disputed Gregory's leadership in the liquor trade, whose names are herewith changed to Plugg and Gamble. It is said they made a much poorer grade of whiskey and could charge only one fourth as much for their merchandise. This led to the Plugg-Gregory family feud which continued over a period of years during the 1920s, and which has not been depicted in any of the National Park Service interpretive displays.

John Plugg reportedly declared the issue by pouring salt in Joe Gregory's mash and also by tearing his mash barrels. Soon afterward a Gregory boy was dragged from his horse while riding in the woods and beaten by two members of the Plugg family. When he returned home with blood streaming, Joe Gregory and his boys struck out after the Pluggs. Thereupon the shooting started in earnest.

The Gregory clan was particularly itchy. They were all stirred when one of their number had his horse shot from under him. Earl Gregory kept his pistol with him at all times, even once when he was sitting at a wake for a dead friend. In the midst of his lamentation John Plugg entered. Earl saw that he was armed and shot him five times in the stomach. Self-defense, witnesses said, and Earl went free.

The Olivers then stepped into the fray. John Oliver, who carried the mail on horseback, and his father, William H. Oliver, "Preacher Will," of the Primitive Baptist Church (he died in 1940 at the age of eighty-three), despised whiskey and all those who made it. Whenever John smelled a still from afar, he would set down his mail pouch and commence tracing the aroma up a branch or creek until he located the scene of the crime, which he promptly reported to revenue agents. It was felt around the community that his devotion to decency, or possibly his father's, accounted for simultaneous raids upon business operations of both the Gregory and Plugg distillers. Apparently in retribution, the barns of Preacher Will and John Oliver were burned to the ground in the dead of night.

Joe Gregory and his son Dave were arrested and charged with barn burning. Some said the Pluggs had turned them in, or perhaps had been responsible themselves and had framed the Gregory father and son. The high sheriff and deputy, known as the low sheriff, offered a good word, but the Gregorys were sentenced to the penitentiary for one year. After serving less than six months, they were pardoned by Governor Hill McAlister, who personally demonstrated his forgiveness by conducting them from Nashville back to Cades Cove, and then returned to the capital city with a large container of well-aged Gregory mash.

In the pre-park years of the 1920s about ninety-odd families, or seven to eight hundred persons, lived in Cades Cove and the surrounding hills and hollows. Many were self-respecting landowners, literate people who had pride in their consolidated school, one of three schools in the Cove, and the center of their social activity. Once a month, on a Friday night, "speaking" would be the big event, featuring recitations, speeches, and debates, both for young people and grownups. There would also be spelling bees from the famous Blue Back Speller and competitions with teams from schools in surrounding communities. The churches (two of which are still standing) were the rendezvous for harp singing, especially noteworthy when the Lawson sisters performed; Leanna, or "Leanner," Lawson put on quite a show by greasing the outside of her throat before the congregation.

Early in the century there had been flumes above the Cove, floating squared or slabbed logs to the mill at Townsend. Later, many Cove men worked winters, from November to March, on logging operations in North Carolina, returning home on weekends and in summer to tend their fields.

A few of them tended cattle on the mountain during the summer, when large herds were brought to the Smokies, mostly from Knoxville and Blount County. The herdsmen would enjoy the cool summers with their shepherd dogs while they received fifty cents per head for cattle and twenty-five cents per head for sheep, leaving their sons and wives to care for their farms down below. Wagon roads from Cades Cove to Gregory and Spence fields were used to "pack" sackloads of salt on muleback to the herdsmen in their cabins. These men were quite comfortable, sometimes coming down every week or so. They would use the scrawny wood of the three-needle pitch pine or the two-needle table mountain pine to provide quick heat for coffee, eggs, and biscuits.

For most in the Cove, subsistence farming was the main way of life. They raised enough food for their families, but found it difficult to scrape together fifteen or twenty dollars for their tax payments. They bartered their eggs, chickens, apples, fatback, sowbelly, cured hams and shoulders for salt, sugar, snuff, and tobacco. There were the usual diseases, such as typhoid and tuberculosis. Around the higher, isolated hollows marriages between cousins were not uncommon; or, in rare instances, even closer relationships, such as between the father and his daughter, who bore him two children, and between the young son and his mother, who bore his son.

At the sophisticated level of the Cove most girls were married at a tender age, although two exceptions were Kate Lawson and Becky Cable, both of whom lived until the 1940s, when they were well into their nineties. John P. Cable brought his three sons, Jim, Dan, and John, and daughter Becky from Carter County, in the vicinity of Roan Mountain. Becky was sixteen at the time; it was said her father had broken off a girlhood romance for her and that she never forgave him or looked at another man.

John Cable built the overshot grist mill and the first frame house in Cades Cove, a unique structure now known as the Becky Cable House, with a roundabout entrance to each room from the porch and a winding stairway inside. Cable ran it as a general store, with merchandise brought from Maryville, twenty-six miles away by ox team. After their father's death, Becky shared the house with her brother Dan's family, until he lost his mind and was committed to the Eastern State Hospital. Thereafter, she devoted herself to raising Dan's children. One of them, mentally retarded, was in the habit of watching chickens by the hour; since he had never been toilet trained, or housebroken, he usually was kept in one room of the house. Although she owned considerable mountain property, life was hard for Becky. Besides raising her brother's young ones, she worked in the fields with the vigor of a man, plowing, mowing, and forking hay.

Kate Lawson, however, who had inherited the home place from her father, never worked in the fields, but passed her time in knitting and spinning. In her later years she was seen riding horse and buggy around the Cove, dropping the reins here and there for a session of knitting and talking to herself.

The two were about the same age and often turned up at quiltings together. Today they are part of the legend of Cades Cove.

But more impressive than the legend is the very survival of Cades Cove. This fragment of living history, preserved inside the boundaries of a park dedicated to nature preservation, is strictly one of a kind, a memorial worthy of the finest qualities of the early pioneers.

XXV

The Sanctuary

The Great Smoky Mountains have been tenanted by living creatures for 200 million years, or perhaps longer, ever since the humblest forms of life appeared on the land of North America.

Life has always found sanctuary in the Great Smokies, from the beginning, down through the glacial ages, to this day.

The primeval portions have endured as a sanctuary of nature, a composition of endless themes and variations in the life cycle, a grand theater of universality. In these forests death needs no apology, but has a beauty of its own in advancing through history as the nourishing helpmate of birth in the folds of earth.

All these creatures play their roles together. The rocks, oldest of all, provide a haven for mosses and lichen, which crawl over and decompose them. The fallen tree feeds fungi, bacteria, and mushrooms of every color. Termites, earthworms, ants, millepedes, and slugs enrich, aerate, and build the soil, preparing it for the growth of fibrous-rooted plants, for seedlings of all kinds, for the succession of life.

They are all intertwined, the humble plants and towering trees of the forest, the insects, birds, reptiles, fish, and mammals, carrying food one for the other, or carrying seeds to perpetuate another's species, or furnishing shade when it is required.

"Our globe, like the totality of creation, is a great organism," Arnold Guyot wrote, "all the parts of which are purposely shaped and arranged." Thus, all of these forest creatures are woven into the fabric of the universe. They need and feed the land and air, and are in harmony with the light and dark of heavens and the flow of waters.

The genius of the Smokies, however, is inherent not only in the untouched primeval portions. This sanctuary of nature is also a place of restoration, or "comeback." Those areas once disturbed, or even destroyed, by man have rejoined their own.

When a mountaineer's cabin was abandoned, the paper wasps arrived; then came the phoebe birds, the white-footed mice, the wood rats, the insects and spiders. The wood rotted, the roof fell down, the floor caved in. Each stage of life prepared the way for the next in the tedious cycle of successive growths. The first year was dominated by horseweed and finger grass, followed by ragweed and heather aster, and by broom sedge. The scrawny scrub pine succeeded the broom sedge, while the apple and fruit trees deteriorated into gaunt and ghostly relics. In about ten years the first hardwood trees, small species like the dogwood, made their presence felt. But the tulip trees grew rapidly and in two or three decades a vigorous young forest had risen. In the dark, moist, and rocky gorges the eastern hemlock proliferated, then reached high for sunlight. Given seventy-five years, a first-class forest, teeming with life, will have claimed its place where the cabin was abandoned.

"But that organism of creation comprises not nature only," said Guyot. "It includes man, and with man the moral and intellectual life." It is, indeed, as a testament of man's faith and intellect that the Smokies have come to us. Despite a past of violent disharmony, through enlightenment and sacrifice man moved to establish a concept of sanctuary in these mountains.

Here, then, is a sanctuary for both nature and man, having achieved harmony and a rare degree of mutual respect.

As to the future, shall we do less than the generation that sacrificed in order to establish this pattern?

It is in man's power to reverse the pattern in order to provide for his own immediate pleasures and profits.

It is also in his power to solidify the concept toward which he and nature have been working in harmony—and to so arrange man's contact with this country as to yield values to civilization that transcend by far the mere levels of "recreation" and play.

The issue is very much alive, even while this book approaches its publication in mid-1966. As I near the final paragraph, the public has been advised that hearings are imminent on the new Wilderness Act as it applies to the Great Smoky Mountains National Park. The immediate issue is whether to go ahead with construction of a proposed road from Bryson City across the park to Tennessee. In a broader sense, we shall write the record of our age in the pages of history; we shall demonstrate the degree of our respect for the ancientness of these mountains, and for the right of generations hence to see them in their natural state.

Suddenly all the struggles of the Kepharts and Cammerers are alive again. It is our chance to prove worthy of a heritage and to establish a mark for the future.

As all creatures are useful and good in the total structure, so too is humankind. Approaching the Great Smokies, the testing ground of man's continuing faith, I enter not as a stranger, but as one who belongs, with respect, with the sense of "the moral and intellectual life," with wonder and reverence at the marvels of this natural sanctuary.

The Great Smokies are
within 600 miles of half
the U.S. population.

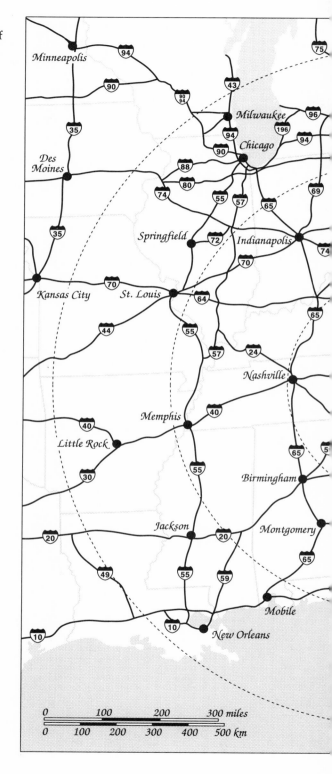

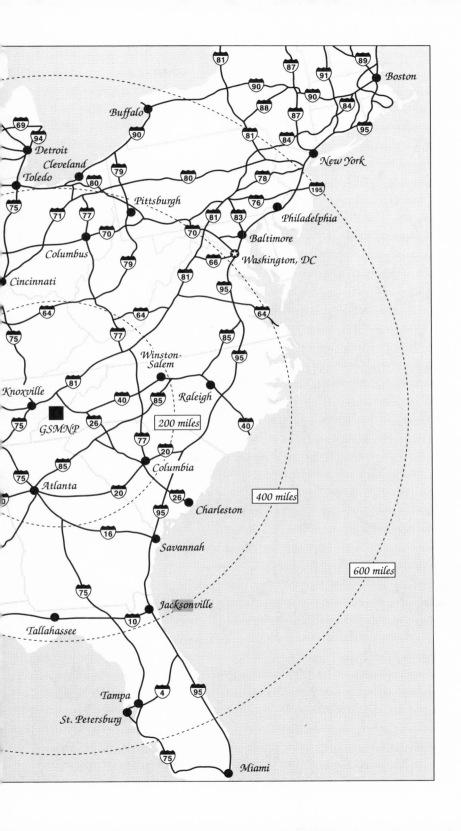

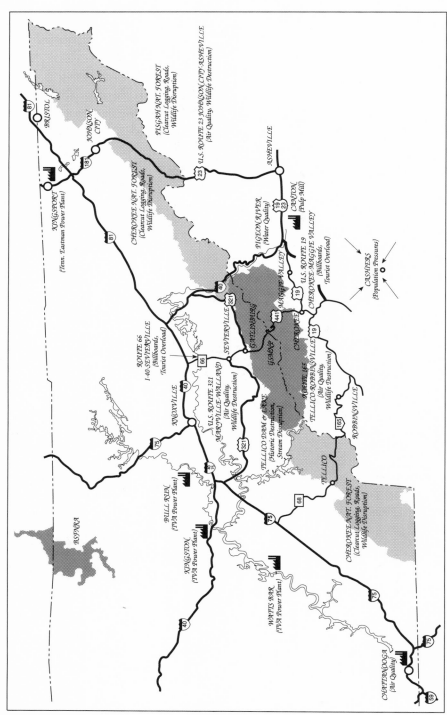

Stresses on the Smokies.

Open Options—an Epilogue

In September 1975 five maintenance workers, while lounging on their bunkhouse porch in Cataloochee Valley following a day on tough backcountry trails, watched three deer at ease on a path less than a hundred yards away. Suddenly the deer fled. Then the workmen were startled to see a grayish colored animal, a large cat with long tail, bound across the trail and vanish into the woods after the deer.

The men scrambled from the porch and followed the animal's path. They found only its tracks in the mud along a creek bottom, but these native mountaineers were convinced they had observed a panther, and so they reported to park headquarters.

This took a modicum of courage since sighting a panther in Appalachia till then had been largely regarded like sighting the Loch Ness monster, a vision best kept to oneself. Naturalists and biologists had long denied the panther's existence, or capability of existing in the national park. Anyone suggesting otherwise was subject to ridicule. Once when a ranger called in and said, "I think I just saw a mountain lion," the park dispatcher retorted, "Have another drink and you might see its mate."

Fifty years ago it was not uncommon for mountaineers to catch sight of a panther (or "painter" in the vernacular) three or four times a year. The Cherokee called it Klandaghi, "Lord of the forest." Panther Creek, Panther Mountain, Cat Run, Painter Branch, and Painter Creek are familiar place names in the Smokies and neighboring Nantahalas across the Little Tennessee River. More recently, however, the Eastern panther was assumed to have followed the trail into oblivion of the great auk, Laborador duck, heath hen, passenger pigeon, and sea mink.

The Cataloochee sighting was not the first (nor the last) reported, but it was advanced as the collective experience of five individuals. It triggered a new sense of awareness of the largest, rarest, and most secretive of wild American cats. Throughout Appalachia resource managers became conscious of their opportunity and responsibility. In a study undertaken for the Forest Service, George Lowman, a consulting biologist, urged complete protection as "the most necessary step." He wrote as follows: "As much of each national forest as possible should be maintained in unbroken undisturbed tracts. Certainly any type of habitat reduction should be avoided."

The panther was taken seriously in the park as well. In December 1976 Superintendent Boyd Evison reported that a deer had been killed by a panther. "The pattern of this kill left no doubt in our minds that it was performed by a mountain lion. It is the first material sighting of the animal of this nature." In a subsequent statement the superintendent went further: "It appears that nature has succeeded where the National Park Service feared to tread. There is no reasonable doubt that there *are* cougars in the park; and it seems likely they have been here for some time. Very little is known about their habits and needs in this kind of country, but the park, if kept free of excessive development, offers the best sanctuary for cougars north of the Everglades and east of the Rockies."

Because most of the Great Smokies have been protected in undisturbed tracts, our generation is free to determine whether the panther should be sacrificed to progress, or saved, or how best it should be saved. The options are open. But in Cataloochee, the very scene of the key sighting, that option was nearly lost. As the *Quarterly News Bulletin* of the Carolina Mountain Club reported in the third quarter of 1974:

> Again, a lovely mountain area is threatened. Land developers, motel operators, politicians, highway builders, some chambers of commerce, and senior citizens interested more in dollars than in the out-of-doors are pushing for construction of a paved highway from Interstate 40 into Cataloochee Valley in the Great Smoky Mountains National Park. The National Park Service is also recommending the road.
>
> This fragile valley cannot stand any more visitors than it is now getting. It would be ruined by the ravages of litter, stream pollution, game poaching, land development, drug abuses, etc., that always come with crowds in primitive areas. This would be a catastrophe.

The National Park Service recognized the same threats. In an "environmental assessment," the bureau forecast that if the road were built this little valley would be subject to noise pollution, air pollution, soil erosion, stream siltation, temperature inversion (by trapping and concentrating auto emissions), loss of primitive character, destruction of natural vegetation and of wildlife habitat, and then, for reasons of its own, said it had decided to let a construction contract virtually forthwith. The Department of Natural Resources of North Carolina commented critically that this precipitous decision made a mockery of the Park Service program of master planning and regional planning then underway. But it took a law suit by a group of citizens of Haywood County, North Carolina, to block construction of the access road. It may indeed one day be built, but the option to save the habitat of the panther still remains open.

The Great Smokies and their surroundings in Southern Appalachia are abundant in treasures of flora and fauna, still little known or understood. The Smokies themselves are the best catalogued because they have been set aside for preservation purposes. Here have been found insects and spiders new to science; twenty-seven or twenty-eight indigenous types of gastro-pods, the lowly slugs; the unique spider of Cades Cove, found only here and across the world in China; a large number of distinctive salamanders, reptiles, and amphibians—the whole chain of life from the lowest of living things up to the bear and panther. But in other areas, still unprotected and uncatalogued, prospects are different. Once defaced or disrupted their values are lost.

The future will be able only to speculate over what species might have been found at Copper Hill, Tennessee, a manmade badlands south of the Smokies, where fumes from the copper works early in this century killed everything as far as the eye could see; now Copper Hill is a monument to man's ability to eliminate with chemical waste every vestige of life from earthworms to trees.

In 1969 the Duke Power Company preempted the Keowee-Toxaway area, a wild region in southwestern North Carolina. Ten years later the power company would have had a much more difficult time, considering the beauty of the region, with its deep river gorges and diverse flowers, and shrubs.

The Keowee-Toxaway region was visited and described by William Bartram and, a few years after him, by André Michaux. Oconee bells, or *Shortia galacifolia*, one of the rarest known wilderness plants in North America, was found by Michaux in 1787, probably at the juncture of the Horsepasture and Toxaway rivers, which join to form the Keowee. The attractive little plant was given its scientific name by Asa Gray, while inspecting Michaux's collection in Paris in 1839. Gray and others searched for it in the wild, but not until one hundred years later was it rediscovered, growing in the most restricted acid humus settings along shaded mountain streams.

The power company generously catalogued such resources, but then proceeded to obliterate the entire scene to make way for a network of generating plants and reservoirs. In clearing and preparing the basins, loggers removed 32 million board feet of mixed hardwoods and soft-woods. Yellow poplars, some measuring 7 feet in diameter, 200 feet in height, and over 200 years in age, tumbled before the chain saws. The presumed discovery site of the Oconee bells in due time was flooded by the backwaters of Lake Jocassee. Nevertheless, Duke Power announced with pride that one section of the ancient forest would be saved "for naturalists and lovers of the untouched outdoors," a considerate gesture, but mostly in public relations, since it covers all of fifteen acres.

The world might never have known a species of fish called the snail darter nor to probe and ponder its special role in nature had the Tennessee Valley Authority been allowed to complete the Tellico Dam in the shadow of the Smoky Mountains. Initiated in the 1960s this project was intended to open new industrial sites and create jobs, although within a 50-mile radius almost two dozen impoundments already surround the Little Tennessee River and many industrial sites are not being used. Federal agencies seem determined to build or underwrite factories and then to find something for them to make, whether the specific product is needed or not, and all the while factories elsewhere may be idle, though the factories employ machines more than people anyway.

Tellico would have flooded fertile bottomland, farms, a major tree nursery, and some of the most important archaeological sites in the Eastern United States—the Overhill Cherokee homeland, including the ancient capital of Echota, or "Chote the metropolis," and nearby Tuskegee, birthplace of Sequoyah. TVA tried to dismiss its opponents as "a handful of selfish trout fishermen trying to deprive the region of progress," but the Association to Save the Little Tennessee was fighting to save a fragment of natural heritage, the last stretch of the river that remained undammed, in free-flowing condition.

The snail darter is part of that heritage, though no one knew it existed at all until a University of Tennessee biologist discovered the three-inch-long species in 1974. This may not have been the most earth-shaking scientific discovery, but the snail darter was destined for fame in preservation and politics. In 1975 the Department of the Interior declared that completion of Tellico Dam would "totally destroy the habitat of the darter" and that protection must be accorded priority under terms of the Endangered Species Act of 1973. The validity of the act to save a seemingly obscure fish was sustained in the Supreme Court and against attacks in Congress; TVA in the late 1970s backed off and opened consideration of broader options than completion of the dam.

Though Congress in 1979 decreed completion of the dam, the lesson of the snail darter transcends the case itself: that species and their surroundings are inseparable, that the seemingly undistinguished are as worthy as the "desirable" or more visible. A snail or a snail darter is plainly an implicit piece of a river in the same way that a moonrock is a piece of the moon. The survival of the snail darter in the Little Tennessee—and only in the Little Tennessee—enables the curious to investigate the darter's place and purpose there in the clean, gravelly shoals with cool, swift, low-turbidity water.

Through the 1970s various parcels of the Southern Appalachians were set aside for the future under terms of one law or another. The Chatooga River, a classic whitewater stream which forms in the mountains of North Carolina and then flows between Georgia and South Carolina into Georgia, became part of the National Wild and Scenic Rivers System. So did the ancient New River in northwestern North Carolina and southwestern Virginia, even after it had seemed lost to commercial hydropower development. The Obed River, a deep-gorge river in a true wilderness setting, and the Big South Fork of the Cumberland River (where the Army Corps of Engineers had planned to build the highest dam in the East), both on the Cumberland Plateau of Tennessee, were added to the National Park System. In an age where most rivers are crossed by highways, fenced in by farms and fields, fouled with effluent of cities and factories, or dammed by concrete, these streams flow through wild country; where unaffected by logging or mining, their waters are clean and clear.

The Wilderness Act of 1964 and the Eastern Wilderness Act of 1974 served as the vehicles to identify and protect additional areas, large and small. Among these are the Cohutta Wilderness, astride the Tennessee-Georgia border, a composition of rugged, steep-sloped mountains, laced with deep gorges, waterfalls, and the Conasauga and Jacks Rivers, covering 34,500 acres (which makes it the largest protected mountain wilderness outside the Smokies), and the Joyce Kilmer-Slickrock Wilderness, astride the North Carolina-Tennessee border, embracing within its 15,000 acres one of the most impressive remnants of the nation's virgin forests and the deeply sculptured valley of Slickrock Creek; but then there are natural gems of smaller size, like the Gee Creek Wilderness in Tennessee, about midway between Knoxville and Chattanooga, covering 2,570 acres.

Other areas need attention, too. Mount Mitchell, 65 miles north of Asheville, is the highest peak east of the Rockies, rising 6,684 feet above sparkling streams and waterfalls and forests that shelter rare plants and wildlife. "I've looked at a lot areas and none was more majestic and beautiful than the Mount Mitchell area," observed Representative Roy A. Taylor (a life-long resident of nearby Black Mountain), when he, before retiring from Congress in 1976, successfully sponsored legislation authorizing a study of a proposed new national park.

The Nantahalas, which compare to the Smokies themselves, may also be worthy of such attention, as should Roan Mountain, north along the North Carolina-Tennessee border, one of the most distinctive mountains in the entire Appalachian chain. Roan embraces grassy balds, natural rhododendron gardens, and hillsides covered with flame azalea in the spring and mountain ash in the fall.

Once these areas were protected by their own remoteness; now they must be saved by desire and design. Most of these lands already are in public ownership, the summit of Mount Mitchell as a small state park and the bulk of the remainder in the Pisgah, Nantahala, and Cherokee national forests, where pressures for logging and other commercial uses chronically preempt preservation.

Soils in the highlands are not sufficiently deep or fertile over large enough areas to justify intensive timber management, nor subdivision development on available pockets of private land. But qualities that make these high places a liability for production make them a natural for preservation and compatible human enjoyment.

In 1978 and early 1979 a substantial number of citizens of Yancey County, in the environs of Mount Mitchell, voiced disapproval of the proposed park. "Residents feared future development might have been hampered. The best reason for approval of the Mount Mitchell Park would have been to limit development," editorialized the *Hendersonville Times-News* (on March 24, 1979). "The idea that land should be kept forever wild presents a hard decision to those accustomed to making a living off the land, but the present is not as important as the future and that calls for resources not only to be conserved, but preserved."

In the final analysis, it is impossible to decouple a natural treasure, such as Great Smoky Mountains National Park, from the technological society around it. The accelerated development of the world should give pause and inspire a deeper exploration of the meaning of preservation.

The esthetic experience of release from cares is highly dependent on the context of the outdoors. But a changing context can radically alter, if not destroy, the total experience. There is, of course, more at stake than enjoyment or esthetics. To cite a guest editorial by Merrimon R. Doster, executive secretary of the Franklin Area Chamber of Commerce, appearing in the *Asheville Citizen-Times* of April 9, 1972:

> We cannot let ourselves be lured into swapping our quality of life for any quantity that could possibly result in deterioration of our environment. If a new industry will increase incomes, raise living standards, strengthen our institutions, enhance the quality of life in general, then we want and need it, but if it pollutes a stream—we can't afford it. If it dirties our air—we don't need it. If it defaces a mountain—we cannot tolerate it. If it reduces the dignity of our citizenry—we must fight it to the end.
>
> All our resources are natural—majestic mountains—pure water— clean air—grand scenery, and above all, decent, intelligent people. Our people are the grandest resource we have, for it is within their power and choice to either conserve or destroy all the rest.
>
> If we are to plan for the development of a tourist industry, we must first build the tools with which to work. The last tool to be used must

be the first one developed. This is a method to stop when growth has reached that point of maximum efficiency, where resources are used but not abused. The cold hard fact is ever before us that when our resources are expended they cannot be replaced.

To save the resources—the plants, panthers, soil, scenery, and the rest —through conscious intent constitutes an unselfish act of a generation in keeping faith with itself. It insures a legacy worth passing down, a choice of open options the future has the right to expect.

Bibliography and Notes

References to the Great Smoky Mountains and environs have appeared in written works for more than two hundred years. With due credit to the old chroniclers who saw the natural scene in the raw, and who came face-to-face with the events of history, some of the more recent literature has also proved extremely helpful as source material.

The abundance of source material is partly due to the excellent group of devoted local historians, who have diligently explored maps, court records, and documents, and to the comprehensive collections assembled at such establishments as the Lawson McGhee Library in Knoxville and the North Carolina Room, a unit of the Pack Memorial Public Library, in Asheville. In addition, the very existence of the Great Smoky Mountains National Park has stimulated and crystallized many facets of scholarship, a remarkable development considering the mountain range was so little known by name until the park movement of the 1920s.

Among most recent books these are especially worthy of mention:
The Cades Cove Story, by Randolph A. Shields. Great Smoky Mountains Natural History Association, Gatlinburg, 1977.
Highland Homeland, by Wilma Dykeman and Jim Stokely. Government Printing Office, Washington, D.C., 1978.
Out Under the Sky of the Great Smokies, by Harvey Broome. Greenbrier Press, Knoxville, 1975.
Hiker's Guide to the Great Smokies, by Dick Murlless and Constance Stallings. Sierra Club Books, San Francisco, 1973.
Valley So Wild, by Alberta and Carson Brewer. East Tennessee Historical Society, Knoxville, 1975.

The following books, booklets, and periodicals have been especially helpful and are recommended for popular and practical reading:
Appalachian Trailway News, published by the Appalachian Trail Conference, Washington, D.C.; references in frequent issues.
Birth of a National Park, by Carlos C. Campbell. University of Tennessee Press, Knoxville, 1960.
The Blue Ridge Parkway Guides, by William G. Lord. Stephens Press, Inc., Asheville:
From Asheville to Great Smoky Mountains National Park, 1963.
From Boone-Blowing Rock to Asheville, 1959.
Camping and Woodcraft, by Horace Kephart. Macmillan Company, New York, 1917 (twentieth printing, 1960).
Great Smoky Mountains National Park, by Arthur Stupka. Natural History Handbook Series No. 5, National Park Service, Washington, D.C., 1960.

Hiking in the Great Smoky Mountains, by Carson Brewer. Holston Printing Company, Knoxville, 1962.

Indians of the Americas, by John Collier. W. W. Norton & Company, 1947. (Abridged version, Mentor Books, 1961.)

The Living Wilderness, published by the Wilderness Society, Washington, D.C.; references in frequent issues.

The Names and Lore of the Great Smokies, by Paul M. Fink. Jonesboro, Tennessee, 1956.

National Parks Magazine, published by the National Parks Association, Washington, D.C.; references in frequent issues.

Notes on the Birds of the Great Smoky Mountains, by Arthur Stupka. University of Tennessee Press, Knoxville, 1963.

Our Southern Highlanders, by Horace Kephart. Macmillan Company, New York, 1913 (seventh printing, 1957).

The Travels of William Bartram, Naturalist's Edition, edited by Francis Harper. Yale University Press, New Haven, 1958.

The Winning of the West, by Theodore Roosevelt. G. P. Putnam's Sons, New York, 1889. (Selections, with an introduction by Harvey Wish, Capricorn Books, New York, 1962.)

Trees, Shrubs, and Woody Vines of Great Smoky Mountains National Park, by Arthur Stupka. University of Tennessee Press, Knoxville, 1964.

The following books and booklets have also been useful and will be of help for specialized interests:

The Annals of Haywood County, by W. C. Allen. Waynesville, North Carolina, 1935.

Annals of Tennessee, by J. G. M. Ramsey. Reprint (from the original published in Charleston in 1853) by Kingsport Press, Kingsport, Tennessee, 1926.

"The Cherokee Nation of Indians: A Narrative of their Official Relations with the Colonial and Federal Governments," by Charles C. Royce, *Fifth Annual Report of the Bureau of American Ethnology*, 1883–84. Government Printing Office, Washington, D.C., 1887.

Cherokees of the Old South, by Henry T. Malone. University of Georgia Press, Athens, Georgia, 1956.

Gift from the Hills, by Lucy Morgan, with LeGette Blythe. Bobbs-Merrill, New York, 1958.

Handicrafts of the Southern Highlands, by Allen Eaton. Russell Sage Foundation, New York, 1937.

History of the American Indians, by James Adair, edited by S. C. Williams (from the original published in London in 1775). Watauga Press, Johnson City, Tennessee, 1930.

Steve Mather of the National Parks, by Robert Shankland. Alfred A. Knopf, New York, 1954.

Message from the President of the United States Transmitting a Report of the Secretary of Agriculture in Relation to Forests, Rivers, and

Mountains of the Southern Appalachian Region. Government Printing Office, Washington, D.C., 1902.

My Wilderness, East to Katahdin, by William O. Douglas. Doubleday & Company, New York, 1961.

"Myths of the Cherokee," by James D. Mooney, *Nineteenth Annual Report of the Bureau of American Ethnology,* 1897–98, Part I. Government Printing Office, Washington, D.C., 1900.

North Carolina Guide, edited by Blackwell P. Robinson. University of North Carolina Press, Chapel Hill, North Carolina, 1955.

Old Frontiers: the Story of the Cherokee from Earliest Times to the Date of Their Removal to the West, by John P. Brown. Southern Publishers, Inc., Kingsport, Tennessee, 1938.

A Preliminary Guide to the Greenbrier-Brushy Mountain Nature Trail, by Stanley A. Cain. (Mimeographed) Prepared under the auspices of the Smoky Mountains Hiking Club and the Department of Botany, University of Tennessee, Knoxville, 1937.

Smoky Mountain Folks and Their Lore, by Joseph S. Hall. Norman Printing Company, Asheville, 1960.

Tribes that Slumber, by Thomas M. N. Lewis and Madeline Kneberg. University of Tennessee Press, Knoxville, 1960.

Additional specific references of books, booklets, personal interviews, and correspondence are referred to in the notes below. Where any of the above works are mentioned frequently, the author's name is used to identify the source, such as *Roosevelt, Mooney,* or *Royce. The Message from the President* will be *1902 Forest Report.* The notes, organized by chapters, together with references in the text, will readily identify the major sources. The conventional apparatus is followed in order to provide supplementary information and to identify sources of particular pertinence. The first figure represents the page reference and the second the paragraph. An incomplete paragraph, even a single line, at the head of a page, is counted as the first.

Part One

THE FIRST HALF-BILLION YEARS

I. *Chimney Tops.* Harvey Broome and John Morrell are two principal sources of this chapter and the book, through many hikes, drives, conversations, and correspondence.

5:2. The average annual precipitation atop Clingman's Dome has been measured at 83 inches. A Climatological Survey of the United States Weather Bureau at Gatlinburg Station, covering the years 1921–53, notes that: "Greatest rainfall occurs during the summer primarily in the form of showers and thundershowers, whose formation is aided by rough terrain. A second maximum of precipitation occurs during the winter and early spring in response to the more frequent passage of large-scale storms over the state (Tennessee) during these months. Driest months are in the fall when slow-moving, rain-suppressing high pressure areas are most frequent." Summarizing weather studies over a sixteen-year period, the Survey tabulated the mean number of clear days for one year at 142, partly cloudy days at 114, and cloudy days at 109.

6:1. Writing on "Origins of the Wilderness Society" in *The Living Wilderness* (July 1940), Broome recalls that in August 1934, Robert Marshall, of the United States Forest Service, while on a field trip in the Appalachians, traveled from Knoxville to Clingman's Dome in the company of Broome and Benton MacKaye, a regional planner with the Tennessee Valley Authority. They discussed the need for a new organization to protect established foot trails in the East from the encroachment of motor roads. "But the project agreed upon that afternoon was Bob's broader suggestion for uniting 'all friends of the wilderness.'" Marshall returned to Knoxville in October for a speech at the annual meeting of the American Forestry Association. During a field trip, Broome, MacKaye, Marshall, and Bernard Frank (associate forester of TVA) discussed a statement of principles. A letter dated October 19, 1934, enrolled the four other founders of the Wilderness Society: Harold C. Anderson, Aldo Leopold, Robert Sterling Yard, and Ernest Oberholtzer.

7:3. An interesting report of this trip and the period, "'Pre-Discovery' Visits to the Great Smoky Mountains," by William M. Johnson, appears in the Bulletin of the Potomac Appalachian Trail Club (October 1945).

8:2. According to *Logging* Magazine (Autumn 1916), "Eighteen miles of standard gauge on hewn oak ties separate Townsend from Elkmont. The entire system is laid upon rock ballast and glitters with 36-degree curves with a few 28-degree reverse curves. The road follows the Little River, the roughest, rockiest, and rip-roaringest river in the United States. It is doubtful whether any spot in America can vie with these eighteen miles for scenic splendor, with the single exception of the Grand Canyon of the Colorado."

II. *Approach to Soco Gap.* Reference to ancient Indian events and locations is from *Mooney*, including his glossary of Cherokee words. Description of the Blue Ridge Parkway benefited from the excellent *Blue Ridge Parkway Guides.* General descriptions of Appalachian geology and geography are in "The Great Smoky Mountain Wilderness," by Robert Sterling Yard, *The Living Wilderness*, March 1942; and "North Carolina's Mountains," by Bill Sharpe, *The State*, May 30, 1953. The chapter on "Topography and Geology of the Southern Appalachians" (pp. 111–21) in *1902 Forest Report* presents the surprising amount of knowledge assembled at the turn of the century. The geologic forces are treated in "The Mountains Appear" (pp. 3–6), a chapter of *Natural History Handbook.* An important and detailed technical account by geologists familiar with the area is "Stratigraphy of Ocoee Series, Great Smoky Mountains, Tennessee and North Carolina," by Philip B. King, Jarvis B. Hadley, Robert B. Neuman, and Warren Hamilton, *Bulletin of the Geological Society of America*, August 1958. The interpretation of the evolution of watercourses is based on "Rivers," by Luna B. Leopold, *American Scientist*, December 1962.

18:1. Fraser fir or "balsam" appears very similar to the balsam fir of northern New England and Canada. But the species are distinct. Fraser fir is distinguished from red spruce, its neighbor, by its upright cones and blunt aromatic needles, which are green above and lined with gray below. A scattering of blisters is evident in many of these trees. Red spruce grows to greater height and diameter; its cones are pendant, the sharp-pointed needles are the same shade of green above and below, and bark blisters are never present.

18:1. Atop Richland Balsam, the highest peak in the range, the chiseled figures "6245" are still visible where they were carved in a rock by a Waynesville friend of the geographer Arnold Henry Guyot. Guyot was only slightly off in measuring Richland's elevation, since determined to be 6410 feet.

III. *Bartram.* In pursuit of the affairs of William Bartram, the author visited Nantahala Gorge, the scene of the meeting with Attakullakulla, and the house at No. 106 Tradd Street, in Charleston, built in 1772 by Captain John Stuart. Source material on the Bartrams, father and son, includes: *John Bartram, His Garden and His House*, by Emily Read Chesterton, John Bartram Association, Philadelphia, 1953; *Bartonia*, Proceedings of the Philadelphia Botanical Club, An Account of the Two Hundredth Anniversary of the Founding of the First Botanic Garden in the American Colonies by John Bartram, Philadelphia, 1931; *John Bartram, Farmer-Botanist*, by Stevenson W. Fletcher, John Bartram Association, Philadelphia (mimeographed, undated), and *The World of Washington Irving*, by Van Wyck Brooks, E. P. Dutton & Company, New York, 1944. References to Boone are from *Daniel Boone, Master of the Wilderness*, by John Bakeless, William Morrow & Company, New York, 1939, an outstanding portrayal of frontier times. The principal Cherokee references in this chapter are from *Brown, Mooney,* and *Royce*.

21:3. "As is always the case with tribal geography, there were no fixed boundaries, and on every side the Cherokee frontiers were contested by rival claimants." *Mooney*, p. 14.

"It is impossible at this late date to define with absolute accuracy the original limits of the Cherokee claim. In fact, like all other tribes, they had no definite and concurrent understanding with their surrounding savage neighbors where the possession of one left off and those of the other began. The strength of their title to any particular tract usually decreased in proportion to the increase of the distance from their villages; and it commonly followed, as a result, that a considerable strip of territory between the settlements of two powerful tribes, though eliminated by both, was practically considered as a neutral ground and the common hunting ground of both." *Royce*, p. 140.

22:4. The marker is located on U. S. Highway 19 at Beechertown, between 600 and 700 feet below Tulula Gap, which is on the upper rim of Nantahala Gorge near the headwaters of Tulula Creek. This creek enters Cheoah River, which flows northward to join the Little Tennessee.

22:6. Linnaeus called John Bartram "the greatest natural botanist in the world." In this period, the plants and trees of America were the rage of Europe. Naturalists were dispatched to study and collect specimens. "Whenever I looked to the ground, I everywhere found such plants as I had never seen before," wrote Peter Kalm, a pupil of Linnaeus sent by the Swedish Royal Academy. "When I saw a tree, I was forced to stop and ask those who accompanied me how it was called. I was seized with terror at the thought of ranging so many new and unknown parts of natural history." (*America in 1750: Peter Kalm's Travels in North America*, Wilson Erickson, Inc., New York, 1937.)

24:2. Stuart was born about 1700. He was one of the Scottish colonists who came to Georgia with Oglethorpe in 1733. As a soldier he rose through the ranks; in 1742, during the Spanish invasion of Georgia from Florida, he was placed in command of Fort William on Cumberland Island. While Oglethorpe conquered the main body of Spaniards on St. Simons Island, Stuart successfully repulsed twenty vessels of the invasion fleet. Years later, after Attakullakulla saved his life, Stuart was appointed superintendent of southern tribes, a vital post in frontier diplomacy.

27:3. Ginseng, or "jen-shen," the Oriental root of life, is an ancient Tertiary plant growing naturally only in eastern Asia and in eastern North America. The plant itself is inconspicuous in the shady hardwood forests. It grows about a foot tall, producing three-leaf stalks, each bearing five leaflets. It blooms in mid-summer, with clusters of greenish-yellow flowers, followed in autumn by bright crimson berries. The Chinese believe the root cures a variety of ills, prolongs life, and has aphrodisiac qualities. After the Chinese had decimated their own supplies of jen-shen, European traders became aware of its value. In 1715, it was discovered by the French in Canada, where shipments to the Orient began. As early as 1784, an American ship, the *Empress of China*, departed for Macao with a supply of ginseng in her hold to exchange for tea, ginger, silk, and camphor. An estimated 95 per cent of ginseng currently collected or grown in the United States is exported to the Orient, according to the United States Department of Agriculture. However, during the three-year period 1960–62 such exports averaged only 151,000 pounds of dried root per year. The average price per pound during that period was slightly under $18. It is known as a difficult plant to cultivate.

29:3. Peter J. Hanlon, supervisor, and William Nothstein, staff officer, of North Carolina National Forests, have endeavored to trace Bartram's course. They advise: "Reading of Bartram's book left us in doubt about the route he followed after leaving Cowee. If he was headed for Tulula Gap, he took a long way to get there by going through Wayah Gap and Old Road Gap. To reach Wayah Gap from Burnington Falls, he would have gone through Harrison Gap and down Shingle Tree Branch, or possibly down Arrowwood Creek. It is likely that such a circuitous route was followed so that he could spend nights at Indian villages and cover a wider area for his botanical observations."

IV. *The World Is a Ballroom*. The title of this chapter is derived from *The Cherokee of North Carolina: Living Memorials of the Past*, by William H. Gilbert, Jr., Smithsonian Publication 4289, Washington, D.C., 1956. Dr. Gilbert writes (p. 541): "The so-called Friendship Dance gives one the impression that for the Cherokee all the world is a ballroom and all the men and women merely dancers, each with his exits and entrances. This is in a way a community opera in which the drama and the music induce a state of emotional exaltation which commemorates the ancestors and assures them of the loyalty of the present generation to the principles of the race."

In addition to *Bartram*, another early picture of Indian life was prepared by James Adair, a well-respected Scotch-Irish trader, a keen observer and historian. His work, *History of the American Indians*, was originally published in London in 1775. *Memoirs of Lieutenant Henry Timberlake, 1756–1765*, originally published in London in 1765, reprinted (Samuel Cole Williams, editor) by the Watauga Press in 1927, and by Continental Book Company, Marietta, Georgia, 1948, presents the recollections of a young Virginia officer who spent several months in the Cherokee Overhill settlements and afterward conducted two delegations of Cherokee leaders to England. His work includes a map on which he located Ford Loudoun, Chote and outlines the course of what is now called Abrams Creek draining Cades Cove in the Great Smokies.

Other sources that have been especially helpful in this chapter include: *Notes on the State of Virginia*, by Thomas Jefferson, edited by William Peden, University of North Carolina Press, Chapel Hill, North Carolina, 1955; *The Eastern Cherokees*, by William H. Gilbert, Jr. (based on John Howard Payne manuscripts in Newberry Library, Chicago), Bureau of American Ethnology Publication 133, Washington, D.C., 1943; *Oconaluftee Indian Village*, an interpretation of a Cherokee community of 1750 (mimeographed), compiled and written for the Cherokee Historical Association by Thomas M. N. Lewis and Madeline Kneberg, Cherokee, North Carolina, 1954; and "Burial Mounds of the Northern Section of the United States," by Cyrus Thomas, in the *Fifth Annual Report of the Bureau of American Ethnology*, Washington, D.C., 1887. "Indian Trails in the Southeast," by William E. Myer, in the *Forty-second Annual Report of the Bureau of American Ethnology*, Washington, D.C., 1928, covers the Great Indian Warpath and its several branches.

37:1. The Portuguese narrative of De Soto's expedition, with the word Achelaque, was published in 1557. A French document of 1699 refers to the "Cheraqui." Cherokee has been an English form at least since 1708.

37:2. Adair theorized that the Cherokee were remnants of the "lost tribes of Israel." John Haywood (*Civil and Political History of Tennessee*, Knoxville, 1823; Methodist Publishing House, Nashville, 1891) thought they were a tribe from southern Asia or the ancient Near East who settled on the lower Mississippi and then were merged with a savage people from the north. "The Cherokee tribe has long been a puzzling factor to students of ethnology and North American languages," wrote Professor Cyrus Thomas. "Whether to be considered an abnormal offshoot from one of the well-known Indian stocks or families of North America, or the remnant of some undetermined or almost extinct family which has merged into another, appear to be questions yet unsettled." He felt he had traced them as a mound-building group to the upper reaches of the Ohio River and to the Mississippi River and its upper sources near Lake Superior. John R. Swanton later classified the Cherokee as a subtype of the Creek, based on art motifs and basketry of southern origin. "The danger of inferring racial movements from cultural evidence is likely to be present here, however," comments Dr. Gilbert, "and we must hold in reserve our final judgment as to the origin of the Cherokee and his civilization."

40:5. Among his achievements, Bartram presented in *The Travels* a complete list of birds known to him as inhabiting the country from Pennsylvania to Florida and west to the mountains; it was considered the first major worthy ornithological endeavor by a native-born American.

V. *Little Carpenter.* Attakullakulla is described in *Old Frontiers.* He was well known to leading contemporaries of his day and appears in many accounts, including one written by Felix Walker, friend and follower of Daniel Boone. Walker observed Attakullakulla closely at the treaty-signing with Richard Henderson. Later Walker settled on the North Carolina side of the Great Smokies (see Chapter VI). The family connections of Cherokee leaders are drawn from the research and writing of Lewis and Kneberg (both formerly of the Department of Anthropology at the University of Tennessee) for the Cherokee Historical Association. The official version of De Soto's itinerary is contained in the *Final Report of the United States De Soto Expedition Commission,* 76th Congress, first session, House Executive Document 71, Washington, D.C., 1939.

45:2. *The Narrative* was published at Evora in 1557 and translated from the Portuguese by Richard Hakluyt, of London, in 1609. *Royce* notes (pp. 135–36) that the expedition traveled through the province of "Chalaque" northward for five days until he reached the province of "Xualla." "The earliest map upon which I have found 'Chalaqua' located is that of 'Florida et Apalache' by Cornelius Wytfliet, in 1597. This location is based upon the narrative of De Soto's expedition, and is fixed a short distance east of the Savannah River and immediately south of the Appalachian Mountains. 'Xualla' is placed to the west of and near the headwaters of the 'Secco' or Savannah River." Considering the many ideas and conjecture regarding De Soto's travels, an official Federal commission undertook to review all evidence. The commission, headed by Dr. John R. Swanton, presented its final report in 1939; it resolved that the Spanish party traveled through Georgia, Tennessee, and Alabama and encountered Cherokee Indians—though not as far north as the Great Smokies.

49:6. Captain Stuart married Susannah Emory, quarter-breed granddaughter of the pioneer trader Ludovic Grant. They had one son, who inherited from his father the bushy shock of red hair, and was called Oo-no-dota, Bushyhead. His son, Reverend Jesse Bushyhead, led one of the emigrant bands to the West in 1838. (See p. 92).

VI. *The Early Settlers.* The principal sources for the patterns of settlement down the Great Valley; descriptions of backwoods society, and of the Virginia-Tennessee military expedition, were *Ramsey* and *Roosevelt.* Also helpful were *William Byrd's Natural History of Virginia,* edited by Richard C. Beatty and William J. Mulloy, Dietz Press, Richmond, Virginia, 1940; *Early Travels in the Tennessee Country,* by Samuel C. Williams, Watauga Press, Johnson City, Tennessee, 1928; *Lost State of Franklin,* by Samuel C. Williams, Watauga Press, Johnson City, Tennessee, 1924; *Conquest of the Old Southwest,* by Archibald Rutledge, Century Company, New York, 1920. The battle of King's Mountain is covered, additionally, in "Patrick Ferguson's Rifle," by John Scofield, in *The American Rifleman,* December 1941; *King's Mountain,* National Park Service Historical Handbook Series No. 22, Washington, D.C., 1955; and *American Revolution 1775–1783,* by John Richard Alden, Harper and Brothers, New York, 1954.

60:3. John Heckwelder, a Moravian missionary, was astounded by settlers who told him: "An Indian has no more soul than a buffalo; to kill either is the same thing, and when you have killed an Indian, you have done a good act, and have killed a wild beast." Pioneers occasionally fed dead Indians to their dogs "to make them fierce." On the other hand, red hunters tortured their enemies to death as part of a public ritual, hoping also to face torture bravely themselves.

60:4. White desperadoes made nearly as much trouble as the Indians; for the frontier attracted people who were rejected by society, as well as those going out to build a democratic frontier society. Horse thieves were active; plundering of one kind led to plundering of another kind.

65:2. Various accounts, including *Roosevelt,* state that Sevier led his horsemen "through the deep defiles and among the towering peaks of the Great Smoky Mountains." Such an incredible feat, according to Paul M. Fink, was highly unlikely at that time. *Ramsey's* account indicates that Sevier's forces skirted the eastern boundaries of the Smokies, then crossed the Balsam Mountains at Balsam Gap and followed the headwaters of the Tuckasegee River to the Indian towns.

66:5. Sevier was found corresponding with the Spanish about a loan to keep the state of Franklin solvent at a time when Spain was trying to undermine American settlement west of the Mississippi by inciting the Indians and encouraging union with the westerners.

68:1. Blount was born in North Carolina in 1749, served as a paymaster during the American Revolution, and represented North Carolina at the Constitutional Convention of 1787. Despite qualities of "great address, courtly manners, benignant feelings, and a most commanding presence," attributed to him by the historian Ramsey, he was impeached July 7, 1797. Besides conspiring to wage war with Spain in favor of Great Britain, he was accused of attempting to incite the Cherokee against Spain and the United States. His trial lasted from December 17, 1798 to January 14, 1799.

69:2. Walker gave the word "Buncombe" to the English language during a debate on the floor of the House of Representatives in Washington. While his colleagues wanted to shut off discussion and proceed to other business,

Walker insisted upon "speaking up for Buncombe"—on the grounds that his constituents expected him to do so.

VII. *Lonely Cathedrals.* The journeys of Bishop Asbury are detailed in his *Journals and Letters,* edited by Elmer T. Clark and others, Abingdon Press, Nashville, Tennessee, 1958 (first published in entirety in 1821). The best description of the old Cataloochee Trail is a report submitted to the superintendent of the Great Smoky Mountains National Park in 1940, entitled "The Cataloochee Aboriginal Trail and Its Uses and Development by White People," by Hiram C. Wilburn. Portions of the trail were retraced and unearthed by Mr. Wilburn and Mark Hannah, park ranger of the Cataloochee district. Description of settlement on the North Carolina side was aided by "Pioneer History of the Great Smoky Mountains National Park," by Robert Lambert, a report to the superintendent, 1957; and on the Tennessee side by "Settlement and Early History of the Coves of Blount County, Tennessee," by Inez Burns, the East Tennessee Historical Society Publications, September 1959, Knoxville. "A Brief History of Methodists in Haywood County," by Reverend T. F. Glenn, appearing in *The Annals of Haywood County,* recalls camp meetings of the countryside. Material on firearms is from *Rifle Making in the Great Smoky Mountains,* by Arthur I. Kendall, National Park Service Popular Study Series, History No. 13, Washington, D.C., (undated). Old pioneer craft ways are from *Vegetable Dyeing,* by Mrs. Emma Conley, Penland School of Handicrafts, Inc., Penland, North Carolina, plus personal interviews with crafts authorities, notably Miss Lucy Morgan, Webster, North Carolina, and Douglas Ferguson, Pigeon Forge, Tennessee. John Parris, newspaper columnist, has written many interesting articles on old ways and beliefs in the *Asheville Citizen* and *Citizen-Times,* collected in *Roaming the Mountains,* Citizen-Times Publishing Company, Asheville, 1955, and *My Mountains, My People,* Citizen-Times Publishing Company, Asheville, 1957.

73:4. Bishop McKendree, of the Tennessee Conference, was the first native-born Methodist bishop and one of the founders of the Camp Meeting Movement. He hoped to Christianize the Indians. The Reverend Boehm was the son of Martin Boehm, one of the founders of the United Brethren Church.

74:3. "Shook was powerfully converted after the old-fashioned Methodist style," according to Reverend T. F. Glenn (*The Annals of Haywood County,* p. 218). "Whilst under deep conviction for sin, he went out into the cornfield to plow. He prayed and wept as he worked. Finally the burden of guilt was lifted and his soul was flooded with joy. He shouted and praised the Lord as he continued to work. He dropped the lines, left his plow, lost his hat, and shouted all over the field. That was a happy, triumphant day for the new convert, but the horse played havoc with his corn."

78:4. Thomas letter book, 1839–40; Terrell papers, Duke University Library.

79:2. Toll rates listed in Acts passed by the General Assembly, state of North Carolina, 1831–32, pp. 82–84.

VIII. *Genius of the Species.* The advancement of the Indians in their "civilizing period" of the early nineteenth century is extremely well told in *Cherokees of the Old South.* Mooney, as in all periods covered by him, is a principal source. Charles Lanman, the secretary to Daniel Webster, who visited the Smoky Mountains in 1848 and spent several weeks with Will Thomas, discussed varied aspects of Indian life, and Yonaguska in particular, in his *Letters from the Allegheny Mountains,* New York, 1849. Three biographies worth noting are *Sequoyah,* by Grant Foreman, University of Oklahoma Press, Norman, Oklahoma, 1938; *The Raven, Story of Sam Houston,* by Marquis James, Bobbs-Merrill, New York, 1929; and *Andrew Jackson, Border Captain,* by Marquis James, Bobbs-Merrill, New York, 1933.

81:2. Article Fourteen of the Treaty of Hopewell represented a new departure for the white man, too. It pledged: "That the Cherokee nation may be led to a greater degree of civilization, and to become herdsmen and cultivators, instead of remaining in a state of hunters, the United States will, from time to time, furnish gratuitously the said nation with useful implements of husbandry. . . ."

81:3. Roosevelt's *The Winning of the West* has done little for the image of the Indian in the patina of history. In the preface he stressed that for him it was "emphatically a labor of love to write of the great deeds of the border people." Essentially, he admired frontier heroics and the physically elite; as a historian, he associated himself with contestants who appealed to him. As he stated in the preface, "We guarded our herds of branded cattle and shaggy horses, hunted bear, bison, elk, and deer, established civil government, and put down evil-doers, white and red, on the banks of the Little Missouri and among the wooded, precipitous foot-hills of the Bighorn, exactly as did the pioneers who a hundred years ago built their log cabins beside the Kentucky or in the valleys of the Great Smokies." Though conceding that wrongs were committed against the Cherokee (as well as the Nez Percé in the West), Roosevelt derided defenders of the Indians—"the weaker race"—as being "foolish sentimentalists."

85:5. Charles Lanman in his *Letters* stretched the trance into fifteen days, with the 1200 Indians marching around the sleeping chieftain.

86:2. A daughter of Yonaguska, named Kata'lsta, survived until James Mooney's day. See Chapter XI.

90:2, 3. The Cherokee Nation *vs.* the state of Georgia (1831) and Samuel A. Worcester *vs.* The state of Georgia (1832) are found in the United States Supreme Court Reports, 5 Peters 15–18 and 6 Peters 559–61. The momentous judicial decisions by which the diminishing power of the Indians was adjusted to the framework of American law resulted largely from the work of Chief Justice John Marshall.

90:6. ". . . Mr. Schermerhorn's apparent design was to conceal the real number present and to impose on the public and the government upon this point. The delegation taken to Washington by Mr. Schermerhorn had no more authority to make a treaty than any other dozen Cherokee accidentally picked up for the purpose. I now warn you and the President that if this paper of Schermerhorn's called a treaty is sent to the Senate and ratified you will bring trouble upon the government and eventually destroy this (the Cherokee) nation. The Cherokee are a peaceable, harmless people, but you may drive them to desperation, and this treaty cannot be carried into effect except by the strong arm of force." Major W. M. Davis to the Secretary of War; quoted by Edward Everett in the United States House of Representatives, May 31, 1838; *Royce*, pp. 284–85.

91:3. Memorial to Dudley, April 3, 1837, E. B. Dudley Papers, North Carolina Archives, Raleigh.

91:3. *Mooney* lists, on the basis of his personal investigation, the other four forts in North Carolina as: Fort Scott, at Aquone, up the Nantahala River from Fort Lindsay, in Macon County; Fort Hembrie, at Hayesville, Clay County; Fort Delaney, at Valleytown, Cherokee County, and Fort Butler, at Murphy, also in Cherokee County.

IX. *Professor Guyot Charts the Hills.* The life and accomplishments of Professor Guyot are comprehensively reviewed in "Memoir of Arnold Guyot, 1807–1884," by James D. Dana, *Biographical Memoirs of the National Academy of Science,* Vol. 2, 1886 (read before the National Academy April 21, 1886), reprinted from the Smithsonian Report for 1886–87 as Smithsonian Publication No. 707, Washington, D.C., 1889. One should also read Professor Guyot's own expressions of his early adventures in "Memoir of Louis Agassiz, 1807–1873," by Arnold Guyot, *Biographical Memoirs of the National Academy of Science,* Vol. 2, 1886 (read April 1878). A major contribution to Smoky Mountains material is *Arnold Guyot's Notes on the Geography of the Mountain District of Western North Carolina,* by Myron H. Avery and Kenneth S. Boardman, Publication No. 10, Appalachian Trail Conference (reprinted from *North Carolina Historical Review,* Vol. XV, 1938), Washington, D.C., 1938. Other Guyot sources employed in this chapter: *Meteorology,* by Marcus Benjamin, Smithsonian Publication No. 1086, Washington, D.C., 1897; "Arnold Guyot, Teacher of Geography," by Robert L. Anstey, *Journal of Geography,* December 1958. "With Professor Guyot on Mounts Washington and Carrigan in 1857," by S. Hastings Grant, *Appalachia,* June 1907; and "Arnold Guyot's Explorations in the Great Smokies," by Myron H. Avery and Paul Fink, *Appalachia,* December 1936.

For place names of the Great Smokies, the foremost expert is Paul M. Fink, whose extensive writings include: "Smoky Mountains History as told in Place Names," in two parts, *Bulletin Appalachian Trail Club,* October 1935, and January 1936; "Early Explorers in the Great Smokies" (read before East Tennessee Historical Society, May 6, 1932), in three parts, *Bulletin Appalachian Trail Club,* April 1937, June 1937, January 1938; *The Nomenclature of the Great Smoky Mountains* (with Myron H. Avery), East Tennessee Historical Society Publication No. 9, Knoxville, 1937, and *The Names and Lore of the Great Smokies.* In the case of landmark called Charlie's Bunion, the author was aided by a personal interview with Charlie Conner, for whom it was named. Through the courtesy of Dr. Kelly Bennett, of Bryson City, it was possible to obtain an extremely useful unpublished manuscript by Horace Kephart on "Origin of Place Names of the Great Smoky Mountains," accompanying correspondence of February 1929, with Will C. Barnes, Secretary, United States Geographic Board, and correspondence of June 1930, with Verne Rhoades, Secretary, North Carolina Park Commission. Sources on Thomas Lanier Clingman included the *North Carolina Guide* and "The Man for Whom They Named Clingman's Dome," *Raleigh News & Observer*, September 29, 1957. An intriguing book is the *Autobiography of Joseph Le Conte*, D. Appleton and Company, New York, 1903; unfortunately, despite the prominence of the peak named for him, Professor Le Conte had very minor bearing on the Great Smokies.

98:2. "Nature was his main teacher," wrote Guyot of Agassiz. "From her he knew God as a personal mind; all wise, all powerful. Each specific form or plant to him was a thought of God. The life system was God's connected system of thought, realized by His power in time and space."

98:2. In tribute to the epochal achievement of Agassiz and his glacial theory, Guyot wrote: "By his sagacity, he found glaciation where it was not suspected before; pointed it out to the astonished and unbelieving English geologists on their own soil; found it in North America, traced it with undoubted evidence in the temperate regions of South America, and believed, though hardly with sufficient reason, that he had seen it on the vast plains of the Amazon. He proved the phenomenon to be well nigh universal."

100:3. One of the first Americans to engage in systematic weather observations was John Bartram. At the time of Dr. Joseph Henry's proposal "to organize a system of observations which shall extend as far as possible over the North American continent," various scattered meteorological studies were already underway. Guyot has sometimes been called the "father of the Weather Bureau." This is not quite true. Before Guyot, a scientist employed by the War Department and the Navy, Professor James P. Espey (known as the "Storm King"), co-operated with the Smithsonian in starting its observation system in 1849.

100:3. The volume of meteorological tables (Smithsonian Publication No. 538) went through four editions under Guyot's direction until 1884. It was widely used by physicists and meteorologists in the United States and Europe.

101:2. Another, and the highest peak named Mount Guyot is 12,305 feet, located in Tulare County, California.

102:3. One of the three North Carolina commissioners was Colonel Robert S. Love, of Waynesville, founder of the great land speculation. In 1834 he was kicked by a horse and was crippled until his death in 1845.

102:4. Guyot presented his classes, an upper-class elective, on the first floor of the Library Building, now Stanhope Hall. In his memory, a new building, Guyot Hall, housing the departments of geology and biology, and the museum he founded, was dedicated in 1909. In front of Nassau Hall, a polished boulder four feet wide, three feet high, and three feet deep bears this inscription: "Glacial boulder from Neuchâtel, Switzerland. Presented in 1890 in memory of Arnold Guyot by his former students at the University of Neuchâtel."

102:4. Clingman was a heroic-tragic figure. Born in Huntersville, North Carolina, in 1812, he was graduated from the University of North Carolina at the head of his class, and was chosen at the age of twenty-three to represent his home county, Surry, in the state legislature. After moving to Asheville, he was elected to the state Senate and, starting in 1843, to five consecutive terms in Congress. In 1858 Clingman was appointed to a vacant seat in the United States Senate and was elected to a full term two years later. However, at the outbreak of the Civil War he joined the 25th North Carolina Volunteers as a colonel, serving later as a brigadier general. As dramatically as his star had risen in youth, so did it decline following the Civil War. He died homeless and impoverished in Morganton, November 3, 1897–in the same city and but four years after his contemporary, Will Thomas.

104:1. Little is known in the environs of the Great Smokies about Professor Le Conte, for whom a peak of major prominence is named. He was born in 1823 on a coastal plantation near Midway, Georgia, of a large, science-minded family. After graduating from the University of Georgia in 1841, he became a physician but presently discovered his tastes were "more scientific than practical." He went to Cambridge, Massachusetts, to become a student of Agassiz in geology and zoology. "Think of the galaxy of stars in Harvard at that time!" he wrote many years later in his autobiography. "Agassiz, Guyot, Wyman, Gray, Peirce, Longfellow, Lowell, Holmes and Felton–with all of whom I was on the most intimate terms. . . . The effect of this intellectual atmosphere was in the highest degree stimulating, giving incredible impulse to thought." In his autobiography, he made absolutely no reference to the Great Smokies by any name, or to a personal experience relating to them. "The summer of 1858 was spent by my brother's family and my own at Flat Rock, North Carolina. This beautiful place is the summer resort of some of the most cultured families of Charleston and the low countries generally, some of whom have here charming houses and grounds, with fountains, artificial lakes, etc. We were often invited to dine with those delightful people. I took advantage of this opportunity to visit Asheville, to climb Black Mountain [Mount Mitchell] the highest peak of the Appalachians, 6710 feet high, and to run down the French Broad River. The scenery in this region, in which Biltmore was subsequently located, is the finest I have yet seen in the United States." (p. 174) In 1869 he joined the staff of the new University of California, beginning many outdoor and scientific adventures in the western mountains. He was a prolific popular and scholarly writer on many subjects, including geology, optics, evolution, and medicine. He was elected president of the American Association for the Advancement of Science, and also of the Geological Society of America. Professor Le Conte was so popular a classroom figure that, starting in 1895, when he was seventy-two, his students made an annual practice of commemorating his birthday by decorating his lecture table with gifts (variously including a portrait of Agassiz, flowers, and valuable works of art). He was an active, enthusiastic member of the Sierra Club; he died in 1901, as he might have wished, while on a hiking trip with the club in the Yosemite country.

107:2. "He [Clingman] caused Mr. Collins to cut a path of six miles to the top, which enabled me to carry there the first horse, kindly loaned me by Col. Robert G. A. Love, that was ever seen on these heights. It would seem natural that the names of the three gentlemen of the party and not only one should be recalled as being applied to the three highest peaks that comprise this group. The central or highest peak is therefore designated as Clingman's Dome, the south peak next in height as Mount Buckley, the north peak as Mount Love." Guyot in a letter to the *Asheville News*, July 18, 1860.

111:3. Avery and Boardman were intrigued by the conclusion of the manuscript, on the "Military Importance of the Southern Mountain Region," in which Guyot urged the Government to seize the entire mountain region and available passes in order to thwart the Confederacy. In 1863 the United States Coast Survey did indeed publish a map, "Mountain Region of North Carolina and Tennessee," with a legend acknowledging that the "mountains and interior valleys of western North Carolina are primarily from a map furnished by Professor Arnold Guyot, the result of his explorations of that region during the summers of 1856, '59 and '60."

111:4. Professor Dana felt that Guyot never received full credit for his work and original conclusions, chiefly because of difficulty of setting down his ideas in English and securing proper publication. Like the *Notes on Geography of the Mountain District*, he left much work incomplete. "It is well known to most members of the Appalachian Mountain Club," he wrote to that group in 1879, "that ever since 1849 I have devoted the greater part of my summer vacations to the investigation of the Appalachian system, and to the measurement of its altitudes from New Hampshire to Georgia. The larger number of the results obtained, however, still await a full publication, which has thus far been prevented from the want of the necessary leisure for a final revision."

X. *Rise and Fall of Little Will*. For many years the principal source of information for inquiries into the affairs of Thomas has been *Mooney*. The ethnologist conducted several interviews with the so-called "white chief," in his lucid moments, and with persons intimately associated with him, including Captain James D. Terrell. Students have also drawn from the accounts of other contemporaries: Charles Lanman, who spent several weeks in Quallatown on his tour of the southern states in 1848 and apparently made several excursions into the Smokies with Thomas; Thomas' daughter, Mrs. A. C. Avery, who wrote a sketch about him in the *University of North Carolina* Magazine, May 1899, six years after his death, and Colonel William Stringfield, his brother-in-law and comrade-in-arms of the Thomas Legion, many of whose recollections appear in *The Annals of Haywood County*.

However, in 1956 Miss Mattie Russell, of the staff of the Duke University Library, completed a doctoral thesis entitled *William Holland Thomas, White Chief of the North Carolina Cherokees*. It served to introduce a substantial amount of valuable material unavailable in the sources mentioned above. Miss Russell has done extensive research into official documents and communications: the incomplete diary which Thomas maintained from 1833 to 1863; a file of his letters and account books, many of which were collected by Dr. W. E. Bird, of Cullowhee, and deposited in the Manuscript Division of the Duke University Library, as well as the papers of James D. Terrell, which are also at Duke University. Through the courtesy of the Cherokee Historical Association, the author has had the opportunity to review Miss Russell's thesis, the value of which is herewith acknowledged. Finally, a document of Thomas' own authorship was made available by George M. Stephens, of Asheville. This is the *Explanation of the Rights of the North Carolina Cherokee Indians*, submitted to the Attorney General of the United States in Washington City in 1851. In 1947, the Stephens Press made a facsimile reproduction of 500 copies of this rare booklet, and then destroyed the plates.

114:2. Certificate from Land Commissioners, October 16, 1820; Cherokee Lands Sale Book, 1820–29. Both in North Carolina Archives, Raleigh.

114:3. According to the 1850 census, Thomas ranked second in land ownership in Haywood County to James R. Love. By 1869, he held deed to approximately 115,407 acres in North Carolina, probably including the 50,000 acres belonging to the Cherokee. Deed from Thomas to William Johnston, June 30, 1869, Thomas papers; *Royce*, p. 315.

115:3. *Explanation of the Rights*, p. 5.

116:3. Occasionally he would remain with the Cherokee in council all night, then proceed to Washington via a combination of horseback, train, and boat. On one return trip from the Capital, his diary shows the following itinerary: At 8 A.M. on March 9, 1858, he left Washington for Baltimore, from which port he sailed aboard the steamer *North Carolina* at 5 P.M. After being seasick all night, he landed at Norfolk at daybreak, March 10, then transferring to the railroad at Portsmouth. On reaching Raleigh, he conferred with the Governor, and remained in the state capital until shortly after daylight. He proceeded to Charlotte, and from there rode until 8 P.M. of the following day before reaching Asheville for the night. Next day he rode to James R. Love's at Waynesville, and finally arrived home at Cherokee on March 14.

116:4. Contract among Thomas, Schermerhorn, and Benjamin F. Curry, May 20, 1836, Thomas papers.

118:3. Letter from Lieutenant Andrew Jackson Smith, November 5, 1838; General Winfield Scott, November 6, 1838; letters of Colonel W. S. Foster, in *Historical Register and Dictionary of the United States Army*, 1903, p. 894; report of T. Hartley Crawford, February 22, 1844; *Washington Globe*, issues of November 17, 1838 and January 4, 1839.

118:5. *Royce*, p. 258, quoting letter of War Department to Hugh Montgomery, Cherokee agent, May 27, 1828, and to General William Carroll, May 30, 1829.

119:6. The claim was taken through the Indian commissioner and finally to Congress, where it died in 1846, Senate document 120, p. 788; Thomas account book, 1836–37; Russell thesis, p. 95.

120:3. Thomas to Gilpin, March 25, 1840 (Thomas papers).

122:4. Execution dockets, Superior Court, *Russell*, p. 217.

123:1. *Russell*, p. 258.

124:4. *Mooney;* Thomas to Breckinridge, April 27, 1862 (*Russell,* p. 217).

125:3. R. B. Vance to Thomas, November 4, 1863.

127:1. *O. R. Series,* Vol. XXXII, pp. 75–76; Thomas to A. T. Davidson, January 22, 1864.

127:2. *O. R. Series,* Vol. XXXII, p. 137.

127:4. Charges drawn at headquarters, 65th North Carolina Regiment near Kinston, May 11, 1864; *Russell,* p. 388; Vance to Seddon, December 13, 1864; Vance letter book, 1863–65, pp. 308–09.

128:2. Testimony in the "Matter of Arbitration between James R. Thomas, guardian of W. H. Thomas, and R. V. Welch and the heirs at law of James R. Love," Thomas papers.

130:1. Joe Jennings, longtime student of Indian history and former superintendent of the Cherokee Reservation in North Carolina, in a letter to the author provides this pertinent observation: "The validity of the statements in this appeal are, I think, questionable. Thomas' financial affairs were in such a tangle, particularly those connected with the purchase of Indian land, that I doubt he could have given the Indians a clear title even if he had been completely sane. The Report of the Commissioner of Indian Affairs for 1869 contains a report of S. H. Sweatland, the United States special agent who visited the settlements of the North Carolina Cherokee for the purpose of bringing the tribal roll up-to-date, and making payments to those entitled to be on the roll (pp. 452–59). This report shows that Thomas regularly received 10 per cent of all the money distributed; it also shows that some Indians in Cherokee County had received from Thomas deeds for their land, some had received bonds, and some had received only memoranda."

130:2. Section 3 of the Act of July 27, 1868, reads: "And be it further enacted, that the Secretary of the Interior shall cause the Commissioner of Indian Affairs to take the same supervisory charge of the Eastern Band of North Carolina Cherokees as of other tribes of Indians." This provision recognized their existence as a tribe and brought about a clear title of present land holdings.

130:4. Although the Indian claims supposedly were resolved by the suits of 1874, between the time of the award and the execution and recording of deeds, many of the title papers were strangely lost or otherwise went astray. New grants were obtained from the state of North Carolina by white people who had settled on part of these lands. New suits had to be instituted by the Federal Government to recover portions of these lands for the Indians. (House document 128, 53rd Congress, 2nd session, p. 4.) In 1894, Congress appropriated $68,000 to settle the title to the lands in the Qualla Boundary.

XI. *Mooney as More than Footnote.* The biographical material is partly from the memorial article, "James Mooney" (unsigned, though by John R. Swanton), in *American Anthropologist,* Vol. 24, No. 22, 1922. However, the reports of the Director of the Bureau of American Ethnology treat with "Work of James R. Mooney," in the *Tenth Annual Report,* 1888–89;

Eleventh Annual Report, 1889–90; *Twelfth Annual Report,* 1890–91; and *Thirty-sixth Annual Report,* 1914–15. In addition to his classic "Myths of the Cherokee," appearing in the *Nineteenth Annual Report,* other major writings of Mooney include "Sacred Formulas of the Cherokee," in the *Seventh Annual Report,* 1885–86, and "The Ghost Dance Religion," in the *Fourteenth Annual Report.*

The Cherokee outlook toward religion in the present day is dealt with in *Cherokees at the Crossroads,* by John Gulick, Institute for Research in Social Science, University of North Carolina, Chapel Hill, North Carolina, 1960. This study was made by a group of ten persons, mostly anthropologists, with support from the Ford Foundation from June 1956, through August 1958.

135:3. James Blythe served also as Indian agent, apparently the only Cherokee ever appointed by the Government to the position.

141:1. "The secretiveness of the Indian doctors is perhaps one reason why discussion of them among the people seems to be difficult and to cause uneasiness. Combined with this is the apparently common belief that Indian doctors do, or can, practice black magic and witchcraft." *Cherokees at the Crossroads,* p. 96.

Part Two

THE CIVILIZED AGE

XII. *Horace Kephart.* Those who knew Horace Kephart intimately shared their candid recollections for the preparation of this chapter. George Kephart, Chief Forester of the Bureau of Indian Affairs, was interviewed in his Washington office on the family life in St. Louis and subsequent long estrangement. Helen Angel, the late Stanley W. Black, Dr. Kelly Bennett, Granville Calhoun, all of Bryson City, reviewed his life and times in the community. Other sources were Horace M. Albright, Walter Damtoft, John O. Morrell, William T. Rolen, and George M. Stephens (the last on both Kephart and George Masa). In addition were the revealing writings of Horace Kephart. One little known is entitled, "Horace Kephart by Himself," an autobiographical sketch published in the *North Carolina Library Bulletin,* June 1922; privately reprinted in 100 numbered copies in 1923, by I. K. Stearns, at Bryson City.

146:1. The respect shown to mules by southern farmers and mountaineers is borne out by statistics. In 1900 the United States had a total of 3,000,000 mules. In 1950 the total had declined to 2,000,000, and in 1960 to 1,300,000, but of those still remaining 90 per cent were in the ten southern states. Enthusiasts of the mule believe the horse is inclined to overeat and to founder when the going is rough. The mule, on the other hand, is considered wise enough to avoid overwork; the animal is viewed as being an exponent of good judgment, rather than of stubbornness.

147:5. ". . . During the great number of years that he spent living out in the open, he brought a keen and trained mind to the study of each day's incidents and experiences, and the solutions of problems as they arose; and he thereby gained a wealth of knowledge and outdoor 'instinct' possessed by few other men of his time. His books on different phases of outdoor living are the most widely read and quoted of any in this field." *American Rifleman*, June 1931.

150:1. Miss Mary Noailles Murfree (1850–1922), of Murfreesboro, Tennessee, spent most of her summers at Beersheba in the Cumberland Mountains, but apparently also visited Cades Cove. *The Prophet of the Great Smoky Mountains* was published in 1885. For an evaluation of Miss Murfree's pioneer role in regional literature, see *Times of Melville and Whitman*, by Van Wyck Brooks.

150:3. The Adams Mine was owned by Walter Scott Adams, of New York, who established a copper industry on Sugar Fork in 1899. Later, the Fontana Copper Mine, centered on Eagle Creek, was operated by the Tennessee Copper Company, which shipped the raw materials to its plant at Ducktown, Tennessee; this operation continued from 1926 to 1944, when Fontana Lake was impounded. See further reference on p. 378.

154:1. "Despite her skill as a novelist, Miss Murfree was not entirely successful in representing the speech of the Smoky mountaineer. With allowance for the years which have passed and the changes which a dialect may undergo, it is still difficult to believe that the people of the Smokies ever spoke quite as she makes them. Kephart, too, is disappointing, despite his manifest absorption in the speech of the hills-man and the abundant linguistic observations contained in his note-books. He seems to have been impressed particularly by what would look like good dialect on paper. . . . These journals, however, are valuable as testimony of linguistic conditions in Swain County and often confirm the existence of forms in the Smokies which have now become rare or obsolete." *The Phonetics of Great Smoky Mountain Speech*, by Joseph S. Hall, King's Crown Press, Columbia University Press, New York, 1942, pp. 3–4. Hall visited the Smokies in 1937 and in 1939–40 on a Columbia University fellowship and with aid from the National Park Service; he conducted a systematic, valley-by-valley study of speech patterns.

155:1. Kephart reached his peak of fame in the early and mid-twenties. In the foreword preceding his article, "Horace Kephart by Himself," in the *North Carolina Library Bulletin*, the editors explained: "The autobiographical sketch was prepared at the request of the Library Commission. An appeal was made to Mr. Kephart for material to meet the demands of the study clubs, and later for a more complete sketch for inclusion in the *Bulletin*. North Carolinians have been keenly interested in Mr. Kephart since the publication of *Our Southern Highlanders*. His early reading experiences and his library career will be of special interest to librarians."

160:3. He died without money. His friends formed the Horace Kephart Memorial Association in order "to satisfy an indebtedness upon the estate" and to assume responsibility for the Kephart library and camping collection, which later were deposited at park headquarters in Gatlinburg.

XIII. *The Loggers' Day.* The best work by far on the general subject of this chapter is the 1902 *Forest Report*, a classic study of the resources of Appalachia. Anyone interested in this period of this region should also consult

Breaking New Ground, by Gifford Pinchot, Harcourt Brace and Company, New York, 1947, and *The Biltmore Story,* by Carl Alwin Schenck, American Forest Historical Foundation, St. Paul, 1955. The specific area of the Great Smokies is covered in *Logging in the Great Smoky Mountains,* by Robert S. Lambert, a report to the park superintendent (typescript), 1958, 1960, and *Logging on Little River, 1890–1940,* by Robert S. Lambert, East Tennessee Historical Society Publications, 1961. The history of the principal logging company of the area is contained in *This is Champion,* Champion Paper and Fibre Company, Hamilton, Ohio, 1959. Interesting observations are found in "Appalachian Comeback," *Yearbook of Agriculture,* United States Department of Agriculture, Washington, D.C., 1949. The author was privileged to interview Walter Damtoft, the early chief forester of Champion Paper and Fibre Company, A. C. Shaw, his successor, and J. Herschel Keener, woods manager for many years, and to receive correspondence from Mr. Damtoft.

169:3. In *The Biltmore Story,* Schenck tells about logging devastation on the Cherokee lands (pp. 148–50): "The Indians showed me their forests, the most glorious stands of tulip trees with an undergrowth of tall beeches. . . . But the Indians were wards of the Great White Father in Washington and were forbidden to sell any of their property without his consent. A few years later a native lumberman obtained many of these trees by supplying the Indians with some liquour, saws, and axes. Thereupon trees were cut down and the Great White Father was forced to sell them for the benefit of his wards in order to prevent the cut logs from rotting in the woods."

XIV. *Coming of the Park.* The official account of the park appears in the *Final Report of the Southern Appalachian National Park Commission* to the Secretary of the Interior, Washington, Government Printing Office, Washington, D.C., 1931. Many portions of the long story are covered in detail in *Birth of a National Park,* by Carlos C. Campbell, who was intimately associated with park movement through the years. Events in North Carolina are traced in "The Appalachian Park Movement, 1885–1901," by Charles Dennis Smith in *North Carolina Historical Review,* January 1960, and "North Carolina's Role in Establishment of the Great Smoky Mountains National Park," by Willard B. Gatewood, Jr., *North Carolina Historical Review,* April 1960. The developments leading to passage of the Weeks Law are covered in the 1902 *Forest Report; Breaking New Ground,* by Pinchot; and *Whose Woods These Are—the Story of the National Forests,* by Michael Frome, Doubleday & Company, New York, 1962.

Other sources have been: "Gifford Pinchot at Biltmore," by Harold T. Pinkett, *North Carolina Historical Review,* July 1957; *Steve Mather of the National Parks,* by Robert Shankland; interview with Robert Sterling Yard in *Appalachian Journal,* September 1925; "A National Park in the Great Smoky Mountains," by Robert Sterling Yard, *National Parks Bulletin,* November 1925; *Great Smoky Mountains,* a publication of Great Smoky Mountains Conservation Association, Knoxville, 1925; *The Great Smoky Mountains National Park—Economic Regulation of Stream Flow, Water Sup-*

ply, and Hydro-Electric Power, by Charles E. Ray, Jr., Great Smoky Mountains, Inc., Asheville, 1926; *Report of the North Carolina Park Commission to Governor O. Max Gardner,* Raleigh, January 2, 1933; *Suncrest Lumber Company vs. North Carolina Park Commission et al,* Circuit Court of Appeals, Asheville, November 27, 1928; *How Are We to Obtain Fast Growth of the Right Kind of Timber?* by Reuben B. Robertson, address before first National Commercial Forestry Conference, Chamber of Commerce of the United States, Chicago, November 1927; plus interviews with Horace M. Albright, Walter Damtoft, John O. Morrell, Charles E. Ray, Jr., Verne Rhoades, and A. C. Shaw.

178:1. Verne Rhoades was land appraiser and project chief of the Smoky Mountain Purchase Unit before becoming supervisor of the Pisgah National Forest. He was succeeded by assistant project chief Walter Damtoft, who later joined the Champion Fibre Company.

179:3. "Within a short time there will be a National Park established in the Southern Appalachian Mountains. Doubtless the new park will be called Grandfather Mountain National Park." *First Annual Report of the Director of the National Park Service,* 1917.

181:5. Members of the commission were E. C. Brooks, Raleigh; John G. Dawson, Kinston; Harry Chase, Chapel Hill; Mark Squires, Lenoir; Harry Nettles, Biltmore; Plato Ebbs, Asheville; D. M. Buck, Bald Mountain; A. M. Kistler, Morganton; Frank Linney, Boone; E. S. Parker, Greensboro; and J. H. Dillard, Murphy.

182:4. "Colonel Chapman is often referred to as 'father' of the park. The genealogy is, however, rather confused. Perhaps the more appropriate term for him is 'foster-father,' for Mr. and Mrs. Davis should be regarded as the 'parents'. . . ." *Campbell,* p. 18.

185:3. Virginia park proponents had the continuing edge of being located closer to Washington. In January 1925, a body of 200 Virginians, led by their governor, arrived in Washington to call on President Calvin Coolidge and establish a lobby for the Shenandoah site. Supporters of the Smoky Mountains park then turned to their Congressional delegations for help. The result was the agreement to place both parks on equal footing.

186:3. "In the end economic law will prevail, and the people who are concerned with securing for Tennessee a national park of the first order will do well to grasp from the start the great problems which will concern the increased prospects, not only of the neighborhood itself, but of the state. In my opinion, there is no reason why Tennessee should not make this national park, which will cost her nothing after once title is passed to the National Government, an income asset which in time will rank high among her assets." Robert Sterling Yard, interview in *Appalachian Journal,* September 1925.

193:5. While in Gatlinburg, Ford was attentive to the wit of Wiley Oakley, a guide, yarn spinner, and professional Smoky mountaineer. Oakley promised soon after to name his next child Henry Ford Oakley. When the baby was a girl, she became Mrs. Henry Ford Oakley. But the child died. He had one son named Colonel David C. Chapman Oakley, Colonel being the child's first name. Cammerer once told Oakley that if the mountain man had another son he would like the child to be his namesake. "With pleasure," replied Oakley. "Write your full name with the correct spelling on a sheet of paper." It was "Honorable Arno B. Cammerer," but apparently Honorable was never born.

197:3. The same year that Champion sold its mountain land, Dr. Charles Holmes Herty, of Savannah, Georgia, made important laboratory discoveries that revolutionized the pulp and paper industries through use of pine fibers. Within a few years Champion and other large corporations developed extensive pine plantations as a profitable source of pulpwood throughout the Piedmont South. It is not likely this was anticipated, however, at the time of the sale.

198:1. "The final settlement involved a considerable compromise on the part of the Champion Fibre Company and of the park's representatives. If, in the minds of some people, the amount was excessive, there may still be satisfaction in the knowledge that a large part of it is now being expended in furthering the industrial resources of this section. Whatever sacrifice the Champion Fibre Company made will, we hope, be more than offset in a very few years by the satisfaction of seeing the forest which it helped to conserve become the most popular playground in the world, attracting millions of people and creating a new prosperity for western North Carolina." Walter J. Damtoft in the *Champion Log*, April 1932.

199:4. The first park men on the scene, even before Eakin, were John Needham, who took temporary charge of the North Carolina portion, and Philip Hough, on the Tennessee side.

202:3. There still remained a serious problem covering 45,920 acres in the Hazel Creek and Eagle Creek watersheds, belonging to the North Carolina Exploration Company, a subsidiary of the Tennessee Copper Company, owned by the Guggenheim mining interests of New York. This area had somehow been excluded from the park boundary, even though it lay logically on the "park side" of the Little Tennessee River. During World War II the Tennessee Valley Authority decided to flood the valley as part of its construction program of Fontana Dam, the source of power for the Oak Ridge atomic laboratory. Facing eviction, the residents of Proctor filed a suit against TVA that went to the United States Supreme Court before the Government could proceed. As a result, the National Park Service received 44,000 acres (transferred from TVA) in return for a pledge to construct a new road, after the war, replacing one that was flooded, between Bryson City and Fontana. The Park Service later sought to convince Swain County to accept improvement of Route 129 along the south shore of Fontana Lake, pleading that a road on the north shore would disturb a large parcel of wilderness with choice trout streams. This proved unacceptable and in the early 1960s construction proceeded four miles into the park. The mountains were slashed, natural beauty destroyed, the landscape scarred with cuts and fills—and a halt was called. This opened the way to a controversial alternate proposal for a transmountain road from Bryson City to Tennessee which is now under consideration. Nor had the last 1920 acres, extending from Matt Mountain Ridge down Pinnacle Creek to Eagle Creek, been acquired by the Park Service from the North Carolina Exploration Company.

XV. *Why the Rockefeller $5,000,000?* The conservation activities of John D. Rockefeller, Jr., are covered in *A Contribution to the Heritage of Every American*, by Nancy Newhall, Alfred A. Knopf, New York, 1960. These wide-ranging activities are also described in "John D. Rockefeller, Jr.," by Horace M. Albright in *National Parks* Magazine, April 1961. Much more valuable, however, have been interviews with his associates and collaborators in conservation, Kenneth Chorley in particular, but also Horace Albright, Edwin M. Kendrew (for many years senior vice president of Colonial Williamsburg), and Sam P. Weems. References to Harold L. Ickes are based on his own words in *Secret Diary of Harold Ickes*, Vol. 3, Simon and Schuster, New York, 1964.

Other sources include "Grandfather Mountain," by James B. Craig, *American Forests*, May 1948, and "Shall Grandfather Mountain Be Saved?" by Harlan P. Kelsey, *National Parks* Magazine, April–June 1944.

The chapter about his father was read in manuscript by Laurance Rockefeller.

211:5. On March 30, 1928, a check for $5,000,000 was deposited in the Equitable Trust Company (now Chase Manhattan Bank) of New York in the name of the Laura Spelman Rockefeller Fund, with a letter of instructions ordering it to be paid on the basis of: (a) One dollar for every dollar received by Tennessee and North Carolina from the sale of bonds; (b) One dollar for every dollar in cash contributions by the park commissions of the two states, or by the two promotional groups, Great Smoky Mountains Conservation Association and Great Smoky Mountains, Inc.; (c) $500,000 to match acquisition of the 75,000 acres of land in the Little River Lumber Company tract, already made by the Great Smoky Mountains Park Commission.

XVI. *Crucifixion of Ross Eakin.* The *Congressional Record* of April 17, 1939, contains the debate over Senator McKellar's amendment to withhold the salary "of the present superintendent of the Great Smoky Mountains National Park." This includes the Audit Report of H. E. Myers, Regional Fiscal Supervisor, a transcript of Mr. Myers' testimony before McKellar, and correspondence with the Director of the National Park Service (pp. 5999–6037). Senate Resolution 131, to investigate the conduct and administration of Superintendent Ross Eakin, was introduced, with detailed charges, by Senator McKellar on May 16, 1939, and referred to the Committee on Public Lands and Surveys. The *Congressional Record* of June 30, 1939, contains the McKellar-Vandenberg exchange over this resolution on the Senate floor. Campbell in *Birth of a National Park* describes the defense of Eakin by park supporters in Knoxville. A memorial tribute to Arno Cammerer appears in "The National Park Service," Extension of Remarks of Hon. Edward T. Taylor, of Colorado, in the House of Representatives, *Congressional Record*, June 28, 1941, A3363–A3366. Much of the Ickes material is from Vols. 2 and 3 of his *Secret Diary;* other material is from personal interviews with Park Service officials.

226:9. Eakin's successor was Blair Ross, former superintendent of Shiloh National Battlefield, Tennessee; he served as superintendent of the Great Smoky Mountains National Park from May 1945 to December 1949.

227:6. Following the appointment of Newton B. Drury as Director of the National Park Service in 1940, Ickes wrote in his *Secret Diary* (Vol. 3, p. 213): "Probably Demaray was disappointed that he was not to be moved up, but he took it very well. I told him that he was paying the penalty of being too efficient in the job that he now has. He is the detail man in the National Park Service and an excellent one. I would not know how to fill his place if he should go. Yet, while he is a good detail man, he is not the type of man, in my opinion, for Cammerer's place."

XVII. *Social Workers in High Places.* The story of Pi Beta Phi in Gatlinburg has been told in two booklets, *Pi Beta Phi Settlement School,* compiled by Pearl Cashell Jackson, Gatlinburg, 1927, and *Thirty Years on Little Pigeon,* by Agnes Wright Spring, Gatlinburg, 1942. Even after many years, *Handicrafts of the Southern Highlands,* by Allen Eaton, continues to be the definitive work on early crafts. Interesting recent booklets on the subject are *The Story of the Penland Weavers,* by Bonnie Willis Ford, Penland, North Carolina, 1954; *Crafts in the Southern Highlands,* by the Southern Highlands Handicrafts Guild, Stephens Press, Asheville, 1958; and *Tennessee Mountain Crafts,* by Helen Krechniak, Tennessee Department of Conservation, Nashville, 1964.

232:2. "I wish earnestly to make such disposition of Pisgah Forest as will maintain in the fullest and most permanent way its national value as an object lesson in forestry, as well as its wonderful beauty and charm." Mrs. George W. Vanderbilt to the Secretary of Agriculture, May 1, 1914; records of the Forest Service.

235:3. Before the decision was made to establish the settlement school, Miss Mary Lansfield Keller, of Pi Beta Phi, ventured to Gatlinburg in company with the county superintendent of schools. It was a hazardous journey from Sevierville. "The entire population turned out to meet Mr. Drinnen and me, and those bearded, dark-eyed men meant business when they found out I was neither a religious propagandist, a Catholic, nor someone to sell them goods. They did not understand why the fraternity was interested, but if 'them women' wanted to give them a school they were mighty sure they would be glad to have it for their children. They were slow to speak in public, and I gained much more information afterward on the porch of the Ogle house, where we were taken for dinner and where the men congregated to meet 'that woman.' 'How old be ye?' 'Be ye married?' 'Why be-n't ye married?' 'Ye be old enough,' etc., but it was kindly interest and well meant. After a dinner of snaps, corn dodger, coffee, tomatoes, and pie, we discussed very earnestly the proposition of a school, and if ever people wanted an education these people did." *Pi Beta Phi Settlement School,* p. 15.

XVIII. *Mountain Missionary*. The career of Dr. Thomas is the subject of *So Sure of Life*, by Violet Wood, Friendship Press (National Council of Churches), New York, 1950. Other material is based on conversations with Dr. Thomas; his nurse, Miss Geneva Morgan; Elbert "Eb" Whaley of Emerts Cove, Charlie Rolen of Jones Cove, and other dwellers of the mountain valleys.

253:11. "During the year our bookkeeper found that income from fees was about $1800, but, during the same period, expenditures for drugs and supplies were more than $1900." Report of Dr. Robert F. Thomas, June 1, 1959, to May 21, 1960.

XIX. *Last Day of a Bear*. The habits of the black bear are found in *The Mammal Guide*, by Ralph S. Palmer, Doubleday & Company, New York, 1954. Two interesting articles have been "Man and the American Bears," by Dick Kirkpatrick, *National Wildlife* Magazine, February–March 1963, and "The Animal that Walks Like a Man," by Ronald Rood, *Vermont Life*, Autumn 1961. The events in this chapter are based largely on an experience in November 1963, in the Sherwood Wildlife Management Area of the Pisgah National Forest. Supplementary information was obtained in visits to George and Vaughan Plott, of Waynesville. Also helpful were comments by Neil J. Reid, Chief of Wildlife Management, National Park Service (former Chief Naturalist, Great Smoky Mountains National Park), and Lowell Sumner.

256:3. His own kind is most important. In the case of two famished bears, we may anticipate that the stronger will eat the weaker. . . . "Beware the February grizzly" is a traditional saying indicating that starvation *is* possible for bears.

262:4. George Plott was seventy-eight and Vaughan Plott sixty-five in 1963. They stated that the Plott hound had been registered as a breed with the American Kennel Club and the National Coon Hunting Association.

263:8. Kephart wrote that another bear of note, named Reelfoot, made a practice of despoiling Granville Calhoun's orchards: "This Reelfoot was a large bear whose cunning had defied our best hunters for five or six years. He got his name from the fact that he 'reeled' or twisted his hind feet in walking, as some horses do, leaving a peculiar track."

265:5. "Perhaps as the result of the many rock ledges which constitute good denning sites, the Sherwood Wildlife Management Area has supported a fine population of black bears which provide good hunting by parties with dogs." *Public Wildlife Management Areas in North Carolina*, North Carolina Wildlife Resources Commission, Raleigh, 1961.

XX. *The Boar on the Loose*. Among reports and articles on this "exotic" of southern Appalachia have been *The European Wild Boar in North Carolina*, by Perry Jones (adapted from a masters degree thesis), North Carolina Wildlife Resources Commission, Raleigh, 1959; *Wild Boar Study*, by Leroy G. Stegeman, Cherokee National Forest, Cleveland, Tennessee; "Origins of the Wild Boar," by Buss Walker, *Tennessee Conservationist*, October

1962; and "European Boar Thrive in East Tennessee Mountains," by Samuel J. Rogers, *Tennessee Conservationist*, June 1956. Also helpful has been correspondence with Gil Stradt, Supervisor, Cherokee National Forest, furnishing preliminary findings of a biological study of boar underway as this book was being written; with Kenneth Flewelling, Sherwood Forest, Lebanon, New Hampshire, on habits of boar in a section of the White Mountains; and with William W. Huber, Assistant Regional Forester, United States Forest Service, Atlanta, on his recollections as district ranger of Tellico Plains, and Merle Stitt of the National Park Service.

277:1. Versions of the escape of the boar appear to be based entirely on the recollections and interpretations of McGuire. He died in 1957.

280:4. In 1932, cholera in domestic pigs spread to the wild boar and decimated the population.

281:2. The boar may also have been placed in the park by persons interested in perpetuating the species for hunting.

XXI and XXII. *Revenuer* and *Moonshine Maker*. These chapters were based largely on personal experiences, arrangements for which were made by the Enforcement Section of the Alcoholic Tax and Tobacco Division of the Internal Revenue Service, and on information furnished by this agency. Kephart dwelled at great length on the classic conflict between moonshiner and revenuer in *Our Southern Highlanders*.

284:10. Nothing delights a moonshiner more than to have the last laugh on a revenue officer, but even the Government men sometimes smile when outmaneuvered. "The son of a diverter of raw materials, discovering the observation of his father's place of business by an investigator, supplied the moonshiner with a pair of binoculars to watch the investigator. When the investigator used his own binoculars, he could see the grinning moonshiner giving him a friendly wave." *Raw Materials Hi-Lites*, United States Treasury Department, Washington, D.C., 1958.

281:1. "Taxes cost mebbe three cents on the dollar and that's all right. But Revenue costs a dollar and ten cents on twenty cents worth of liquor, and that's robbin' the people with a gun to their faces." Traditional saying.

290:8. "Once, while in hiding, I observed an old 'shiner watching the flow of his just-started still. Every five minutes he would get up from his stump, go over to the still, and draw off a half tin-cup full, spray it on the fire—then return to the stump. On one such trip he made an adjustment to the still, running the finished product into a clean bucket. When I slipped the cuffs on the 'shiner I asked him to explain what he had been doing with all that sipping and spitting. 'Proofin' 'er, son,' he replied, 'proofin' 'er. I can tell by the 'flash' when she's a-ready!'" Personal recollections of Henry Schneider, Internal Revenue Service.

296:2. Dr. James C. Crutcher, of the Veterans Administration Hospital, Atlanta, Georgia, delivered a paper in April 1958 on "Southern Society's New Disease." This, he said, was lead poisoning resulting from the ingestion of illegal whiskey. Dr. Crutcher cited his own examinations, over a four-year period, of thirty-three patients with symptoms of lead intoxication; twenty-four were diagnosed as due to ingestion of illegal whiskey.

298:2. The moonshiner spoke of the agency as ATU, for its former title Alcoholic Tax Unit.

298:6. Despite prevailing beliefs among moonshiners in this section, neither helicopters nor planes were employed by investigators.

299:5. While he talked, a public official (not of the Internal Revenue Service), but one of the moonshiner's best customers, sat in the mountain rendezvous where this interview took place and proved himself a connoisseur of the product.

XXIII. *For Tomorrow, a Ballad*. Bascom Lunsford is observed at close range in "Minstrel Man of the Appalachians," by Harold H. Martin, *Saturday Evening Post*, May 22, 1948. His voice and fiddle playing are heard in recordings made by the Archive of Folk Song of the Library of Congress; among these are *Songs and Ballads of American History and of the Assassination of Presidents*. The results of a folklorist's adventures away from home are in *English Folksongs from the Southern Appalachians*, by Cecil Sharp, 2 vols., Oxford University Press, New York.

For an understanding of the Cherokee in a modern context, rather than as historical oddities, *The Indians of the Americas*, by John Collier, is essential reading. So too should be "The Case of the American Indian," by Alexander Lesser, *Social Service Review*, University of Chicago, June 1961. References to commercial developments in Cherokee are from *ESC Quarterly*, North Carolina Employment Security Commission, Raleigh, Winter-Spring 1964. The author also benefited from information, and cooperation, provided by the United States Public Health Service, both in Cherokee and in Washington.

The quotation of Dr. Bennett urging "opening" the wilderness of the national park is from one of a series of articles, discussing various park problems, by John Parris, March 27 to April 1, 1955, in the *Asheville Citizen*. The quotation from Justice William O. Douglas is from his book, *My Wilderness: East to Katahdin*, which considers some of the same problems from another viewpoint. *National Parks* Magazine, March 1965, contains proposals for the future of the park and entire area of southern Appalachia.

302:3. The chestnut blight was first observed in this country in 1904, when it affected chestnut trees at the New York Zoological Garden. Studies determined the blight had arrived in the United States sometime earlier on trees imported from China. The fungus disease spread with stunning swiftness wherever the chestnut grew. It wreaked the most complete decimation of any tree in the recorded history of man. In the southern Appalachians most of the damage was done in the late 1920s and early 1930s. By 1940 approximately 85 per cent of the American chestnut trees in the Great Smokies had either been killed or infected by the blight; ten years later, 95 per cent had been infected. Though failing to identify the cause properly, mountaineers recognized the impact of the blight on the biotic balance in the forest. Food supplies were so seriously affected that much of the bear population fled the park. In some watersheds, gray squirrels showed a 90 per cent mortality. On the other hand, flying squirrels found winter nesting in the dead chestnut trees and increased their numbers. As a result of the blight, other kinds of trees, notably the tulip tree in the hardwood coves, have taken the place of the chestnut, thus influencing an entire sequence of changes in the forest community.

In the 1960s chestnut sprouts continued to grow from old stumps in isolated high mountain sections, leading to the hope that "the chestnut will still come back," but the trees were considered foredoomed to death before reaching full growth. After fifty years of experimentation, all efforts to control the disease and to rescue the American chestnut had failed. However, the United States Department of Agriculture in recent years has shown progress in a long-range program to breed a disease-resistant hybrid tree by crossing Chinese chestnut trees with surviving American chestnuts.

303:5. "What better form of music or literature," asked Cecil Sharp, "can we give them [the nation's children] than the folksongs and folk-ballads of the race to which they belong, or of the nation whose language they speak?"

306:8. "For generations, the Indian has been, and is today, the center of an amazing series of wonderings, fears, legends, hopes. Yet those who have worked with Indians know that they are neither the cruel, warlike, irreligious savages imagined by some, nor are they the 'fortunate children of nature's bounty' described by tourists who see them for an hour at some glowing ceremonial. We find the Indians, in all the basic forces and forms of life, human beings like ourselves. The majority of them are very poor people living under severely simple conditions. We know them to be deeply religious. We know them to be possessed of all the powers, intelligence, and genius within the range of human endowment." John Collier, Commissioner of Indian Affairs, in the *Annual Report of the Secretary of the Interior*, Washington, D.C., 1938, p. 209.

307:5. "Once a vigorous people, totaling about 800,000, the Indian population was sharply reduced by tuberculosis, smallpox, dysentery, and other diseases brought by the early white settlers. Today the Indian people are still faced with a burden of disease far in excess of that found in the general population. Most of their illnesses are from preventable diseases which have long been under control in other groups throughout the country." *Indians on Federal Reservations in the United States*, Public Health Service, Washington, D.C., 1960.

309:3. The Cherokee Historical Association was founded in 1948 by the Western North Carolina Associated Communities. In preparing for its first major project, the production of *Unto These Hills*, a total of $20,000 was raised in gifts from the eleven counties of western North Carolina. The legislative appropriation of an additional $35,000 was effected largely through the efforts of Harry Buchanan, the leading figure in the Association. The Tribal Council of the Eastern Band contributed $5000 and leased land to the Association for the outdoor theater.

309:4. Qualla Arts and Crafts Mutual, Inc., organized under the administration of Superintendent Joe Jennings, is now sponsored by the Indian Arts and Crafts Board of the Department of the Interior. It is considered a pre-eminently successful Indian arts and crafts group. The most celebrated artist of Cherokee is Miss Amanda Crow, designer, painter, and versatile sculptor in wood and stone. In addition to maintaining her own studio, Miss Crow has been a year-round teacher of wood carving, under the auspices of the Cherokee Historical Association.

309:5. The Cherokee Indian Fair, long encouraged by the Government, was thwarted by officials of the Bureau of Indian Affairs in the period 1963–64, and was thus discontinued. This event, held annually in October, was the high point of the year for the Cherokee people, their homecoming and their pride. As many as 10,000 persons attended in one day to observe the high quality of Cherokee farm products, the beauty of their arts and crafts, the revival of their games and dances. In this period the Bureau of Indian Affairs required the Historical Association to discontinue a number of services; the Association then decided no longer to undertake any activity involving co-operation of the Bureau.

310:2. "The Indians are citizens with the full rights of citizenship, and many have exercised their freedom to become completely Americanized. But there are many who want and need the freedom to be Indians within the framework of America. For the Indian, the tribal community is the only carrier of his tradition; if it disintegrates and disappears, his tradition be-comes a matter of history, and he loses part of his identity. . . . In a world in which we hope that peoples, however diverse, will choose the way of democracy, we cannot avoid the responsibility for a democratic resolution of the American Indian situation. Our attitude toward the Indians, the stub-bornest non-conformists among us, may be the touchstone of our tolerance of diversity anywhere." Alexander Lesser, in "The Case of the American Indian."

XXIV. A *Slight Case for Exercise*. Most of this chapter is based on walks in the woods with Arthur Stupka, attendance at his lectures, and interviews in his office before his retirement and in his home. Stupka is the author of the *Natural History Handbook*; *Notes on the Birds of the Great Smoky Mountains National Park*; *Trees, Shrubs, and Woody Vines of Great Smoky Mountains National Park*; and *Wildflowers in Color*, with Donald H. Robinson, Harper and Row, New York, 1965. The comprehensive story of the Appalachian Trail appears in *Publication No. 5*, Sixth Edition, Appalachian Trail Conference, Washington, D.C., 1950. The history of the Great Smoky Mountains Hiking Club is related in *Appalachian Trailway News*, May 1948; the history of the Carolina Appalachian Trail Club in *Appalachian Trailway News*, January 1964. The excellent report (typescript) titled *A Study for the Preservation of Mountain Culture in Field Museums of History*, by Charles S. Grossman (undated) is in the files of the National Park Service in Washington; the *Report on Preservation of Mountain Culture in the Great Smoky Mountains*, by Dr. Hans Huth (typescript), 1941, is also in the files of the Park Service. "The People of Cades

Cove," by William O. Douglas, appears in the *National Geographic* Magazine, July 1962.

321:5. Dr. L. R. Hesler, formerly chairman of the Department of Botany, University of Tennessee, pursued studies of fungi of the Great Smoky Mountains and vicinity for over forty years. In 1962, he listed 1975 species of fungi in the park.

325:1. "Throughout Dr. Hesler's long career he was instrumental in attracting a number of outstanding botanists to the staff of the Department of Botany—particularly H. M. Jennison, A. J. Sharp, S. A. Cain, and R. E. Shanks—whose combined activities, especially in the realm of published accounts of the local flora, served to mark an era. It proved to be a most fortunate circumstance that in the early stages of the development of a national park, whose grandeur and uniqueness are based largely on botanical features, there would be a source of information so conveniently located and made up of such distinguished personalities." Stupka, *Trees, Shrubs, and Woody Vines*, p. 6.

327:3. The text of *A Preliminary Guide to the Greenbrier-Brushy Mountain Nature Trail* was written by Stanley A. Cain and others. Dr. Cain, then of the University of Tennessee, wrote extensively on the ecology of the Great Smokies from 1930 to 1945. Later, after serving at the University of Michigan, he became Assistant Secretary of the Interior.

330:6. Soon after establishment of the park, enthusiasts in North Carolina organized the Western North Carolina Great Smoky Mountains National Park Museum Committee. Their purpose was to collect regional artifacts suitable for a museum on pioneer culture. W. E. Bird was chosen chairman, Mrs. John C. Campbell, vice chairman, and George McCoy, of the *Asheville Citizen*, secretary. The committee felt it had been given adequate assurance by the National Park Service that such a museum would be constructed, particularly when Hiram C. Wilburn, of the park staff, was assigned to collaborate in assembling appropriate artifacts. "This final collection, as I recall," Dr. Bird has advised the author, "embraced at least 10,000 separate articles, most of which were excellently representative of the past, and were illustrative of the pioneer years." The museum, as envisioned, was never built, however, causing disappointment and irritation in western North Carolina.

XXV. *The Sanctuary*. For the crisis of the mid-sixties, see "The Great Smokies Park and the Wilderness Act," *Living Wilderness*, Autumn 1965; "Wilderness in the East," editorial in the *New York Times*, December 5, 1965; "Beauty or the Bulldozer?" by Michael Frome, *American Forests*, February 1966; and "Has N.C. Spoiled Its Beauty?" by Chester Davis, *Winston-Salem Journal*, March 10, 1966.

ACKNOWLEDGMENTS

A number of those to whom I am deeply indebted are mentioned in the text and/or the Notes. The fact that their names do not reappear here does not diminish appreciation to them.

As a general observation, the average, ordinary people of the Great Smokies could not have been more generous or co-operative, despite their reputation for being suspicious of strangers. Most of them answered all questions; they volunteered useful information. The less they had, the more they were willing to share of their time, food at the table, a bed for the night, or an invitation to church services and harp singing. (This also involved, unfortunately, a long session devoted to sampling the mountain product described in Chapter XXII.)

I am grateful for the personal, as well as official, assistance furnished by members of the staff of the National Park Service, from headquarters in Washington to ranger districts in the field. It was my privilege to be on close terms with Fred J. Overly, superintendent of the Great Smoky Mountains National Park during the period of most extensive research, as well as with his two immediate predecessors, Edward A. Hummel and John Preston, and to be well received by his successor, George W. Fry. With David deL. Condon, assistant superintendent, and Neil J. Reid, chief park naturalist, who served in the national park as contemporaries of Mr. Overly, I also enjoyed warm personal relations. Many arrangements and facilities for research were made through the interest of my longtime friend, A. Clark Stratton, Associate Director of the National Park Service, and George B. Hartzog, Jr., Director of the Park Service (a former assistant superintendent of the Great Smoky Mountains National Park). I appreciate, also, the help furnished by Gil Stradt, Supervisor, Cherokee National Forest, and by Peter J. Hanlon, Supervisor, North Carolina National Forests, and his associates, Monte Seehorn, wildlife biologist, and Lindsay Rogers, of Canton, fire-tower specialist; and the help of the Internal Revenue Service, through Joseph S. Rosapepe, Director, George B. Coffelt and Henry Schneider, of the Public Information Division, and John Lathem, chief, and Earl Branum, of the Enforcement Section; and of the Public Health Service, through Mrs. Jean Nowak, Miss Annabelle Price, and Dr. Robert Bokat.

Carol White, the devoted general manager of the Cherokee Historical Association, provided much of the background information on the Cherokee, as well as many forms of guidance. I am also grateful to O. A. Fetch, general manager of Fontana Village, and his associates; Douglas Ferguson, the potter of Pigeon Forge; Hiram C. Wilburn, of Waynesville; John Parris, of Sylva; Earl Shaub, of the Tennessee Department of Conservation; Miss Miriam Rabb, of the North Carolina Department of Conservation and Development; the late George McCoy, a pioneer booster of the national park; Miss Myra Champion, of the Pack Memorial Library, Asheville; and Dr. Jean Stephenson, of the Appalachian Trail Conference, Washington, D.C. Also, Miss Edith P. Alley, of Maggie Valley; T. Edward Pickard and Luke Wright, of the automobile clubs in North Carolina and East Tennessee; Genevieve C. Cobb, Librarian, and David Landman, of Princeton University.

Dr. W. E. Bird, President Emeritus of Western Carolina College, Cullowhee, North Carolina, read the manuscript in its entirety, and made invaluable comments and suggestions. Howard A. Stagner, Assistant Director, National Park Service, also read the manuscript in its entirety, and provided criticism that constructively influenced key sections of the book. Joe Jennings, of the School of Graduate Studies, East Tennessee State University, Johnson City, former superintendent of the Cherokee Indian Reservation, reviewed much of the script, and particularly the sections dealing with the Indians. Kenneth Chorley reviewed the chapters relating to John D. Rockefeller, Jr., and to events in establishment of the national park in which he was involved. The manuscript was also reviewed in entirety or in part by Edward A. Hummel, former superintendent of the Great Smoky Mountains National Park (and later Western Regional Director of the National Park Service), Harvey Broome, John O. Morrell, in behalf of the Great Smoky Mountains National Park, Donald Robinson, Arthur Stupka, Victor Cahalane, Robert Rose, and Dr. Robert Linn. I owe many thanks to all of them.

Finally, I appreciate the patience, tolerance, and encouragement of my editor, Samuel S. Vaughan, and of his associates, Miss Anne Hutchens and Miss Lucia Staniels; and, as always, the partnership of my wife.

Index

Place names and other geographic features mentioned more or less casually throughout the text are included in the index when they are treated in substantive manner.